An Illustrated History of
GARDENING

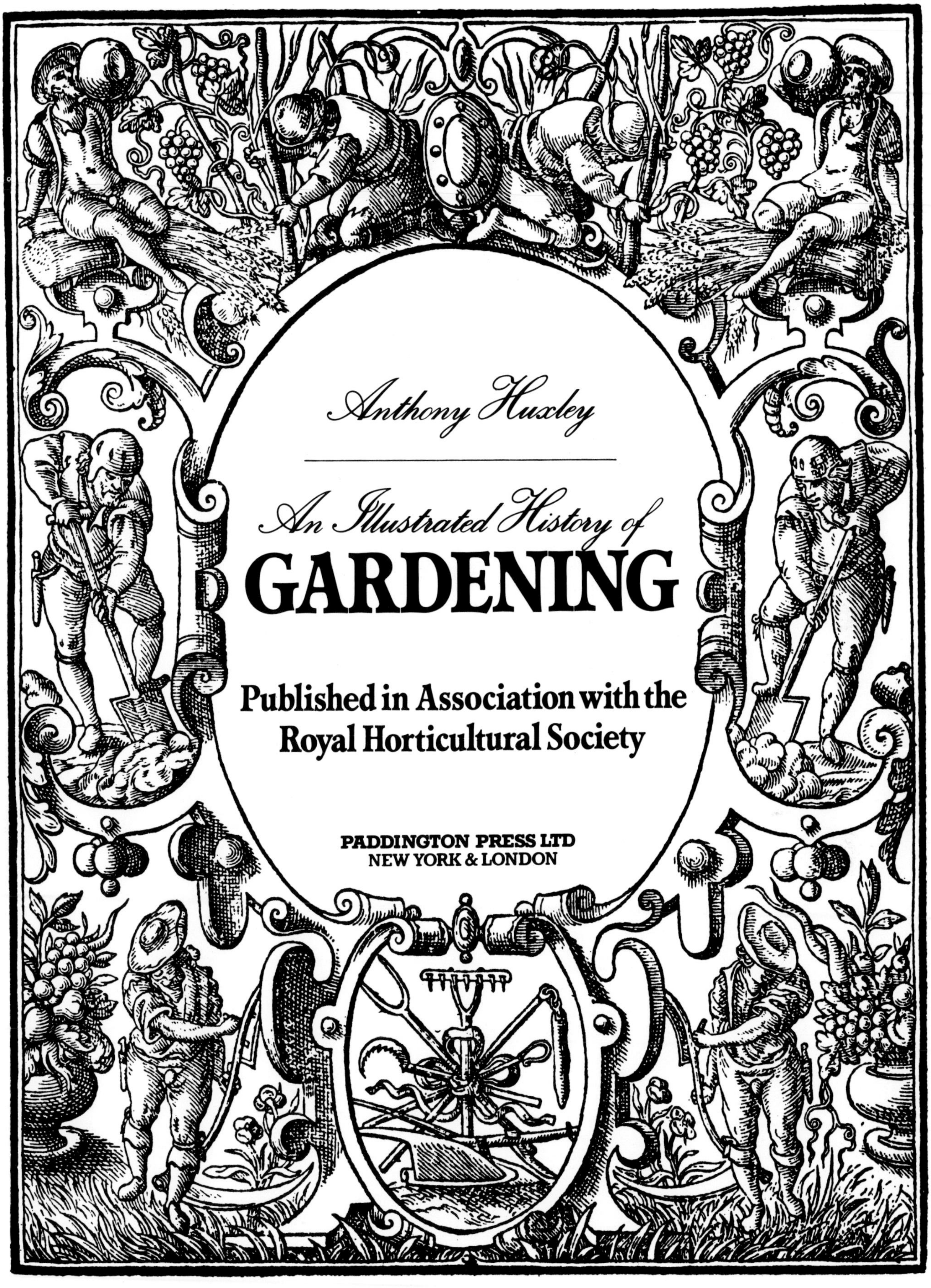

Anthony Huxley

An Illustrated History of

GARDENING

Published in Association with the Royal Horticultural Society

PADDINGTON PRESS LTD
NEW YORK & LONDON

Library of Congress Cataloging in Publication Data
Huxley, Anthony Julian, 1920–
An illustrated history of gardening.

Bibliography: p.
Includes index.
1. Gardening–History 2. Gardening–History–
Pictorial works. I. Title.
SB451.H87 635.9'09 78-5961
ISBN 0 7092 0322 5
ISBN 0 448 22424 0 (U.S. and Canada only)

Filmset in England by BAS Printers Limited,
Over Wallop, Hampshire
Printed in Hong Kong
Color separations by Modern Reprographics Ltd., Hull, England
Designed by Richard Johnson

IN THE UNITED STATES
PADDINGTON PRESS
Distributed by
GROSSET & DUNLAP

IN THE UNITED KINGDOM
PADDINGTON PRESS

IN CANADA
Distributed by
RANDOM HOUSE OF CANADA LTD.

IN SOUTHERN AFRICA
Distributed by
ERNEST STANTON (PUBLISHERS) (PTY.) LTD.

Contents

Introduction

"GOD ALMIGHTY FIRST PLANTED A GARDEN, AND INDEED it is the purest of human pleasures. It is the greatest refreshment to the spirits of man."

Sir Francis Bacon's words of well over three centuries ago are still worth repeating. The millions of men and women who garden today are following in a noble tradition, and this book tells the story of their heritage – the roots, the history, and the progress of this ancient occupation. The art of gardening and the history of garden design have formed the subjects of numerous books, and the discovery and introduction of plants have also been written about at length. But the history of gardening methods, the actual ways and means of making plants grow, has barely been touched on, and this book fills that gap.

The theme of this book is the development of tools and implements of all kinds, and of beds, containers, hedges and fences, of the ways of sowing, planting, controlling pests, watering and feeding, of training, forcing and protecting. Before a garden can be enjoyed for its beauty alone, much hard work must be accomplished. Before his garden can be filled with pleasure-giving plants, the gardener must know his craft. Gardeners are first of all artisans, only secondarily artists.

This book is illustrated entirely from works, whether books or paintings, of the periods concerned, or in a few cases by pictures of tools or devices still extant. The illustrations are a very important part of the book and much time has been spent in searching for them. A large proportion of those collected here, from various countries and periods, have not been reproduced since their original publication.

Just as I have used contemporary illustrations, I have quoted freely from the most important and original contemporary authors. Some of the quotations may seem quaint, especially in their original spellings, but they have a freshness and directness, all too seldom found today, which rephrasing would lose. We must remember as we read these words from authors of so long ago that they were often the first to write about the technique they are describing. In past centuries gardening writers were scarce or, like the Romans Columella and Pliny, virtually unique. In more recent times we can see an ever-increasing flood of gardening writers among which a few "giants" rise up, notable for their industry and originality, such as the British John Claudius Loudon (1783–1840) or, more recently, the American L. H. Bailey (1858–1954); and it is to such authorities that I have gone for information.

Gardening began at very different times in various parts of the world. In this book I have sought my examples from widely different cultures, and it has been impossible to avoid many chronological jumps, for this cannot be an account in which matters are described in strict sequence of time. The subject matter of the different chapters alone creates a recurring recapitulation of history.

It is particularly fascinating to note how different cultures invented basically similar devices when there was no apparent possibility of contact, a fact which perhaps finds its best example when comparing China with the rest of the world. It is also chastening to realize how very late European civilization asserted itself and gave rise to the kind of garden which is inevitably that given most prominence in these pages by a Western writer. And North America, not colonized until the seventeenth century, of course emerged as a gardening civilization even later. North America, however, provides a unique example of what occurred when people with a relatively advanced knowledge of husbandry settled in virtually virgin land.

There are, of course, many points in history when an originally utilitarian gardening method leads to artistic embellishment and finally to a distinct art form. For example, the basic plant bed, rectangular and conscribed solely for the need to attend to all its parts without stepping on its plants, gradually assumes more ornamental surrounds and forms, and at one period becomes pure design, completely eliminating plants in the most esoteric kinds of knot. Water conduits and basic irrigation lead to decorated spouts and basins, to fountains and cascades, and finally to elaborate waterworks created entirely for their own sake. The training of plants such as vines and other fruits points the way to their ornamental use, while the simple hedge is first clipped and finally emerges as topiary.

In such cases, a few examples of the final art form are given in these pages, but in general as soon as method becomes art it has no further place here. Thus the reader will not find any account of decorative waterworks, statuary, garden ornament for its own sake, gazebos, temples, bowers or garden furniture, nor will he be told how to lay out a border or a parterre – although many of these subjects appear in illustrations demonstrating some tool or technique in action. The study of *how* gardening is and has been done, rather than its results in flowers, fruit, decoration and design, provides quite enough material without recounting what has been described admirably elsewhere.

Although most readers will be well aware of current gardening practice, I have tried to bring the various themes up to date, for one must not forget that history only stopped yesterday. But I have used illustrations of modern equipment sparingly, for it is the forgotten past which fascinates. The student of the ways and means of gardening cannot fail to be amazed by how little is really new and how much astonishingly old in principle.

There has always been a lot of work involved in the craft of gardening, and much of it is devoted to the essential need for growing food. But once the gardener has some leisure he can cultivate plants for diversion and decoration as well as sustenance. Whichever he does, the gardener is joining in nature's creative process and making his own life at once more comfortable and more beautiful. That is why more and more of us yearn for a plot or yard in which to make plants grow, turn to community gardens or allotments, or grow plants in pots indoors. And that is why Bacon regarded gardening as such a "refreshment to the spirits of man."

Chapter One
Origins

TO DEFINE "GARDEN" AND "GARDENING," IT IS NECESSARY TO GO back to the beginnings of agriculture. Man began to cultivate plants when he started to live in settled communities and to abandon the earlier subsistence based on hunting, or collecting animal food and wild vegetable material.

The earliest cultivators seem to have lived around Jericho in Palestine about 8000 B.C. Early farming can be traced at various points around this focus a little later: at Jarmo on the Iraq/Iran borders, and at Çatal Hüyük and Hacilar in central Anatolia, from around 6500 B.C.; in northern Mesopotamia and in Crete from 6000 B.C. – the latter probably predated on the Greek mainland; in Cyprus and Egypt beginning about 5000 B.C. In the Orient, Chinese agriculture began no later than the fifth millenium B.C. The dead Indus Valley civilization in the west of the Indian subcontinent flourished from 2500 B.C.; and cereal cultivation in India may have occurred very much earlier. Organized cultivation was practiced in South America from around 2500 B.C.

This earliest agriculture was carried out in areas around the villages. Even today one can get a very good idea of their probable appearance, when flying over less developed areas of Turkey and Iran where the fields develop around the community either concentrically or, occasionally, in triangular segments expanding from the center. In due course these early agriculturists developed simple implements – the digging stick, elementary hoes and mattocks, and also the prototype plough pulled by an ox.

In Southeast Asia and South America, this early agriculture was devoted to roots, such as yams and taro, and to local fruits, including the banana when it was introduced. Such plants are extremely easy to grow and increase in a warm, humid climate, their cultivation calling for only the simplest digging or hole-making implements. This diet was easily and satisfactorily supplemented with small animals, fish, snails and the like, and these still constitute the basis of the South American and Asian peasant diet, although rice is now an additional staple, having been introduced from China where it was cultivated as early as 2400 B.C. (Some authorities believe this occurred as early as 4000 B.C.) Even today

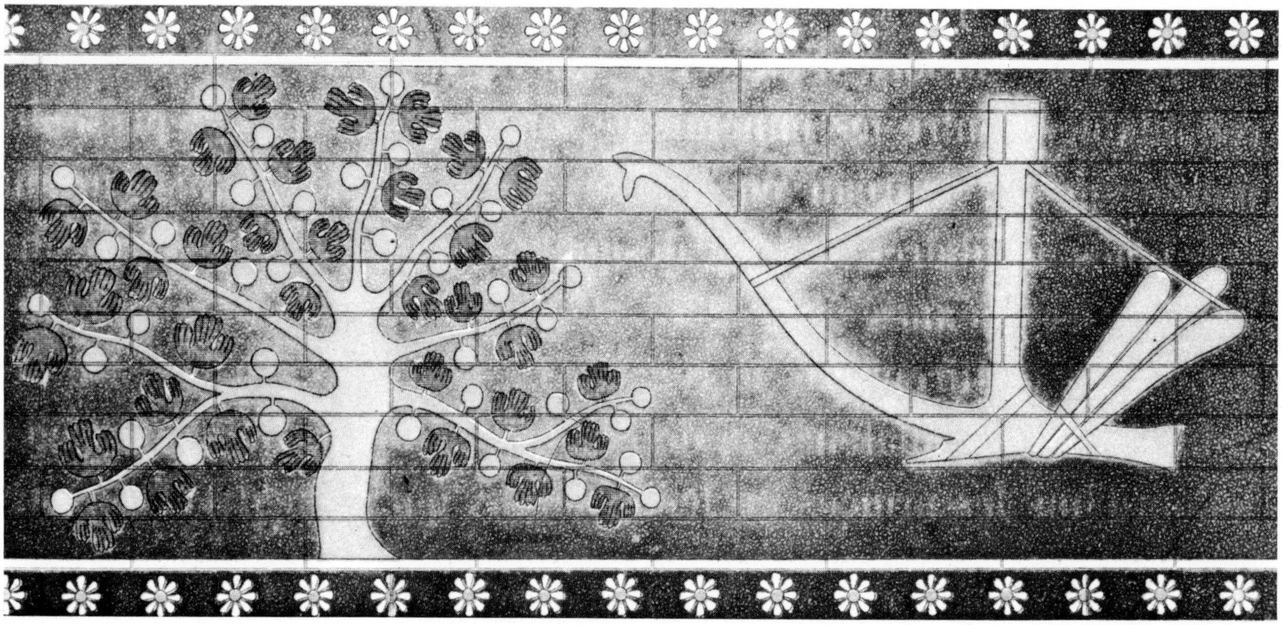

All gardening derives from agriculture, and implements like this Assyrian seed plough of around 700 B.C. *precede gardening tools.*

plots in Southeast Asia or South America tend to be devoted entirely to vegetables and fruit – and to involve a minimum of planning.

A garden in our terms is more than that, and its origins are more readily sought in the Near East. There agriculture was concerned largely with cereal grains, which were supplemented not only with meat and milk from goats, and later sheep, but also with wild fruits – such as figs, grapes, pomegranates, apricots and almonds, depending on the altitude at which the people lived. By degrees, doubtless springing from rejected pips and stones, the plants producing these fruits became massed around the villages, exactly as one can see today from the Lebanon to Afghanistan. And, again presumably growing from spat-out seeds, they were nearly always found close to the dwellings.

At some point in the evolution of villages, houses came to have walled or fenced enclosures or yards around them, probably initially to pen goats and sheep. The seedling fig or vine would provide welcome shade here, the vine lending itself to training on some kind of simple structure. In The Bible we read of "every man" sitting under and eating of "his own fig tree," while Noah is credited with the first cultivation of the grape. (In scientific terms this occurred in the Neolithic period.) Wine obviously became very important, for vineyards are mentioned frequently in the Old Testament.

The Hittites certainly had "garden cities" from early in the second millennium B.C. These were townships of growers clustered together for safety. The vegetable plots and orchards were never far from the houses, so these antique towns were relatively widely spread by our standards, the average fruit farm being two to four acres in area. Growing fruit and vegetables was apparently far more important than the cultivation of field crops to these people. At any rate, gardens and vineyards were apparently worth twenty times as much as ordinary farmland, and there were severe penalties for damaging fruit trees, an act that was considered barbaric.

But we do not yet have a garden. A garden can be said to exist when the shade-casting tree in the enclosed yard was deliberately placed, and was accompanied by plants deliberately grown for food, progenitors of our vegetable crops. Such might have been the "bitter herbs" frequently referred to in The Bible, and used to accompany meat dishes – wild lettuce, chicory, sorrel, dandelion, watercress and mint. Onions, and probably flavoring plants like dill and coriander, were certainly grown very early.

Medicinal herbs were also cultivated in antiquity. There is a Sumerian herbal record of the third millennium B.C. The first Chinese herbal is believed to have been written around the same time. Five hundred herbs were known, grown and recorded in Egypt in the days of Imhotep (around 2700 B.C.), and some seven hundred a thousand years later. By the first century A.D., knowledge had slipped back: the great Greek herbalist Dioscorides only records some five hundred herbs, although he mentions about one thousand drugs. In Anglo-Saxon times, some five hundred herbs can again be identified from the literature. From the ninth century A.D., the Arabs were prominent in herbal knowledge, and they transmitted much to Europe via Spain.

Grown in neat rows, like the cereals in the fields, these plants needed watering. Water would often be supplied from an irrigation channel, and the Sumerians again first brought irrigation to a fine art.

A Sumerian legend of the third millennium B.C. tells how the goddess Iranna falls in love with a gardener called Shukallituda. He was a diligent worker, setting out his plant beds, digging irrigation channels and watering; but then high winds blew sand from the mountains into his face, blinding him and destroying his garden. On consulting the heavens, the goddess told him what to do: in five or ten corners of his garden he must plant trees to provide both shade and shelter. "The shadow lies on the ground at dawn, in the afternoon and at dusk . . . it never runs away." So, in legend, first appears the windbreak.

It is this sort of combination – enclosure, shade, trained vine, vegetables in rows, and water – which perhaps first constituted a garden, although it is impossible to give any kind of accurate date for this elementary stage.

Communities have to raise themselves above subsistence level before they can really afford to grow – or even to appreciate – plants not strictly utilitarian. It was in Egypt – certainly by 1500 B.C. – that civilization first made the utility garden decorative in its design, with walls, regular beds and pools, and planted trees. Shortly later the Egyptians added plants grown for their flowers alone. In contrast to such enclosures, the Assyrians and Babylonians made vast parks, partly for pleasure, partly for hunting, and these were later developed by the Persians.

We have more or less strong evidence of the scale of gardening from ancient Egypt; from the Mesopotamian region occupied in succession by Sumerians, Hittites, Assyrians, Babylonians; and later from Persia. But whether other cultures really had decorative gardens early on is a matter of surmise. Much of their husbandry must have been similar to today's unplanned smallholdings in South America and Southeast Asia.

The first record of a Greek garden is to be found in Homer's *Odyssey* (eighth–ninth century B.C.), describing that of Alcinous – admittedly a royal one. It was surrounded by hedges, and "in it flourish tall trees; pears and pomegranates and apples* full of fruit, also sweet figs and bounteous olives. Here too a fertile vineyard has been planted. . . . Beyond the last row of trees, well-laid garden plots have been arranged, blooming all the year with flowers. And there are two springs; one leads through the garden while the other dives beneath the threshold of the great court to gush out beside the stately palace; from it the citizens draw their water." The first archaeological record of a Greek garden is that of the Temple of Hephaistos. The temple was completed by 444 B.C. near the Athenian Agora, but the garden with its planting pits and flower pots (page 137) probably dates from the third century B.C.

The ancient love of the Greeks – notably of the Minoans and Myceneans – for flowers and trees in natural landscape is evidenced not only in Homer's works, but also in innumerable murals and decorations on pottery. But the earlier Greeks in particular had few, if any, private gardens; perhaps they were too gregarious, and in any case land was usually owned by the family, not the individual. Later, in the fifth and fourth centuries B.C., they planted many trees to shade and decorate their meeting places and monuments; Cimon (507–449 B.C.) was notable for the planting of "shady walks." Athens certainly had large market gardens outside the city walls for both food and flowers, the latter essential for the garlands and wreaths used in most ceremonies, public or personal. However, the poet Dicaeogenes is known to have made a private garden early in the fourth century, and Epicurus did the same a few decades later, to be copied by other wealthy, pleasure-loving citizens. Although they did not record anything about practical gardening until late Hellenistic times, it is clear that it was Greek gardeners who taught the Romans much about the subject, including some of its more esoteric aspects like topiary (the art of clipping shrubs into ornamental shapes).

The Romans, with their advanced technology, elaborate architecture and high standard of living, had, by the second century B.C., developed farming, market gardening and decorative gardening to new levels, and laid the foundations of the gardening ideals which were built up, after intervening centuries of strife and ignorance, in Renaissance

* Although "apples" usually appears in translations, it is very unlikely that the Greeks actually grew apples. Quinces or azaroles (a kind of hawthorn) are more probably meant.

Europe (fourteenth–sixteenth centuries).

Thousands of miles to the east, the Chinese civilization, as skillful as that of Rome in very different ways, was elaborating its own very specialized gardening. As with the Romans, gardening was very much for the rich – cheek by jowl with the palaces of Ch'ang-an and their parklands were the slums where no tree or plant could survive.

A similar pattern of beginning, upsurge, and climax in gardening can be traced in more or less detail in every culture which has become civilized. The final stage of collapse back into subsistence farming after conquest and pillage is, alas, all too frequent. In each of these stages a similar pattern of technical development can be traced – from elementary plough, hoe, digging stick and mattock to ingenious tools and techniques of all kinds. Obviously the interaction of different cultures increased as world-wide communications improved, but there are very few examples of a whole existing set of techniques being imported into a conquered or a virgin land. The Moguls, conquering Persia and India, probably assimilated more than they introduced; and it was only the Pilgrim Fathers, settling in New England, and the various other colonists in the New World, who brought a ready-made horticultural technology to a country accustomed only to the most primitive methods.

Chapter Two
How Gardens Developed

IN VIRTUALLY EVERY CULTURE THERE SEEMS TO HAVE BEEN A concentric development of communities, with gardens eventually becoming closely associated with houses, agricultural fields lying beyond, and grazing lands for the domestic herds remaining on the perimeter. In the early days of history, when communities were still far apart, local raiding was perhaps less common than the massive invasion of foreigners. Therefore the fields and gardens were not closely guarded; even the villages had no real fortifications in many cases, although Jericho was a very early example where elaborate fortification did exist. The local raiding party would be met by direct assault from the villagers; the foreign invader could only be fled from or succumbed to. Fields themselves might, of course, be walled, as they are still in many parts of the world; but this was mainly to prevent loose animals and local troublemakers from spoiling the crops or helping themselves.

But communities grew in size and number and, as the Tower of Babel legend reminds us, tribes developed in which communities were aggregated, each tribe with different customs and perhaps dialects. The more people there were, the more ready some were to prey upon others – the warlike and less work-minded attacking the achievements of the peaceable agriculturists and smallholders. In such circumstances, the village at least becomes fortified, even if this allows the invader to pillage the fields and orchards. A large, prosperous community is able to build a big wall around both houses and personal plots, but the agricultural land always remains outside.

Personal plots themselves may be found in a band outside the walls, or in a separate area within the walls but beyond the houses. The garden closely associated with a house – once we have left the earliest simple communities – is almost always a product of advanced civilization.

Europe in the Dark Ages is very much an example of this process of development, evidenced both in the fortified towns and, in microcosm, in the innumerable castles that local lords built to ensure their own safety and that of the vassals who tilled the surrounding land, who would come into the great courtyard from their hovels if danger threatened. Here, they and their animals would be reasonably protected by the high, immensely thick walls, moats and, of course, the lord's private army.

Most of the castle's land would necessarily be outside the walls, but in many cases there were utilitarian plots close to the inner walls which might, in the grandest cases, be surrounded by another wall providing immeditae protection from casual thieves. In smaller castles there would be little room for any garden plots within the inner walls, but it became increasingly the style to provide more space for gardens within these walls, with areas for vegetables, fruit and, in particular, herbs.

These herbs were vital to life in many ways. In the first place, they, and imported spices, concealed the taste of bad or poorly preserved meat, which might have been stored for many winter months. Without the people knowing it, eating these herbs must have kept scurvy and other vitamin deficiencies at bay. Certainly some other vegetables (in the modern sense) were eaten, and a little fruit, but meat, birds and fish were undoubtedly the main items of diet, and they were seldom cooked without herbs. The diet of the very poor was unbalanced: food was largely bread or, when the wheat harvest failed, acorns, tree bark, grass seed, and perhaps flour eked out with soil.

A great number of herbs were used medicinally. Some were real remedies, many more were imagined ones; and medicine was a combination of herbal potions and applications with mumbo-jumbo. But from the earliest times, in every culture, magic and medicinal herbs were cultivated – and if a medieval castle had no other plot within its walls, there would be one for herbs.

As the rule of law became more effective, and the danger from local wars and marauding bands lessened, the fortifications naturally became reduced. Castles became fortified manor houses, where the semblance of protection was given by a high wall and often a moat, but where little protection would in fact have been afforded against serious attack. Outer walls were dismantled, or no longer built, so that the building looked out into the surrounding country rather than inward upon its own courtyard. Around it would be spread its gardens, in which the proportion of decorative to utilitarian plants steadily increased. The defensive moat often became an integral part of a decorative scheme, and there are examples where plots could only be reached by boat – a pleasing diversion, no doubt, on long summer days.

Medieval towns started with the gardening disadvantage that they too had to be protected by strong outer walls, and as many houses as possible were packed within them. In such cases, very few houses could have gardens – perhaps only those of important people. Once the dangers of outside attack receded, the town began to spread beyond the walls, and one can see at once how much larger the cultivated areas became at this point of release, as the new housebuilders took advantage of the hitherto undeveloped countryside.

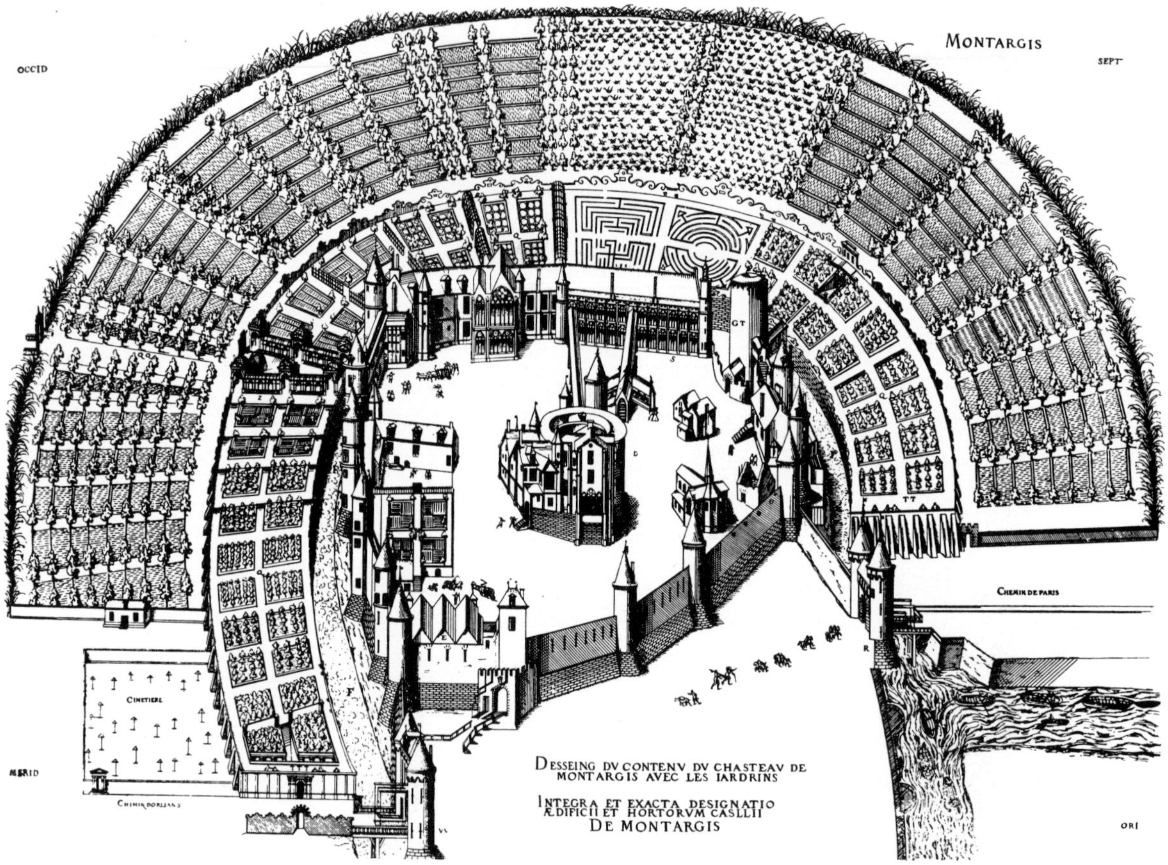

ABOVE: *The two little gardens within the castle walls at Montargis, France, are remnants from the Middle Ages. The plan shown dates from after 1560, when the terrace nearest the walls was devoted to ornamental gardens, while the outer terrace was for vegetables and fruit.*

RIGHT: *In this imaginary scene from 1495 the rather ill-defended little castle and its yard are surrounded by wattle fences; beyond is the "pleasaunce" with a simple arbor.*

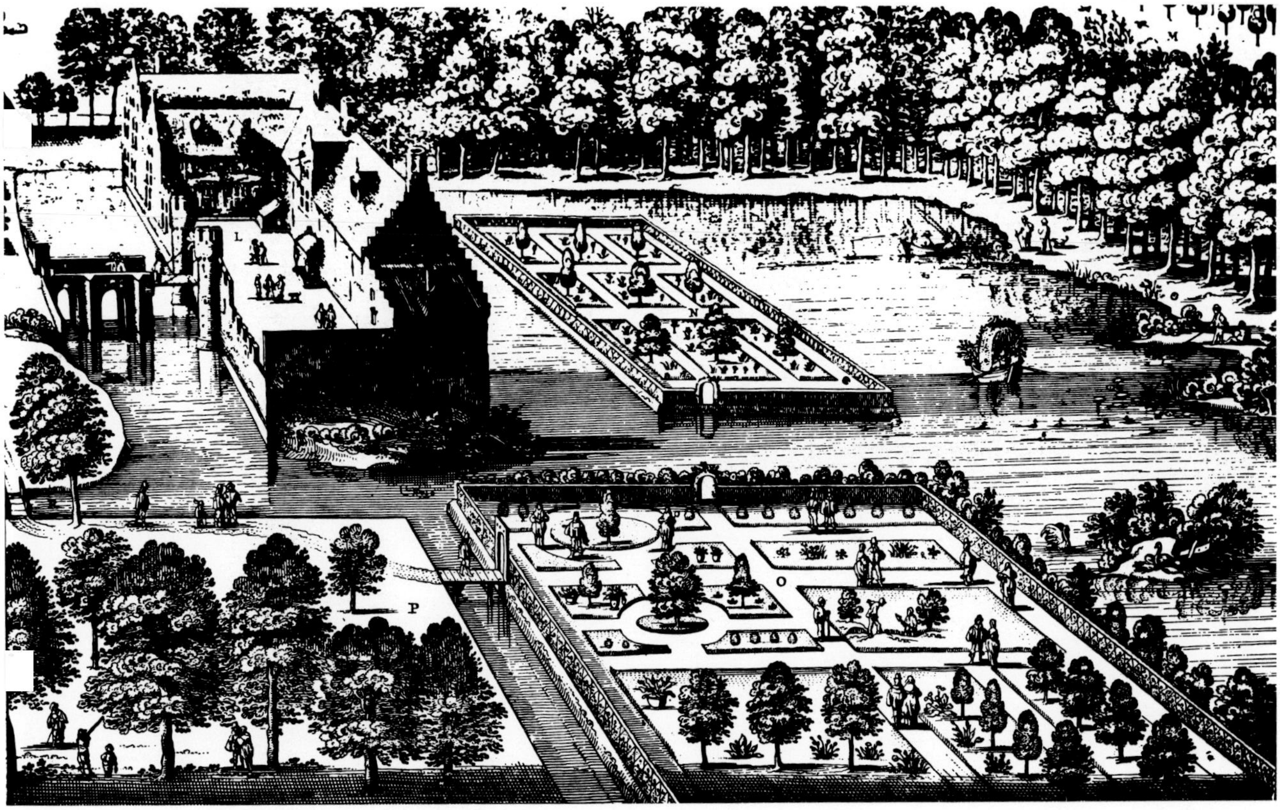

The castle of Wacquem, Flanders, was defended by a wide moat and drawbridge. By 1560 the water had become a decorative element dividing up the various garden areas, one of which could only be reached by boat.

Towns built after the need for fortification had dwindled further show a vast change in plan, with the houses of the better-off at least all having individual gardens, although obviously restricted in some measure by space limits and street plans. The Norman Domesday Book (1086) mentions both *horti* (gardens) and *hortuli* (little gardens) in fair number. By the reign of Henry II (1154–1189), the senior citizens of London at least are known to have had relatively large gardens attached to their houses.

Sometimes development sprawled steadily away from the original fortified center, and one imagines that no town planning of any description was involved. Roadways follow old tracks, and sometimes lead into large undeveloped areas; houses have their own gardens, and often additional separate plots not closely tied to the house.

MONASTERIES

Just as lords, barons and kings shut themselves up within walls, so did the religious communities, the monasteries not so much seeking protection from attack as imposing seclusion upon themselves. Within the monastery walls, the whole community was frequently entirely self-supporting. There would be orchards, vegetable grounds, some space for animals, and the all-important plots of healing herbs. The stricter the order, the more likely was it that these would be communal; in less severe monasteries, each monk might have his own personal plot and, in some unusual cases, this might be associated with his personal dwelling. Individual gardens were normally the prerogative solely of the abbot or prior, although officials such as the precentor, sacristan, almoner, and even

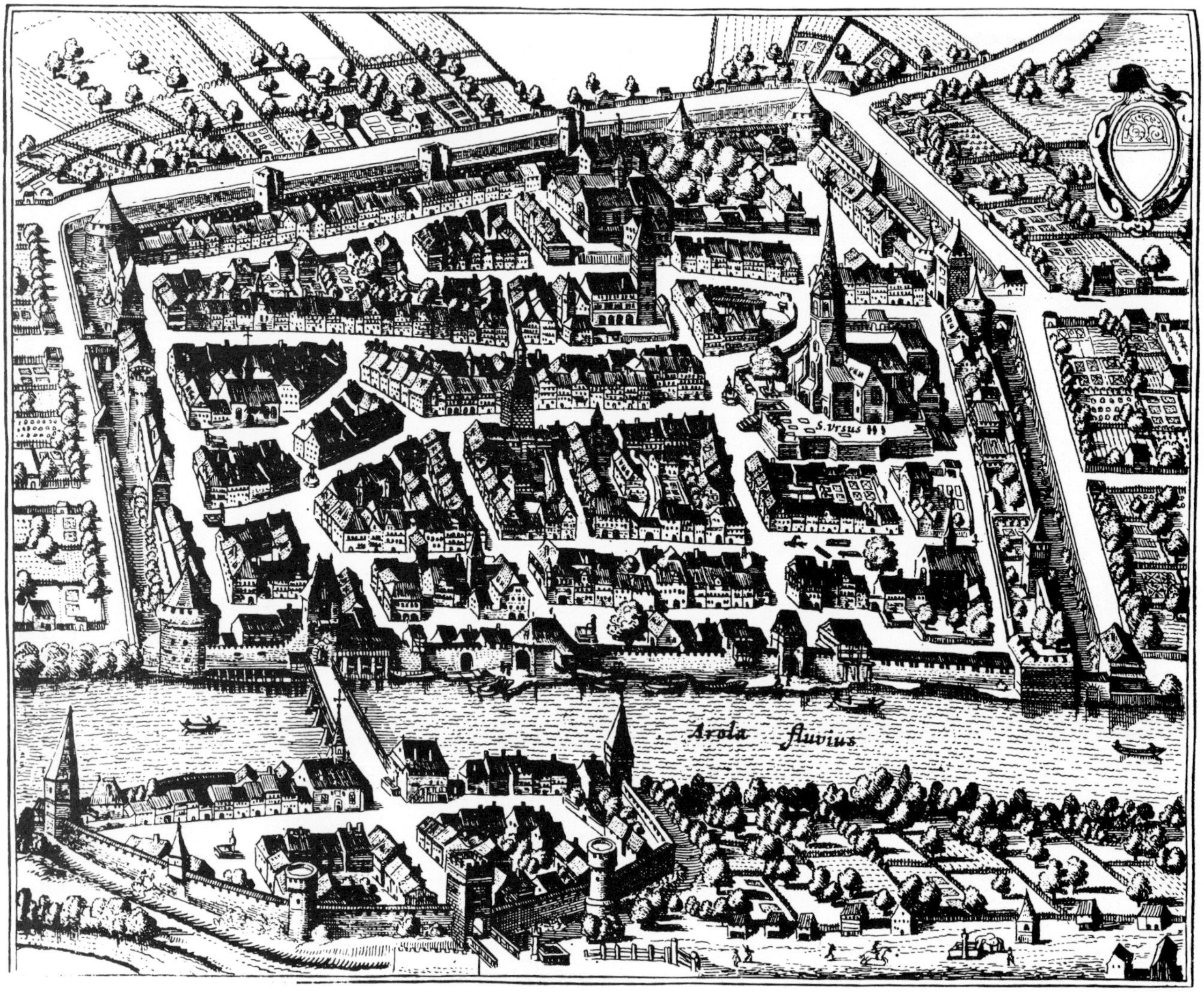

In the Middle Ages, a town like Solothurn (now in northwestern Switzerland) had a moat and massive battlemented walls with many guard towers. It is interesting to note the small extension across the river, equally well fortified. As danger of attack from raiders outside lessened, small, unprotected farmsteads with extensive gardens became established outside the old walls.

OPPOSITE: *A myriad of small gardens, most of them laid out formally, occupy the courtyards of the royal palace of Isfahan, Persia, in 1712.*

the cellarer might rent a garden. The sacristan's garden had to supply flowers for the church, and that at Winchester in southern England was actually known as "Paradise." Many European monasteries, of course, also had vineyards and the associated wine-making equipment, and many distilled liqueurs from alcohol and secret mixtures of herbs. Some of the great monastic beverages, like Benedictine and Chartreuse, are still with us. The Benedictines probably contributed more to horticulture than the other orders: forbidden to eat meat, they had to cultivate large quantities of fruit and vegetables, so it was just as well that manual labor was obligatory.

The ninth-century monastery of St. Gall, in present-day Switzerland, is not only one of the oldest, but also one of the few for which we have a plan – the first European garden plan to be handed down (pages 22–23). It has a double interest, for it demonstrates that monastery gardens were based on those of the Roman *villa rustica*, or agricultural estate, with special emphasis on fruit and nut trees and a vegetable garden. St. Gall also provides us with the first garden book – a poem called *Hortulus* (*The Little Garden* – the diminutive implies something regarded

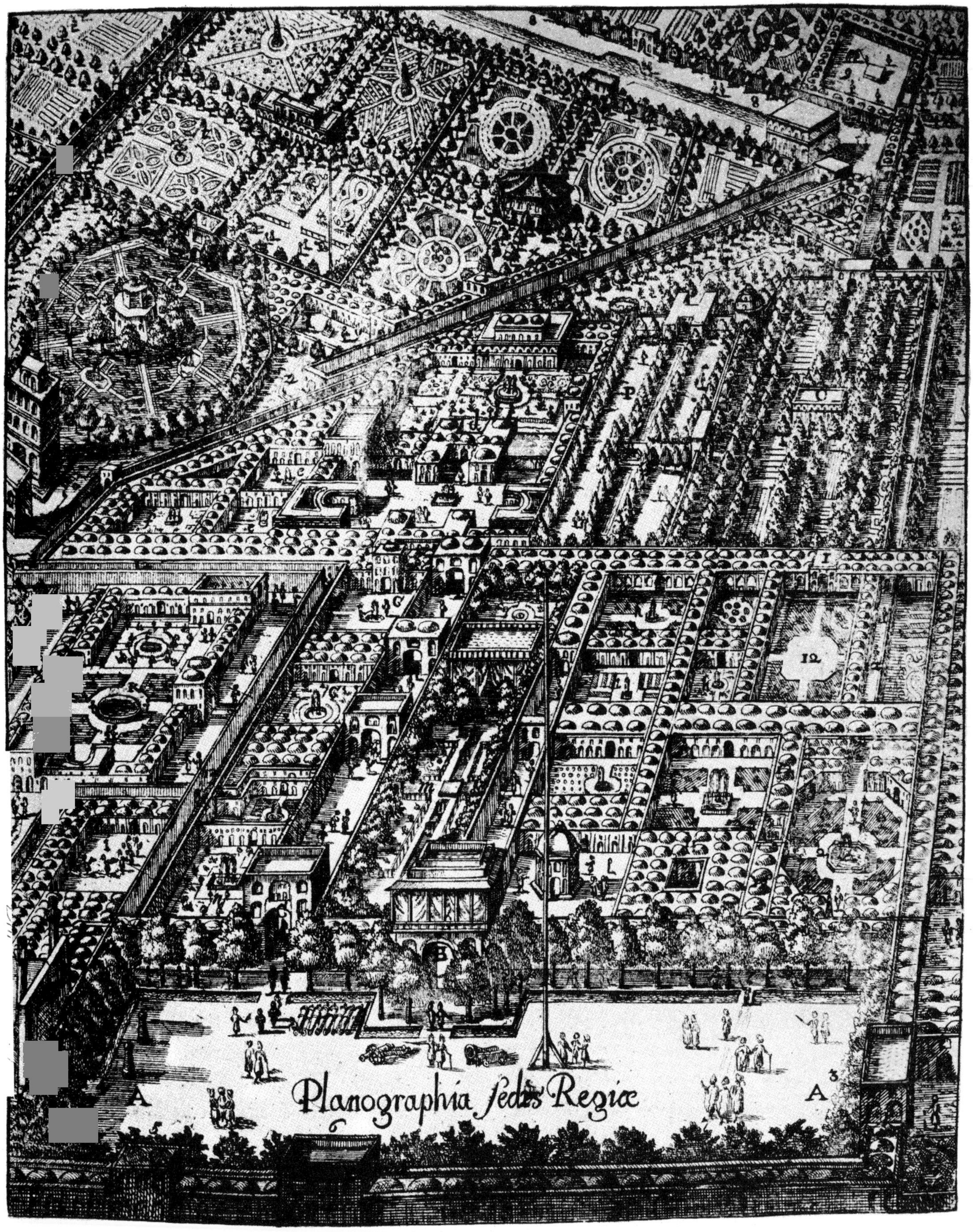
Planographia sedis Regiæ

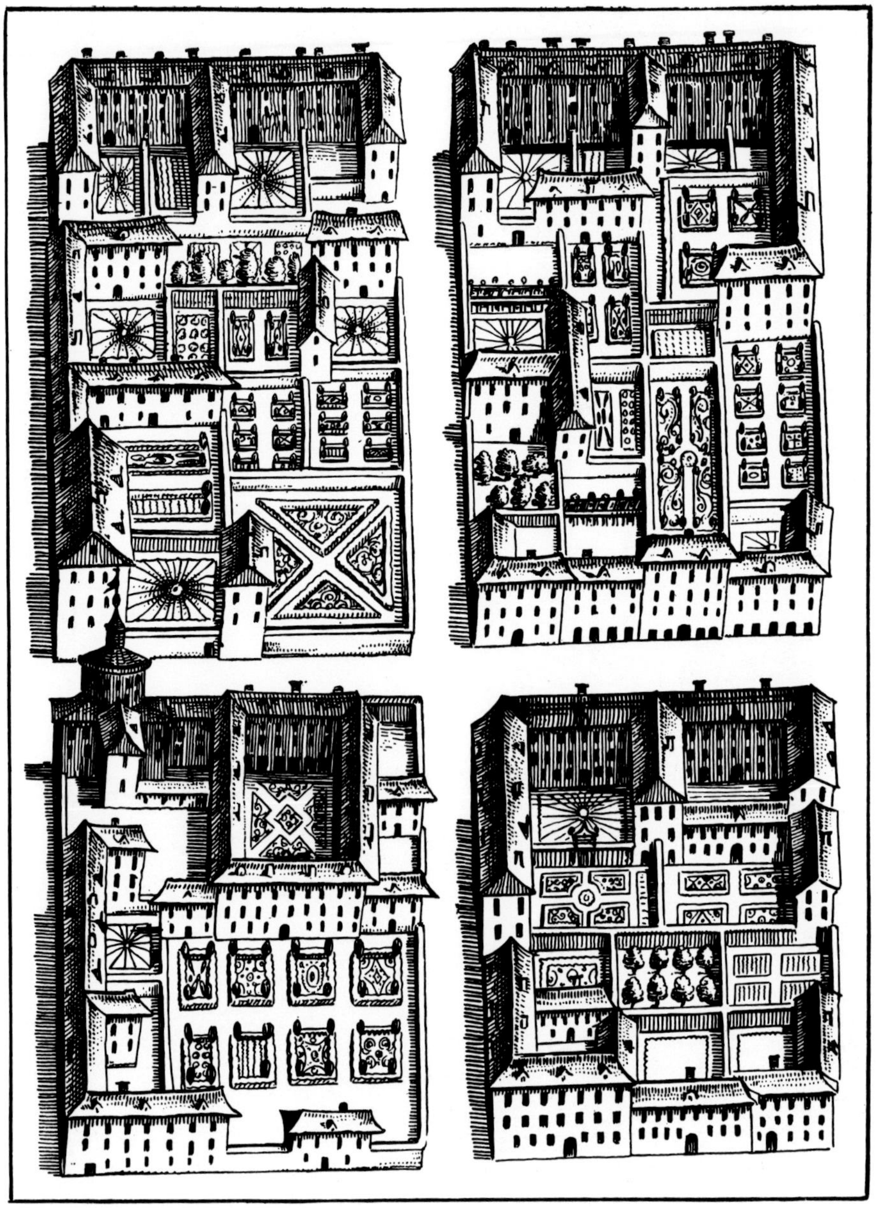

Rebuilt after a fire in 1659, Turin was perhaps the earliest "garden city," with houses laid out on a grid pattern and, as this detail shows, almost everyone having a garden.

with affection) by the monk Walahfrid Strabo, who died in 849, having been tutor to Emperor Louis's son, and later abbot of the closely associated monastery of Reichenau.

Apart from their emphasis on food and medicinal plants, most monastery gardens had a fish pond, and also a garden of leisure where the monks could rest and meditate in off-duty hours.

The monasteries, far more than the castle owners, maintained older gardening traditions but, perhaps even more importantly, they also kept many plants in cultivation that would otherwise have been lost for long periods. And, by their frequent intercourse with each other, and with the crusader orders, they constantly brought more unfamiliar plants into Europe. The Knights of St. John, the Hospitallers and the Templars owned many gardens in England alone. Present-day London names evoke

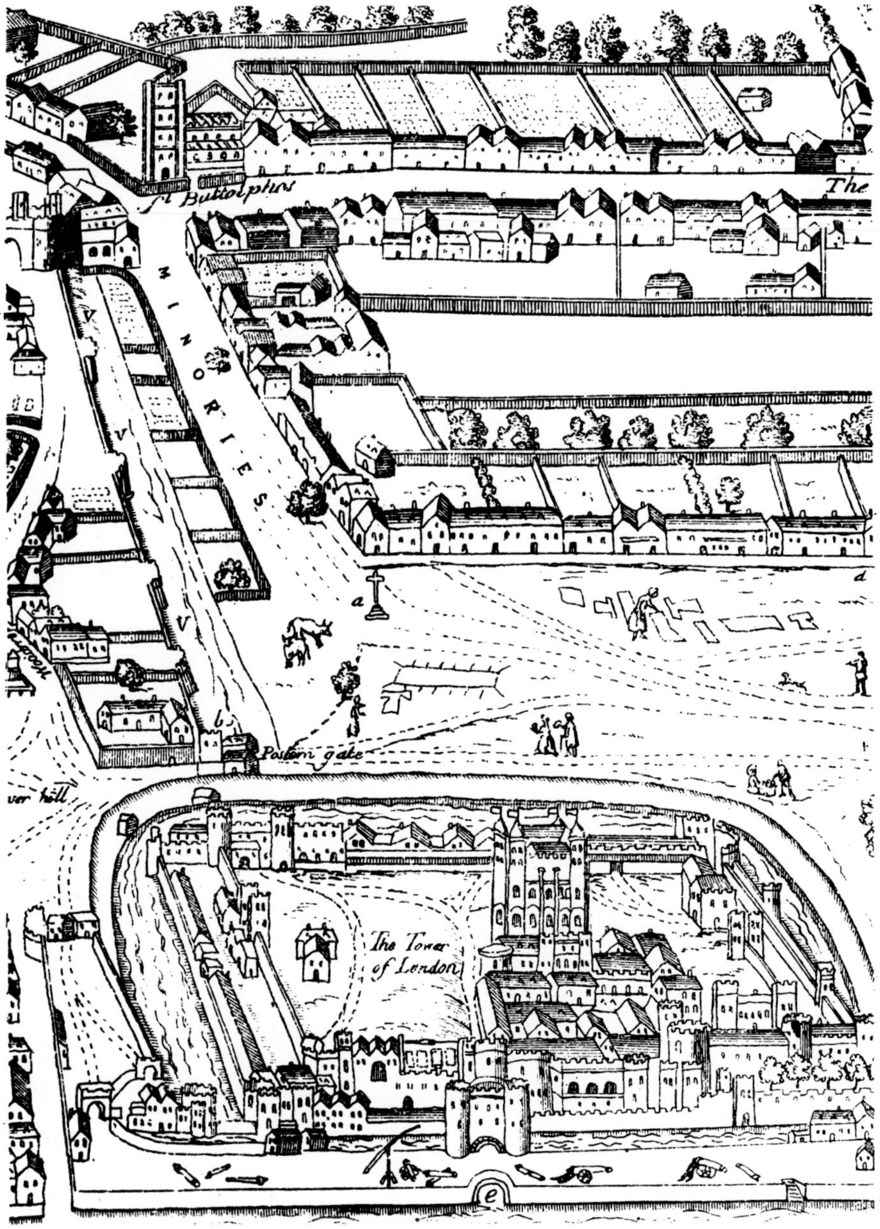

The earliest houses, with gardens and associated fields, spread away from the fortified nucleus of the Tower of London. (From Ralph Aggas's map of 1560.)

them: Black Friars was a Dominican property, and the Temple was owned by the Knights Templar. But the gardens have since disappeared.

HERB GARDENS

When, in the twelfth and thirteenth centuries, wars were not so frequent in Europe, an interest in gardening revived. Small commercial gardens for herbs, other utilitarian plants, and flowers for church decoration developed from the monastic gardens. A medieval herb garden could be a very simple affair, with the plainest of square beds, small enough for every inch to be reached without having to step on the soil, and with adequate pathways in between.

But a real apothecary's garden was altogether more elaborate. The garden itself was often decorative, perhaps boasting a fountain and ornamental plants in pots, as well as the cultivation of herbs. But the main items were the distillery, where essential oils were distilled from the plants,

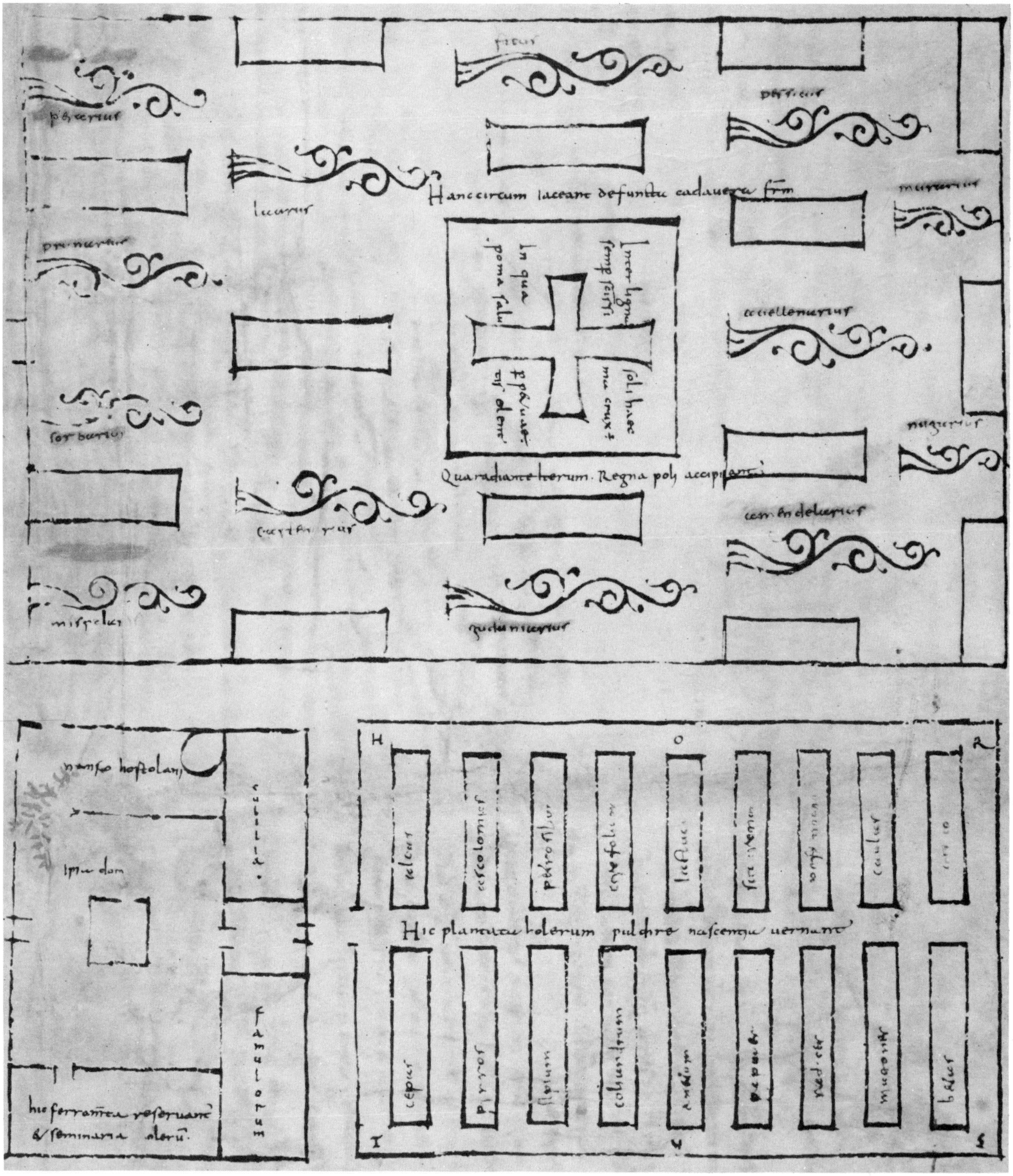

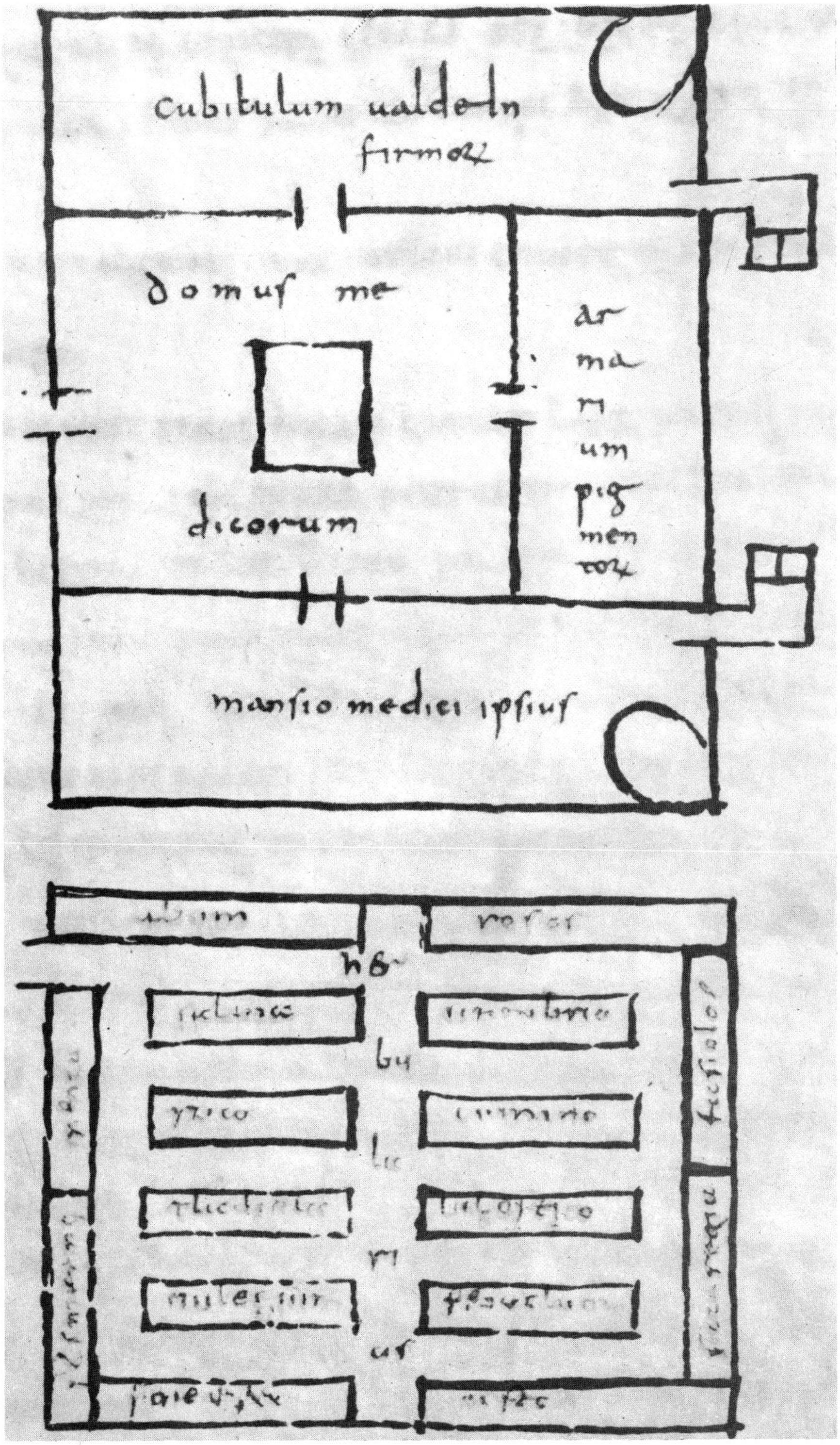

One of the oldest garden documents is the plan of St. Gall monastery, dated A.D. *820. The garden areas in this large foundation are shown on the opposite page. Above is the cemetery, where the scroll shapes indicate fruit trees – apple, pear, plum, service tree, medlar, chestnut, fig, quince, peach, hazel, almond, mulberry, walnut, and a bay laurel, apparently planted between the graves. This orchard adjoins the vegetable garden, with eighteen neat beds and, left, the gardener's dwelling, toolshed and seed store. These areas were in the southwestern corner of the whole, while the physic garden (near left) was in the southeastern corner. Here there were sixteen beds of herbs, including lilies and roses, and adjoining them was the doctor's house. The infirmary was above these.*

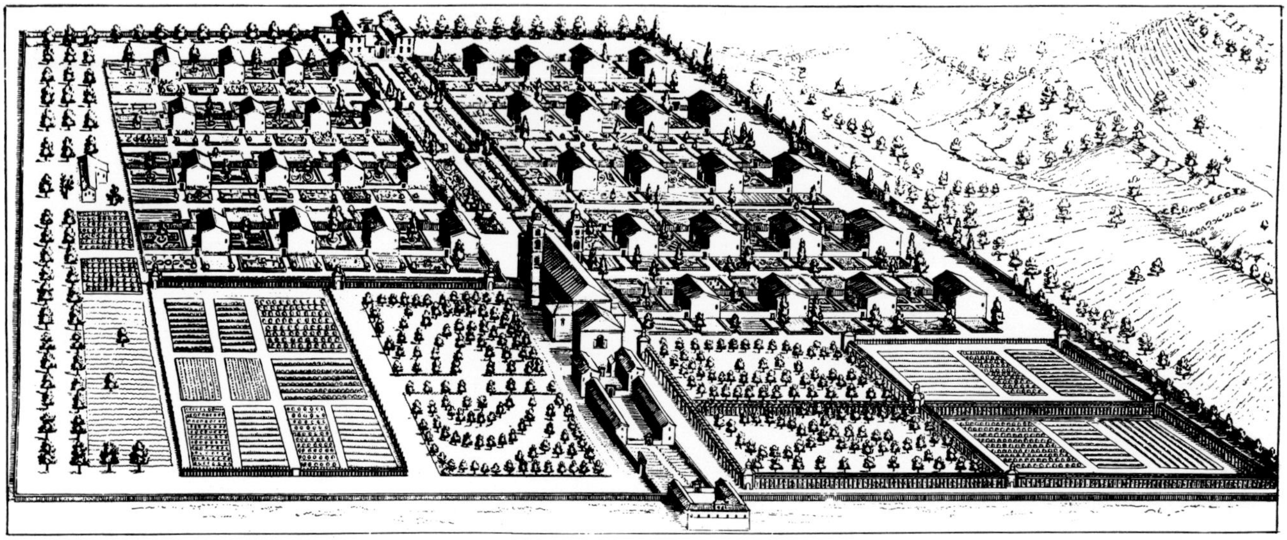

An extraordinary "garden city" style of hermitages near Turin, where, apart from communal orchards and crop fields, each monk had his own separate cell with garden attached. These gardens seem to have been both utilitarian and decorative.

and the pharmacy or laboratory, where tinctures, cordials, oils, "waters," syrups, powders and ointments would be prepared. Judging by contemporary illustrations, these might actually be associated with a kind of hospital, and would be thronged by the doctors of the day, earnestly searching for new cures and tonics, not to mention such desirable mixtures as "Celestial Potion," "Elixir Vitae" or "Aqua Mirabilis."

Herb gardens were also vital parts of the home garden, as we can read in Thomas Tusser's *Five Hundred Points of Good Husbandry*, published in 1573:

> The nature of flowers dame Physick doth shew,
> she teacheth them all to be known to a few.
> To set or to sowe, or else sowne to remove,
> how that should be practised, learne if ye love.

This is for March; rather surprisingly he described "stilling" (distilling) under May – presumably to be carried out later in the year as each herb matured:

> The knowledge of stilling is one prety feat,
> the waters be holesome, the charges not great.
> What timelie thou gettest, while Somer doth last,
> thinke Winter will helpe thee, to spend it as fast.

A herb garden full of flowers would be a pretty sight, but it was entirely utilitarian, ready to cope with illnesses of all kinds, wounds and other accidental hurts, fevers, melancholy and other forms of mental illness. The preparation of herbs was a very important duty of the lady of the house, and Tusser lists twenty-five "necessarie herbes to growe in the garden for physick," seventeen "to still in sommer," some twenty "strowing herbes" – plants which could be swept up periodically, to strew on floors (likely to be fouled in so many ways). He also catalogs over forty "seedes and herbes

A physic garden of 1531 shows preparation and distilling of herbs at left; in the center doctors confer, and at top left there is a patient in a "hospital."

An apothecary's garden, or physic garden – illustrated in 1500 – where herbs were grown and their essential oils and essences distilled. Note the primitive wattle fence around it.

OPPOSITE: *The original plans of colleges resemble those of monasteries in the positioning of their cloisters and gardens: Jesus College, Oxford, in 1707.*

for the kitchen," twenty "herbes and rootes for sallets and sauce," and another twelve "to boile or to butter."

We can trace a direct line from the monastery garden to the early gardens of English university colleges, where a rather similar arrangement of plots was often carried out, although naturally these became steadily more ornamental. This is hardly surprising, since the buildings themselves, usually based on a quadrangle, were architecturally derived from the cloistered courtyards of monastic foundations.

PLEASURE GARDENS

The final development of the garden is its use for pleasure rather than plain utility – a use which, as I have suggested earlier, develops only when the culture concerned has some excess of wealth and time. Very often, of course, these surpluses are limited to the upper crust – the royal families, nobles, aristocracies – while the peasants toil for their basic essentials, paying tithe or tax to their rulers. And this, of course, is a pattern we see repeated in vastly different epochs as civilizations rise and fall. Gardening in its widest sense is certainly an expression of a civilization becoming mature; one hopes that it is not also a symbol of the beginnings of its decadence.

The development of the pleasure garden in different cultures and ages has, of course, little bearing on horticultural method or technique. But one must, I think, bear in mind the purposes for which gardens have been designed, and pleasure is certainly among these – from the simplest levels of enjoying shade and coolness to those of appreciating plants and flowers for their own beauty. These purposes, as well as the completely utilitarian ones of providing food and medicine, must be kept in mind if one is to appreciate the historical development of gardening.

The design of gardens owes much to ancient symbolism, which becomes more pronounced as one moves east. Chinese and Japanese gardens were very formal and symbolic, while the gardens of ancient Egypt and Persia combined symbolism and relaxation more equally. A great many garden designs are based on the cosmic cross, whose first literary appearance is in the second chapter of Genesis: "And a river went out of Eden to water the garden; and from thence it was parted, and became into four heads." We find a garden divided into four parts by water to be a recurring theme. The Persians frequently made, and still make, carpets depicting such gardens, with a river or canals forming a cross; and the four-square Tudor garden is seemingly a direct descendant of this. Four is a basic number in the symbolism of numbers – it is the number of creation, and there are the four corners of the earth, four seasons, four winds of heaven, and so on.

OPPOSITE: *A detail of the gardens at Trinity College, Cambridge, in 1688, showing checkerboard beds, possibly for herbal plants.*

This four-square conception made many early gardens heavily symmetrical, as is very clear if we study plans and reconstructions of early Egyptian gardens of the second millennium B.C. The plants in these plots – fenced and later walled – were almost all for food, including grapes, dates,

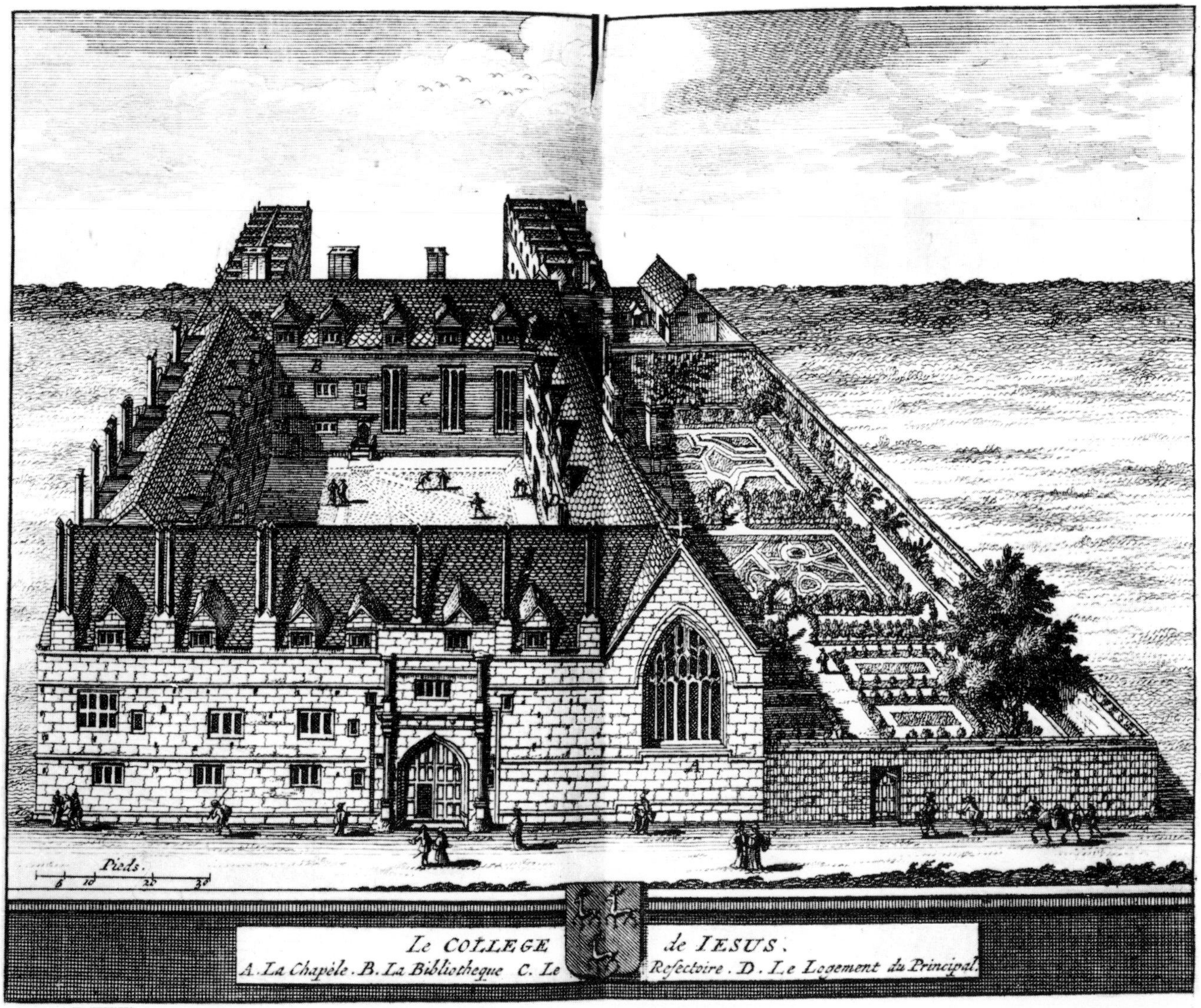
Pieds.
5 10 20 30
Le COLLEGE de IESUS.
A. La Chapèle . B. La Bibliotheque C. Le Refectoire . D. Le Logement du Principal.

figs, sycomore figs, and pomegranates. The vines were always grown on the pergola system, which does not seem to have been used for anything else. The pools held both fish and fowl, also for the table. Royal and, especially, temple gardens had extensive plots of medicinal herbs, and many plants, including trees, for providing incense. (The Egyptians were the largest users of incense in the world's history.)

Besides all these plants grown for home use, the gardens also provided shade, coolness, and the relaxation which a people of such discipline would find in strictly ordered walks, pools, and ranks of trees and vines, all enclosed behind high brick walls. The gardens often had pavilions in which one could sit and survey the scene. Such elaboration was the prerogative of the wealthy – royalty and high officials; the middle classes grew vegetables and fruit in much smaller plots, but shade was equally important, and there was usually at least one tree shading the well.

The Egyptians certainly loved flowers, as is demonstrated by their murals portraying court ladies wearing Egyptian lotus blooms (waterlily, known as the queen of flowers) on their heads. Various other blooms are depicted in containers, and there is also the touching evidence of preserved funeral garlands. The flowers concerned, however, grew wild in Egypt at the time, and usually sprang up as weeds in the gardens. The herb plots probably provided other kinds as a bonus.

But some flowers and exotic trees were actively cultivated, for inscriptions record the activities of Ramses III (1198–1166 B.C.) when creating a new city in the Delta. Here he apparently founded public pleasure grounds with "wide places for walking with all kinds of sweet fruit trees, laden with fruit, a sacred way, beautiful with flowers of all lands. . . ." And among his gifts to Heliopolis were "great gardens, planted with trees and vines . . . grounds with olive trees . . . groves and copses with date palms, ponds planted with lotus flowers, rushes, grasses, and flowers of all land for thy beautiful face." Elsewhere Ramses recorded that he imported plants from outside the kingdom in honor of the god Amun. Certain trees were grown in temple gardens, each temple confining itself to one kind which was cultivated as a sacred grove. Altogether, Ramses donated no less than 514 gardens or garden sites to various temples.

Although the garden plans are very stylized, it does seem possible that they sometimes included a kind of bedding scheme, where flowering and foliage plants were grown in blocks. Small shrubs were also grown in large earthenware pots, a practice developed under Ramses III and undoubtedly picked up later by the invading Romans, who carried the fashion back home. Still later, the use of ornamental pots became widespread during the European Renaissance, and it survives to this day.

Besides pot culture and the symmetrical garden on one level, the Egyptians introduced another style which became immensely important in Renaissance Italy – that of the terraced hill so grandly elaborated by Queen

Hatsepshut at her temple of Deir-el-Bahri in about 1540 B.C. Here great stone terraces, linked with ramps and stairways, were laid out to include trees, plant beds and pools, backed by many pillared arcades.

ZIGGURATS

Deir-el-Bahri brings to mind the ziggurats of ancient Mesopotamia, but whereas the former was taking advantage of a hillside to make a more impressive structure than could be constructed on the flat, the ziggurats were really artificial hills. The people who made them came from hilly country and had always placed their temples in high places; in the fertile but featureless "land between the rivers" they had to build upward. Ziggurats were in essence rectangular, widely terraced pyramids of up to seven stories, with a temple at the summit. Ziggurats were certainly made in the reign of Sargon I (*c.* 2350 B.C.). The apparently similar "hanging gardens of Babylon" were, according to one account, made by Nebuchadnezzar II (604–561 B.C.) for his Median wife who pined for her native wooded hills. Another account, however, attributes them to the reign of Semiramis (814–810 B.C.).

At any rate, the ziggurats were built to be cultivated: around the temple was planted a sacred grove, and on the terraces were trees, shrubs and vines planted in rows. The hanging gardens, described by Strabo as consisting "of vaulted terraces raised one above another," incorporated drainage and irrigation channels. According to Diodorus, the topmost terrace held the main garden, while additional trees were planted on the ramps between terraces. The planting area was, if we can believe the Greek historian, waterproofed with a layer of reeds heavily coated with asphalt, on top of which were two layers of tiles and a final covering of lead sheets. A considerable depth of soil was augmented by further soil in the hollow structural columns, while "certain engines" drew water from the Euphrates through hidden conduits. Such pyramids must have been an impressive sight, rising, covered with verdure, above the plain.

PARKS

Besides such artificial tree cultivation, the succeeding Mesopotamian civilizations had, from earliest days, parks of various kinds. In the Gilgamesh epic of the third millennium B.C., there is a reference to a kind of park, in this case apparently surrounding a sacred grove and a sanctuary. Later, to the Assyrians at any rate, a park was very much a place where trees, often imported ones, were planted formally. Tiglath-Pileser I, who flourished around 1100 B.C., boasts of planting "trees that none of the kings my forefathers have possessed . . . carried off from the countries I conquered . . . in the parks of Assyria have I planted them." A few hundred years later (660 B.C.), there is a bas-relief of Ashurbanipal, reclining on a couch, feasting with his queen (on a chair) in the royal garden after a victory. This garden was huge, filled with vines, fruit, spice plants and herbs, and was surrounded by a vast park. The royal couple each apparently hold flowers in their left hands, so one surmises that flowers may have been cultivated, although the main gardening interest of all these peoples was clearly trees, along with food and herbal plants.

From the parks of ancient Mesopotamia, which were also used partly for hunting game, came those of the Persians. They called them *pardes*, a word from which our "paradise" is derived via the Greek *paradeisos*. Xenophon, writing of Cyrus the Great who reigned from 553 to 529 B.C., describes how "the Persian king is zealously cared for, so that he may find gardens wherever he goes. Their name is Paradise, and they are full of all things fair and good that the earth can bring forth." It is clear that the Persians were very active planters of trees, creating shady, regular groves. The planting and care of trees was as important a part of their education as was the study of arms and warfare. However, the private gardens that surrounded Persian homes and palaces probably derived from those of Egypt, which the Persians conquered in 525 B.C., and had a similar geometrical layout.

GREECE

We now turn chronologically to a very different kind of civilization – that of the Greeks and Romans. Often warring these peoples may have been, but the benefits of life were more equally spread among the population. I have already quoted Homer's description of the garden of Alcinous and mentioned the scanty records of private Greek gardens.

The standard Greek house was composed of small rooms surrounding an inner courtyard, which was the main area of activity during the day. This courtyard would usually contain some trees, large terracotta containers holding other plants, and some statues – not a very elaborate garden, but the beginnings of one.

It was a remarkable mixing of cultures that made later Hellenistic gardens so interesting – not primarily in Greece itself, but in Asia Minor, Egypt and North Africa. Alexander's conquests made available many exotic ideas from Persia, itself inheritor of the Mesopotamian traditions, and from farther east, while of course the Ptolemies had many centuries of gardening behind them. In these lands, decorative gardening and the cultivation of newly introduced plants became a passion; artistic and social associations almost entirely effaced the early religious ones.

ROME

These were the models which the Romans copied, assimilated, and developed almost beyond recognition. They were not really innovators themselves, but they were always excellent farmers and smallholders, with a tremendous love of plants and the land. When their townships grew up, the average citizen would have a *hortus* or smallholding entirely devoted to fruit and vegetables, some to be consumed by his family, any surplus to be sold. Richer families combined the smallholding with a farmhouse, the *villa rustica*. In these earlier days, there was no single word for "gardener." The vegetable grower was *olitor* or *holitor*, the tree tender *arborator* or *frondator*, the vineyard specialist *vinitor*.

Decorative Roman gardening began in the first century B.C. under the influence of Cicero and his circle. Town gardens were developed from the Greek model, with a number of courtyards surrounding and interlocking with the house itself – the *villa urbana.* Stylization was the order of the day, with rectangular beds, straight alleys and paved walks, edgings of box and ivy, much use of ornamental plants (acanthus, for example, in blocks to provide pattern rather than an individual feature). There were large plant containers, ornamental urns, statues, pools and fountains. Where space was restricted, the garden was sometimes given another dimension by beautiful painted *trompe-l'oeil* murals representing garden or natural scenes. This was evidently practiced at Pompeii where "postage stamp" gardens as small as 7½ by 1½ feet – really glorified window boxes – were amplified by a painted wall or fence. Many houses also had raised or rooftop gardens to make maximum use of space, and it was not unknown for a Pompeiian to make a new window for the purpose of enjoying a neighbor's garden.

The Romans were the first to develop gardens as essential extensions to their houses. Martial, in the first century A.D., jokes at a rich man whose garden was so full of plants, walks and fountains that his house lacked space for eating and sleeping – just as in the modern lyric by Flanders and Swann, where "the garden's full of furniture and the house is full of plants."* But apart from the wealthy, the ordinary Romans were so fond of plants that the innumerable apartment dwellers in the multi-storied *insulae* or apartment houses in the city grew plants on windowsills, balconies and roofs, just as we do today.

It was only in the first century B.C. that the general or ornamental gardener made his literary appearance (in the writings of Cicero); he was called *topiarius* because one of his main functions was to train the ivy so extensively used, as well as to look after evergreen trees and shrubs. It was not for a century or so that the word was applied in its modern sense to a clipper of evergreens. Topiary rapidly became a major addiction of the Romans, and it was apparently as elaborate as anything to be seen in later periods.

The gardens of the wealthy outside the town during the first century A.D. had seemingly no limit to their extent and lavishness; they soon spread over much valuable agricultural land, to the concern of serious agronomists like Columella. Some of the larger villas had gardens very like the classical ones preserved in Italy today, with enormous parterres, tree avenues and the gamut of fantastic waterworks, often enhanced by terracing on hillsides. The rich Romans apparently also had elaborate funerary gardens; one mentioned in a second-century will had orchards and ponds, with three gardeners and an apprentice to look after it.

People in hot countries often must have eaten outside the house in the shady courtyard, cooled by a fountain playing in the pool or canal.

* From *At the Drop of a Hat,* "Design for Living," Michael Flanders and Donald Swann, Angel 65042.

Eating and drinking, card playing, music making and courting take place in a fifteenth century "garden of love" set in a forest park full of wild animals, adjoining two castles. A stream runs through the flower-filled meadow; wine bottles are cooling in the water. Note the low turf seats with wooden back rest in the foreground.

Doubtless, other leisure activities also took place there. The Romans were perhaps the first culture to make real use of gardens for sheer pleasure. The basic enjoyment of eating was accompanied by music, dancing, miming, and often, in the decadent years, by postprandial orgies of varying degree.

Many medieval and later illustrations depict similar activities in gardens of varying sophistication. The "pleasaunce" of the early Middle Ages was usually described as an orchard, but was much more than a collection of fruit trees; other kinds of tree were often found there. The pleasaunce was used for receiving guests, playing games, and sometimes staging tournaments, for dancing, singing and, on occasion, for large dinner parties. Gradually the orchards were replaced by altogether more formal designs, "gardens of pleasure" with elaborate fences and arbors, private corners, turf seats, fountains, and a main grassy area with wild flowers in and around it. These were also the "gardens of love" of the troubadours, where courtiers wooed their ladies in their intense but physically restrained manner.

During this period the civilizations of the nearer East, notably the Arab and the Byzantine, continued to develop decorative gardening, culling both their ideas of design and their plants from the immense range assimilated from the Romano-Hellenistic and the Persian garden. Their gardens were enclosed, formal, and almost always included pools and fountains. The Arabs were also intensely technical. A book by the eleventh-century Ibn Bassal discusses water supply, manures, soil and its preparation, and describes numerous vegetables and ornamental plants, as well as all aspects of tree culture, including grafting and seed sowing.

Some of these ideas came to Europe with pilgrims and, later, with

The simple life – eating to music in the late fifteenth century.

An outdoor revel around a banqueting table in a formal bower, part of a public park (Holland, around 1600).

crusaders. Those of the Arabs usually reached Europe via Spain and the Moorish occupation. Thus we find the garden of Charlemagne (741–814) resembling a Persian park or paradise, complete with menagerie; and that of Henry I of England (reigning 1100–1135), at Woodstock, was a vast park with animals from "divers outlandish Lands." When Petrus Crescentius (Pietro de Crescenzi) wrote the most important medieval gardening treatises (in 1304 and 1306), he devoted space to describing something very similar to the Eastern "paradise." When the Normans conquered the Saracens in Sicily in 1094, they found similar park gardens, full of pleasure pavilions – "the first purely secular pleasure gardens of medieval Italy," according to Georgina Masson – and reinstated them.

Most elementary gardens in Tudor England resembled the formal courtyards of the Persians and the Moguls, although many contained a hint of the fantastic, almost a spirit of frivolity. Soon, however, the designs of Renaissance Europe overtook this symbolic symmetry. The Renaissance sought its inspiration in the classical period, and a great deal of subsequent garden design – whether on the lavish or townhouse scale – stems from Roman originals (including the great open landscapes of eighteenth-century England).

CHINA

I must now go back in time and thousands of miles to the east, where the Chinese civilization, as skillful as that of Rome in very different ways, was elaborating its highly idiosyncratic garden style. It is known that, during the Han dynasty (about 206 B.C.–A.D. 220), hunting parks, artificial hills, and complex water gardens with strangely shaped rocks were being constructed. The houses were in the center of an elaborate jigsaw of enclosures, with architectural features such as bridges, richly decorated pavilions, carefully designed walls and paths. The Emperor Wu Ti (187–140 B.C.) collected in his vast grounds plants, notably rare trees, from all over his vast empire which extended from Central Asia to Korea. Although the descriptions of this and similar gardens are vague, they were clearly so sophisticated that their origins must be much earlier, although no records exist. The record is also poor because of the ancient custom that a son would not continue living in a property when his father died, so that gardens rapidly went back to nature, and the rocks would be removed to decorate new gardens.

The earliest gardens were those of the rulers; later every wealthy family created one, while hermits, poets and philosophers devised smaller plots of studied simplicity. As with those of the nearer East, they had religious significance as well as recreational purpose, being an expression of Taoist nature worship. The pleasures the Chinese enjoyed in them were of a much less earthy, more meditative kind than those enjoyed in Rome and Europe. In essence, these gardens were romantic landscapes and – just as in England in the early eighteenth century – their design ran parallel with idealized landscape painting. Their features included lakes or ponds, streams, islands, waterfalls, clumps of trees or bamboos, grottoes and pavilions. Country gardens combined wide views with small intimate areas; cities also had fine gardens, which perforce relied more upon architectural design.

Later, under the influence of Buddhist monks who always placed their monasteries in sites of natural beauty, a rather more naturalistic style arose. But Chinese gardening in general has always been remarkably conservative. One of its most extraordinary aspects is the love of usually enormous, well-weathered or water-sculpted rocks, sometimes used singly like statuary in the West. One rock can be made to represent a whole mountain.

The Chinese cultivated the rare trees and herbaceous plants which could be found in such variety in their country, the most important of these originally being the chrysanthemum and the tree peony or moutan. The flowering plants were grown in regular beds or, more often, in pots artistically arranged around house or pavilion so that every stage of their growth could be observed.

JAPAN

Of the Japanese, historian Edward Hyams has written that they have carried garden art "much farther into the realm of the abstract than any other people." Although their ideas were derived from Chinese gardening, via Korea, the end results are quite distinct. According to the Swedish art historian Osvald Sirén, the Chinese influence was "assimilated to the Japanese feeling for style and in accordance with national needs."

The earliest Japanese gardens probably date from the third century A.D.; there are written references to a sixth-century garden and to royal gardens of the seventh century. The basic ingredient of these antique Japanese gardens seems to have been an island in a lake, with bridges for access. From about A.D. 800 to 1186, Japanese gardens were often lavish and extravagant, with artificial lakes and mountains. Some were landscapes outdoing reality – "picture gardening" very similar in principle to that of early British landscape gardening. Later, a combination of symbolism, tradition, superstition and Zen Buddhism (introduced around 522) controlled Japanese garden design, resulting in places for quiet meditation, with planting often reduced to a handful of trees among rocks, water (or raked sand to symbolize it in "dry landscape"), stepping stones, and certain architectural features. But one must never forget that all this is based, in however stylized a form, upon an innate love of nature and an intimacy with it. The smallest area is regarded as garden-worthy by the Japanese and, if there is no space around a house, they resort to miniaturization of both gardens and plants (bonsai).

SOUTH AMERICA

Meanwhile, on yet another continent, there flourished what was perhaps the world's most isolated gardening culture – that of pre-Columbian America. From around 2500 B.C., the widespread Inca empire, in the Andes of South America, was based on successful horticulture rather than on large-scale agriculture. At this very early period, they grew many vegetables and fruits, as well as utilitarian plants for medicine, contraception, dyes and poison. Rulers and high officials had elaborate gardens about which the Spaniards wrote in lavish terms all too lacking in detail. They clearly had water channels, pools and basins, sometimes made of silver and gold. William H. Prescott, in *History of the Conquest of Peru*, writes of "groves and airy gardens . . . stocked with numerous varieties of plants"; he comments also on the "parterres" filled with artificial plants made of gold and silver.

And farther north, the Aztecs, living in the Valley of Mexico (Tenochtitlan) in the twelfth to thirteenth centuries A.D., were passionately fond of decorative plants, and seem to have made extensive botanical gardens, arranged in some kind of system, of the myriads of wild species. The royal gardens were again based on water, with fountains, canals and lakes. They seem to have been largely rectangular in plan, but the flowers grew so abundantly in the squares and on trellises bordering the paths that the formality must have been greatly obscured. Prescott again, in *History of the Conquest of Mexico*, describes a "labyrinth of sweet-scented groves and shrubberies . . . ample basins . . . overhung by light and fanciful pavilions. . . . Montezuma's gardens stretched for miles." Beyond the water and the formal beds, there seem to have been parks of rare trees surrounded by a wall.

The smaller private houses of the Aztecs had courtyards and roof gardens which greatly impressed the Spaniards on their arrival. Prescott wrote that "the flat roofs . . . were protected with stone parapets, so that every house was a fortress. Sometimes these roofs resembled parterres of flowers, so thickly were they covered with them, but more often these were cultivated in broad terraced gardens, laid out between the edifices." These gardens reminded some of the conquistadors of the hanging gardens of Babylon. And the gardens of independent Tezcuco (present-day Texcoco) at this period displayed horticultural taste and knowledge of a kind virtually unknown in Europe. Cortes himself described the gardens as "the largest, freshest and most beautiful that ever were seen."

Virtually nothing remains of all this. As Bernal Diaz de Castillo wrote, "No future discoveries will ever be so wonderful. Alas! today, all is overthrown and lost, nothing left standing." Even from the sketchy descriptions, one can surmise that these gardens, so wantonly destroyed by the Spaniards, paralleled those of India and Persia.

But however wonderful the gardens were, and however much they impressed the conquerors, they do not seem to have influenced European design.

NORTH AMERICA

Certainly they did not influence the early European colonists of America. These people are of particular interest to gardening history because they represent the only occasion on which there were brand new settlements in virtually virgin territory, by people with a relatively advanced knowledge of husbandry.

Earliest to be permanently settled by white men was Florida, where the Spaniards established a settlement at St. Augustine in 1565. The governor imported tools, seeds and plants, and within twenty-five years St. Augustine became a busy city with numerous gardens and orchards. It and the other Spanish colonies established along the Florida and Georgia coasts became the first American testing grounds for European plants, citrus fruits and peaches being especially important to the Spaniards. When, in 1763, Spain ceded Florida to England, an English writer noted that the gardens they left behind were "well stocked with fruit trees, figs, guavas, pomegranates, lemons, limes, shaddock, bergamot [i.e., bergamot orange], China and Seville oranges, and potherbs."

Not much is recorded of the Spanish gardens in the numerous coastal settlements. The Spaniards were, after all, soldiers rather than gardeners. But every house seems to have had a garden, and further cultivation was done by the priests who followed the soldiers with missions, built patio-style with large enclosures within a square of buildings or high walls.

Much the same occurred on the West Coast, where the first outposts were those of Spanish Jesuits who created missions in Baja California from 1697 onward. Considering the difficult climate and inhospitable terrain, they did wonders of cultivation in the gardens and orchards surrounding their missions. Of San Xavier, outstanding in this respect, an early observer wrote that "almost all productions of both temperate and torrid zones throve side by side with astonishing exuberance." Much of this success can be attributed to the knowledge of irrigation of one of the founders, Padre Juan de Ugarte.

In 1767 the Jesuits, expelled from Spain and her territories, were replaced by Franciscans, and two years later these established new settlements in California proper. Unfortunately, as Victoria Padilla has written,* "so busy were the padres keeping records of conversions and vital statistics that they made little note of the trees, shrubs and plants they raised" – nor of their tools and methods. But their success as cultivators is, again, reported by other observers, like the English navigator George Vancouver who wrote of a visit in 1793 as follows:

> . . . the garden at Buena Ventura far exceeded anything I had before met with in this region, both in respect of the quality, quantity, and variety of its excellent productions, not only indigenous to the country, but appertaining to the temperate as well as the torrid zone;

* In *Southern California Gardens: An Illustrated History*, University of California Press, Berkeley, 1961.

> not one species having yet been sown, or planted, that had not flourished, and yielded its fruit in abundance, and of excellent quality. These have principally consisted of apples, pears, plums, figs, oranges, grapes, peaches, and pomegranates, together with the plantain [banana], cocoa nut, sugar cane, indigo, and a great variety of the necessary and useful kitchen herbs, plants and roots. All these were flourishing in the greatest health and perfection though separated from the seaside only by two or three fields of corn, that were cultivated within a few yards of the surf. The grounds, however, on which they were produced, were supplied, at the expense of some labor, with a few small streams, which as occasion required, were conducted to the crops that stood most in need of water. Here also grew great quantities of the Indian fig, or prickly pear. . . .

The prickly pear was in fact used by the Franciscans to make impregnable hedges, which grew to twelve feet wide and twenty feet tall, around their grounds. Besides the edible plants listed above, they also grew many flowers.

These Spanish mission gardens declined during the early nineteenth century, following the secularization of the missions in 1822. But, as Victoria Padilla again observes:

> Although the sphere in which they worked was limited, the Franciscans left an indelible imprint on the land they had sought to cultivate. For three-quarters of a century their missions had been the only developed areas in an otherwise primitive region. It was they who planted the first orange grove and gathered the first grapes for wine: it was they who showed that the olive would flourish and bear fruit. They introduced the palm and the pepper tree into California gardens, as well as many plants closely associated with the "Golden State." The influence of the padres did not die with their missions; left behind was a heritage more valuable than the gold discovered later in the mountains. The padres proved that California's greatest treasure lay in a soil capable of producing crops that would bring more wealth than all the minerals within the hills. They did reveal that the "Garden of the Hesperides" was not entirely a myth.

This brief "golden age" of gardening is in marked contrast to the experiences of the Pilgrims when they landed at Plymouth, New England, in 1620, to be followed by the Dutch in New Amsterdam (now New York), the Swedes in New Jersey, and others. They were not, in fact, the first colonists: Jamestown Island had been colonized in 1607, but these earlier settlers were after gold and had neither experience of gardening nor inclination to practice it. They lived mainly on what they found, only slowly beginning to garden seriously. In the winter of 1609–1610, they endured the "Starving Time" in which only sixty of the original five hundred survived. The marriage of John Rolfe to Pocohontas led to these earlier settlers learning about tobacco cultivation and improving on the Indian agricultural methods, with the result that by 1620 some forty thousand tons of tobacco had been shipped to England.

But in Plymouth, although the Pilgrims had a disastrous first winter, it is recorded that, as early as March 7, 1621, they planted "garden seeds," and so effectively started European-style gardening in New England. They found the local Indians, who were peaceful and settled, excellent gardeners already, with unfenced fields and plots of neatly cultivated crops among and around their curiously modern-looking huts. The Indians cultivated a wide variety of vegetables and fruits, using digging sticks, elementary hoes and a kind of mattock (further described in Chapter 4). Most of the crops were developed from the profuse natural flora, but some plants (such as the peach) had reached them from earlier Spanish plantations in Mexico and Florida. Some Indians practiced a simple rotation of land (rather than a rotation of crops on the same land), but most moved on when the ground was exhausted.

Although the settlers commented on the variety of the native edible flora, they were even more impressed by the rich soil – at Salem if not at the original settlement at Plymouth – and the splendid crops it very rapidly grew. Naturally, they primarily grew crops to which they were accustomed, of which they had brought stocks of seeds, but they cultivated many of the local fruits and vegetables, including wild vines and corn (maize). In many places settlers bought surplus corn seed from the Indians, often exchanging or partially paying with agricultural implements such as hoes – which the Indians greatly desired – and "trading hatchets." Perhaps the most widely grown plant of all was the pumpkin, whose general use is celebrated in contemporary doggerel:

> For pottage and puddings and custards and pies
> Our Pumpkins and parsnips are common supplies;
> We have pumpkin at morning and pumpkin at noon;
> If it were not for pumpkin we should be undone.

What a prospect!

Needless to say, food – agricultural crops and vegetables and fruit which could be grown in the gardens which each household rapidly made around their homesteads – was the prime consideration at first. By 1629, when one William Wood visited the settlements, about which he published *New England's Prospect* in England four years later, there were "very good arable ground, and hay grounds, faire Corne-fields, and fruitful Gardens."

Even so, this took quite a while to achieve. The earliest fields, newly cleared from forest, were full of stumps and roots and were

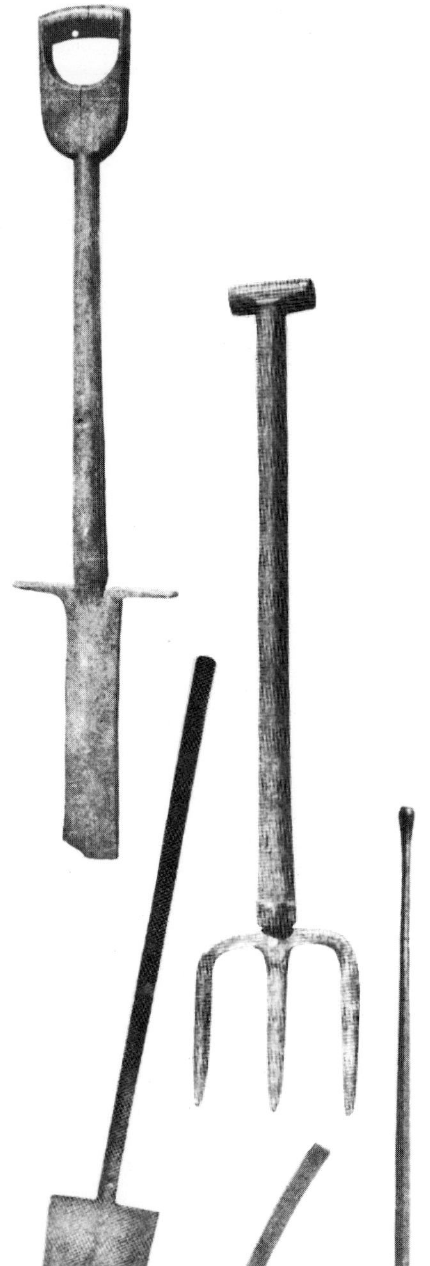

impossible for clumsy homemade wooden ploughs; the initial cultivation was carried out with heavy hoes. Since there were no fertilizers, fields lost their first fertility quite quickly, and new ones would then be cleared and brought into cropping.

There is an interesting account of such early activity in one of the earliest records of cultivation in America, Edward Johnson's *Wonder Working Providence of Sion's Saviour in New England* of 1654:

> The Winter's frosts being extracted from the Earth, they fall to tearing up roots and bushes with their howes, even such men as scarce ever set hand to labour before, men of good birth and breeding, but coming through the strength of Christ to war their warfare, readily rush through all difficulties.
>
> After they have found a place of aboad they burrow themselves in the earth for their first shelter, under some hillside, casting the earth aloft upon timber; they make a smoky fire against the earth at the highest side, and thus these poor servants of Christ provide shelter for themselves.

Naturally most of the early tools were primarily agricultural, and these were used in the earliest gardens; but there were also implements for the garden itself. An inventory taken in 1657 of the tools owned by Theophilus Eaton, governor of New Haven colony, Connecticut, lists "A pr. of garden Sheares, 3 sickles and 5 hooks, 3 hoes, 2 sithes, 2 stone axes, with brick axes and trowels. A plow and Plow irons." Such early tools were probably those originally brought across the Atlantic; as these wore out they had to be made on the spot, and were often more clumsy than their originals. Always important were the hoe – a heavy tool, no doubt made by the village blacksmith – and the lighter mattocklike adze. There would be spades, short stubby "spading forks," rakes, a relatively huge "dock digger" or "burdock," watering pots of various sizes, barrows made by the local carpenter, and flower pots of all shapes and sizes from the local potter.

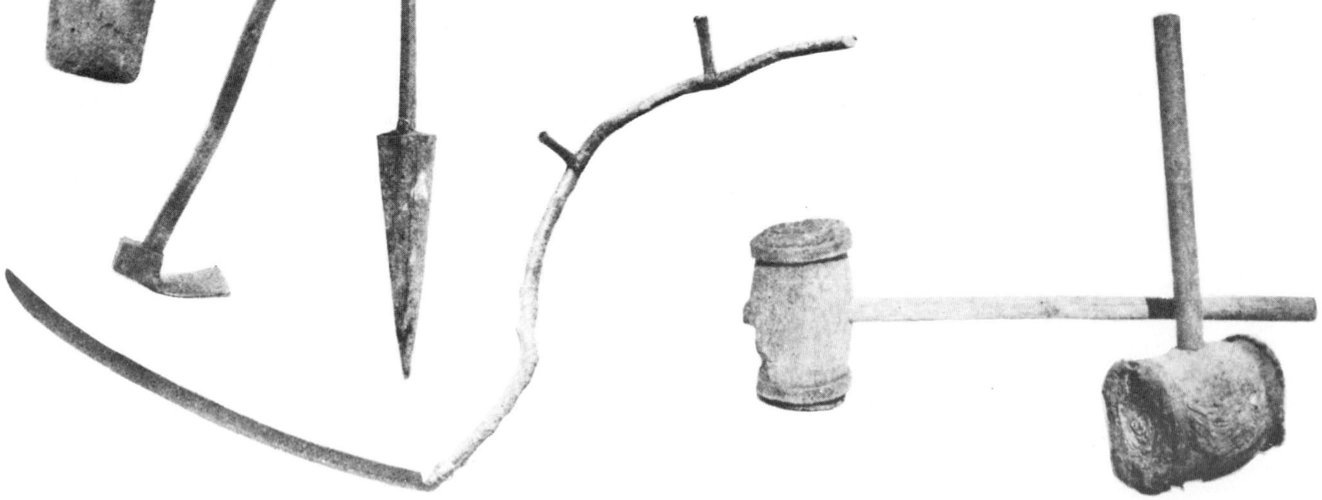

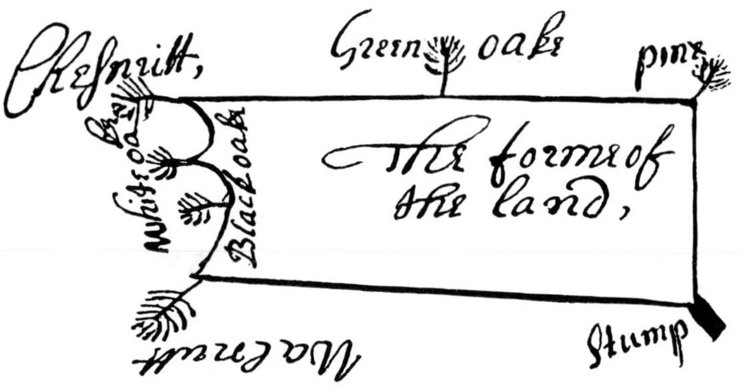

A land grant of 1681 from Providence, Rhode Island, includes this sketch map and records "The northwestern Corner being bounded with a pine Tree . . . the North Easterne Corner Bounding with an old Walnutt stumpe . . . the South Westerne Corner with a Chestnutt Tree . . . And on the South Easterne part with Three Trees (Viz) a White oake Tree . . . a Black oake Tree . . . and a Walnutt Tree . . ."

Not least important among the early tools were the posthole digger and the "beetles" to drive in the posts, because one of the first things the settlers did was to erect fences. This followed, of course, the allotment of land to groups of settlers. In the Plymouth colony, we read of plots being allotted "to every person half a pole in breadth, and three in width. We thought this proportion large enough for houses and gardens to impale them round." Early regulations were very concerned with the establishment of fencing. This was mainly for protection against Indians, wild animals, and the encroaching wilderness, but also to protect private plots from livestock which was allowed to wander about in common pasturage (something the Indians came to understand very slowly). Fences were also needed as proof of ownership of parcels of land. In Rhode Island settlers were instructed to fence their own planting grounds, orchards and gardens, and their own dwelling houses "if desired." In Connecticut fences in front of houses had to be "a five rayle or equal to it," and "the general fence a three rayle." Later on, regulations permitted "a good three rayle fence, four feet high, a good hedge or pole fence, well staked, four and a half feet high." In Virginia early ordinances were for fences of paling $7\frac{1}{2}$ feet high.

Fences around planting grounds were very commonly the type described as "worm" or "zigzag," in which horizontal poles were laid on crossed uprights forming a zigzag pattern. Washington's diary for 1760 records that he "Laid in part the Worm of a fence around the peach orchard." The botanist and traveler Peter Kalm noted in 1771 the extravagant use of wood in such fences, saying "one will imagine how the forests will be consumed, and what sort of appearance the country will have forty or fifty years hence; . . . especially as wood is squandered away in immense quantities . . . for fewel." The familiar rail fence, consisting of posts and split rails, was also widely used, another cause of "squandering" timber. Such fences often had no gates across public roads, only drawbars, because hinges and nails were expensive and difficult to obtain. Many states, such as Virginia, finally made it compulsory for landowners to provide gates.

Some landowners made ditches or "water fences"; others created

OPPOSITE: *Tools used by early American settlers, most probably dating from the eighteenth century.* FROM TOP TO BOTTOM: *A dock-digger or burdock with hand-wrought iron head 12 inches long and $2\frac{1}{2}$ inches wide; the handle is a later addition. A three-pronged spading fork with 8-inch tines. A spade, made of two thin sheets of iron welded at the edges. An adze with solid blade 8 inches long, 5 inches wide. A posthole digger entirely of iron, with point 15 inches long, weighing around 40 pounds.* BOTTOM RIGHT: *"Beetles" of lignum-vitae and oak to drive in posthole diggers and the posts themselves.*

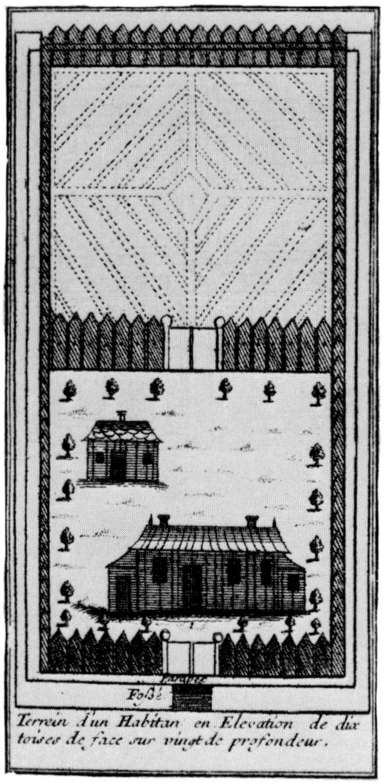

A plot in a Louisiana plantation in 1753 is enclosed in a pointed palisade fence. The lower half has trees within the boundaries, while the upper, separated from the house by another fence, contains some sort of regular patterned garden.

hedges, either by the ancient method of "laying" or "plashing" existing young trees (this involves partly cutting through the stems and laying them horizontally), or by planting. Wild species, like barberry and honey locust (robinia), were often used; but the most popular hedge plant seems to have been osage orange (maclura). Later, imported hedge plants like privet became popular. Fieldstone walls were made where stone was plentiful.

The maintenance of these boundaries remained of great importance in the settlements for a long time. In Rhode Island ordinances stated that "for a hedge, or a hedge and ditch, or a ditch only, the sufficiency of them shall be judged according to the viewers' judgments. And for that purpose, four men shall be chosen . . . to see and view the fences when men shall have occasion to look for damage done by other men's cattle or other men's fences joining upon them. . . ."

Most early settlements – certainly the coastal ones – were of scattered farmsteads, and each would have a house, barn, various outbuildings, an orchard, kitchen garden, and a herb garden which later developed into the flower garden. As the outstanding American horticulturist U. P. Hedrick commented in *A History of Horticulture in America to 1860*, "the fact of holding title, of paying rent neither to overlord nor king, of being subject to laws he helped to formulate, gave a New Englander a love for his land that few tillers of the soil in other colonies could enjoy in so high a degree – a feeling very conducive to planting gardens and orchard."

Settlements inland, frequently hacked from a virgin forest like that at Savannah, Georgia, in the 1730s, would be arranged in blocks, each house having a rectangular garden patch either in front or behind; agricultural development went on outside as the forest was gradually cleared. But in New England less formal villages developed, although as time went by, and the menace of both Indians and French from Canada became greater, these tended to be fairly compact, with streets of houses surrounded by gardens, and trees, notably the elm, planted along the streets and around the village common pasture.

We must remember that, throughout the early years in the eastern states, the original natives from time to time did dispute territory with the settlers. Rhode Islanders had a bad time of it in particular, for the Indians frequently attempted to destroy planters' gardens, to burn farmhouses, and to kill or abduct settlers. During "King Philip's War," 1675–1676, women and children were sent away, all ornamental and pleasure gardening was abandoned, and all cultivable land that could be protected was used for crops. Plantations and extensive vineyards in Virginia were wiped out in the Indian massacre of 1622. When, in 1665, a Dutch settler in New Amsterdam saw an Indian woman taking a peach in his garden and shot her dead, another massacre took place which again laid waste to settlements throughout the area.

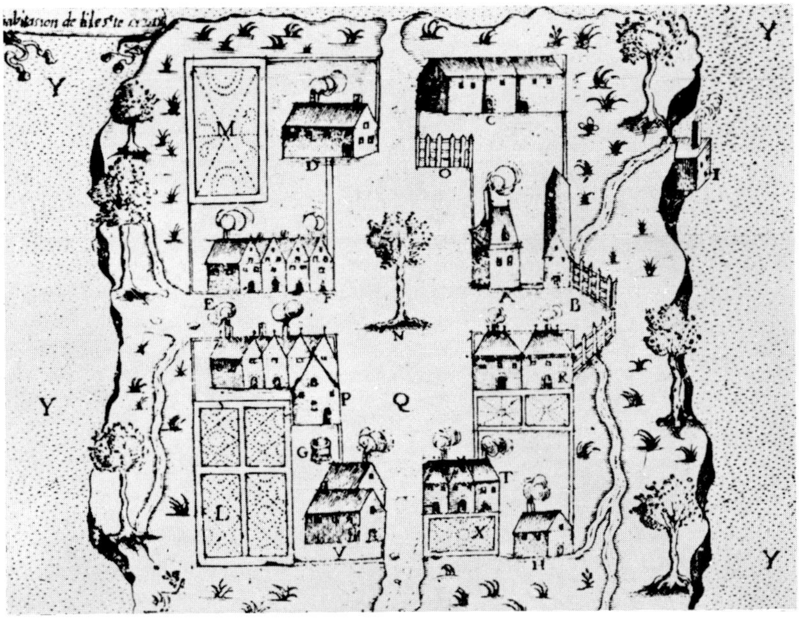

LEFT: *This drawing of 1604 shows possibly the earliest gardens planted by Europeans in what is now the northern United States (at L, M, X and adjoining the houses R). It is of the short-lived French settlement on an island in the St. Croix River.*

BELOW: *A view of the riverside settlement of Savanah, as it was spelled then, in 1734, showing each little house with its own fenced plot.*

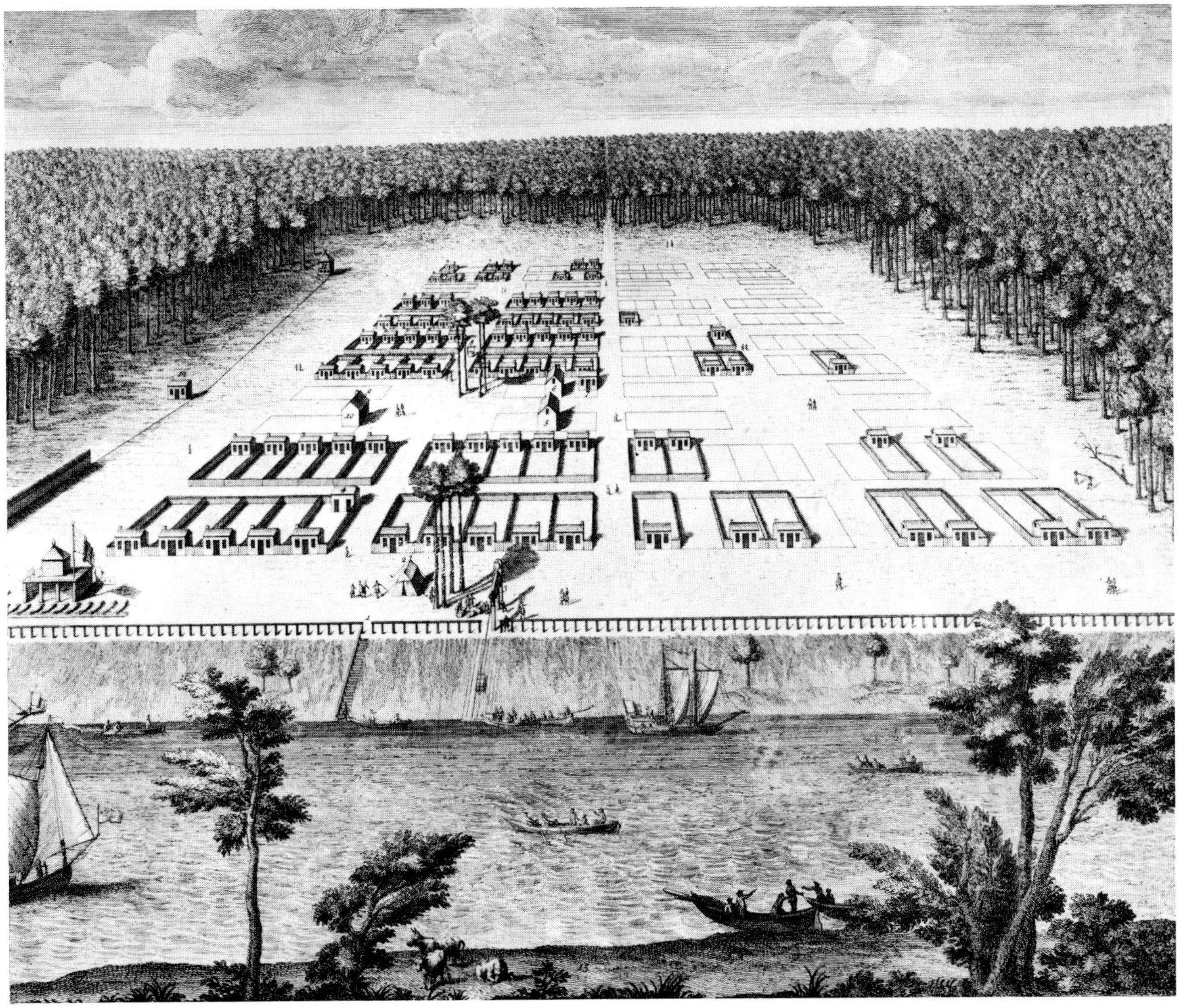

A plan of the Louisiana concession in the Yazoux River in 1754. Adjoining the typical four-cornered fort is a garden enclosed in a stout palisade; instead of being utilitarian as one might expect, the plots within are in fact elaborate decorative parterres.

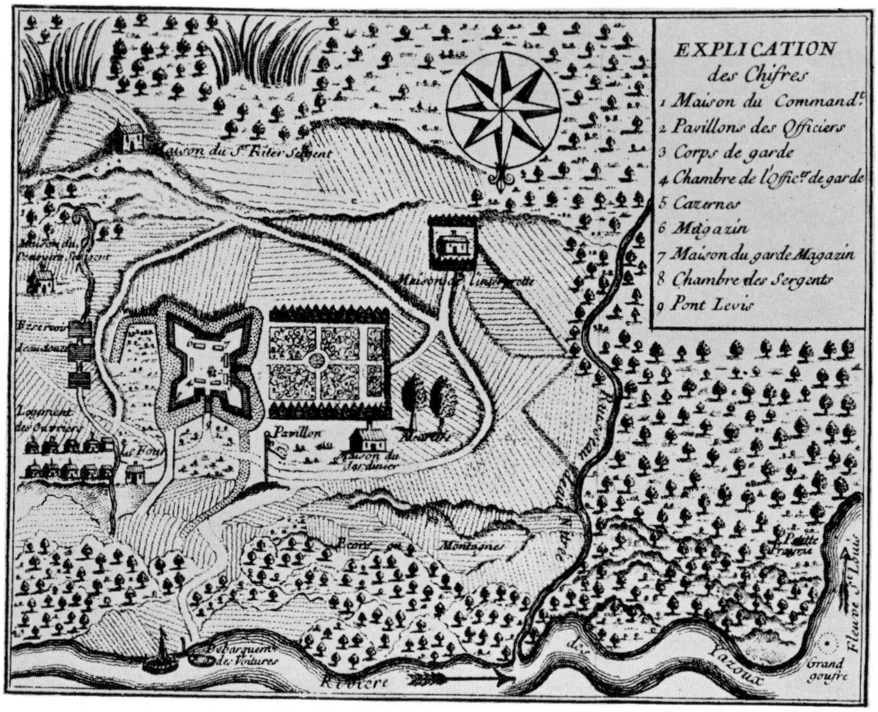

Disputes among the settlers themselves were another source of trouble. In 1692, for example, English settlers pillaged the crops of their French Huguenot neighbors and tried to destroy their gardens, with the result that by 1700 most of the French had left the area. Later, the Revolution brought yet more problems, with both sides demanding food from local farmers and planters. (And, of course, even later, the Civil War resulted in yet more destruction.)

The military themselves were important gardening pioneers. In the second half of the eighteenth century, the hundred or more forts held in America by the British all had extensive fruit and vegetable gardens, as did those held by the French. Often there were decorative plantings as well, because the soldiers had more time for cultivation than the settlers trying to wrest a living from the land.

The American settlers naturally used the agricultural and horticultural manuals of their countries of origin. One of the earliest books available was *The Whole Art and Trade of Husbandry* by Conrad Heresbach, sent to America in 1620. In the eighteenth century, Philip Miller's famous *Gardener's Dictionary*, first published in 1731, was perhaps the most popular book of all. Many books published in the New World were partly, and sometimes extensively, based on European texts. While the first American book on kitchen gardening, *A treatise on Gardening* by John Randolph Jr., was published in 1780, not until Peter Henderson's *Gardening for Profit* in 1867 was there really an original text that was fully practical, especially in the New England climate.

In New England the frontyard flower garden or forecourt recommended in current English garden books was made everywhere. The garden would typically be a rectangle with the house or cottage against one boundary, the opposite boundary edging the track or road; all would be fenced with split wooden pickets – usually whitewashed – or "payles" – vertical pointed-topped planks. As the years go by, one can trace a development to more complicated layouts with grass areas or additional paths, but for a long time the American garden remained rectangular and very symmetrical.

Apart from vegetables and fruit, the settlers grew as many herbs as they could – usually potherbs for cooking on one side of the garden, medicinal herbs on the other. These were, of course, habitual in the Old World, and were more than ever necessary in the primitive conditions of first settlement, with relatively poor housing, insanitary conditions, and the danger of exposure. These were the plants first grown in the forecourts, together with a few favorite flowers, such as hollyhocks, lilies, crown imperials and peonies. Pinks, irises or iceplant (*Sedum spectabile*) would line the straight path from garden gate to house entrance and, in places near the sea, box would be used for edgings. On either side of the porch, there would be a shrub – most often a lilac and a rose.

Of the settlers, the Dutch were perhaps the most efficient agriculturists and gardeners. They brought in many more ornamental plants and started to cultivate the handsomer wild species which make a New England field, even today, resemble a herbaceous border.

A Mrs. Grant, who lived in Albany, New York, from 1758 until the Revolution, wrote a book called *Memoirs of an American Lady* in which she described an early Dutch town full of gardens which stretched along the shore of the Hudson River. Mrs. Grant emphasized that "the care of plants, such as needed peculiar care or skill to rear them, was the female province. Everyone in town or country had a garden. Into this garden no foot of man intruded after it was dug in the spring. I think I see yet what I so often beheld – a respectable mistress of a family going out to her garden, on an April morning, with her great calash, her little painted basket of seeds, and her rake over her shoulder, going to her gardens of labors. A woman in very easy circumstances and abundantly gentle in form and manners would sow and plant and rake incessantly."

It took a long time, of course, before there were home-grown seeds available; for two centuries at least, all the seed was imported across the Atlantic, together with fruit bushes, "sparrow grass" or asparagus roots, bulbs and pot plants. They would be sold in the general stores and later by the nurserymen who gradually came into being, chiefly at first to propagate fruit trees. The earliest nursery of importance was Prince's on Long Island, begun in 1730.

For a long time, nursery trees were all grown from seed or suckers, which allowed for selection of strong frost-hardy trees. Grafting was not practiced at first, presumably because of lack of suitable scion material.

Hedgemaking was always a preoccupation of American gardeners. Here are four examples from a whole set of different methods published in 1892 – from top to bottom, training an arched fence; making a plashed fence by hand (a machine for this was also available); a plashed fence full grown, with supporting posts; and a cactus hedge, "a favorite for Texas and the west."

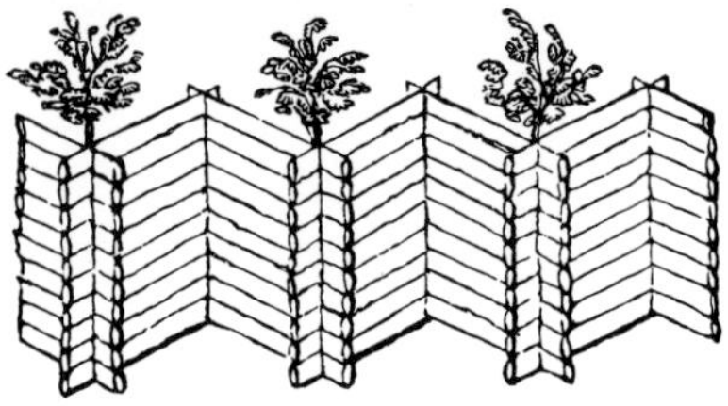

TOP: *The simplest of fencing surrounds the tiny front garden of this Rhode Island house built in 1659.*

ABOVE: *A rather stylized drawing of a Canadian zigzag timber fence with fruit trees in the sheltering embrasures.*

But, even without this method, the cultivation of fruit trees had been one of the most extensive aspects of commercial horticulture since the early days of settlement.

Colonies kept springing up all along the American seaboard and further inland as the years went by. The later development of gardens in Canada followed much the same pattern as in New England, although there settlers seem to have been much slower to make neat gardens. Their earliest plots probably grew an informal mixture of herbs, vegetables and a few flowers, and were usually fenced with osiers braided together. Later they built fences without posts or rails by laying heavy pieces of timber – rough, but cut into equal lengths – one over the other in a zigzag arrangement. The embrasures these fences formed on the leeward side were used to shelter fruit trees. J. C. Loudon, the most remarkable, prolific and influential gardening writer of his time (1783–1843), incidentally, quotes a contemporary source, describing the early nineteenth-century gardens of North American "farmers or small proprietors" as "universally of the most slovenly description, and full of weeds; nevertheless they are prolific in ordinary vegetables . . . and orchard fruits."

It must, no doubt, have been difficult to find time to weed in those early days; farmers everywhere still find it so. But even by the early years of

the eighteenth century, Williamsburg, capital of the Virginia colony, boasted of a governor's palace, "a magnificent structure . . . finished and beautified with Gates, fine Gardens, Offices, Walks, a fine Canal, Orchards . . ." (Hugh Jones, *Present State of Virginia*, 1724). The gardens were typically English, with walks, arbors, knot gardens and box hedges. Outside the city great plantations developed, copied, as far as possible, from estates in England. Many have since been restored, including Monticello, Gunston Hall, and Washington's Mount Vernon.

By the end of the eighteenth century, New England was full of fine country estates, complete with attractively planted gardens laid out in the latest European style. There is a nice description of Manhattan Island by the Reverend Timothy Dwight, dated 1791 in his *Travels in New York and New England*: "The Island of Manhattan . . . is set with cheerful habitations, with well-stocked gardens, and neat enclosures, while the heights, and many of the lower grounds, contain a rich display of gentlemen's country seats connected with a great variety of handsome appendages [i.e., gardens]. No part of the United States has such a numerous collection of villas within so small a compass; nor is any ride in the country made so cheerful by the hand of art, as is the first six miles of the Bowery Road; and indeed the whole distance to Haarlem Bridge." Alas, things have changed.

None of this development in North America is particularly surprising. It does, however, present a telescopic version of garden development all over the world, which from the earliest days must have benefited more or less from previous expertise. It shows clearly how very much man, or at least Western man, values his own fenced plot, and how symmetrical-minded he is even under arduous circumstances.

OPPOSITE: *A greenhouse and a grape arbor feature in the grounds of this country gentleman's place at Washington, New York, between 1830 and 1840. There is a pinetum to the left, protected by a spruce windbreak, and, in the right foreground, a worm fence.*

Chapter Three

The Parts of the Garden

THERE ARE FEW GARDENS WHICH ARE NOT DIVIDED INTO DISTINCT parts with different functions, and this has been the case since the time of ancient Egypt. The simple garden may only have sections, such as a paved terrace, a grassy area with a shade-giving tree, a vegetable and a fruit plot. It is not a matter of much more sophistication to divide the garden up physically into further distinct plots. Quite apart from utility areas, a "pleasaunce," such as the medieval ones mentioned in the last chapter, had many sections for various diversions, for privacy, and for the basic pleasure of changing scenes, surprising visitors at each new division.

BEDS

But the first part of a garden which must have taken shape was the bed in which plants were grown. As soon as one grows vegetables and herbs at all seriously, it is apparent that they must be in lines or rectangles to allow easy access with tools and to permit harvesting, and that the plants must be a certain distance apart to give each adequate light. Once this is done, the lines or groups of vegetables become separated by trodden areas – paths – and the cultivated sections become elementary beds.

Such separation does not exist in the casual vegetable gardens of people in hot, humid countries; but man has an innate sense of formality, and beds very soon become regular. In Egypt the garden itself was entirely formal, and planting was done in rectangular beds; the vegetable gardens were often divided into many small square plots or mud compartments filled with garden mold. Part of the formality in such cases derived from the need to irrigate with a maximum economy of water and channels.

The curving wall and the flat one, in a Roman house at Timgad, North Africa, originally formed a deep flower box surrounding part of the central courtyard.

Simple beds of rectangular form, often arranged in a more or less pleasing pattern, can be seen in the gardens of the St. Gall monastery and of medieval herbalists. The Greeks had borders of parsley; the Romans had regular utilitarian beds "so contrived that the hands of those who weed them can easily reach the middle" (Columella), and they also used raised beds or ridges for sowing. They were probably the first to have really stylized beds, either rectangular or curved, made of handsome stonework and beautifully integrated into garden design. In Europe curved beds did not appear until after the Middle Ages.

Medieval beds might be anything from a couple of inches to a couple of feet deep, edged or supported in various ways as described a little

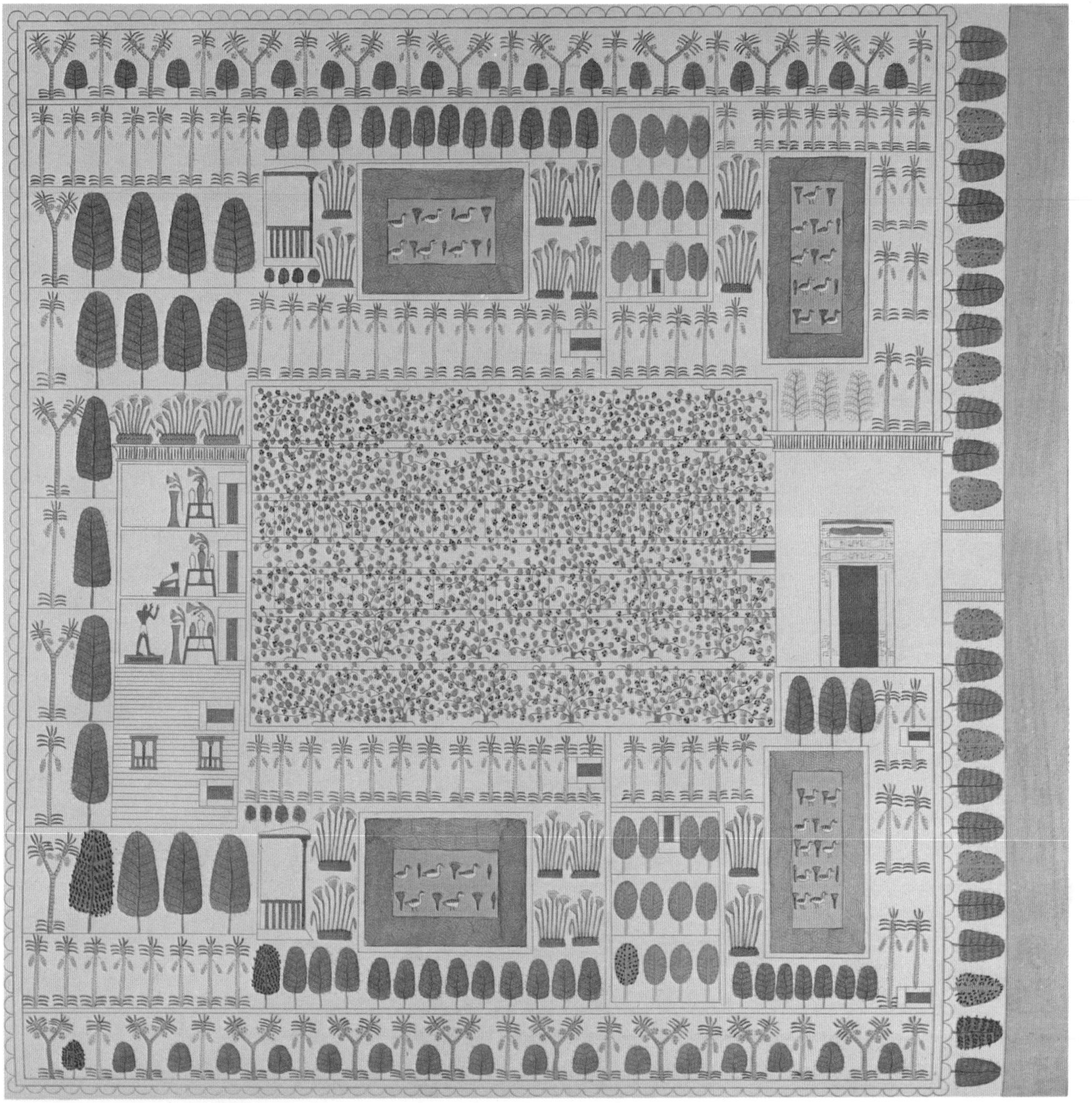

ABOVE: *The garden of a high official of the Egyptian pharaoh Amenhotep III (about 1400 B.C.). It is entirely surrounded by a high wall, with shade-providing trees along the side in which the main gate opens, at right. In the center is a vineyard and beyond it, left of center, the official's house. There are date palms (with single trunks), doum palms (with forked trunks), and various other trees. Four pools are filled with waterlilies and waterfowl; two of them have adjacent sitting pavilions. There are beds of papyrus beside the pools and at one end of the house. The thin double red lines represent internal walls, which form a series of enclosures. This very early formal garden, combining purposes of utility and relaxation, is totally symmetrical.*

LEFT: *A detail of a small private garden of the same date. The fishpond is edged with papyrus and the mixed trees around include (bottom left) a grapevine.*

The small garden of the House of the Gilded Amorini at Pompeii is, like most of those of the time (first century A.D.), built within a colonnaded courtyard or peristyle. It has a series of concentric dwarf hedges in the center, and a minimum of ornament.

The larger peristyle garden of the House of the Vetti has a good deal of ornament, pools, clipped trees, and florid, curved beds full of shrubs on either side.

The garden room in the Empress Livia's Roman villa was subterranean – a cool place of escape in hot summer. The garden scene of which this is a part ran around all four walls. In the foreground of the fresco a simple wooden lattice fence encloses a green walk; a more complex fence with three repeated patterns surrounds the flowers, shrubs and fruit trees. (Late first century B.C.)

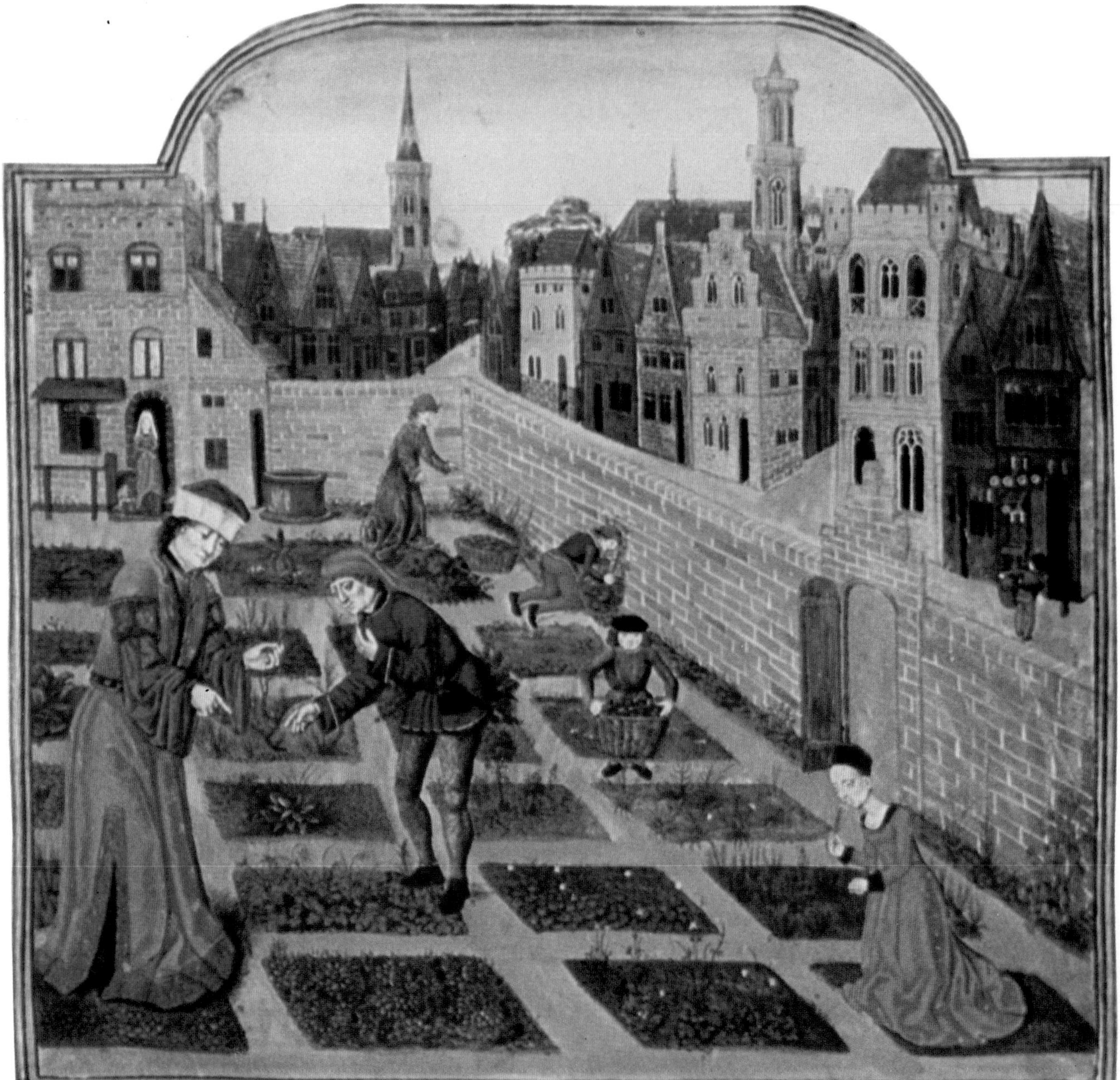

Square beds for utility purposes: a medieval herbalist's garden where the chessboard arrangement of small beds simplified cultivation and harvesting.

OPPOSITE: *The small square flower bed, as seen in this eighteenth-century painting, was a habitual feature of Indian gardens through the centuries. In the center of the four flower enclosures is a pavilion with small pools on either side.*

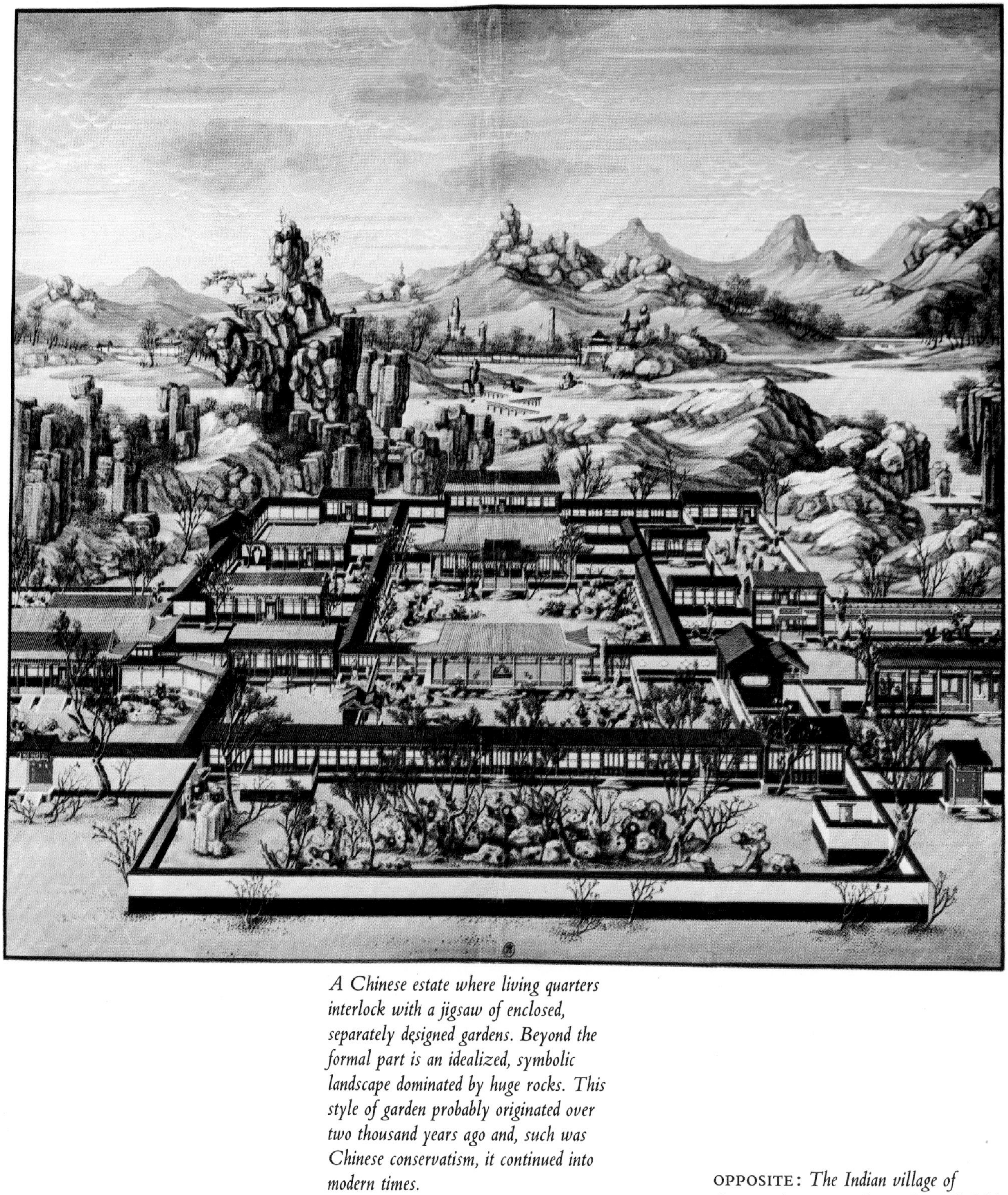

A Chinese estate where living quarters interlock with a jigsaw of enclosed, separately designed gardens. Beyond the formal part is an idealized, symbolic landscape dominated by huge rocks. This style of garden probably originated over two thousand years ago and, such was Chinese conservatism, it continued into modern times.

OPPOSITE: *The Indian village of Secoton, drawn in 1585, with small fields of corn in different stages of maturity immediately around the huts and ceremonial places. In the background, a beehive. This was the kind of native agriculture found by the first European settlers in North America.*

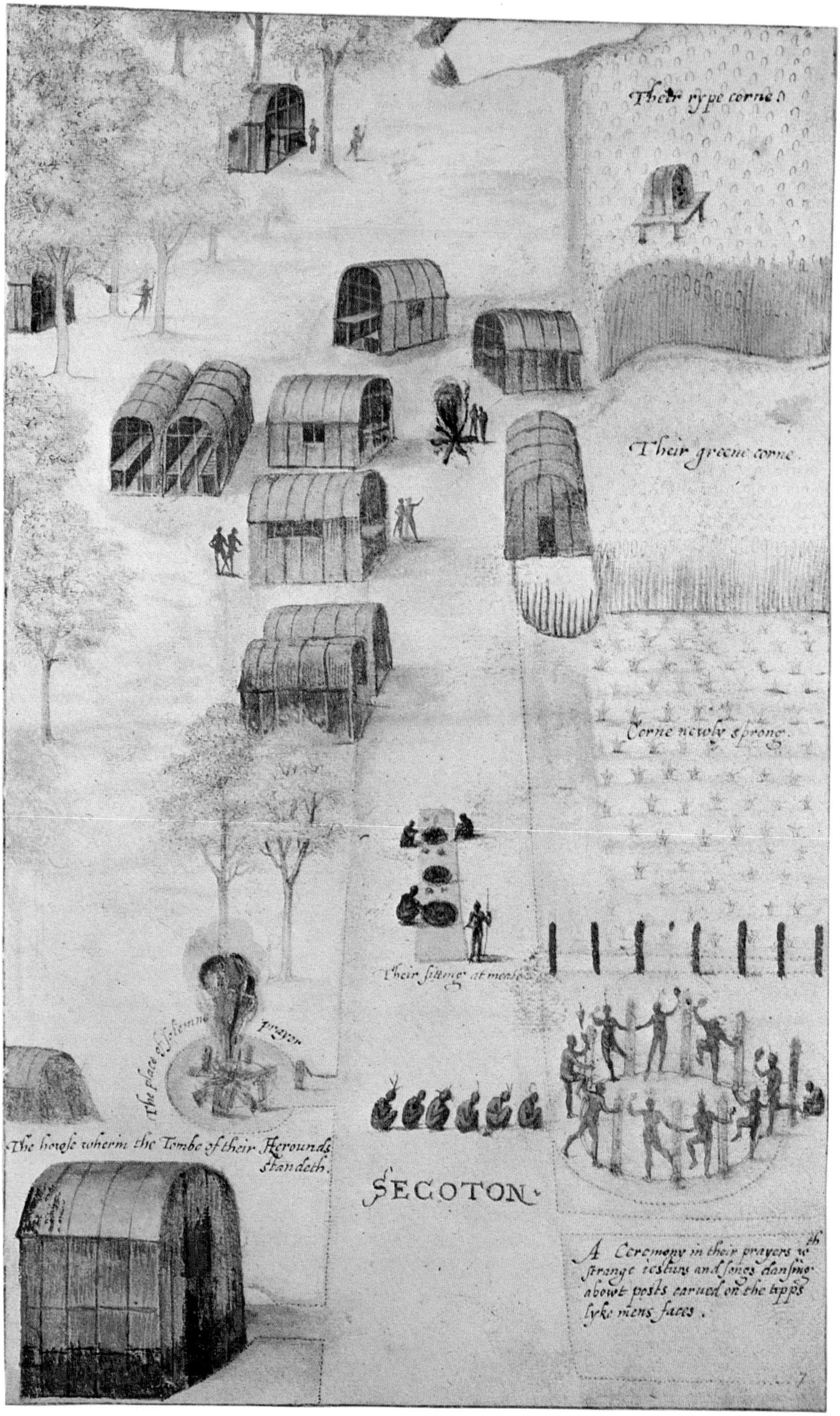
Their rype corne
Their greene corne
Corne newly sprong
Their sitting at meate
The place of solemne prayer
The howse wherin the Tombe of their Herounds standeth
SECOTON
A Ceremony in their prayers wth strange iestures and songs dansing about posts carued on the topps lyke mens faces

A Canadian homestead in Ontario in 1847. Even at this date the garden is very simple, with wooden fences enclosing the kitchen and herb gardens in front of the house and an orchard to the right.

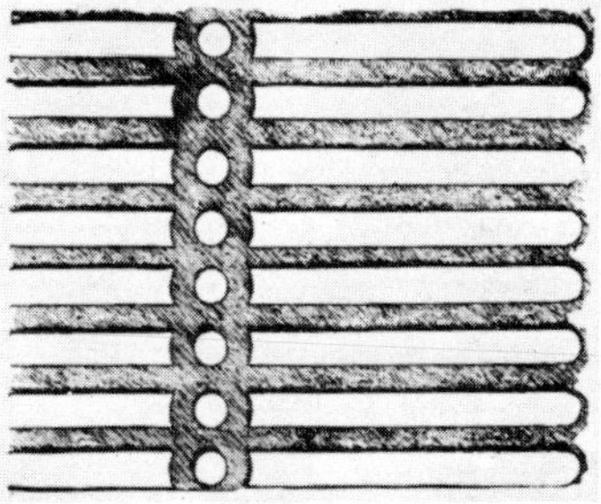

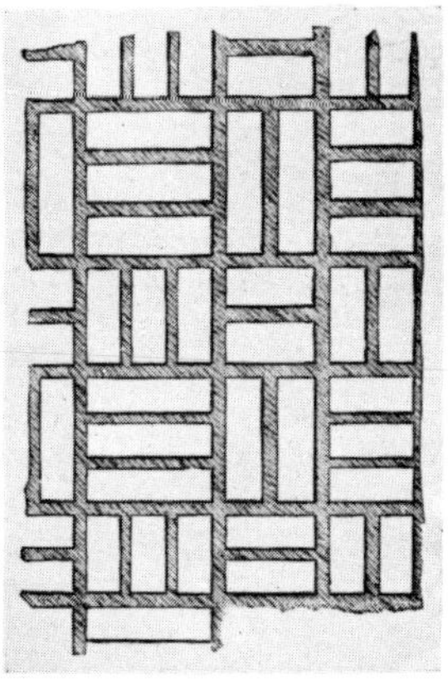

later. The raising of beds was not simply ornamental: it was to assist in drainage. William Lawson (who wrote the first book on gardening in the north of England, in 1618) later explained that this is why gardeners "raise their squares . . . if only they knew it." In doing this, the gardeners were in fact following the agricultural practice of making "lazy beds," still to be seen in some parts of Britain, where slightly convex beds of soil are raised a few inches above straight gullies. Something apparently very similar once occurred in Michigan and, to a lesser extent, in Wisconsin, where today can still be seen large areas of raised patches of ground. These are about seventeen inches above the surrounding gullies, arranged in plats or blocks of parallel beds, usually round or rectangular, but in some case curvilinear or scalloped. These plots, presumably agricultural, each occupied an area between twenty and three hundred acres, and their symmetry distinguishes them from any system of agriculture or horticulture north of Mexico. No artifacts which might date them have been found, but the age of trees now growing over them shows that they were abandoned some time before A.D. 1500.

The very high beds of medieval gardens would often be of turf and were presumably sat upon in the manner of turf seats (described in Chapter 8); they might be arranged all along the boundary walls of the garden or subsidiary enclosure, form short sections along the walls, or be placed more toward the center of the garden. One of the most common bed patterns is the chessboard of squares which recurs again and again in almost every culture; also common are oblong beds placed in strict alignment – clearly more pleasing to the eye, even if still somewhat stiff.

Gradually some variation begins to be seen. Squares and rectangles are placed in a manner that is still formal but less regimented; beds of differing proportion are placed together; and eventually the rectangle is abandoned in favor of shaped beds forming an intricate pattern.

One curious phenomenon of the late Middle Ages and early Renaissance is the use of such separate beds either for single specimens of plant or, at best, a small number of plants in a relatively large area. This is called "sparse planting." Many kinds of plant were so treated, like the

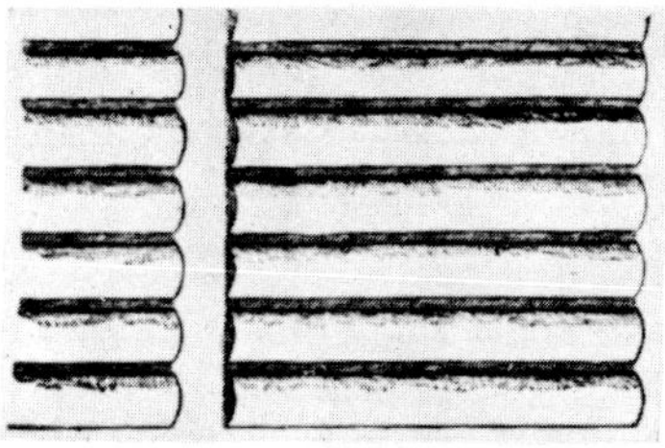

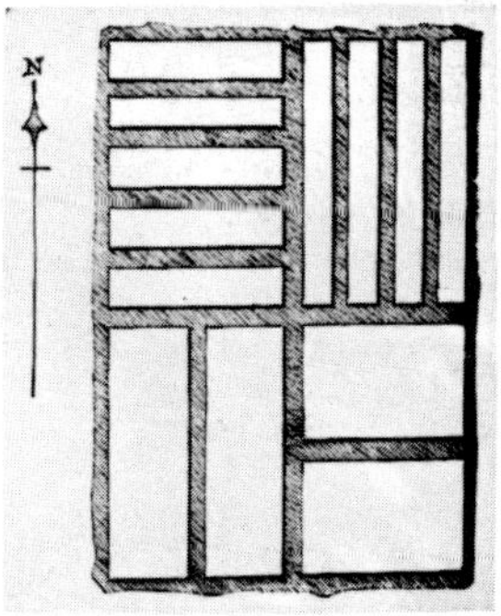

Examples of the precolonial "garden beds" in various parts of Michigan, in which the beds, divided by gullies, were raised about seventeen inches above ground level. Nothing is known of the culture which produced these large, remarkably symmetrical agricultural arrays.

A Nuremberg garden of the mid-seventeenth century shows an old-style garden in which the strictly regular beds each contain one kind of plant. However, there are also rare exotic plants in pots, brought out from the greenhouse for the summer.

bulbs on page 60, but the idea was reserved especially for trees and shrubs, which of course would be more apt to fill out a small bed, rather in the way that we use "specimen plants" today.

EDGINGS

The Romans often used stone for edging their plant beds. In Europe, much later, it was more common to use wood or metal. Among the earliest materials used both for edging beds and for external fencing was wattle – interlaced boughs and twigs, especially the pliable growth of osier willows. Horizontal boards were frequently used, held in place with long vertical wooden pegs nailed firmly to them. (Originally placed on the outside of the beds, they were later and less obviously put within them.) Wood palings, often with the tops cut into a triangle, might be used vertically. Low metal lattices were often used alongside wooden boards, creating a visual contrast. Such wooden and metal edgings were frequently painted in bright colors. Some pictures of beds show low balustrading, presumably of stone but also possibly of wood, on what were well-separated pillars.

Other materials employed for edging included strips of lead, tiles, large cobblelike stones (for level beds), and even shankbones of sheep, placed with the knucklebones uppermost. John Parkinson, herbalist to King Charles I of England, in his *Paradisi in sole* . . . of 1629, admired round whitish pebbles "for durability, beauty of the sight, handsomeness in the work, and ease in the working," commenting on animal jawbones, as used in the Low Countries of Europe, as "too gross and base." One early drawing shows a plot edged with human skulls, but we can hope that this is an allegory. A New York garden of the nineteenth century is known to have had horse and cattle skulls fixed to the fence posts – not as mere ornaments, "but a most hospitable arrangement for the accommodation of the small familiar birds."

In the Far East, wood seems to have been the favorite material for

Although contemporary with the Nuremberg garden opposite, this Ulm garden shows many design developments. The beds, set in paved walks, form a pleasing pattern; there are arbored walks, a grotto and, almost obscured behind, a small summerhouse for dining.

edging beds, which were very often arranged in chessboard pattern. While in India beds were usually massed with flowers, in China each was more often devoted to a single plant.

The alternative to all these inert materials was, of course, the use of living plants as edgings. Thrift, cotton lavender, germander and box were among the favored subjects – plants either growing very compact naturally or capable of being trimmed to shape.

KNOTS AND PARTERRES

The increasing use of plant edgings led to more and more elaborate designs of beds, culminating in "knots" or "knotts" (the word is first recorded in 1494), where a pattern – resembling what one could make of knotted cord – was created by the clipped edging plants. The pattern was originally infilled with flowers or, as in the case of the French *potager*, with vegetables. These knots became so elaborate that they were later made solely for the patterns they could provide. Sometimes plain earth was left between the clipped plants, or the areas were filled with colored earth or sand, gravel or turf. This technique was especially used when the knot represented a coat of arms or other heraldic device. Materials included sand, powdered tiles, coal, coaldust and chalk mixed (for blue), and broken bricks. Such knots, which were designed to be looked down upon from the upper floors of the house, or from "mounts," led to Francis Bacon's famous jeer: "These be but toys: you may see as good sights many times in tarts."

The word *parterre*, first used in France in 1549 and in England in 1639, denotes any level garden area containing ornamental flower beds of any shape and size. The parterre, which was developed initially in Italy, was usually a separate unit in a garden design, typically rectangular, and separated from other parts of the layout by stone balustrades or clipped

ABOVE: *The wood-edged beds in this Dutch garden of 1670 – scene of much preparatory activity for summer – create a formal pattern.*

ABOVE RIGHT: *"Sparse planting" in a very elaborate Dutch bulb garden of 1614.*

hedges. Its individual beds were frequently laid out as knots, though some part of the pattern might be reserved for flowers, or be devoted to an appropriately shaped pool. The large gardens of the sixteenth and seventeenth centuries might have whole series of knot or parterre areas separated from each other by hedges, often part of a huge plan that would include hedge mazes.

Designs steadily became more and more elaborate and florid, and obviously needed an amount of upkeep fantastic by our standards today, for the edging plants had to be constantly trimmed and the areas in between weeded or otherwise kept tidy. On the plus side, knot gardening provided a permanent decorative feature in days before bedding plants as we know them were available, and its design compensated for any lack of color.

There was a huge reaction against knots and associated formality later on, and these elaborate gardens were largely swept away in favor of open landscape – partly because of change in taste, but also, one surmises, because of the enormous cost of upkeep.

As the fashion for knots and parterre gardens was dwindling in Britain and Europe, it became popular in North America. The typical American garden, after its rectangular phase, slowly began to contain a large number of beds of different geometrical shapes. The beds were edged with box, where that plant was winter-hardy, or with raised boards. Sometimes the knots were filled with sand or other inert materials, more often with plants. George Washington's famous garden at Mount Vernon, which he worked on from 1759 onward, was described by a visitor in 1799 (the year of his death) as follows: "The garden is very handsomely laid out in squares and flower knots and contains a great variety of trees, flowers and plants of foreign growth collected from almost every part of the world." Most of the care of the flower garden was, incidentally, almost certainly in

Setting out simple knot beds with the aid of pegs and a garden line beside fruit trees conscribed by an espalier fence at right (1701).

In the restored Renaissance garden at Château Villandry, France, the vegetable garden or potager *(top of photograph) is composed of neat beds with low plant edgings. Note the orange trees in tubs by the château, and the symbolic box parterres in the foreground.*

Mrs. Washington's capable hands. There was an elaborate parterre which the English architect Benjamin Latrobe described, admitting its perfection but disliking it, since on the other side of the Atlantic such creations were no longer fashionable: "For the first time since I left Germany I saw here a *parterre* stripped and trimmed with infinite care into the form of a richly flourishing *fleur-de-lis*, the expiring groan, I hope, of our grandfathers' pedantry."

FLOATING GARDENS

One of the most extraordinary aspects of plant cultivation involving a kind of bed is that of the floating garden, which developed in very different parts of the world. When the Spaniards faced the Aztecs, their principal target was the capital city of Tenochtitlan – now Mexico

RIGHT: *Plans of the flower and kitchen gardens laid out by George Washington at Mount Vernon, Virginia, from 1759 onwards.*

BELOW: *One of the box-hedged parterres at Mount Vernon, a replanting of the original fleur-de-lis motif described by Benjamin Latrobe, a contemporary visitor.*

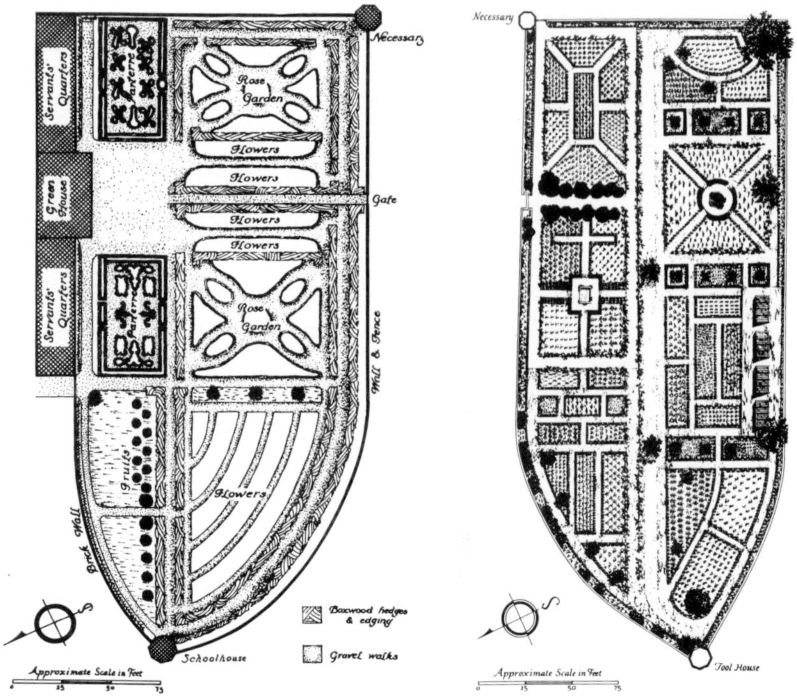

City. It could be likened to a Central American Venice, with buildings built on piles spreading out from the lake island on which it had started life, and canals replacing streets as the city spread outward. This pile-building was a relic of days when the Aztecs, then poor and weak, settled on the marshy lake shores of Mexico; what little real land they possessed was used for crops. To make additional cropping areas, they constructed soil-bearing rafts: their basis was reeds on a framework of roots bound together; their top hamper, three or four feet deep, was fertile lake mud. Some of these were simply extensions of the foreshore; others were mobile. By joining rafts, they ended up with incredible floating islands, called *chinampas*, up to three hundred feet long. On them maize was first grown, later luxury vegetables, flowers, and even fruit trees. The lake was so shallow that the gardener of each raft could punt it about between his home and the market, and the movement of dozens of these huge green rafts around the city must have amazed the Spaniards – as it did Humboldt in 1804. *Chinampas* still exist, incidentally, in the floating gardens of Xochimilco outside Mexico City.

A very similar form of gardening developed, and still exists, in Kashmir (northern India), on the lakes around the capital Srinagar where there is little agricultural land between the town and the mountains. Here reeds and other vegetation are bound together in long, narrow strips on which mud is piled. As with the Mexican *chinampas*, a combination of natural buoyancy and decay keeps them afloat. Normally these strips are moored alongside each other with a narrow band of water in between, in which the gardener maneuvers his *shikara*, a small canoe propelled by a large paddle wielded at the front. The strips are fixed by willow stakes driven through them, permitting up and down movement when the water level changes. Only occasionally are the islands moved, out of some necessity, and then they are towed behind a *shikara*. To walk on one of these strips is rather unnerving, for one sinks down a foot or more into the water (they are not so deep or solid as the Mexican ones).

At any rate, many crops are grown on these floating islands. Further intensive cropping of vegetables and flowers, which the Kashmiris love as much as the Aztecs did, can be seen on the embankments, or *bunds*, built up from mud scooped from what must have been a vast marsh rather than a lake in its early days. These *bunds* project into the lake with canals between and around them, and on them are grown poplars, practically the only timber trees to be seen in the Vale of Kashmir; willows which, along with rushes, provide animal fodder; waterlily leaves and other plants pulled from the lake; and crops. Every inch of this reclaimed ground is used, and one can see cucumbers and squash hanging over the water, their stems supported on stout sticks pushed into the *bund* edges at an angle.

CONTAINERS

Besides growing plants in soil, whether in natural ground, on the terraces of hanging gardens, or in the mud of floating gardens, it is possible

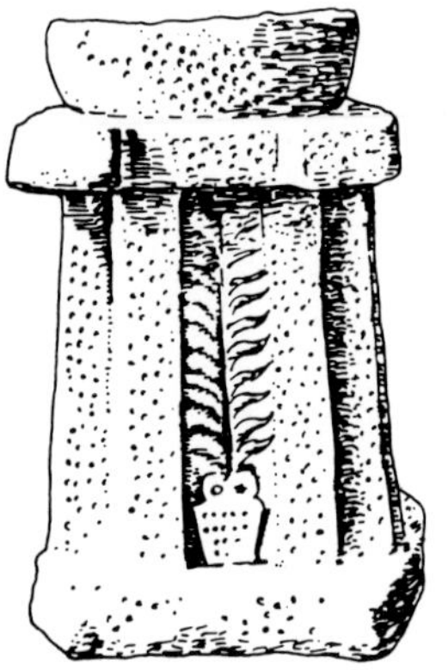

Possibly the oldest representation of a plant container in the world: an altar from the Maltese temple of Hagar Qim, dating from the second millennium B.C.

to do so in containers. The use of earthenware pots in Egypt under Ramses III has already been mentioned. The earliest apparent representation of a pot-grown plant is found in the famous decorated altar from the Maltese temple of Hagar Qim (before 2000 B.C.), which depicts an upright leafy plant seemingly growing from a bucket-shaped pot.

The Chinese appear to have had pots from their early gardening days. (They, incidentally, also made floating gardens on occasion, for growing rice.) The Greeks certainly grew a few ornamental plants in large terracotta pots placed in their courtyards. And earthenware flower pots of a special kind were found associated with the plantings of the Temple of Hephaistos in Athens, but these were almost certainly used only for propagation purposes as described later.

The ancient ritual of Adonis – originating from that of Tammuz, whose mythology goes back to ancient Mesopotamian times – called for the growing of seedlings in some kind of pot and allowing them to wither, thus symbolizing the death of the god. The Adonis cult, representing the yearly decay and revival of vegetable life, was carried out in the names of various other gods, including Osiris, Tammuz, and Attis, in Egypt, western Asia, and Greece. In some places, such as the Lebanon, these seedlings were usually of wheat, but in Athens the Adonis gardens, made by women from the sixth century B.C. onward, were of herbs including fennel and lettuce.

The Romans used a wide variety of pots and other containers on their roof gardens, which were often elaborate with fruit trees and a fish pond. In larger gardens containers were ornamental rather than functional, although in many cases they probably held plants. Exactly the same use of containers on window ledges, balconies and roofs can be noted in Italian paintings a thousand years later.

At Pompeii some large terracotta pots were found embedded in soil. Each had a hole in the bottom and three at the sides above the base. It seems possible that they were placed in the soil, and roots were allowed to grow out of the holes – very much like the Hephaistos pots mentioned above. They may well have been specifically for lemon trees, for Pliny the Elder mentioned attempts to acclimatize these, which were imported in "earthenware pots with breathing holes for the roots."

Pots of all shapes and sizes, made both of earthenware and painted metal, appear in a great number of medieval European pictures. They often stood on the turf-topped beds or benches, as well as on the ground, and many of them show the use of attractive plant supports (as discussed in Chapter 5). In some cases plant containers appear to be made of wattle, but these were probably more or less immovable, although smaller ones may have been used for transporting plants.

A stout wooden medieval window box. It can only be surmised what plants were to be grown in it.

The most popular material at all times was terracotta, which was capable of being shaped or molded in numerous attractive ways. But as

Urns and ornamental pots of earthenware were an essential part of seventeenth-century gardening, together with the large wooden, metal-hooped tubs in which citrus trees in particular were grown – in shelter during winter, outside in summer. Watering all these containers must have been a very considerable chore.

time went on and technology improved, stone and metal, notably lead, were increasingly used, as well as wood in the form of round or square tubs, especially favored for the cultivation of citrus trees and other fruit. In 1828 the Scottish writer Charles M'Intosh, who was gardener to the king of the Belgians, publicized a square tub, two sides of which were hinged and could be folded down; he recommended this for citrus, camellias and similar plants.

The mass-produced flower pot as we know it today began life in the early nineteenth century, when a wide range of designs was available. Some Victorian pots had the drainage hole raised by means of a deep under-rim, to prevent worms getting in – a useful device which one regrets not having today. Others were molded with channels cut into the base so that water could escape readily onto a hard flat surface. Pot saucers also came into being at this time.

The Victorians not only took over all the ornamental shapes of pots and urns produced in previous centuries, but developed some very florid ones of their own, using both earthenware and metal. Mass production methods brought these into every gardening household. They also devised jardinières, of wire or stouter metal, upon which pot-grown plants could be massed, usually in tiers so that a cascade of bloom and foliage was produced. These were primarily for the conservatory and "winter garden," but could also be used outside.

Another form of container which has been in use for many centuries is the window box. Roman roof and window gardeners used them; they appear in medieval and post-Renaissance paintings, thoroughly

The nineteenth century saw much technical development in clay pots. From left to right, an "annular water saver"; a pot with raised bottom to keep out worms; one with channeled base to help water to escape; and an ornamental pot with separate base to catch surplus drainage water.

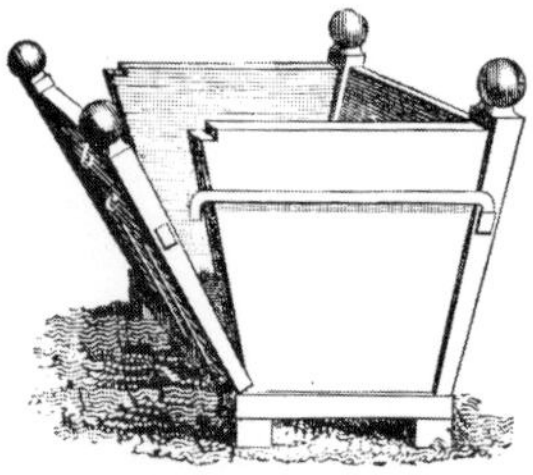

A square wooden plant box of 1828, designed to allow the gardener to examine or prune roots of citrus, camellias and the like without too much difficulty.

modern-looking boxes with stout supports to prevent a disastrous fall on anyone passing by. Again, the Victorians mass-produced them in metal or earthenware, with classical or rustic designs, one of their favorite devices being the imitation of tree stems and twigs.

How long ago the Chinese started pot gardening is a matter of speculation. It was certainly in evidence in the T'ang dynasty (A.D. 618–907), and one imagines for many centuries before. The Chinese, of course, went beyond earthenware and such ordinary materials, and most of their containers were beautiful ceramic pieces. There is a Sung bulb bowl with "transmutation" red glaze in the Victoria and Albert Museum in London. Itinerant flower sellers carried such containers in flat panniers swinging from a yoke on the shoulder; the peddler would take away containers whose plants had finished flowering and nurse them into next season's bloom. Larger, more permanent containers which might hold plants as diverse as shrubs and sacred lotus would often be supported on ornate stands.

A special kind of very shallow container was, and is, used for bonsai, that originally Chinese art now practiced mainly by the Japanese. Although today most people believe the word to refer exclusively to miniature trees, kept dwarf by special techniques of root and branch pruning, bonsai actually means "grown in a tray" and can refer to any plant which will remain small, by whatever means, in such conditions. Plants such as dwarf sweet flags and bamboos were often grown, and there is a special art in turning certain kinds of chrysanthemum into bonsai – a process which is repeated every year, for the upper stems of the chrysanthemum perish in winter. The choice of an appropriate container was supremely important, and many were works of art in their own right, usually rectangular but sometimes oval or with rounded corners. These containers would be set aside in special places; the main collection was housed under a screen of laths to diminish the sun's heat while allowing maximum air circulation, and specially chosen specimens were set out on stone benches or on the edge of a pool.

Container gardening continues to be immensely important. So many people today live in apartments that keeping pots and boxes both outside and inside their rooms is the only way they can grow anything. A vast range of ornamental boxes can be obtained, some directly copied from

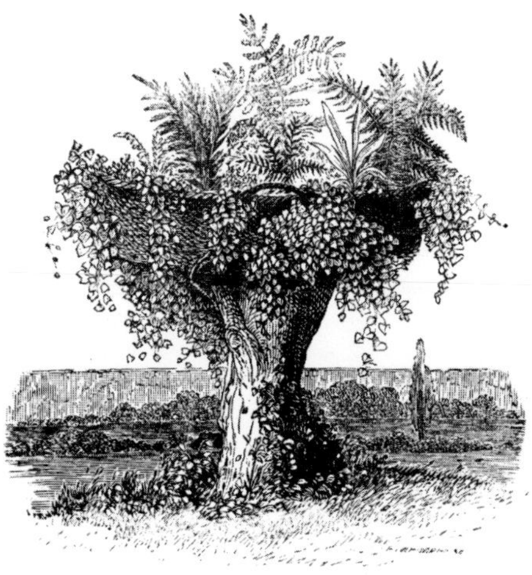

antique originals and reproduced in fiberglass or composition stone, others derived from old originals, and yet more, of course, in keeping with present-day architectural design, made of concrete or cement.

The basic clay flower pot has now largely been replaced by plastic, a nonporous material which keeps the soil damper longer and thus somewhat alters the method of cultivation. But many clay pots are also available; in most parts of Europe they are often imported from Spain and Italy, in the United States from Mexico, where hanging types are especially popular.

Clay pots used to be made by hand, and the number that could be made from the uniform quantity of clay, known as a "cast," was of course different according to the size of pot. From this came the gardener's jargon, now fast disappearing, of "a small sixty" (because sixty $3\frac{1}{2}$-inch pots are obtained from a cast), "a forty-eight" (for 5-inch pots), and so on. The biggest size normally produced was a "twelve," or a 10-inch pot. Today pots are made in molds, and most of them have a vertical outside "collar" or rim. These are called nesting pots because they fit into each other without jamming, so that stacking is much easier and breakages are reduced.

Such pots for cultivation, whether clay or plastic, are available in a wide range of shapes. There is the standard pot, slightly deeper than wide; the pan, much wider in proportion to depth; and the "long tom," about twice as deep as wide, for taprooted plants. Most clay pots have one fairly large drainage hole at the base. The "orchid pot" – seldom seen today – also has additional holes at the side to ensure that the porous compost can never become waterlogged, and to encourage the aerial roots produced by many orchids to grow outside the container. And, in addition to the conventional shapes, plastic ones can be found in more unusual forms: square, squat, half-round for hanging on walls, even artistically flared. Many are now also wick-fed through the drainage hole for self-watering, while large bowls with saucers attached to catch surplus water are beginning to replace traditional wire hanging baskets.

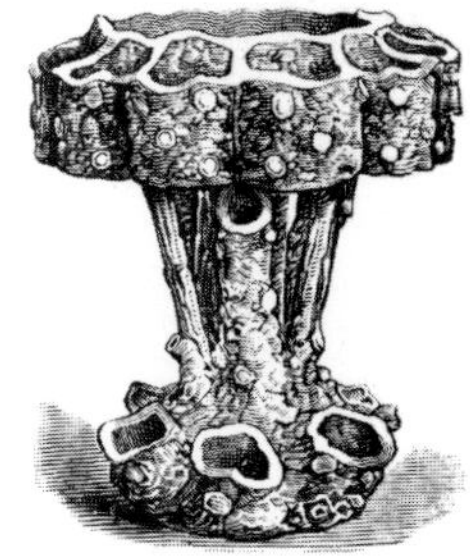

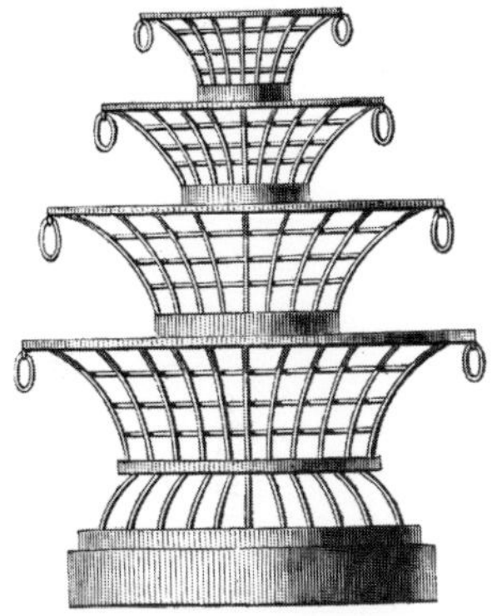

In the latter part of the nineteenth century, there was a tremendous development in ornamental containers, including rustic-style earthenware objects, metal and clay window boxes, and metal jardinières of various styles.

RIGHT: *A roof garden in Verona, about 1708, with many large plants in containers creating a peaceful formal garden.*

BELOW: *Details from the* Annunciation *by Crivelli (died 1495–1500) show pots on window ledges, parapets and balconies.*

RIGHT: *A detail from a painting by Tiepolo (1696–1770) shows a mass of small pots – some rather precariously unprotected – on a laborer's balcony.*

Variously shaped containers, some on elaborate stands, decorate a Chinese courtyard. The one on the left holds a lotus growing in water. Note the weirdly shaped natural stone (left) and the typical tile-topped outer wall.

Nurserymen have shifted from clay pots for growing their plants. Many plants are sold in a material resembling very strong cardboard, called "whalehide," or in other paper compositions. Some materials, like compressed peat, allow roots to penetrate so that pot and all can be planted. Large plants may be potted for display in garden centers in old tin cans with a hole punched in the bottom, and they must be extracted, often with difficulty, from these before planting. The most recent trend is to use thin black polyethylene bags with small holes punched in them for drainage. These certainly hold a well-rooted plant adequately, are cheap and space-saving for the nurseryman, and are easily removed by the customer.

In California in particular, but spreading rapidly throughout the United States and Canada, there is a vogue for selling nursery stock in pots, cans and tubs. This is especially popular with garden centers which do not grow their own plants. At the same time, it enables them to keep the plants alive until sold and makes "cash and carry" sales much easier. Large nurseries, such as Monrovia in California, grow all their own stock in pots and ship by truck even to the East Coast. Garden centers were, after all, an American invention of the 1930s; it was not until after 1950 that they began to be accepted in Britain, becoming firmly established around 1963.

PATHS

With few exceptions, gardens must have paths – paths between beds, among rows or groups of pots, paths to connect features and provide suitable access wherever it is needed. Many of the illustrations in this book will show paths of one kind or another, and it seems almost superfluous to describe them. The original path, naturally enough, is simply earth beaten hard by constant traffic. An all-weather path has to be hard and impervious; older paths were always of stone, as was the paving on terraces and surrounding the different sections of a parterre. At different times, all kinds of materials have been used – pebble mosaic, gravel, cobbles, stone setts, bricks, tiles, large flat stones, concrete, asphalt, composition stone, and various combinations of these. The Chinese invented interlocking paving in sophisticated shapes. An attractively patterned path can be a major decorative feature in a garden.

By the same token, a path does not necessarily just connect *a* to *b*; it can meander or zigzag to provide interest. Meandering walks and paths were especially popular in eighteenth-century European gardens, and George Washington laid down "serpentine roads" and "serpentine walks" at Mount Vernon. The Chinese were especially adept in making paths part of the overall design. To quote Osvald Sirén in *Gardens of China*, "the paths in the Chinese gardens seem in their design to have been dominated by an irregularly winding and undulating system of lines." In the important gardening text called *Yüan Yeh* (1634), we read "the paths meander like playing cats." The pattern of a Chinese path would frequently echo that of the latticed wall panels and the balustrades of the garden pavilions. Sirén describes the general aim as "to cover the path with something recalling a plaited carpet."

Here, of course, we are straying into nonfunctional realms. However, the techniques used by the Chinese are of interest. Their path mosaics were made of brick, stone chips or shingles, stamped into the soil. The bricks might be cut into various shapes, or placed on edge, to create straight-lined figures. Between these lines, the spaces might be filled with shingles or chips of different colors, recalling the knot garden. The *Yüan Yeh* mentions that "even small bits of waste brick may be used for paving. The small square bricks should be collected; they can be used around the plum trees, where they are laid out in a pattern of cracked ice." Elsewhere we read: ". . . one should pave the paths with stones not larger than pomegranate seeds; they will then become beautiful and durable. . . . Some use stones as large as goose eggs to produce the patterns, but such patterns are not lasting, and tend to produce a vulgar effect. . . . The goose-

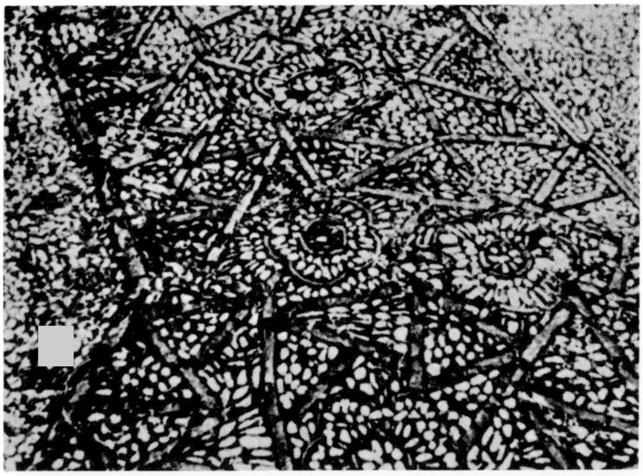

ABOVE LEFT AND RIGHT: *The Chinese were among the first gardeners to make paths not only vital parts of a garden design, but works of art in their own right. These are path-mosaics of brick, shingle and multi-colored stone chips.*

LEFT: *The Japanese often combine stones of different sizes: here the effect is of stepping stones in a stream.*

egg stones may be used in places where one does not walk much; it is best to mix larger and smaller ones, but I fear that the workmen do not understand this. In between the stones one may use roofing tiles with which to form patterns representing herons, deer, lions with globes and so on, but they make a ridiculous impression." Certainly the antique geometrical or stylized patterns that remain are extremely striking without any recourse to animal representations.

The actual making of a path is dependent on a firm foundation, usually incorporating drainage, either through the actual porosity of the material or through a pipe drain in the center. If it is of a solid material like asphalt, it should be slightly cambered to allow water to run off. And it should be flush with any surrounding grass, or even below grass level, to permit easy cutting. Paths in woodlands are often made of turf, and a path in a lawn may consist of well-separated stepping stones laid into the grass.

Steps may be considered in much the same terms as paths. They are frequently a necessity, allowing access between levels, and they can be built in a very decorative manner. They need to be constructed even more rigidly and solidly than a path, and are thus more often of mortared stone or brick on a well-made foundation. In informal situations, like a woodland garden, steps can be made of trimmed logs. Occasionally, some plant, such as thyme, chamomile or aubrieta, is used as the "tread" in informal steps. In the past, curved grass steps were sometimes used in U.S. gardens, notably in the South. One famous example remains in Portsmouth, New Hampshire, in the garden of the Ladd House.

WATER GARDENS

It has already been mentioned how water was – and indeed still is – a vital part of gardens in hot countries. Apart from the dependence of utility gardens upon irrigation, the always separate pleasure gardens of the nobility had conduit-filled pools and often fountains in courtyards, terraces and more open places. Such were essential to people living in great heat much of the time, especially when the ladies of the household would be almost entirely confined to a set of courtyards. The moving water provided coolness, the fountains a continuous pleasing murmur, and trees and walls the essential shade.

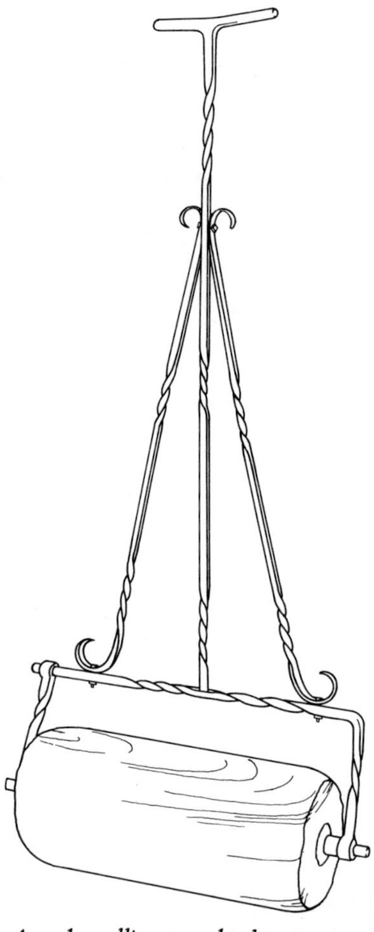

A garden rolling stone dated to 1739, still extant in Massachusetts, was used to keep gravel walks firmly packed down. Philip Miller recommended that "the person who rolls . . . should wear shoes with flat heels that he may not make Holes in the Walks."

Nowhere is this seen more clearly than in the gardens of Mogul India and ancient Persia. Almost every picture of a palace or garden, of a harem or love scene, shows the formalized water garden. As mentioned earlier, these gardens are most often based on the anciently symbolic cross pattern, and Persian carpets often depict beautiful gardens complete with flowers, trees and wildfowl, always in four plots separated by a narrow cross-shaped canal. An Italian visitor to Tabriz in the sixteenth century described the palace gardens as having "a thousand fountains, a thousand rivulets, a thousand rills."

Some of the Mogul gardens that remain in India are extremely beautiful, peaceful places. Basically they were made on the flat, as at the Taj Mahal. One of the most astonishing is the water parterre at Amber, Jaipur, where a terrace of stone divisions etches a water surface into diverse stylized patterns, the whole being raised above the surface of the lake itself. When the Moguls reached Kashmir, they were able to exploit the hillsides that descended to the waters of Lake Dal, and built beautiful terraced gardens such as Shalamar and Nishat. There is an inscription at Shalamar, incidentally, which reads, "If there be a Paradise on the face of the earth, it is here, it is here, it is here!" Springs from the mountain are channeled into wide canals between enormous plane trees (*chenars*); between levels the water flows down sloped cascades. But they are no ordinary cascades; they are *chadars*, where the flat surface has been chiseled to make a pattern, not

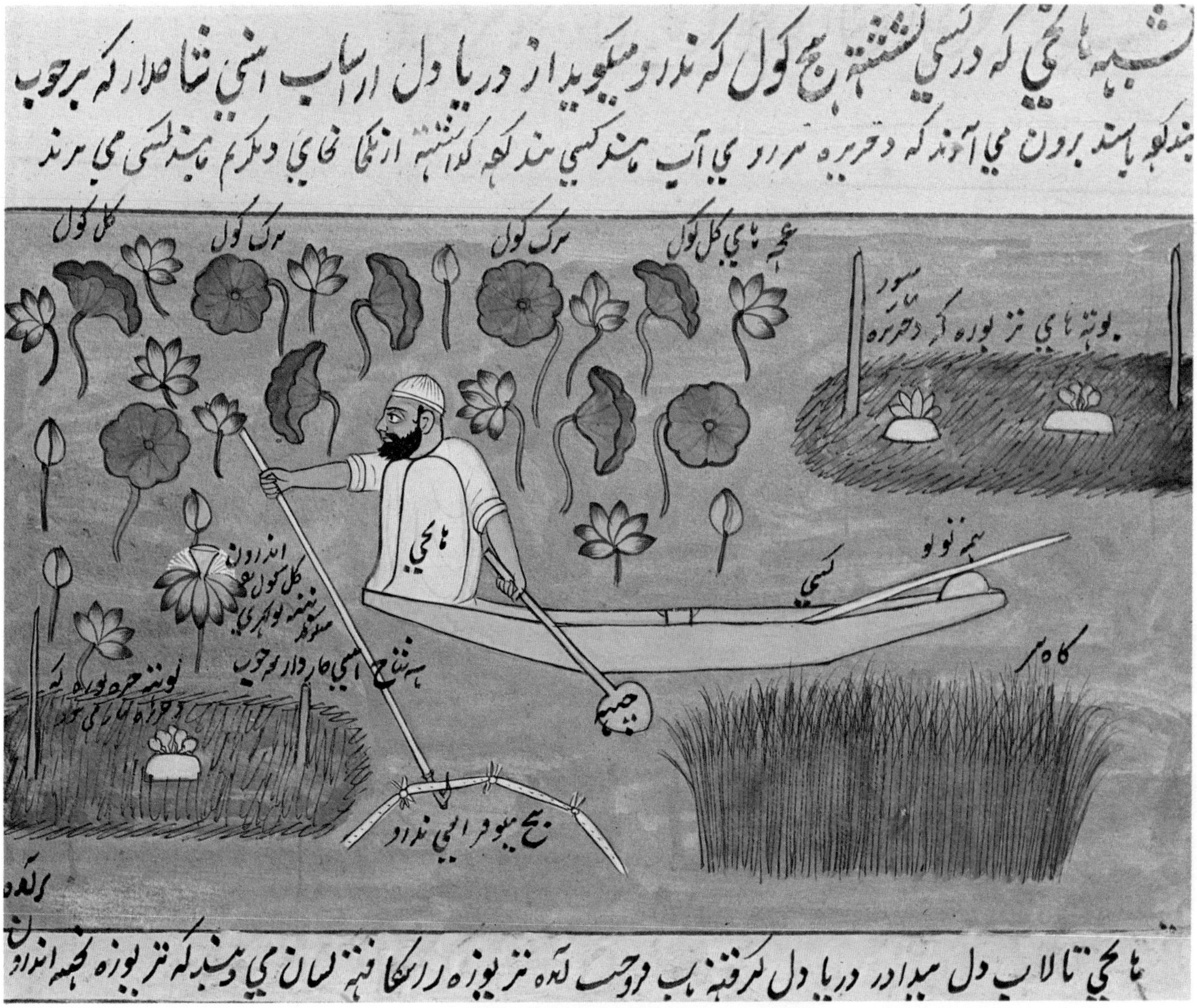

ABOVE: *The Kashmiri gardener has for centuries paddled between his floating gardens, secured to the lake bottom with poles, among the sacred lotus blooms.*

RIGHT: *If the water was too deep for an ordinary rice paddy, the Chinese sometimes made rafts, moored to the bank and covered with soil, in which the rice could grow.*

FAR RIGHT: *The floating gardens of Lake Dal, Srinagar, Kashmir, are still very much part of the scene. This photograph shows an itinerant flower seller in front of a series of floating garden strips, behind which poplars grow on reclaimed soil.*

ABOVE: *Seventeenth-century gardeners plant and dig around simple knot beds in a large enclosed garden: a Swiss glass panel of 1637 from Canton Zug.*

LEFT: *A modern French restoration of a knot bed with box outlines, which interestingly combines some patterned planting with outer sections filled with colored or white stones.*

OPPOSITE: *This painting from an illuminated manuscript of about 1400 depicts a very sturdy, businesslike window box.*

No Indian garden would be complete without a pool and fountain. This Rousseau-esque painting from the Jodphur school depicts a lush private garden of handsome trees symmetrically planted, and also an elaborate fence with several different grille patterns.

A four-way painting of a late seventeenth-century potentate's gardens in the Deccan Plateau, India, with highly formalized planting and splendid ornamental pavilions.

Wooden fences of simple lattice patterns enclose the simplest checkerboard beds in these medieval paintings. In the center, the fence has wider uprights and top members and supports carved animals beside the opening. In the arbor below, the horizontal and upright members are fixed together with twisted osiers.

In this medieval village scene, wattle fences surround plantations of young fruit trees, while men on long ladders pick fruit from old ones. A vine is trained on the front of one of the houses.

Although planting in medieval days was usually rather casual, these vine growers rooted their young plants from cuttings in wicker baskets which they are burying complete in up-to-date container style.

OVERLEAF: *Iron uprights of extremely modern appearance enclose this early sixteenth-century garden of square grass plots. Iron also appears to form the supporting structure of the open arbor walk in the background, although the tunnel arbor at right seems to be framed on wood supports.*

The frequent depiction of the Bathsheba story (left) suggests that in medieval times bathing in a stone pool or tub outside was common, the bathers – often attended by retainers – eating and drinking and listening to music (above).

only in the stone but also in the water that passes over it.

The *chadar* has been used ornamentally by present-day North American architects in modern buildings in New York, San Francisco and Vancouver. Another echo of a *chadar* can be seen in the unique wall waterfall at Longue Vue Gardens, New Orleans, among many other kinds of fountain; water comes out of a slot and runs over the very slightly sloped surface of a brick wall.

Where, in the Mogul gardens, water was allowed to leap over a parapet into a lower pool, the wall behind it was often pierced with alcoves. By day artificial flowers in precious metals would glint behind the waters, by night each niche was occupied by a candle.

It is a remarkable piece of "parallel evolution" that similar gardens were being made at roughly the same time in Renaissance Italy and Aztec Mexico. Of the Aztec gardens almost nothing, sadly, remains, but the Italian are with us to this day, and the parallels are plain to see. These, as already mentioned, are in fact closely derived from Roman originals. Apart from all the elaborate pools and cascades, one appealing feature of Roman water gardening – perhaps a unique one – is described by Pliny the Younger in his villa at Tifernum in Umbria:

> At the upper end is a semicircular bench of white marble, shaded with a vine which is trained upon four small pillars of Carystian marble. Water, gushing through several little pipes from under this bench, as if it were pressed out by the weight of the persons who repose themselves upon it, falls into a stone cistern underneath, from whence it is received into a fine polished marble basin, so artfully contrived that it is always full without overflowing. When I sup here, the tray of whets and the larger dishes are placed around the margin, while the smaller ones swim about in the form of little ships and waterfowl.

Although the climate was obviously not the main reason, water was always important in the gardens of medieval Europe, particularly in the form of a spring emerging in a well, springhead, or in a fountain. From these the water would pass through other parts of the garden in channels and sometimes pools. Springs were sometimes contained in a raised box of brick or stone, and it was apparently customary to place a board across this as an alfresco dining table.

One rather peculiar feature of medieval gardens as represented in contemporary illustrations is the bathing pool. Apart from the numerous depictions of Bathsheba (whom David saw bathing and desired, and whose husband Uriah he sent to certain death in battle), and Susanna and the Elders (she rejected their advances and was then accused of adultery, the elders being found out by Daniel), there are others showing the ladies and gentlemen of the courts and castles bathing stark naked in a stone basin or, occasionally, a wooden tub, attended by retainers both male and female, sometimes playing instruments. On occasion the bathers and clothed guests are depicted dining together. While the bathing pool is directly descended from the garden pools of the East, the happy nudity of the medieval nobility in the company of mixed servants remains perplexing to me, for it seems out of keeping with other customs of the time.

The pools of Near Eastern gardens were clearly used for bathing, but the sexes were usually kept separate. Nevertheless, the sultan or caliph would no doubt enjoy seeing his harem in the pool and, perhaps, disporting himself with them.

The Chinese seem to have been more refined in this respect, even though their gardens were very much based on water. However, this was water for entirely decorative and contemplative purposes; neither the heat of the Indian sun nor the apparent grime of the medieval court were reasons for its existence. There were, however, merrier moments, as when the ruler of Hsai (around 2000 B.C.) filled a pool with rice wine. Boats carried his guests on this alcoholic surface until, at the stroke of a gong, they jumped overboard and drank themselves silly.

The Hellenistic peoples of Asia Minor enjoyed elaborate fountains. Ctesibius of Alexandria invented the waterclock in about 250 B.C. and a hydraulic organ in about 243. (Water organs were to appear again later in sixteenth-century Europe.) His fellow countryman Hero, or Heron, who lived from roughly 147 to 100 B.C., wrote a treatise on waterworks which included a fountain with mechanical singing birds, whose song ceased when a mechanical owl popped up. Other water-operated conceits of this time included moving statues which performed on musical instruments. This tradition of water-operated figures was taken up in seventeenth-century Italian gardens, as at Pratolino, near Florence, a garden notorious for its waterworks and other features. An account by Richard Lasels, an Englishman doing the grand tour, describes how these shows – one showed Syrinx changing into a reed – were "done by water, which sets these little inventions awork and makes them move as it were of themselves."

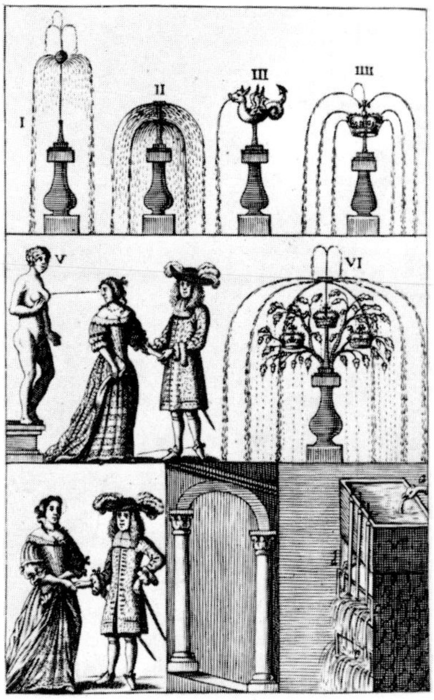

In the sixteenth and seventeenth centuries, fountains played an important part in gardens, and many ingenious and attractive designs were created, such as trees which dripped from every leaf (VI). Garden owners were also very fond of joke fountains, which – like the lady (V) "who at the turning of a private cock shall cast water out of her nipples" – might simply strike one in the face, but more often wet the unwary to the skin. These designs were drawn in 1677.

The fountains of the Muslim countries of the East were beautifully designed, but always geometrical; the Koran forbids the making of images, although I recall a delightful miniature spouting lion in the harem courtyard of the sultan's palace in Damascus. In medieval Europe there was a considerable fashion for copper and lead fountains as well as pools and springheads. Later, fountains became vastly elaborate, apparently capable of depicting the most intricate designs in spraying jets. The water theater at Versailles was perhaps the most elaborate collection of fountains ever put together.

Some garden owners played damp jokes upon their visitors with concealed jets controllable at a distance: seats became flooded; water sprang up under ladies' crinolines from paving; grottoes became showers; artificial trees dripped; and statues sprayed visitors from such unexpected places as their nipples. Such japes are recorded, for instance, from Pratolino, the Alcazar at Seville, and, among others in England, Wilton House in Wiltshire and Dyrham Park in Avon.

ENCLOSURE

The necessity for enclosure – for protection of village, town, castle or fortified manor – has been sketched out earlier. Whether carried out by strong walls or the impenetrable thorny *boma* of the African village, the principle is the same.

The enclosure of gardens stems in part from the same need, although on a smaller scale: a protective enclosure keeps out grazing animals and deters human intruders. Virgil writes of woven fences to keep out destructive beasts, notably the goat; Columella prefers a quickset hedge. Later, the wish for enclosure also arises from the same feeling for neatness and formality which gave rise to the Tudor precept that the garden

A representation of a wattle fence at the end of the fifteenth century. It encloses a garden in which a tiered fountain and beehives are prominent.

formed a frame to the house. A garden without a boundary is like a picture without a frame, especially if it is a small one whose limits can be seen.

In enormous areas like Persian parks, and Roman and European landscape gardens, the boundary is basically protective – usually to keep animals suitable for hunting within. There is in fact a very interesting transition period at the end of the Middle Ages, when the heavily protective outer boundaries of estates were pierced to allow views into the surrounding countryside, views which shortly became accentuated by contrived avenues through the parkland or forest. This could, of course, only happen when the risk of intrusion was very slight, and mostly when the garden owner also owned a vast tract of countryside around.

Medieval Europe gives as good an idea of the possible types of enclosure as anywhere else. In some measure they follow the range of enclosures for beds already described. Wattle fences, made of osier willow shoots braided around upright stakes, were long in use, being cheap, easy to construct, and in fact extremely strong if some active protection was needed. Wattle was on occasion used as part of a fortification.

Wattle was later more or less replaced by wooden palings, nailed very much as they are in fences today against two horizontal rails fixed into strong uprights at intervals. These palings could be straight-topped or triangular. A variation on this, explained at some length by John Worlidge in *The Art of Gardening* of 1677, was to use palings fixed along the edges, and with the top cut into two: "the middle vacancy being about

A rather more convincing wattle fence than the one opposite encloses an orchard. Entry is through a stout wooden gate.

This four-square Tudor garden is enclosed in an outer paling fence, with an elaborately pillared lattice fence within. This is the title page of one of the earliest books on gardening, Thomas Hill's A most briefe and pleasaunte treatise, teachying how to dresse, sowe, and set a garden, *probably published in 1558.*

one-third part of the whole breadth, the two extream parts . . . being cut with square pyramidal points. . . . As you stand against them they appear open, and everything very conspicuous through them . . . but as you view them obliquely they appear full, only their sharp heads open and not unpleasant . . . every motion of your Body from its place begetting a variety in the object." Very subtle.

At Monticello, Thomas Jefferson constructed an outer paling fence in 1809. Ten feet high, it was to keep out both wild and domestic animals. The palings did not have the usual triangular point, but were made with only one slanting cut; also, according to Jefferson's instructions, they were set so close together "as not to permit even a young hare through."

Railings of both wood and iron were extensively used in Europe from the Middle Ages on. Some look almost like modern ranch fencing; others resemble the dreariest of wire fences, with a strong outer border supporting a finer lattice. Metal railings were typically used to train roses, as were diamond-patterned wooden trellis fences.

I have already mentioned, at the end of Chapter 2, the various other kinds of fence, besides the habitual palings, made by the American settlers; around estates or plantations they often used the characteristic worm or zigzag fence, so easy to erect but so wasteful of timber. All this was in marked contrast to the Indians who very seldom fenced their plots. One of the few tribes to do so before the settlers arrived were the Nipmucks on Rhode Island who made small stone walls. When the settlers' livestock made it necessary, the Indians in the neighbourhood finally had to enclose their gardens, and usually did so very competently from stone.

ARBORS

Woodwork expanded in another way, into the arbor or "herber." Originally this resembled the Roman *porticus*, which was essentially a shelter where one could rest or escape from hot sun or rain. They were erections of either wood laths or of trained plants. In a translation of a French work of 1572, we read of "arbours . . . set about with lattise work . . . contrived . . . as it were, into small chappels, or oratories and places to make a speech out of . . . in like sort shall the Garden of Pleasure be set out and compassed in with Arbours made of Jesamin, Rosemarie, Boxe, Juniper, Cyper Trees, Savin, Cedar, Rose-trees and other dainties first planted and pruned according as the nature of everyone doth requires, but after brought into some forme and order with willow or juniper poles, such as may serve for the making of Arbours." One may understandably think the plants suggested are an extraordinary mixture.

Wooden arbors extended, in the late fifteenth and sixteenth centuries, to long tunnels, often of very elaborate construction, which might surround the entire garden, occupying three sides, or sometimes forming a cross in the center. On these tunnels climbing plants would be trained, the result being somewhat like a modern pergola, but with an

Wall paintings at Pompeii depict some typical features of Roman gardens. Pergolas carry vines, or possibly climbing roses, while lattice work divides off individual gardens. In winter (above) the main plant decoration shown is ivy, tied into bunches at the tops of poles. In the summer scene (below) there are some flowers as well as trees. Urns, statues and fountains complete the ornamentation.

LEFT: *A strong, simple open wooden fence encloses one plot; in the other, deep raised beds include two standard roses with horizontal "wheel" supports. Note the long-handled, slightly scooped wooden spade (fifteenth century).*

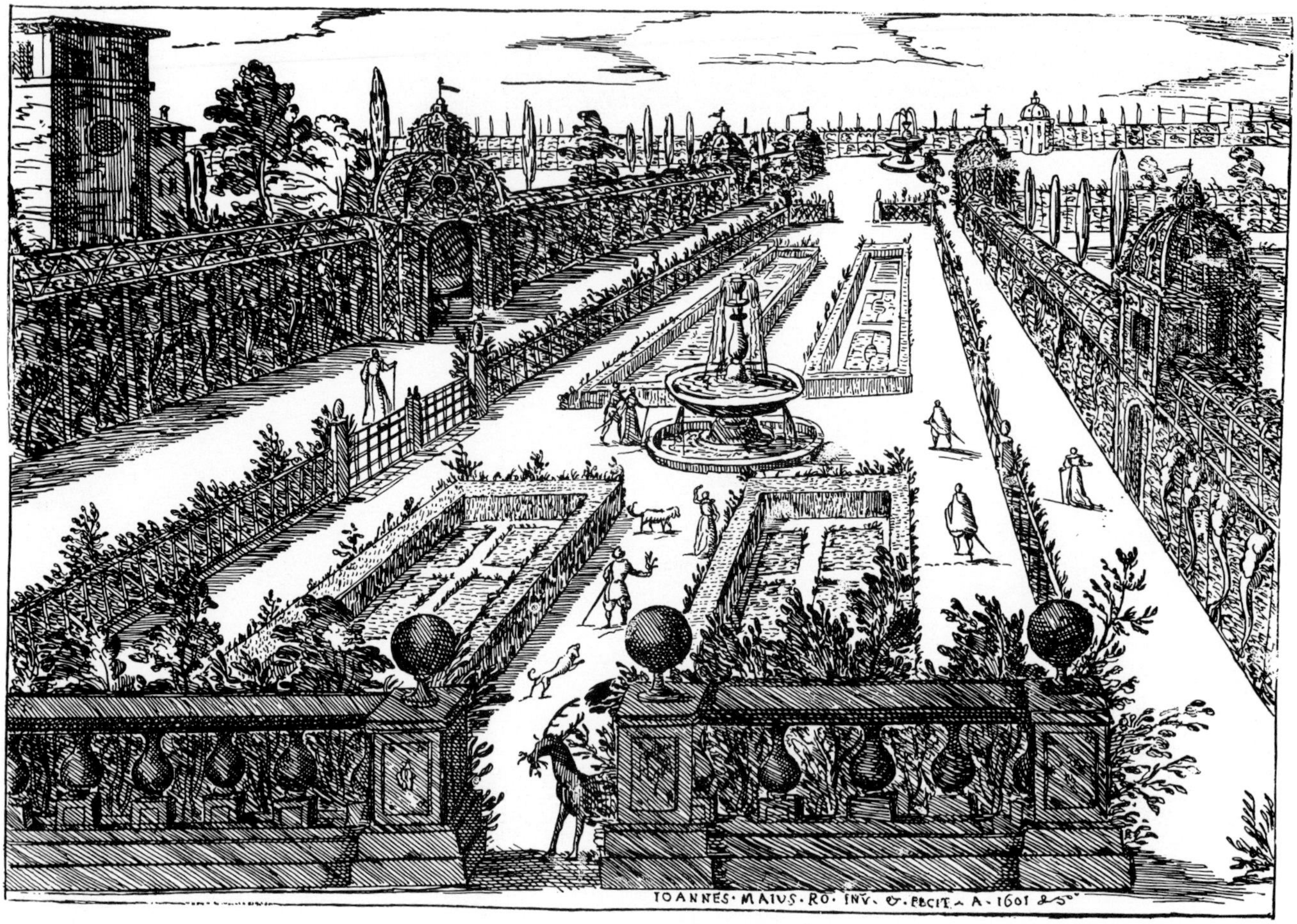

Thick hedges of medium height enclose four individual gardens of formal beds, themselves contained in a wooden fence against which shrubs are trained. Elaborate arbors or galleries surround the whole (1601).

arched top instead of a flat one. (More about this aspect is contained in Chapter 6, as well as information about hedges and pleached trees, which became important as both external and internal divisions.) These various forms of arbor or gallery, as they came to be called, were by the late sixteenth century a very important part of garden decoration, far exceeding the necessities of mere enclosure which a good hedge would provide as well. The poem *The Floure and the Leafe*, once attributed to Chaucer, describes a medieval "hegge" around a private arbor:

> . . . as thicke as is a castle wall,
> That who that list without to stand or go,
> Though he would all day pryen to and fro,
> He shoulde not see if there were any wighte
> Within or no . . . .

Arbors continued to be made in European gardens until the landscape revolution of the eighteenth century, when they largely disappeared, to return in Victorian times. Today their only descendants are the pergola and the summerhouse. But older gardens in the United States still show some fine examples, often of wooden slats in diamond pattern over an arched framework, and sometimes containing bench seats on either

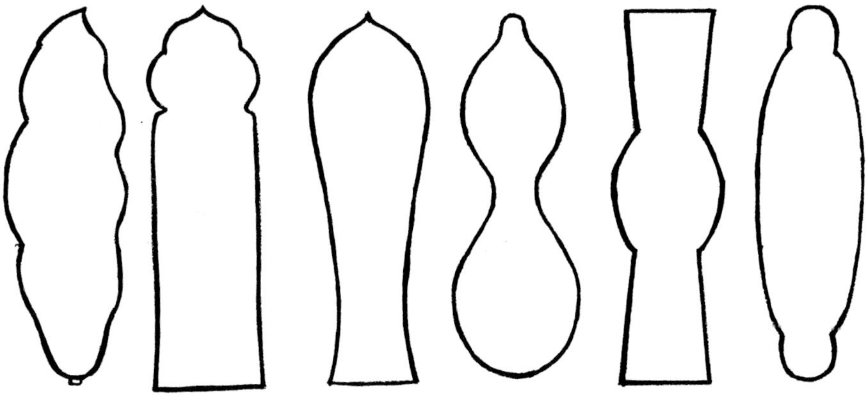

ABOVE: *Internal fencing in Chinese gardens was always of pleasing artistic design, and its arrangement – like that of the paths – was an integral part of the garden composition.*

LEFT: *Chinese gateway outlines. From left to right the shapes are: shell, Ju-i, lotus petal, gourd, flower vase and sword guard.*

side of a central path very like some medieval examples.

The ancient Chinese equivalent of the extended arbor was the definite gallery. These galleries were usually open, and varied from wide verandas in front of buildings to corridorlike constructions connecting the scattered buildings which made up the wide courtyards. Although practical, giving shelter for rest, entertainment or just walking, they were – like everything else in the Chinese garden – essentially decorative elements of the whole composition. They often opened upon or led to beautiful views, constantly changing as one moved from one "frame" of the gallery to another. The *Yüan Yeh* suggests that they were the most important buildings in a garden.

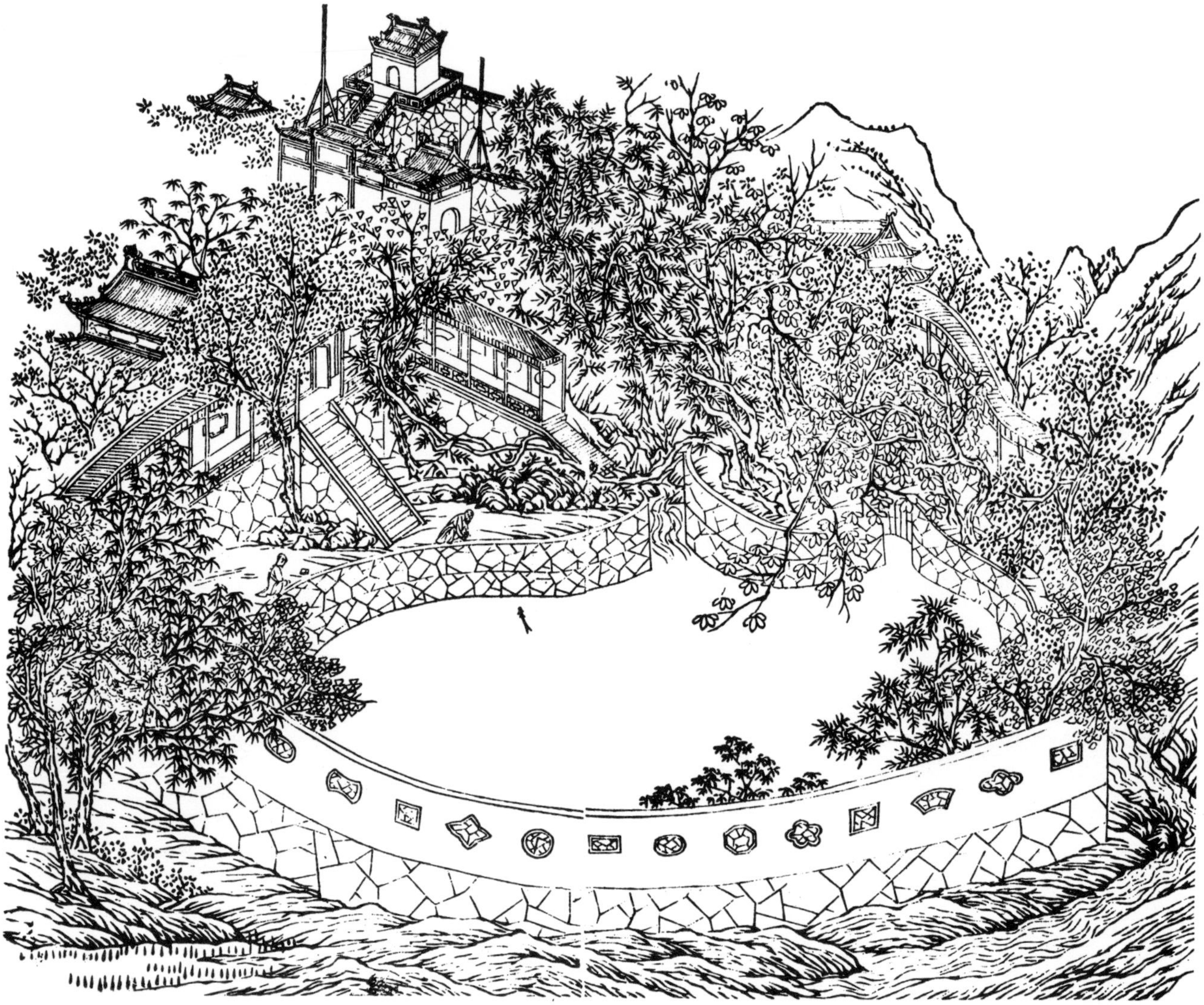

A garden near Peking displays an ornate winding wall, partly of irregular stone blocks carefully fitted together, and partly of white plaster with earthenware-framed openings of different shapes.

In construction they usually resembled the garden pavilions with saddle-shaped roofs, but they could also be flat-topped, when they would have an upper balustrade so that one could climb to this level and view the garden from a higher point. The galleries had no walls; their supports were fairly widely spaced, and their form and ornamentation were often enhanced by brightly painted decoration. Their low balustrades were made of wood or metal in an endless variety of patterns.

Unlike Europeans, the Chinese would never sully these finely wrought buildings with climbing plants. Such clutter would be quite alien to them, and in its inevitable untidiness destroy the carefully calculated calm of the garden itself.

WALLS

The actual enclosures of Far Eastern gardens not unexpectedly also show a great deal of sophistication. Walls surrounding gardens were made of many materials – cast brick, stone, or "earth stamped between boards." But, to quote *Yüan Yeh* yet again, "there are also walls made of plaited bamboo or branches of the jujube bush; such wattled walls are better than trellises; they are more rustic in appearance, and have a fragrance of wood and mountains." These are, of course, what we would call fences.

Solid walls had a great deal of care given to their external finish. Although many had a reddish coloring, white or pale gray was the usual choice. The great manual goes on: "Paper pulp and chalk have of old been used for plastering the walls. Connoisseurs, who wished to give the walls a glossy surface, used for this purpose white wax, which they rubbed or patted into the wall. Today one uses for the ground yellow sand from rivers or lakes, mixed with a small quantity of chalk of the best quality, and over the whole is spread a little chalk as a covering surface. If this is rubbed carefully with a hempen brush, a mirror-bright surface will be produced." This whiteness was a perfect foil for the outlines of trees and bamboos by day, and for their shadows on moonlit nights.

Solid walls in particular would be constructed with ornamental apertures. "The views seen through these apertures should appear unexpected or surprising, and attract the attention at certain points. . . . One should be secluded from all neighbors, but at the same time have a view of the landscape in all directions." These openings were often decorated with patterns made of brick.

Some walls were made of irregular stone blocks, but mostly they were formal, carefully finished, and often surmounted by low balustrading similar to that on the galleries and pavilions. Within the garden itself, the internal divisions were formed by open wooden or bamboo fencing, or occasionally stone balustrading, once again in incredible variety of pattern and often arranged in a zigzag pattern like the paths, thus contributing to the basic design of the garden composition.

In Japan the palace grounds would have thick, high walls made of plastered clay and tiles, supported by a strong timber framework. They had an elaborate wooden cornice and a roof of ornamental tiles. Lesser grounds did without the wooden framing and ornamentation. The use of brick and stone is relatively recent.

The many kinds of fencing in Japan were often similar to that seen today. Frequently a framework of upright posts and horizontal laths would be plastered, the main timbers remaining visible as in Tudor buildings, and supporting a projecting roof of tiles or, more likely, boards. Where privacy was essential in crowded towns, these fence walls might be fifteen to twenty feet high. As in China, they might have shaped openings, and sometimes the upper part was an open lattice or trellis.

Plain boarding with vertical supports was used in many cases, either overlapping as in our close-boarded fences, or butted together, the open joints being covered with thin strips of bamboo or lath. Such fences were usually capped, presumably to prevent rotting due to too much rain. Often a foot or more would be left open at the base, and sometimes a space, filled with upright or diagonal bars, was also left between the top of the

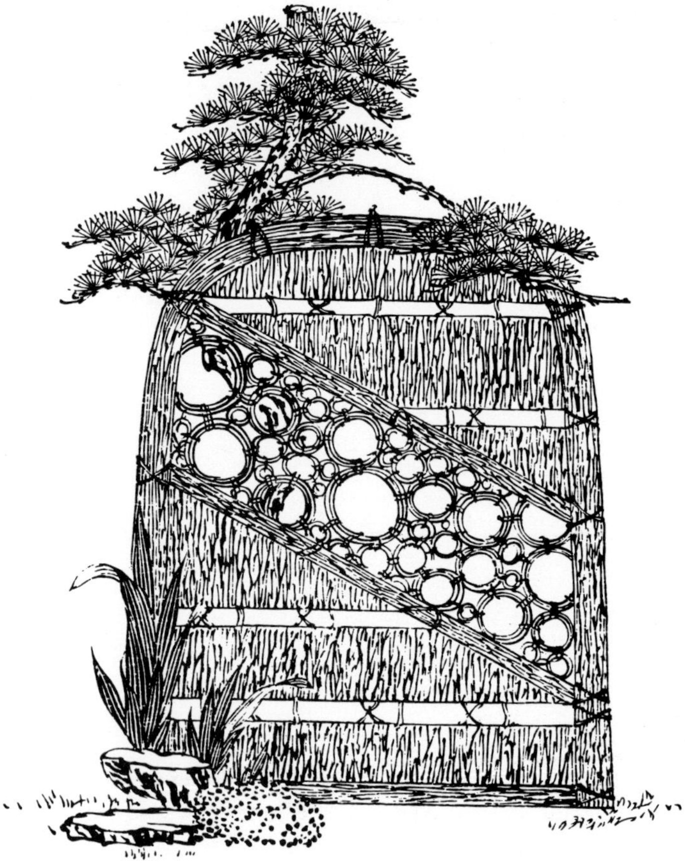

Internal screens, or "sleeve fences" as they were called, of great diversity were favored in Japan. In the "moon-entering" screen (top left) a carefully trained conifer leans through an embrasure. One of the more complex was the "armor pattern" (top right) in which the circles were formed of wisteria shoots, set in vertical reeds with bamboo crosspieces.

fence and the capping.

The Japanese, with their love of natural-looking materials, would enhance wooden boards either by sanding them to leave the harder parts of the grain in relief, or by introducing weather-worn planks from old boats. Sometimes they charred the timber to produce a piebald effect, or roughly chiseled and chipped it.

Split bamboo was, not surprisingly, very extensively used for fences, in a great range of patterns. Upright and horizontal members would be tied together by colored cord at regular intervals, giving yet another dimension to the formal pattern. Sometimes tendrils of vine or wisteria were used for tying, as were bracken fibers. Rustic fences were sometimes made of leafy bamboo shoots, arched in opposite directions and tied together where they crossed.

The Japanese also had tall, thick hedges of growing plants. Although they used many plants, such as box and camellia, which could be clipped in the orthodox way to form hedges up to six feet or so, they also used trees which do not branch low down. These were supplemented by an outer bamboo fence of appropriate height. Sometimes they trained hedge plants, like the small thorny citrus called kikoku, and also climbing plants, on an open bamboo trellis. Such "fedges," as they are occasionally called today, were usually three or four feet tall, and often grown on narrow grassed embankments.

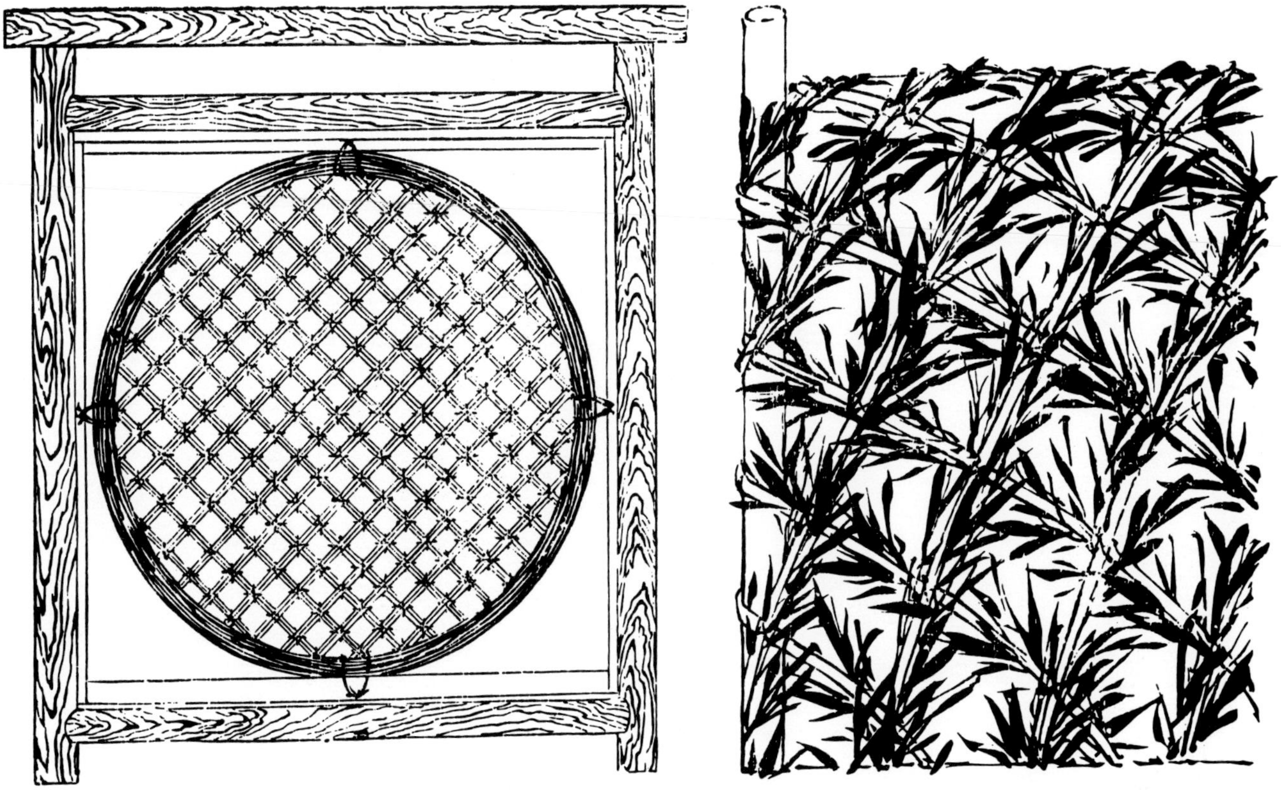

Further examples of Japanese screen fences. One of the few formal patterns was the "round-window clothes horse" (left), while one of the simplest was the "bent branch," mainly of bamboo sprays (right).

Internal screens or divisions, usually more ornamental than functional, but often hiding unsightly necessities, were short units a few feet wide and five to seven feet tall. Usually set up near the house veranda, they had one end attached to a wall or veranda post. Innumerable designs existed in many fascinating shapes, sometimes curved at top or bottom, combining open and solid work, incorporating stylized patterns, and often with a shaped embrasure through which the branch of a choice cherry or gnarled conifer could be seen to best effect. Among the quaint names given to these screens, which the Japanese call "sleeve fences," are "two-stage torch," "leaning plum tree," "round window clotheshorse," "hiding," "looking through," "tea whisk and lattice," and "moon entering" (this last one with an embrasure). Perhaps the most extraordinary is the "armor pattern" in which a diagonal section of circles of different sizes, formed of wisteria shoots, is inserted in a panel of upright reeds with a thicker external binding of reeds and crosspieces of bamboo. Much of this stylization of fencing and screening is still used today in gardens in Japan, where tradition remains so important.

Gates are, of course, essential to enter any enclosure, and they again reach their highest ornamental development in the Far East. Although the outer gate is always necessarily a door, the gateways within gardens and compounds in China were always open. In older gardens they were likely to be octagonal or the circular "moon gate," much copied in Europe today. The Chinese considered this to provide the most perfect frame for a view. Later, many other forms were used, based on the shapes of leaves, flower

Seventeenth-century French designs for latticework screens "made of poles or wands."

petals, seeds, gourds and vases. These developed finally into more bizarre outlines – of swordguards, scepters, musical instruments and shells. These entrances echoed comparable shapes in pavilion windows.

Japanese gateways were usually found only in external walls or fences, and it was considered essential to have both a front entrance and a back one – the latter called the "sweeping opening," because through it leaves and trash were swept out. These lesser gates were simple wooden or bamboo constructions; the entrance would be much more imposing, of wooden timbers, wooden lattice on a stout frame, bamboo, twigs in a lattice framework – an endless variety similar to that of the "sleeve fences."

The walls of later Western gardens are humdrum compared with the subleties and elaborations of their Eastern counterparts. Outer walls are habitually of brick, sometimes of stone and, in appropriate places, in the attractive, ancient flintstone pattern of horizontal lines. Grand houses had, and have, grand walls, with buttresses, niches and sometimes balustrades or ornate patterns of brick or metalwork on top. In-and-out-curving or serpentine walls were sometimes built, primarily to provide sheltered niches for fruit trees (see Chapter 6). At Monticello during the latter half of the eighteenth century, Thomas Jefferson built a very extensive serpentine wall, seven feet high, some of which is still standing. This was not in fact for growing fruit nor, as is widely believed, for economy in use of bricks, but probably in keeping with the current European fashion for avoiding straight lines.

Walls and hedges were sometimes, in the eighteenth and nineteenth centuries, combined. The hedge might be planted on top of an earth wall, which would usually be reinforced with stonework or

sometimes with furze branches. Alternatively, the earth on one side of a constructed wall would be built up and the hedge planted on the summit of the ridge thus created.

Many walls were, of course, for specific purposes, notably fruit culture, and these will be dealt with later (Chapter 6). The training of plants – both fruit and ornamental – over walls is very much a Western idea, as opposed to the Eastern concept where, as we have seen, the walls and screens themselves were so ornamental and stylized that the untidiness of a climbing plant – even that of a strictly trained one – was anathema. In Britain especially, the land of the plantsman, we see both kinds of culture widely carried out – a principle especially desirable today as gardens become steadily smaller and it becomes all the more valuable to make use of this third dimension of surrounding walls. Warm south-facing walls are especially prized because they provide the opportunity of growing many plants – both climbers and others in the wall's immediate shelter – which are too tender to succeed in the open garden.

As with everything they touched, the Victorians elaborated enclosing materials into patterns almost as complex in their way as those of the Far East, reveling especially in their newly discovered mastery over metal which enabled them to make fencing units for both external and internal division. Rustic woodwork also came into its own in late-Victorian and Edwardian days.

I have remarked earlier how the size of an enclosing wall depends upon the lawlessness of the surrounding country. As law and order prevail, the need for immense walls diminishes, and people finally cut vista-viewing gaps in their walls. It was not, however, until the very early

ABOVE: *Edwardian prefabricated rustic fence panels of intricate workmanship. These were constructed entirely of wood which "may be barked or unbarked, according to taste, but should never be painted."*

ABOVE LEFT: *Elaborate wrought-iron panels frame stone urns atop a wall supported by stone pillars (France, late nineteenth century).*

HA-HAS

eighteenth century that walls were in many places entirely done away with. This followed the new fashion for landscaping, where the harsh line of a wall would have entirely spoiled the blending of the man-made landscape with the countryside beyond. William Kent was the first landscape designer to perceive this principle; in Horace Walpole's well-known words, "he leaped the fence, and saw that all nature was a garden." But it was his contemporary, Charles Bridgeman (d. 1738), who seems to have first swept away what he called the "unnaturalness" of walls by using an earlier invention called a ha-ha. This is in effect a sunken fence – a ditch designed to separate a garden from a pasture without the erection of a wall. It keeps farm animals in the pasture, but it brings them right into the view. (A ditch is also appreciably cheaper than a wall.)

It developed from a wall with a ditch on the outer side, designed to prevent animals spoiling the construction or eating plants growing upon it. The origin of the ha-ha and its name is given by John James in his *Theory and Practice of Gardening* published in 1712, an adaptation of a work by the Frenchman d'Argenville published three years earlier. James describes how, in a garden surrounded by walls, iron grilles were set in them at the ends of avenues "to extend the view, and to show the country to advantage." Here we have the vista-viewing gap mentioned above, but still protected against intruders. But, James goes on: "At present we frequently make Thorough-views, call'd *Ah, Ah*, which are Openings in the walls, without grilles, to the very level of the Walks, with a large and deep Ditch at the Foot of them, lined on both sides to sustain the earth, and prevent the getting over, which surprizes the eye upon coming near it, and makes one cry *Ah! Ah!* from whence it takes its name." Clearly the ha-ha was in use for some years at least before this book was published; in France it was sometimes called a *saut-de-loup*.

The fashion for landscape, and the corresponding use of the ha-ha, reached its crescendo in the early nineteenth century (as we can read in Jane Austen's *Mansfield Park*, published in 1814) – a "rage for improvement," to quote Miles Hadfield, which "affected country residences almost by the thousand . . . it was, indeed, the period when every house of any pretensions had its walls (except those protecting the kitchen garden) swept away and a ha-ha substituted." One does not regret the views into the country thus created, but one must sorrow for the vast numbers of formal gardens, parterres and topiary works irretrievably swept away. But that, like miniskirts and platform shoes, is fashion. Unfortunately, it takes an infinitely longer time to rebuild a formal garden than it does to bring back some particular form of dress.

Ha-has were made in various designs. The slope next to the garden was usually vertical or almost so, and typically made of brickwork or stone, with the opposite side more gently sloped. Sometimes the supporting brickwork would be continued upward into a dwarf wall

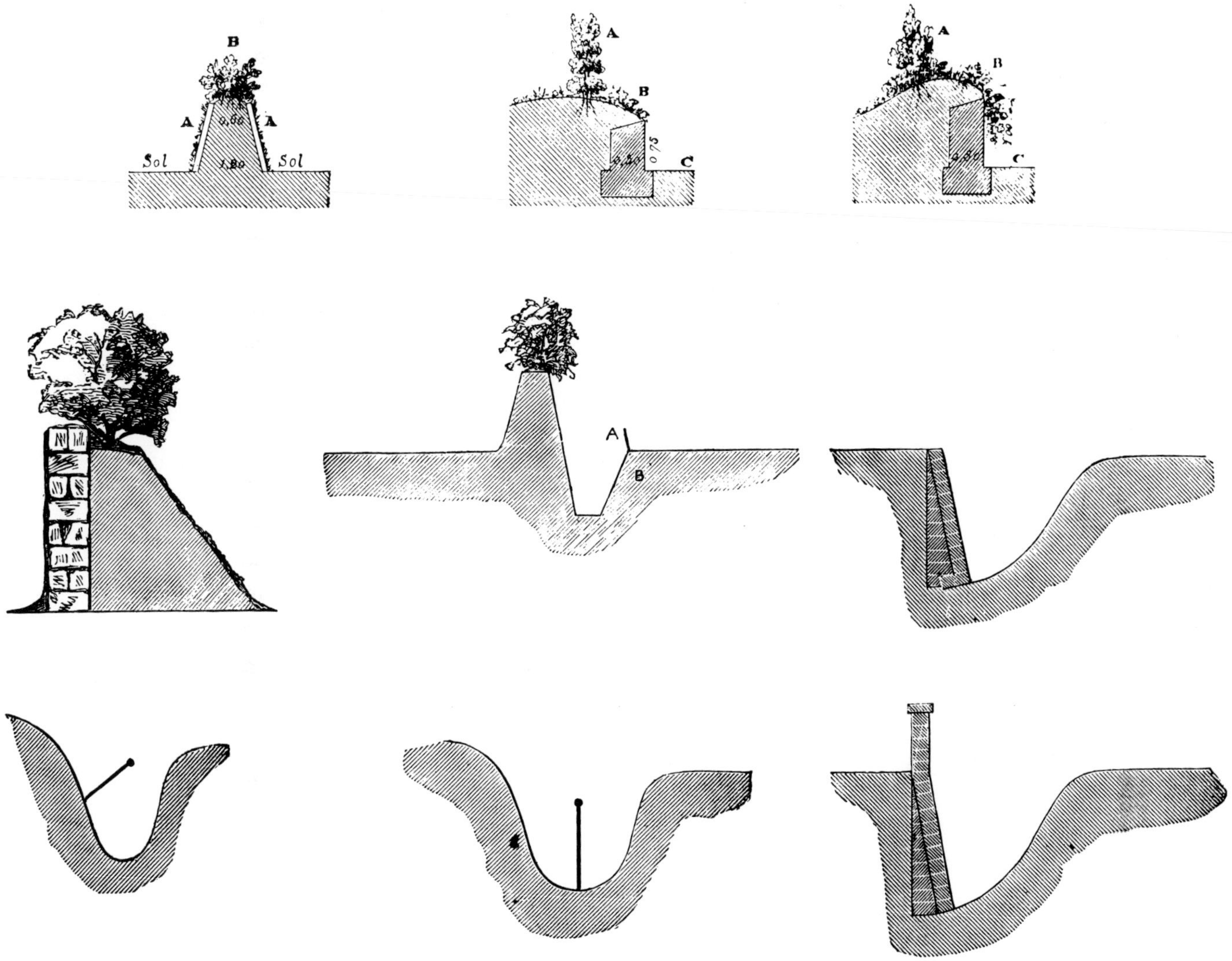

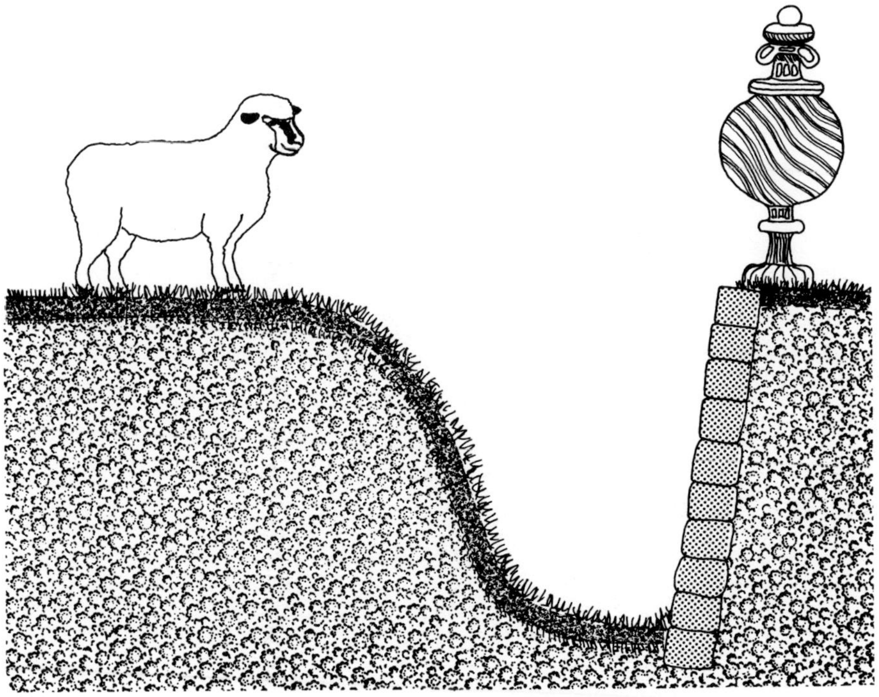

Boundaries took many forms. TOP ROW AND LEFT OF CENTER ROW: *Various combinations of walls and hedges, of earth alone, or reinforced with stonework (shown in section).* REMAINING DIAGRAMS: *Sections of ha-has of various patterns. They were usually without the protective wall but might incorporate a metal fence if security was important. The ha-ha allowed an uninterrupted view from garden into landscape – and the animals could look straight into the garden too (bottom).*

which presumably provided a little safety for the garden visitors. Other ha-has were made with equal slopes on both sides, and these would sometimes be combined with a fence where extra precaution against intruders was deemed necessary.

George Washington, who always followed current European fashion in his gardening, created a ha-ha at each end of the mansion at Mount Vernon in 1765. However, ha-has were never used to a great extent in the United States, any more than high walls were. The tendency was always to open up the view, even when there was none.

MOUNTS

A different way of gazing at the surrounding countryside was the artificial hill or mount. As mentioned earlier, the tradition of building artificial hills is very ancient, with such examples as the hanging gardens of Babylon, the ziggurats and the pyramids of Egypt. Several authors consider that garden mounts have a sacred origin, or result from the tradition of holy hills. This may possibly be the case, but on a more prosaic level the idea of a mount as a viewpoint within a high-walled garden seems sufficient of itself.

Mounts existed in Europe, and especially in Britain, as early as the fourteenth century, when they were features of the gardens of the Louvre in Paris. In his famous essay *Of Gardens* (1625), Francis Bacon makes it plain that he considers it an essential feature of a "princely garden": "I wish also, in the very Middle, a Faire Mount, with three Ascents, and Alleys, enough for foure to walk abreast; Which I could have to be Perfect Circles, without any Bulwarkes or Imbossments; And the Whole Mount to be Thirty Foot high; And some fine Banqueting House, with some Chimneys neatly cast, and without too much Glasse." This last comment may be a backhander at the South Arbor on Henry VIII's great mount at Hampton Court, which contained forty-eight glass lights about $4\frac{1}{2}$ feet long. These were used in a three-storied "lantern arbor" on the summit, which was reached by a spiral pathway. The foundation alone contained 256,000 bricks.

Mounts could also be built in less elaborate gardens. Bacon writes elsewhere in the same essay, "At the End of both the Side Grounds, I would have a Mount of some Pretty Height, leaving the Walk of the Enclosure Brest high, to look abroad in the Fields."

The popularity of mounts continued into the sixteenth and seventeenth centuries, and we find them still being recommended as late as 1728. A prosaic rather than a religious origin is certainly suggested by John Worlidge (1700), when he wrote, "it is not unusual to raise a Mount with the waste earth or Rubbish, you may otherwise happen to be troubled withal, at some convenient distance from your House, on which as on your Terrace-walks, you have the advantage of the Air and prospect, and whereon you may erect a Pleasure or Banqueting-house of Repose." Although many mounts were flat and grassed on top, their summits were frequently used for an arbor.

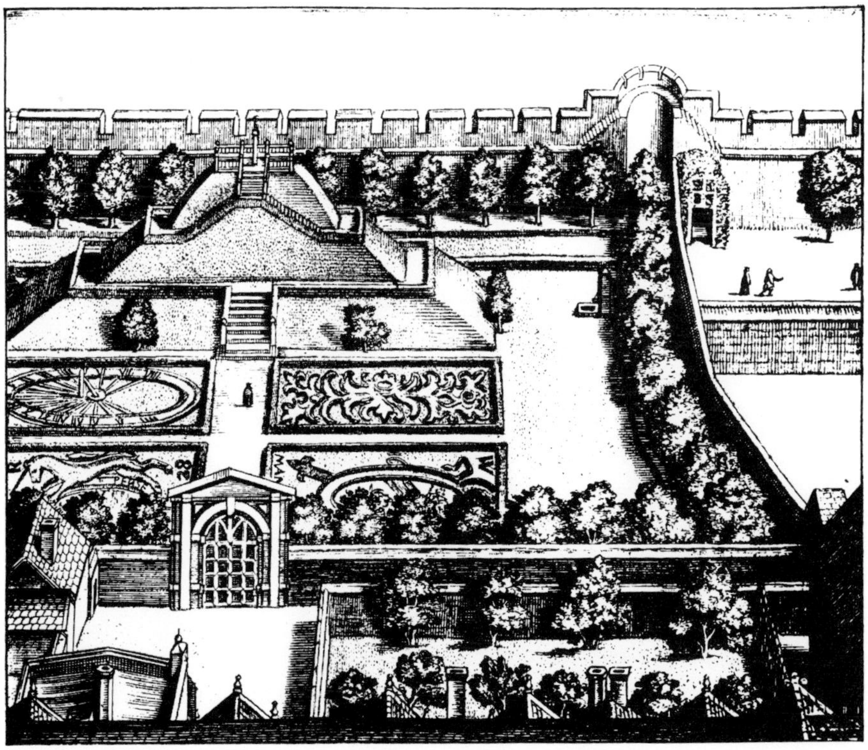

LEFT: *Mounts in the grounds of New College, Oxford, in the seventeenth century. The oblong, terraced mount at the left stands isolated; at right steps lead from a terrace walk to a high viewpoint in an embrasure in the outer wall.*

The mount was often placed symmetrically in the center of the garden, but later it was considered more useful to place it against an outer wall, or in a corner of the walls, so that the visitor could look out not only over the countryside but obtain a bird's-eye view of the garden itself. If there was a park outside the walls, it was suggested that one could even "shoot a buck" from the mount. Sometimes there might be several mounts in one large garden.

Isolated mounts were usually circular, and might be ascended by a steep stair up one side, by a "winding path," or by a spiral ramp. The *Itinerary*, written in 1533 by John Leland, who became Henry VIII's antiquary, describes a Yorkshire garden: "in the orchardes were mountes, opere topiarii, writhen about with degrees like turninges of cockell-shells, to cum to the top without paine." Some authors likened this construction to that of the Tower of Babel. Occasionally mounts were square and then resembled pyramids, with stair ramps at each angle. In recommending the latter, the French author Olivier de Serres (1600) suggests that the terraces should combine a walk eleven feet wide with a four-foot-wide bed for herbs, and also that the mount might be hollow to provide shelter for the plants in winter.

Mounts gradually gave way to "viewing terraces." These might ascend a very high outer wall in tiers, as can be seen to this day at Northbourne Court, in England's southern county of Kent, an Elizabethan layout where there is also a terrace above the garden at the elevated level of the house. (A similar design still exists at Rockingham

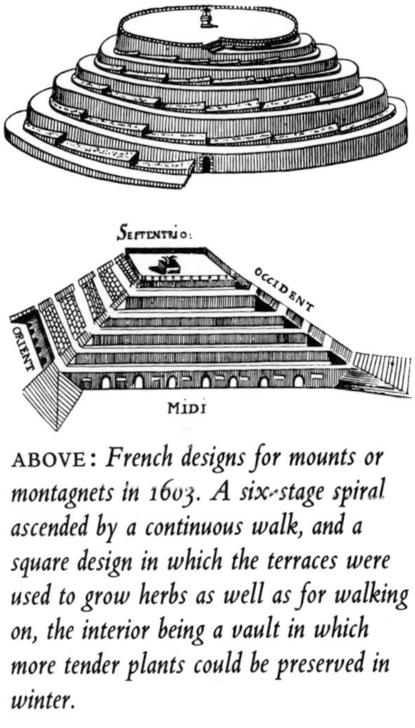

ABOVE: *French designs for mounts or montagnets in 1603. A six-stage spiral ascended by a continuous walk, and a square design in which the terraces were used to grow herbs as well as for walking on, the interior being a vault in which more tender plants could be preserved in winter.*

Castle, Northamptonshire.) Such arrangements were praised by Sir Henry Wotton who wrote, in *Elements of Architecture* (1624), how he found special pleasure in "a garden into which the first access was a high walk like a terrace, from whence might be taken a general view of the whole plot below." Occasionally there would be a low viewing terrace actually across the "whole plot," with views on either side. An example of this can still be seen at Hampton Court.

Although mounts were seldom, if ever, built in Europe after the seventeenth century, a few were made in North America. Washington planned two at Mount Vernon, each to carry a weeping willow – this being a new idea for planting rather than the concept of the mount for viewing. Another ornamental mount is recorded at a Charleston, South Carolina, estate called Goose Creek. An account of around 1740 explains that at "the boundary to this charming spot . . . is a large fishpond with a mount rising out of the middle, the top of which is level with the dwelling house, and upon it is a Roman temple."

TREE HOUSES

It is not perhaps much of a jump from the mount to the use of trees to provide yet another dimension to accessible parts of the garden – the formation of tree houses of various sorts. The Romans seem to have made tree seats, and many are recorded from the Middle Ages. More elaborately, from the Middle Ages onward, trees were made, by special training and cutting out of surplus branches, to provide a room seven or eight feet above ground level, to which one ascended on a ladder. The roof and sides of this arboreal room were created by bending upper branches down and around; the floor would be of planking either supported on lower boughs or on extra supports pushed in underneath. John Parkinson, describing the use of the lime tree for such purposes, tells us in his famous *Paradisi in sole . . .* of 1629:

> It is planted both to make goodly Arbours and Summer banqueting houses, either below upon the ground, the boughes serving very handsomely to plash round about it, or up higher for a second aboue it, and a third also: for the more it is depressed, the better it will grow. And I haue seen at Cobham in Kent, a tall or great bodied Line Tree (*sic*), bare without boughes for eight foote high and then the branches were spread round about so orderly, as if it were done by art, and brought to compasse the middle Arbour: and from those boughes the body was bare again for eight or nine foote (wherein might bee placed halfe a hundred men at the least, as there might be likewise in that vnderneath this) & then another rowe of branches to encompasse a third Arbour, with stayres made for the purpose to this and that vnderneath it: vpon the boughes were laid boards to tread vpon, which was the goodliest spectacle mine eyes euer beheld for one tree to carry.

OPPOSITE: *A monk finds peace and quiet in a small tree house (from an Italian miniature of the late fifteenth century).*

A Japanese tree walk at Kyoto, from which a fresh view could be obtained of the maple trees through which it is built, and of the rest of the garden.

These "roosting places," as they were called (the phrase was also applied to arbors), were especially popular with the ladies of the household. But the modern English garden historian Ralph Dutton comments amusingly: "These Peter Pannish conceits throw an interesting light on the simple mentality of the Tudor Englishman."

The Italians seem to have gone in for elaborate tree seats and balconies; there was a famous one at Pratolino (built 1568–1580), admired by Montaigne, who records seeing them elsewhere in Tuscany and also in Germany and Switzerland. An enterprising American of the late eighteenth century, Mr. John Ross, son-in-law of George Cruikshank, owner of a garden in Haverford Township, Philadelphia, made a "roost" of this sort. Ross's granddaughter described "a long dark walk seven-eighths of a mile in extent, shaded by tall forest trees. . . . Near the beginning of this walk Mr. Ross had caused to be constructed, on a spot ten or twelve feet above the walk, a seat capable of holding twenty persons and a place for a table. On the fourth of July and other warm days of summer he would take his friends there and iced wine would be served. A bell wire, communicating with the house, was arranged to call the servant when wanted and avoid his constant presence."

Persian paintings depict tree houses, sturdily built of boards, in which food was often served to nobles. Then there are Mogul miniatures showing Akbar (emperor of India from 1556 to 1605) in "garden thrones" or *chabutra*, always in the revered *chenar* or oriental plane tree. One miniature shows the emperor on a railed platform, placed just above the first forking of the tree boughs, which is connected to the upper floor of a building close by where his ministers are gathered. There is a close relationship between the living tree and the Vishnu symbolism of the Tree or Pillar of the Universe on which the emperor sat enthroned as Vishnu's regent. We can still see such a pillar in Akbar's hall of private audience at Fatehpur Sikri, the abandoned city not far from Agra. Smaller boxlike rooms in trees served as places for monks and hermits to sit and escape from earthbound thoughts and activities. A simpler tree conversion was to form a room of wood around the trunk at ground level.

The Chinese do not seem to have indulged in such entertaining follies, but the Japanese did, building elaborate structures on tall stiltlike supports among the higher branches of trees. These seem to have been mainly to admire the trees from a different angle, rather than for purposes of entertainment or dining.

The tree house is a dimension of the garden which – apart from the making of tree houses for children – seems to have been almost completely neglected by modern designers. Its loss seems rather a pity. The only example I know of is a half-timbered one which can be seen at Pitchford Hall, Shropshire, England.

This chapter has been devoted to various important parts of a garden, most of which are more or less functional. There are, of course, a multitude of other possible, primarily decorative garden features, such as those quoted by Batty Langley (1728) – walks, slopes, avenues, groves, wildernesses, labyrinths, winding alleys, dales, purling streams, cascades, grottoes, serpentine meanders, precipices, and amphitheaters; there might also be "rude coppices, haystacks, small enclosures of corn, wood piles, rabbit and hare warrens." Few gardens today could in fact find space for most of these romantic conceits; but, as we shall see reviewed in Chapter 10, walls, beds, and especially containers continue to be the basis of modern gardening.

A tree house which still exists at Pitchford Hall, Shropshire, England. The exterior is late eighteenth century, but the framework is of much earlier date.

Chapter Four

Instruments of Gardening

EVERYTHING IN HORTICULTURE AND GARDENING SPRINGS FROM antique agricultural origins, a fact which applies very much to the basic tools of the trade. Leaving aside ploughs and their progenitors, we can trace our gardening tools right back to the bone-digging implements of later Paleolithic times (from 40,000 B.C.), when two main kinds were in use – a rather crude digging stick, such as could be made from the rib of a mammoth cut across diagonally, and a quite sophisticated picklike mattock, with the business end made from either a mammoth rib or the tusk of a young mammoth, firmly bound onto a partly shaped, flat-forked tree branch. Similar bone mattocks were used by Eskimos until quite recently.

Other tools were made of antlers. Mattocks composed of a single sharp horn bound to the perforated end of a stick were used to loosen soil which was then scooped up with a shovel made of the flat part of an elk or reindeer antler, with three holes in a line down the center for the binding to its stick. Later one finds shoulderblades of oxen used in the same way.

Interestingly enough, the digging stick and mattock, though found together in certain Paleolithic sites, later diverged and became symbols of very different cultures. The mattock – still in use in southern Europe and other parts of the world – is lifted over the shoulder and brought down forcefully into the soil. The digging stick, on the other hand, is sunk vertically into the soil and treated as a lever by body pressure, although it could also be used for breaking up the soil surface by picking at it with the more or less sharpened tip. To increase efficiency, the digging stick might be weighted with pierced stones, or it could have a transverse footbar for additional pressure. Two sticks were occasionally mounted close together. More elaborate versions had a curved handle bound onto the main one. Digging sticks were often as tall as a man, and some had a shaped, bladelike end. The digging stick is known from diverse cultures, such as Australia, the Veddah (ancient Ceylon), and the dead South American civilizations. It is basically a tool for soft or sandy soils offering relatively little resistance, whereas the mattock, operated by brute force from a stooping position, will break up hard soils.

Elementary hoes with a triangular flaked-stone head, mounted on a handle with thongs and fixed with bitumen, are known from the fifth millennium B.C. in Mesopotamia. A little later, in predynastic Egypt, we find the angled hoe, originally made by cutting a forked branch just below the fork, then shortening and sharpening one of the branches of the resulting V shape, the other being used as a handle. Later, a simple bit of carpentry enabled a sharpened stock to be hafted at an acute angle onto a plain one, the two being lashed together with cord. An alternative form of hoe, recorded from Egypt a little later again, has a pointed, slightly curved stick, hafted at right angles through a handle of almost the same length. Much later the Incas of Peru used a rather similar but shorter implement, in effect a digging stick with a short curved handle lashed to it, allowing a picking motion with the wrist.

Rather different types of stone hoe were based on a flat "celt" with a ground edge, hafted onto a handle like an ax. These were probably used for elementary cultivation as early as Neolithic times. The adze, a small, mattocklike tool with its blade at right angles to the line of the shaft, was certainly in use in Mesopotamia around 4500 B.C.

North American Indians were still using extremely primitive tools when the first settlers observed them in the sixteenth century. In Virginia a tool for making seed holes was a kind of digging stick – "a crooked piece of woode, being scraped on both sides in fation of a gardener's paring iron." A rather curious record from Florida described Indians using "a kind of hoe from fishes' bones"; perhaps it was in fact the same as that used by the Connecticut Indians – a large clam shell fixed to a long stick of basswood. William Wood wrote lyrically about these natives in 1634: they "exceed our English husbandmen, keeping it [the ground] as cleare with their Clamme-shell hoe as if it were a garden rather than a Cornfield, not suffering no choaking weede to advance his audacious Head above their infant Corne, or an undermining Worme to spoil his Spurnes [roots]." This is in contrast to observations in *Description of the New Netherlands* by the Dutch visitor Adrian Van der Donck in Manhattan Island at almost the same time: "Of manuring, or proper tillage, they know nothing. All their tillage is done by hand and with small adzes they obtain from us. Although little can be said in favour of this husbandry, still they prefer their practice to ours, because our methods require too much labour and care to please, with which they are not well satisfied. . . . All their agriculture is performed by their women. The men give themselves very little trouble about the same, except those who are old. . . ." Management of husbandry by the women of the tribe seems to be almost universal practice among the world's peasants.

The use of metal transformed agricultural implements. It seems unlikely that copper was widely used, for it was too soft, but bronze, although brittle, certainly was. There is in the British Museum a bronze hoe or mattock blade of Mycenean origin, of about 1100 B.C.: it is a stout

An Inca calendar shows digging sticks of various sorts. The women are holding large and rather clumsy dibbers, while a man is making planting holes with a more elaborate tool with a handle and a foot bar.

Mexican gardeners are working with a digging stick, the end of which has been fashioned into a narrow blade, and an elementary hoe or pick of rather curious form.

piece of metal, forming a flat tongue-shaped blade about seven inches long and two inches wide, with its upper end curved over to grip a handle.

The Greeks used general terms to describe the tools they used, which included the *sminue*, a two-pronged hoe or small mattock; the *dikella*, a two-pointed mattock; the *geneis*, an axlike mattock; the *drepanon*, or pruning hook; and the *harpage*, or rake. Their word *skapheion* covers any digging tool.

Once iron appeared everything improved; it was at first wrought, because it was not until the invention of the early blast furnace in the Middle Ages (there was one with water-powered bellows at Liège in 1340) that molten iron could be produced for casting. However, it is equally certain that utilitarian implements of wood, stone, bone, etc. continued long after the introduction of iron, which was at first used mainly for weapons. Iron-socketed ploughshares are known from the Near East in about 1200 B.C., followed by iron axes, picks and hoes with which land was cleared and cultivated. The Romans rapidly graduated from wooden implements to iron-shod ones, or those with "business ends" entirely of iron.

There were numerous metal-headed tools in the Roman armory. Starting with the heaviest, the *dolabra* was a kind of axlike implement for breaking ground – one version was indeed used like an orthodox ax to cut wood; it combined a pick prong and an axlike blade. The *marra* was a heavy, single-headed pickax or broad hoe, used for soil-breaking and tearing up weeds; the *ligo* was a rather lighter implement, sometimes with a simple blade, sometimes two-pronged, also used for clearing weeds – what we might call a grub ax. The *bidens* was a heavy hoe, in essence a kind of

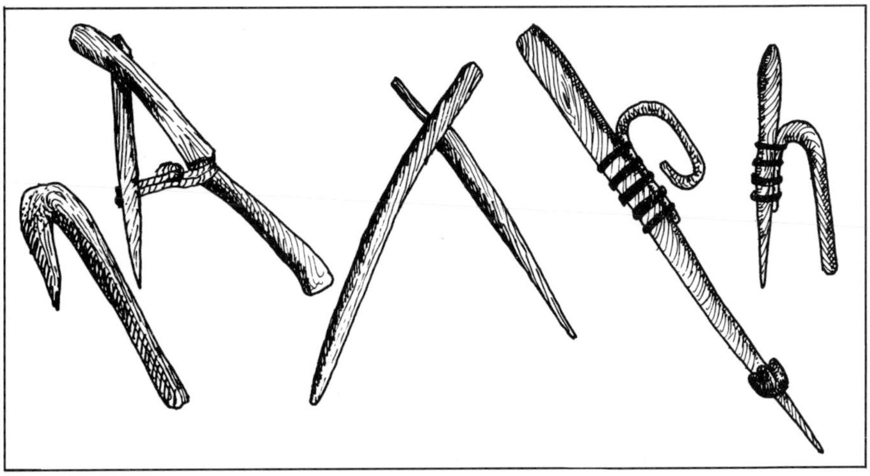

FROM LEFT TO RIGHT: *A very primitive Egyptian hoe made from a forked branch, with sharpened point; a more sophisticated hoe with hafted blade (both Middle Kingdom, third millennium* B.C.*); a much better made type of about 2000* B.C.*; and two Peruvian digging sticks or hoes (both around* A.D. *1500).*

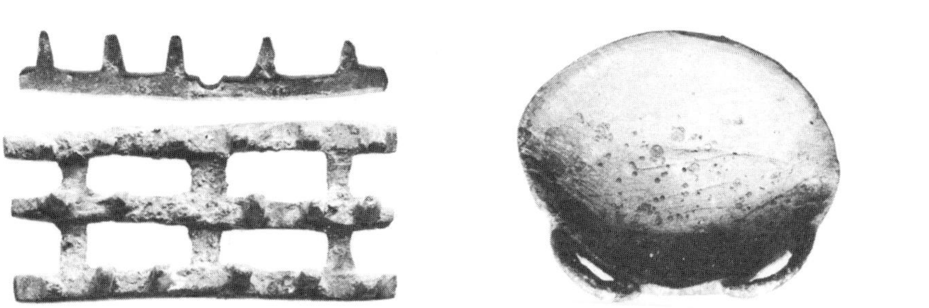

ABOVE AND LEFT: *Models of Roman tools found in a tomb on the Rhine. They were mainly agricultural – like the plough, winnowing dish and harrow (at left) – but many, like the mattock, adzes, sickle and fork (above), would also have been used in gardens.*

mattock with two curved prongs, while the related *rastrum* was a toothed hoe with varying numbers of prongs; thus the *rastrum quadridens* was a four-toothed rake. Some rakes were made of wood, and used to cover seeds with soil – direct descendents of those used in predynastic Egypt. Another hoe, the *sarculum*, rather resembled the *marra* and *ligo* but was much lighter; it was also used to cover up seed and, in difficult or mountainous terrain, to break up soil where ploughs could not be used.

The *pala* was the spade, with a broad blade in the same plane as the handle, curved at the bottom end, and rather resembling a modern shovel; Pliny recommends it for breaking up rushy ground. There was a modified *pala* called a *bipalium*, with a crossbar above the blade, used for trenching, the trench usually being dug at least two feet deep. The position of the crossbar could be varied, being set much higher up the handle when three-foot trenching was needed, as Columella recommends at one point. Trenching was also done with a long-handled gripless spade or *rutrum*.

One might add that trenching – digging out and turning over the soil to two or, exceptionally, three spits (or spade-depths) deep – was prescribed until very recent times. In our lazier days it is most unusual to find gardeners doing more than turning over the top spit and perhaps forking over the second.

The *pastinum* was a two-pronged dibber for preparing soil and setting out plants. There was also the *cylindrus*, a cylindrical rollerstone for levelling ground. Finally, there was the *falx*, a combination of sickle, scythe and, primarily, pruning knife, rather resembling the wooden billhook, to which we will return at an appropriate point.

The sickle itself, primarily a reaping instrument only used now in very rough gardening, is a very ancient tool. In the fifth millennium, we find bones, often straight, in which flint teeth are set. Later the bone is replaced by shaped pieces of wood closely resembling a modern sickle in outline. Bitumen might again hold the often overlapping teeth in place, though in wood it was easier to force them into a slit.

Most of these implements remain with us today in basic form; even the mattock has recently been reintroduced in Britain. The large mattock was a formidable tool, often with a blade on one side of the haft and a heavy pair of prongs on the other. To quote Thomas Tusser once more,

> Go breake up land,
> get mattock in hand.

Spades and shovels were made in an increasing range of shapes and sizes. The Saxons (about A.D. 100) favored a one-sided spade with a flat horizontal top to the blade on which the foot was pressed. Spades could have curved handles, and a top crossbar in a T or a Y shape, formed by a forked stick, or they might have a stick cleft down the center, just as today.

The tools of medieval gardeners were rather clumsy. The mattocks (above) had heavy metal heads, and the spades were of wood with metal sheathing. Note also the wide-bladed sickle and the short knife carried by one gardener.

RIGHT: *The early fifteenth-century rendering of Adam and Eve shows Adam using a one-sided wooden, metal-shod spade, which must have been rather hard on his unprotected foot.*

ABOVE: *Medieval gardeners putting their backs into digging are using clumsy wooden spades with wide metal-shod blades and a T-shaped grip.*

By the end of the Middle Ages in Europe, the divergence between agricultural and horticultural tools is fairly clearly marked. Although the same tools were undoubtedly used on both sides of the fence, as it were, in less prosperous and inventive times like the early Middle Ages, nothing really impedes the separate evolution of tools for these two uses. Agriculture developed more elaborate handtools for purposes such as trenching, as well as ploughs, harrows, clod breakers and so on, usually pulled by animals. The tools of the garden became gradually more refined and more specialized.

LADDERS

The ladder was an early essential in fruit cultivation, even if the ancients preferred to knock down many fruits, like olives, with long sticks – as is still done in Greece, for example, the fruit falling onto large sheets for collection. The Romans certainly had fruit-picking ladders. Many medieval pictures depict the use of ladders – objects whose construction remained almost completely unchanged until metal began to supplant wood for certain purposes in the Victorian period. As Thomas Tusser has written:

Light ladder and long
doth tree least wrong.

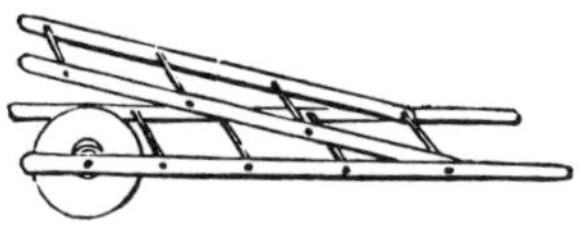

TOP: *A Victorian three-legged orchard ladder, complete with basket-pulley.*
ABOVE: *An early nineteenth-century portable wheelbarrow-ladder.*

The Victorians had an elaborate, three-legged, self-supporting ladder for picking fruit, looking like something out of a full-rigged ship and complete with pulley-operated basket; and they also invented a wheelbarrow ladder which could be used like steps or as an extendible ladder.

In contrast, some utensils could only appear when there was more subtlety in gardening operations. This applies to the sieve, which was only of use when fine soil had to be produced for seed beds, for the cultivation of plants in pots, or possibly for plants like celery grown in trenches dug in the

SIEVES

soil. The Roman Cato describes the use of a sieve (*cribrum*) to cover seeds in furrows with sifted soil. Sieves have not changed much over the centuries; round sieves were early in use, sometimes suspended on a support made from three stout timbers when heavy work was being carried out. The slanted, rectangular sieve which we may consider fairly modern is in fact several hundred years old. It is used by flinging the coarse soil, scooped up with a shovel, against its inclined surface.

Pictures of some early sieves look as though the mesh was made of cord or thongs, but in principle it must mainly have been made of metal wire as it is today, and by the seventeenth century some sieves were apparently made of a disk of perforated metal.

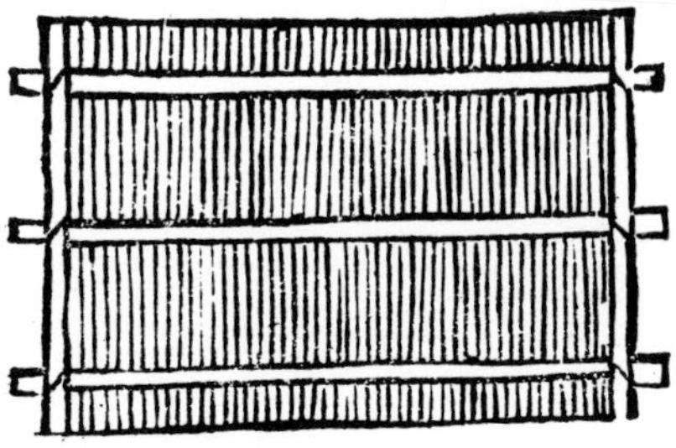

TOP: *A hand sieve of 1630 appears to have holes pierced through a metal disk.* ABOVE: *A square sieve of 1706, specifically recommended for removing stones from soil destined for the flower garden.*

WHEELBARROWS

The wheelbarrow is such a useful implement that it seems incredible that the Romans did not invent it, but they always used baskets as carrying utensils in gardens, while on farms they naturally used carts. Other primitive cultures had various types of sled, pulled by hand or by animal, in which the "chassis poles" formed the pulling part at hand level in front, while the back end dragged along the ground. These implements still exist in places like eastern Turkey, and such sleds must have made those mysterious "cart ruts" in the soft limestone on Malta.

At any rate, wheelbarrows resembling what we know today are depicted from the late Middle Ages onward in a vast variety of shapes – some apparently fanciful. (The first written reference, to a *wilbarewe*, is around 1340.) Some had sides, others had a framework for holding pots, and yet others only a "stopper" board in front. Most were oblong, but some were square. Some seem to have been, in effect, baskets on wheels. Most barrows had the typical single wheel, but some seem to have had a pair at the front. There is an amusing entry in Thomas Jefferson's farm book, comparing the efficiency of the one-wheeled versus the two-wheeled barrow: "Julius Shard fills the two-wheeled barrow in 3 minutes, and carries it 30 yards in $1\frac{1}{2}$ minutes, more. Now this is 4 loads of the common barrow with one wheel. So that suppose the 4 loads put in at the same time

LEFT: *One man can operate a screen sieve by throwing the material to be sifted against the mesh (1706). Compare this method with the more primitive one shown overleaf.*

A coarse-meshed sieve of 1572 is replenished by one man with a long-handled shovel; the other man shakes the sieve to and fro.

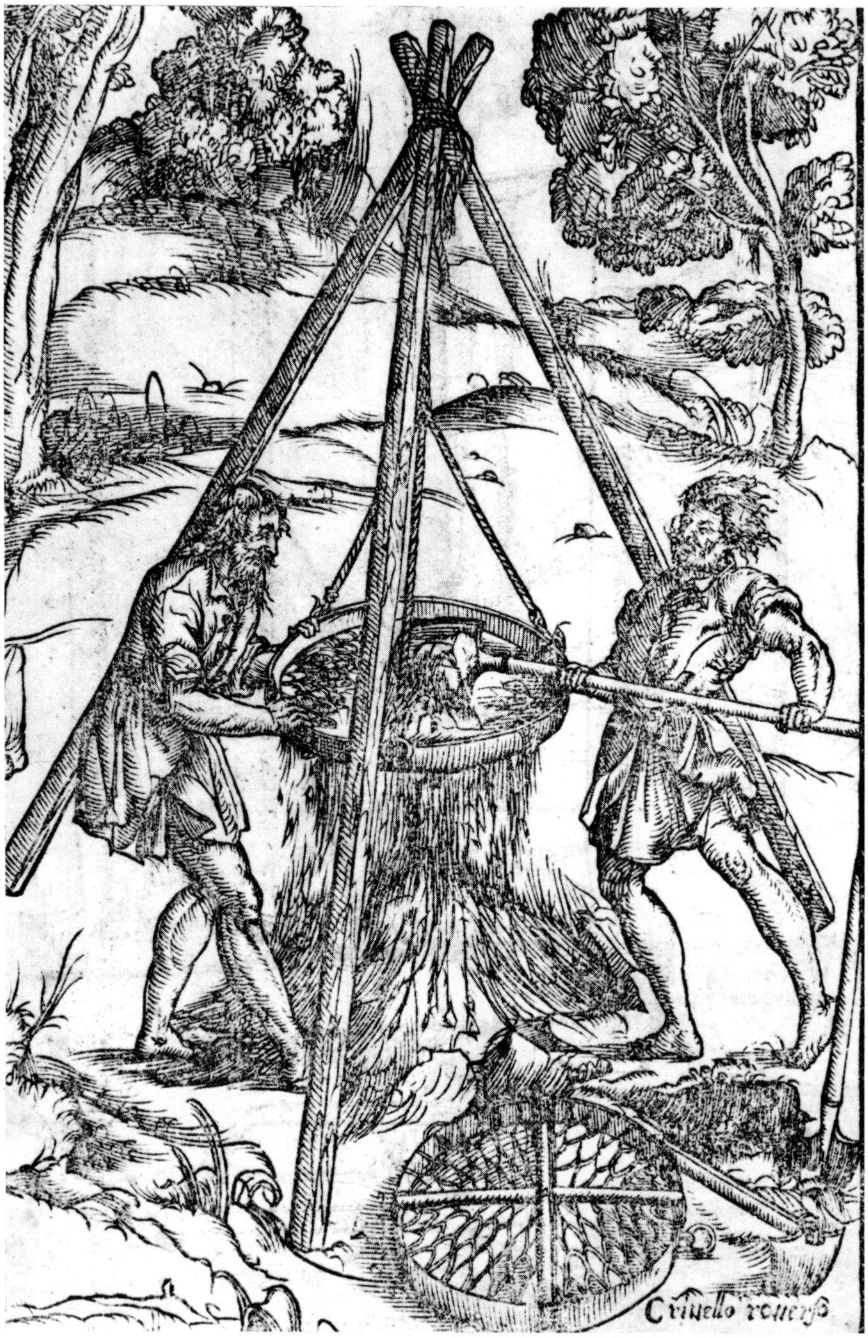

vis. 3 minutes, 4 trips will take 4 × $1\frac{1}{2}$ minutes = 6, which added to three minutes = 9 minutes to fill and carry the same earth which was filled and carried in the two-wheeled barrow in $4\frac{1}{2}$."

Barrows were normally made of wood, but there are references to wrought-iron ones (which must have been very heavy) in Victorian times. In this period too the "separating barrow" was devised, the body of which, secured by bolts, could be unfastened and lifted off, so that the load could go into hothouses where a barrow could not be pushed. Such barrows were made on the stretcher principle, with no wheels, but a pair of upper supports which projected beyond the carrying box on either side. These

The principle of the wheelbarrow seems to have been invented in the Middle Ages. Almost all were one-wheeled, though a three-wheeled example is also shown. The latest development (bottom right) is the modern "ballbarrow," with a large pneumatic ball for a wheel, which can be pushed over rough terrain more easily than a wheel.

ABOVE: *A three-wheeled barrow of 1885, designed for moving very heavy plants.*

ABOVE RIGHT: *The barrow of this Scillies bulb grower of 1953 is clearly homemade.*

included the "haum barrow," with open sides of wood or wicker, for carrying litter, leaves, prunings and "haum" or haulm (that is, discarded plant stems), and the flower pot barrow, with a protective framework above the oblong base. There was also a strong water barrow to carry a tub of water; it was relatively long, so that the tub would not spill by being tilted much out of the horizontal. Yet another late Victorian barrow had three wheels and a low platform on which to transport very heavy potted plants.

The Normandy wheelbarrow of the last century had two wheels and two handles nearly fifteen feet long. A strap fastened to these handles went over the operator's shoulders so that, when he picked up the barrow, almost all the weight was thrown onto the axle and he just had to push.

Modern wheelbarrows may be of wood, metal or plastic, with one or two wheels, and often pneumatic tires. The very latest invention is the "ball barrow" in which the wheel is replaced with a large plastic ball, which spreads the weight more widely and makes the loaded barrow easier to push.

The contrast between the tools shown in early and late Tudor times is remarkable. Within this quite short period, the gardener's armory began to attain massive proportions. Look at the tools and gadgets pictured by John Evelyn in 1659, for example (pages 116–117) – all the basic utensils of cultivation, dibbers descended from the digging stick, rollers, shears, pruners, a pumping engine, glass garden frames and cloches, a

Gardeners working in 1580 were satisfied with a few primitive tools.

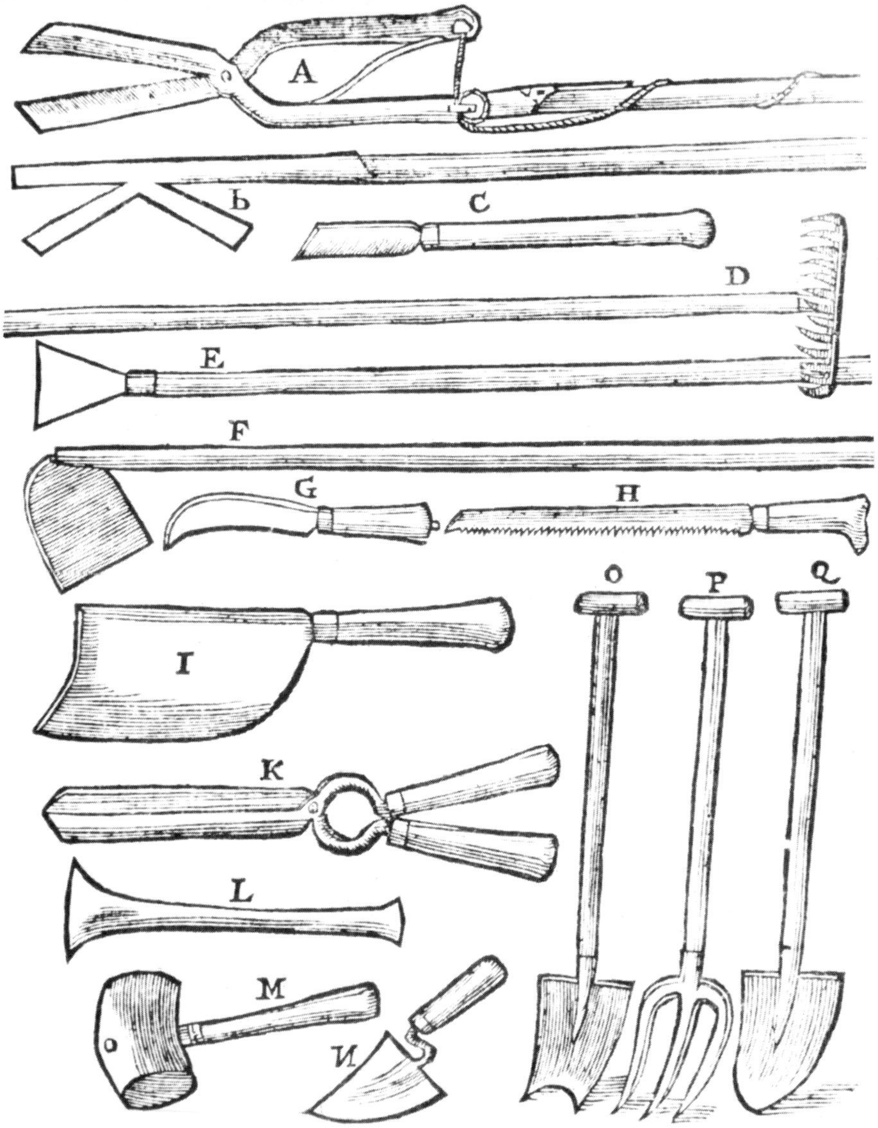

A gardener's armory illustrated in 1649 demonstrates a much wider range of tools. This is possibly the earliest depiction of the triangular trowel and the digging fork.

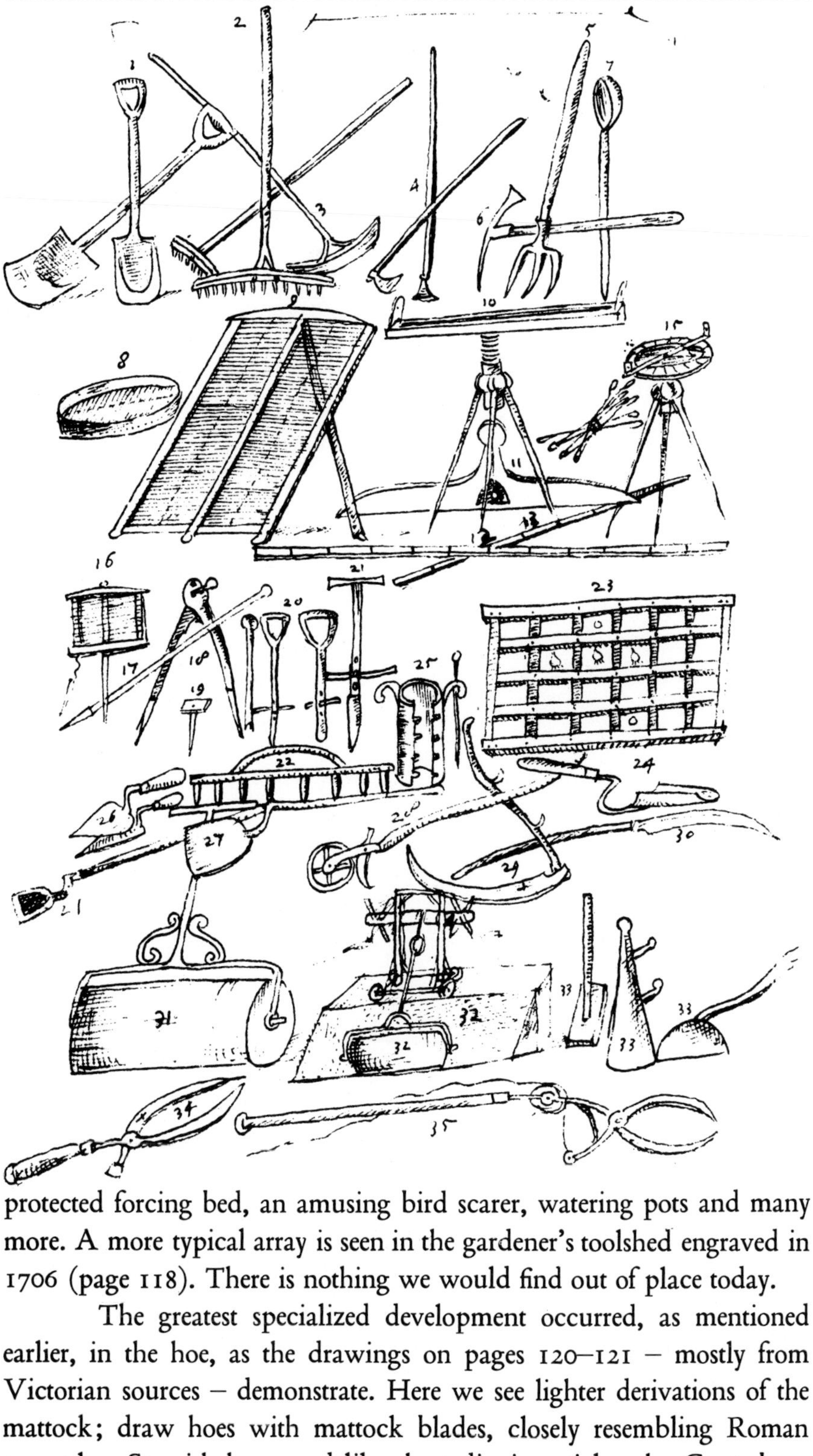

*Sketches made before 1659 by John Evelyn for a book he never completed (*Elysium Brittannicum*) show an amazing range of tools: they include remote-control shears, a range of cloches and frames, a two-spouted water pot, a modern-looking bird scarer and an old four-poster bed employed for raising seedlings. At the top of each sketch are shown the basic garden tools of the time; it is interesting to note that the spades are still metal-shod.*

protected forcing bed, an amusing bird scarer, watering pots and many more. A more typical array is seen in the gardener's toolshed engraved in 1706 (page 118). There is nothing we would find out of place today.

HOES

The greatest specialized development occurred, as mentioned earlier, in the hoe, as the drawings on pages 120–121 – mostly from Victorian sources – demonstrate. Here we see lighter derivations of the mattock; draw hoes with mattock blades, closely resembling Roman examples; Spanish hoes used like short digging sticks; the Canterbury hoe, with three stout prongs at right angles to the handle; and a variety of "thrust hoes" which the operator pushes in front of him rather than pulls. These, especially those for destroying smaller weeds, are perhaps descendants of the smallholder's "breast plough," in which a broadly triangular metal-shod flange was fixed on a shaft some five feet long with a

RIGHT: *The rake is one of several tools which has hardly changed at all over many centuries. Note the vine arbor behind in which some kind of ball game is being played (1580).*

BELOW: *A gardener's toolshed of 1706 shows a number of digging tools without handles, and a coffin-shaped wheelbarrow. Some of the implements on the walls are for surveying.*

two-foot crosspiece. The operator pushed on this crosspiece with his chest, forcing the blade along just below ground level to cut a slice of soil two to three inches thick. This tool went out of use in the middle of the nineteenth century, although one version – the Lincolnshire longhorn hoe – has recently been modernized.

About two dozen different forms of hoe are depicted in Loudon's *Encyclopaedia of Gardening* in its 1834 edition. Some of these are sharp, heavy dragging hoes used in France and Spain "as substitutes for the spade in stirring the soil of the vineyards; and they are better adapted for hilly, stony surfaces, and for women and men who do not wear shoes, than spades."

We still have a fairly wide selection of hoes today, including one or two recent inventions. The "Swoe," with a carefully angled blade capable of being used in two directions, is one useful twentieth-century invention. There are also the Saynor hoe – with a roughly oval blade, sharp all around, centrally fixed – and the push-pull weeder hoe – with a flat oblong blade sharpened on both edges. Both are used horizontally at soil level, and there are in fact apparent precursors of these among early nineteenth-century tools. There is also today an electric hoe which pulverizes soil by vibration.

In Britain there seem to be roughly equal preferences between the draw hoe with blade at right angles to the handle and the Dutch hoe with blade in the same plane, derived directly from the thrust hoe. In the United States, this latter type, known as a scuffle hoe, may be obtained with straight or triangular blades of various patterns, but seems less popular than the draw hoe. This exists in a number of versions, including several resembling small mattocks – one model is even called the mattock hoe – or combining a small mattock blade with one or two prongs. These light descendants of an ancient tool are invaluable since either blade or prongs can be brought into use by the quick rotation of the handle. In the United States, the Canterbury hoe – usually called a "speedy cultivator" – has four-pronged as well as three-pronged versions, and there also can be found hoes with small triangular blades, having no European counterpart.

In his 1834 *Encyclopaedia*, Loudon also shows a wheel hoe with a broad blade slightly inclined from the horizontal, mounted under a pushing chassis with one front wheel. Rather later in the century, many further wheel hoes were devised, some bearing a strong resemblance to much earlier single-wheeled ploughs. Some were designed to be pulled by one man and pushed by another. Very similar tools exist today, both with fixed blades or tines and with star-shaped or pronged blades of various sorts, which "mill" the soil into a fine tilth. Multiple-tined hoes were made both with and without wheels. Some present-day American tools have a bicycle-sized wheel which improves steering and levering pressure.

SPADES

Man has invented nearly as many types of spade as types of hoe. At one time there was a differently shaped spade in use in every county in Britain, as well as different long-bladed shovels for agricultural

FROM LEFT TO RIGHT: *Three nineteenth-century draw hoes. The "Swoe" and an apparent ancestor, the Prussian hoe. A Victorian "surface-stirrer" and the larger modern bent-pronged fork (French). A group of American hand tools of 1928, mostly kinds of hoe. A modern three-tined hand cultivator and two "soil millers" with rotating tines.*

BELOW, FROM BOTTOM UPWARD: *Victorian versions of the mattock – pick-fork, Guernsey prong and hoe-rake. Two Spanish hoes. A group of Victorian thrust-hoes. A modern thrust-hoe blade and an American "action hoe."*

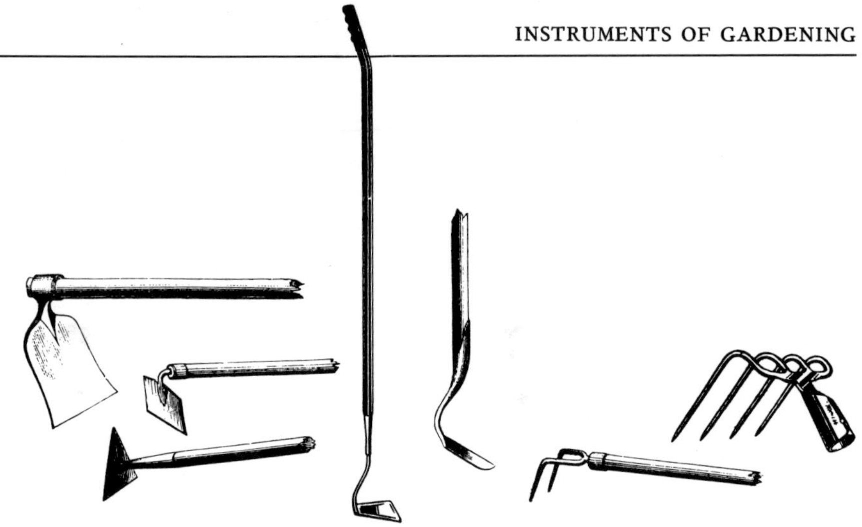

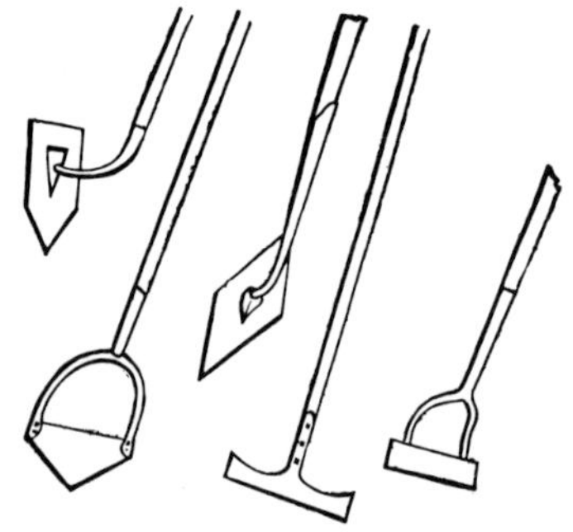

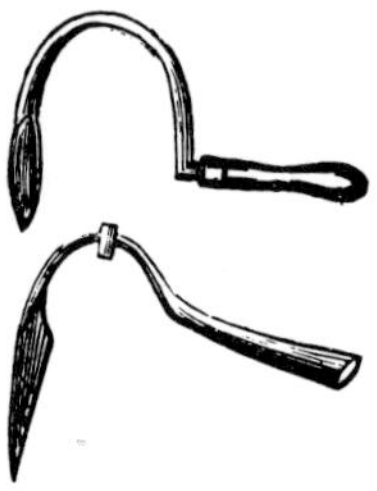

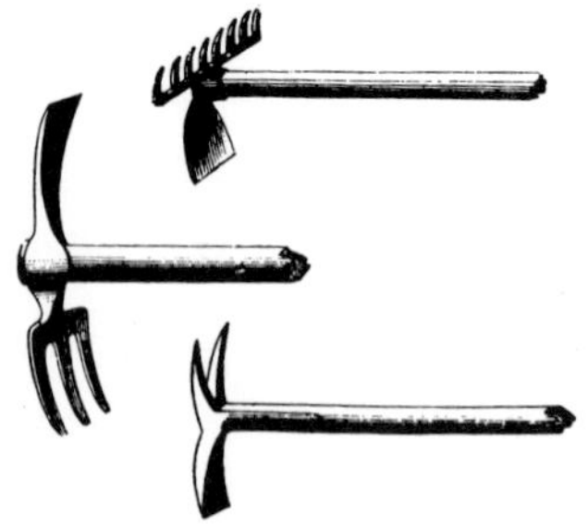

purposes. Even today a leading toolmaker lists twenty-three different spades, including a few specifically used for digging drains; and in the small country of Belgium twenty-two patterns are currently available. The only departures from a straight or slightly curved business end are the shallow-angled point of the "Geestmünder" and the widely notched edge of the "Ground Breaker" type. Variation also occurs in presence or absence of treads, method of fixing blade to handle, and form of upper handle. The T-shaped grip used to be preferred to the enclosed Y- or D-shaped handle because, in earlier generations, when the latter was cut from a solid piece of wood, it did not provide enough space for the large fist of a working man. Until quite recently, northerners in Britain usually used the "T" and southern "softies" the "D."

Among tools with handles, the "D" grip seems almost universal in North America, where the typical flat-bladed spade is also in use, sometimes with a rather longer blade than the European. Spades similar to those used in Europe for drain making, with a long, narrow, slightly concave blade, are sometimes used in gardens, as are various kinds of shovel, with relatively short, broad, round-ended, concave blades – seldom seen in European gardens.

These spade-shovels are usually made with long handles and no grip. European spades are largely made in the same way. When such a tool is in use, the handle is rested on the knee or thigh, which acts as a fulcrum when digging. As one British tool manufacturer said in 1975, "the Continental European thinks that an Englishman who bends down to dig is quite mad. They believe in a much longer handle with a different grip."

In this respect the Europeans and the Americans follow the example of the Romans two millennia before. A spadelike shovel of this type is still in rural use today in Devon, Cornwall and West Wales. An account by the head gardener at Bicton, Devon, in 1843 describes this tool in its primitive state: "Their spade is an ugly, homemade, heart-shaped bit of heavy iron, with a great socket to it; and they form the handle themselves, by cutting a great heavy, lumbering stick out of a hedge, six or seven feet in length, about the size of a Kentish hop pole, so that they can

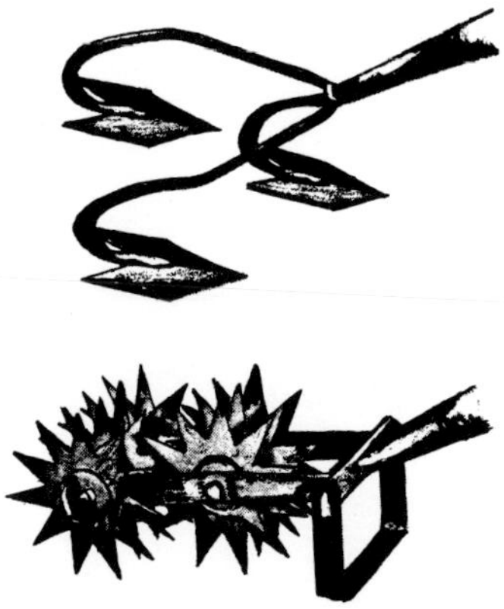

always use it without bending their backs." One wonders whether the American prediliction for long tool handles stems from West-countrymen among the Pilgrims? At least such handles must have been much easier to make than any with hand-grips.

Today an automatic spade has also been devised. It is fitted with a pivot which allows the digger to press the spade into the soil in the normal way, but to throw the soil forward simply by pulling the handle backward, without bending the back. It is thus valuable for the older or partly disabled gardener.

The digging fork has fewer variations, although several different sizes exist. Some have sharply pointed tines, others flat-ended ones; a few have fairly fine tines, but most have more or less broad ones; and sometimes the tines are slightly curved – this is the preferred American type. Here again the only new pattern to emerge recently has been the "Cultifork," in which four fairly small blades are arranged in the form of a sugar scoop – a tool designed for finicky work among plants in borders. In the last century, a fork with two slightly curved tines was used for lifting parsnips and similar root vegetables.

Nearly all American and British forks and spades today seem to have their blade or tines at a slight angle to the handle. The straight-line tool, invaluable for heavy soil, is much more in vogue in Europe.

One fairly recent development has been to fit the equivalent of small handtools, like trowels and handforks, onto very long handles. This permits working in difficult corners without treading on cultivated areas. There is even a telescopic handfork with a handle adjustable from 4 to $5\frac{1}{2}$ feet.

Perhaps the most valuable present-day improvement is the development of stainless steel tools, which last virtually for ever, go into the soil more cleanly, and are much easier than orthodox tools to keep clean. They are, naturally, more expensive than their run-of-the-mill prototypes. Aluminium handles for smaller tools have greatly reduced their weight.

In looking at the development of garden tools and the variations found among them, one is often tempted to ask whether, in a country as

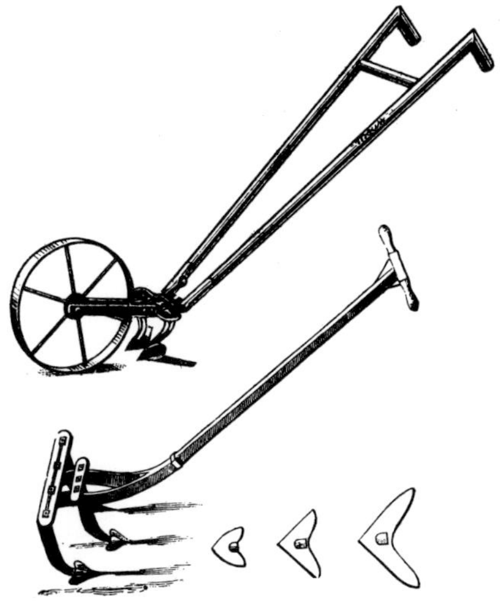

FORKS

FROM BOTTOM UPWARD: *An American garden plow and its accessories. A Victorian cultivator with various accessories. A smaller European wheeled cultivator.*

NEAR RIGHT: *The "automatic" Terrex spade, especially designed for the elderly and those with bad backs, eliminates back-bending with digging.*

FAR RIGHT: *The Cultifork is the only major development of the digging fork. Its "sugar shovel" pattern of tines makes it valuable for working in confined places like borders.*

large as the United States, extending for three thousand miles from coast to coast, any noticeable differences in tools have evolved from region to region. Although its culture was derived basically from that of England, where, although so much smaller, there were several distinct types of basic tool, the United States never developed such regional variations. The only differences found among modern tools are strictly practical ones – based upon their uses. For instance, potato and beet-digging forks have widely spaced flat tines to avoid damaging the vegetables; cotton seed forks are closely spaced and have a dish shape; stone pickers are curved and closely spaced. Onion hoes are narrow and sharpened on three sides; tobacco hoes are also narrow, but one-edged; and orange grove hoes are triangular scuffles sharpened on all sides.

Having now covered the tools of soil breaking, digging, raking, producing fine tilth and keeping the soil free of weeds, there remain a few other specialized areas.

SURVEYING

Among these must be mentioned, if only in passing, the instruments of surveying and leveling which were essential as soon as gardens of any size and elaboration were designed. While the average gardener makes do with a garden line on a reel and pin, and perhaps a spirit level, the sophisticated planner has various kinds of measure, parallel rods, ground compasses, more elaborate levels, staffs to lay out straight lines, and so on. (I have not illustrated any of these, for they are instruments

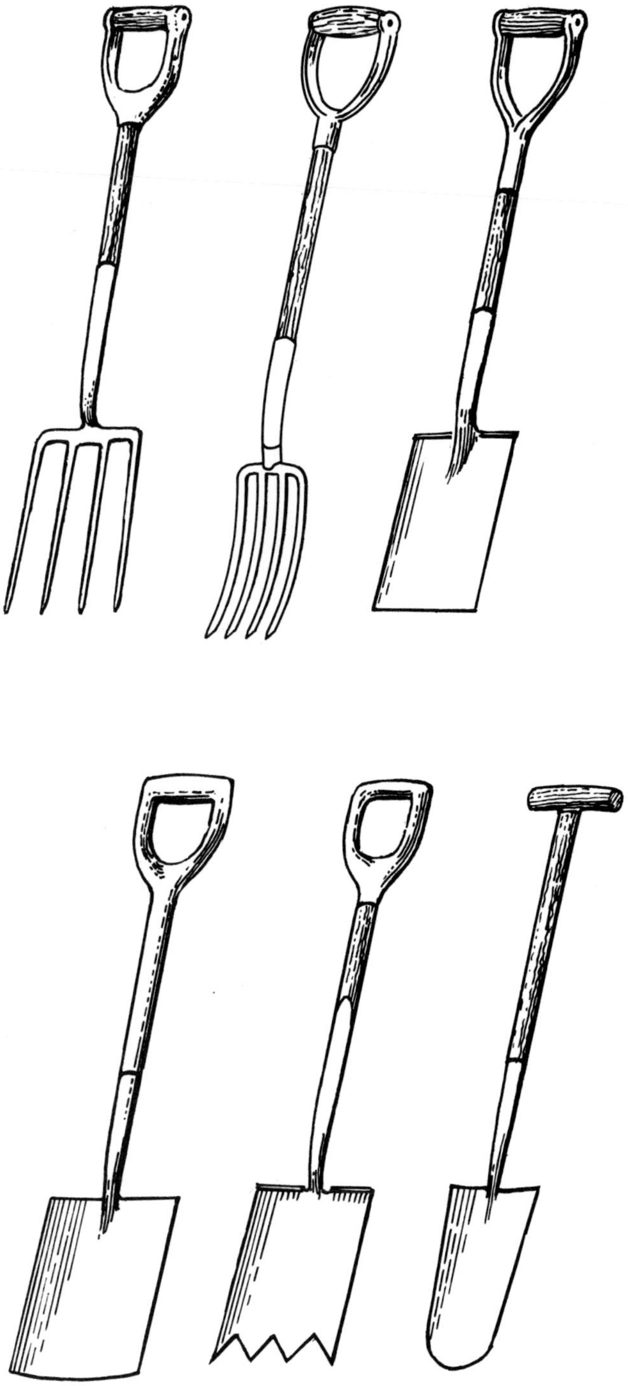

ABOVE: *A British sharp-pronged digging fork; an American broad-tined example; and a typical American spade.* BELOW: *A broad-bladed British spade; the European "Ground-breaker" spade; and a British transplanting spade.*

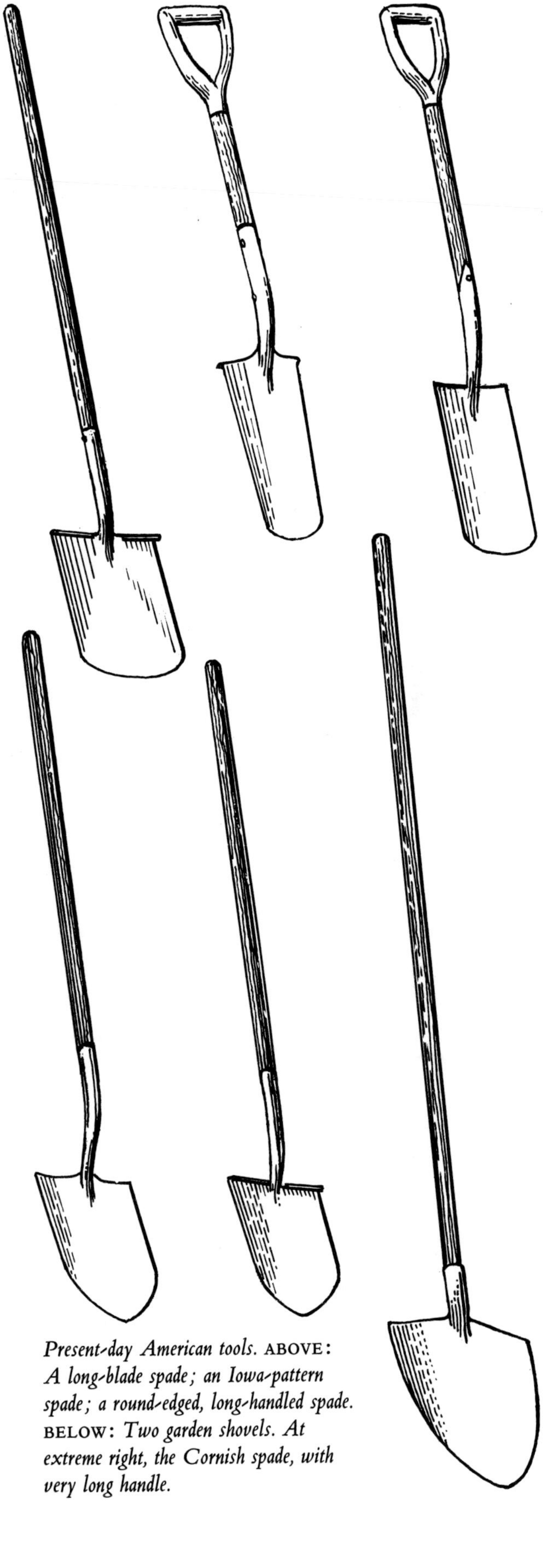

Present-day American tools. ABOVE: *A long-blade spade; an Iowa-pattern spade; a round-edged, long-handled spade.* BELOW: *Two garden shovels. At extreme right, the Cornish spade, with very long handle.*

The board-topped poles in this scene are there to assist a landscape designer in considering where he will place trees. J. C. Loudon (1834) further suggested he should use strips of white sheeting to represent water, and frames partially covered with boards to show the effect of buildings.

Fruit-gathering devices of the turn of this century (right) differ little from the modern French ones (below), although the three lowest are manually operated from the end of the supporting pole. More modern French inventions (below right) are a handy device to assist in raspberry picking and a bilberry picker.

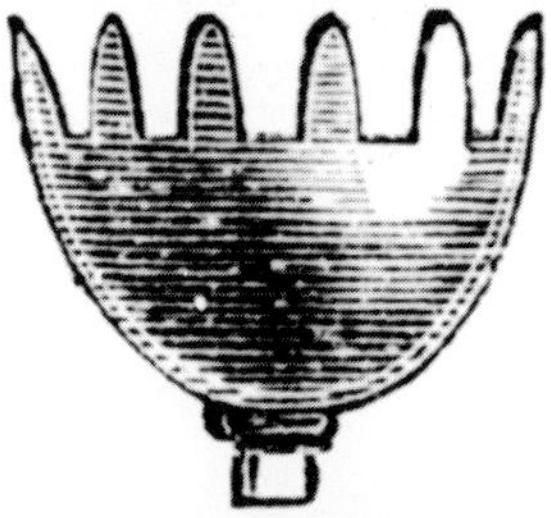

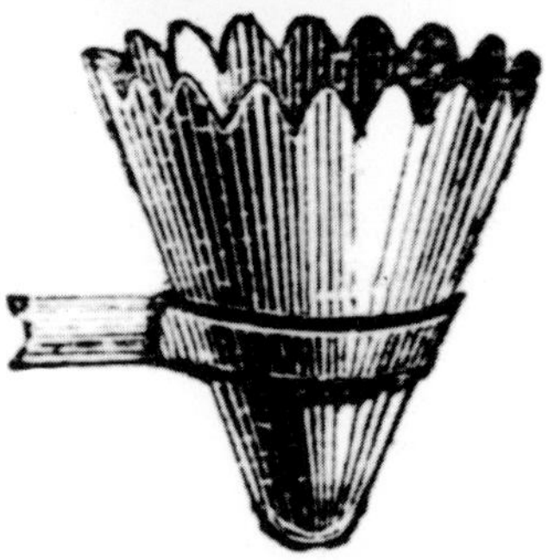

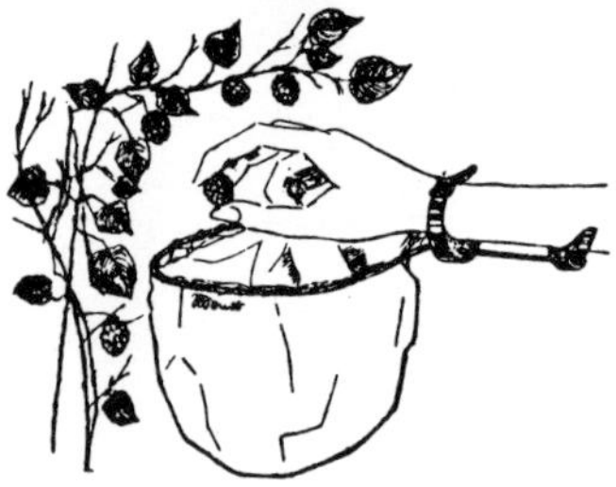

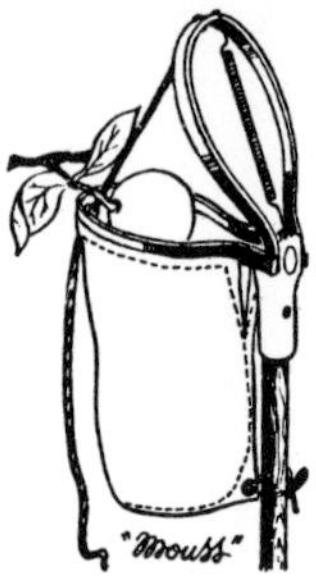

FRUIT PICKING

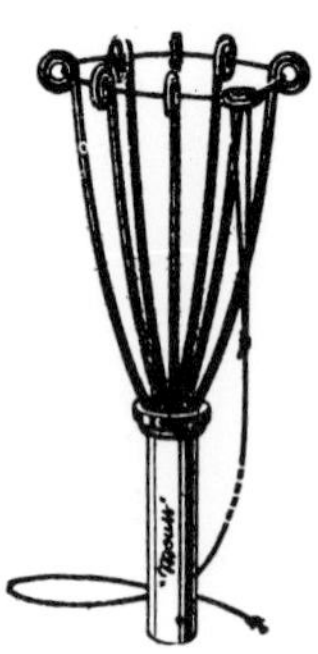

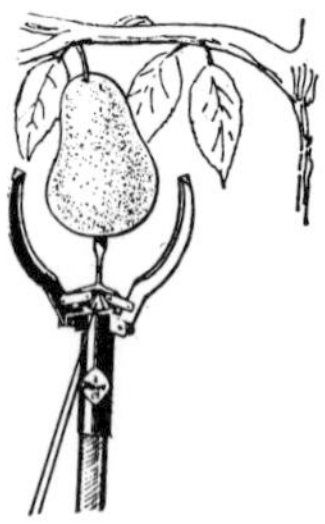

used in occupations other than gardening.) However, before surveying instruments came into being, it was customary for the designer to dig a channel in the ground to accommodate his stomach, so that his eye could be at ground level.

Harvesting is, of course, a climactic operation in gardening, and nowhere more than with delicate orchard and berry fruits. In 1618 William Lawson wrote that the fruit picker should have "a gathering apron like a poake before you, made of purpose, or a wallet hung on a bough, or a basket with a sive bottome or skin bottome, with lathes or splinters under, hung in a rope to pull up and downe; bruise none, every bruise is to fruit death; if you doe, use them presently. An hooke to pull boughes to you is necessary, breake no boughes."

Elaborate fruit gatherers began to be produced in many forms in the nineteenth century. They included grape gatherers of scissorlike form operated by a cord at the end of a pole, which were later enhanced with a pair of flattened forceps, or with a basket below the clippers. Mostly, however, they were simple hand-shaped, round or tubular "catchers" which one pushed under the fruit so that it was prised off without the complication of finding its stalk and cutting it.

Such fruit gatherers continue to be patented today, following the principles of those made a century before. One did away with the need to lift the picker down every time two or three fruits were gathered, and had a long plastic sleeve along the pole which allowed a succession of fruits to find their way to ground level. The French have a particularly useful gadget for collecting raspberries and similar fruits, in which a bag is supported beneath the picking hand; and another for gathering bilberries, and presumably other small fruits like currants, with a number of fine metal bars arranged in scoop form.

BELOW: *Early nineteenth-century remote-control gatherers designed for grapes or flowers.* BOTTOM LEFT: *A very elaborate gatherer with clippers and a basket.* BOTTOM RIGHT: *The forceps for picking delicate fruits are metal rings padded with soft leather.*

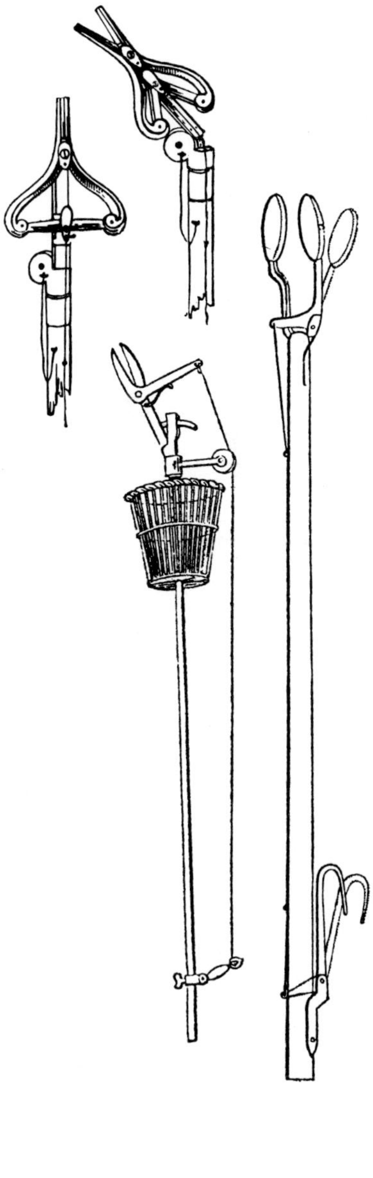

LABELING

Another important necessity to the serious gardener was the label or tally with which plants could be identified. One imagines that something of this nature must have been in use since Babylonian and Egyptian times when collections of herbs were first grown. Or did they just learn to recognize them? I have been unable to find any reference to plant tallies for such cultures, nor for that of the Athenians, nor that of the Aztecs with their elaborate, systematically arranged gardens.

One is surprised that the early monastic gardens such as St. Gall, and those of medieval and later herbalists, seem to have had no labeling system. Nor is one recorded in early European botanic gardens, the first of which were at Pisa (probably 1543) and Padua (1545), and in which there were a great number of small beds. It is perhaps more likely that all the information was written into books rather than displayed by the plants. John Evelyn in 1641 records seeing the "Catalogue" of a Netherlands' "Garden of Simples" (i.e., herbs).

The French appear to have been using tallies in the eighteenth century, if not earlier. These were, in fact, great wooden sticks, in which Roman numerals were cut with a knife, read upward from the base. Tens were indicated by further notches. Such tallies were, of course, cross-references to a written record. In the early nineteenth century, various improvements on these Roman-numbered tallies were made, incorporating various codes of horizontal and transverse notches and smaller cuts.

From these incised tallies developed the written number stick, just like a modern white-painted wooden label – but with a record number, rather than a name, written upon it. Such nineteenth-century tallies were of wood, copper, lead, cast iron, or square blocks of brick or stone with numbers engraved upon them.

One of the earliest name labels was in use in the Glasgow Botanic Garden early in the nineteenth century, and consisted of a cast-metal spike

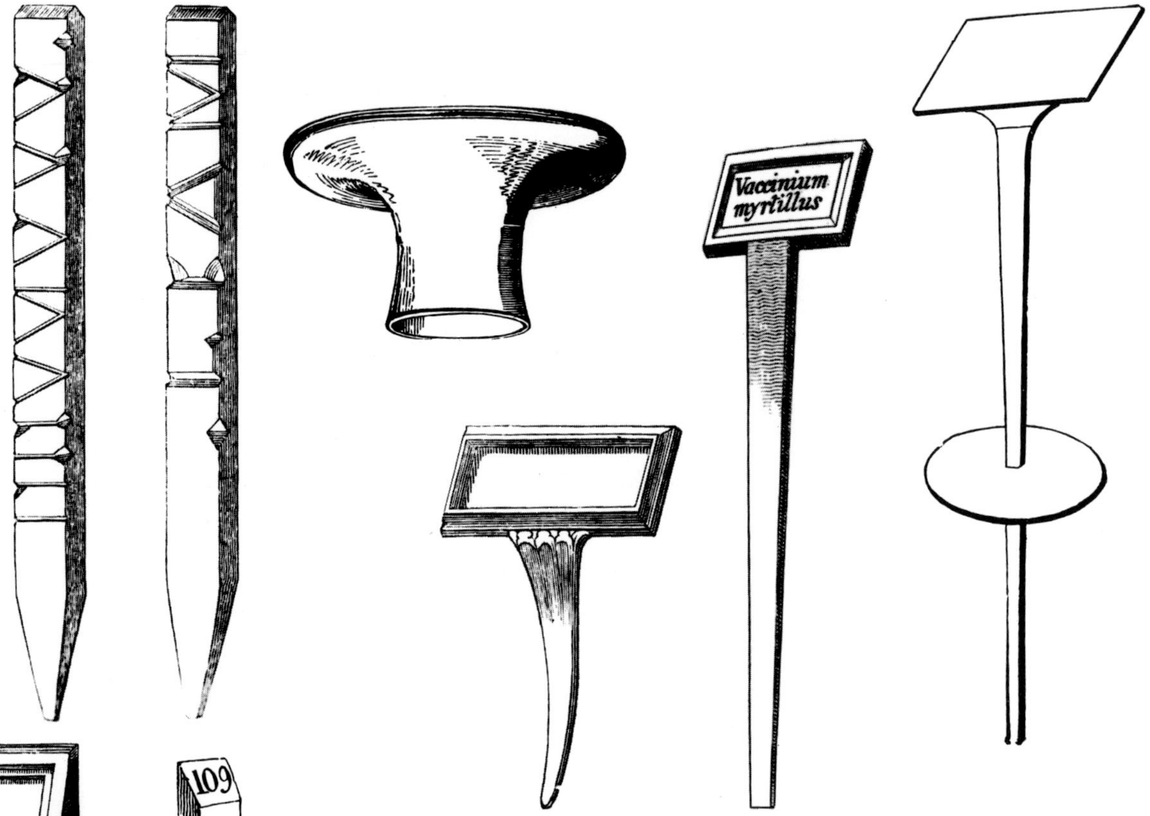

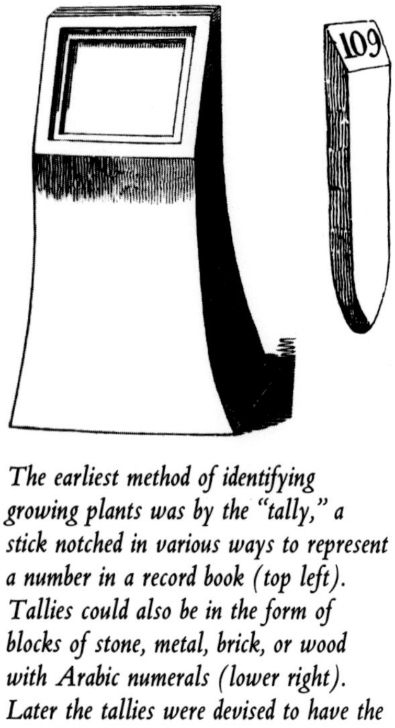

The earliest method of identifying growing plants was by the "tally," a stick notched in various ways to represent a number in a record book (top left). Tallies could also be in the form of blocks of stone, metal, brick, or wood with Arabic numerals (lower right). Later the tallies were devised to have the actual plant name written, or more usually, inserted in or upon a block or shaped label of some sort (remainder of drawings), often varnished or covered with a tiny glass pane. A rather specialized label from Florence (top, middle) is of glass; the name, written on paper, was pushed into the flat top, and the base fixed onto a metal rod stuck in the ground.

with a square head forming a hollow box. In the box, the name of the plant, written on paper, wood, tin or earthenware, was placed, and a piece of glass was then fixed above it with putty. Labels on a similar principle were made more cheaply of earthenware, with broad bases so that they could sit firmly on the soil without sinking into it, or they were shaped like a long square prong to be pushed partly into the soil. In the Pitti Palace, Florence, labels written on paper were placed into small glass bottles fixed onto the end of iron rods – "a complex mode," to quote Loudon, "and one which can only succeed in climates like Italy." Glass tube labels were, however, still advertised in France in 1911.

By degrees, labels of kinds more familiar to us today came into use. As Loudon writes, they could be of "deal, metal, earthenware, leather, horn, bone, ivory, etc." – and in our day plastic. On these the name would be written or impressed, and they were then hung on the plant itself or to the wall or rail on which it was trained. Loudon remarks, "the difficulty in the case of hanging labels on trees, is to find a durable tie, or thread; and, for this purpose, untanned leathern thongs, or pieces of catgut, are preferred: silver or lead wire may also be used, the former for select plants, and the latter for commoner uses."

Many kinds of metal labels, including those made from lead, have come into use in the twentieth century. Special machines now exist to indent lettering on long narrow pieces of lead. (One snag with these is the extraordinary fact that squirrels eat these otherwise indestructible labels,

easily looped around a branch or pushed into the ground.) Light aluminium labels are particularly useful because of the ease with which they can be inscribed with pencil.

The tools to which we are accustomed, almost all with metal heads on wooden or, often today, lightweight metal handles, are in general use throughout the Western world and the countries where its civilization has left a mark. The digging stick is a remnant in less advanced cultures, including primitive tribes in Australia and Africa. In the Far East, tools basically resembled those of the West, though differing from them in detail. In China, wood was used for a longer time – one must bear in mind that many Eastern tools were used in the relatively soft conditions of paddy fields – but metal hoe-rakes with long handles have been known from at least the time of the Han dynasty. Although handles were usually straight, some were elegantly curved. Metal was slower in coming to Japanese gardens, but a Tokyo scroll of 1590 depicts rice farmers using mattocks and spades with a kind of iron "glove" fitted over the basic wooden tool.

It is nice to note, among the Chinese tools depicted, an elegant leaf gatherer of netting, with two cords which would close up the device when full, long before the leaf bags of canvas or similar material of the present century, or the modern leaf sweepers working either with a brush which rotates when the two-wheeled implement is pushed or on exactly the same principle as a vacuum cleaner.

The basic implements of gardening can be seen to have evolved much like living creatures – along lines created by new opportunities and by new demands. Their principles are much the same the world over, but local conditions and traditions have produced variations on themes.

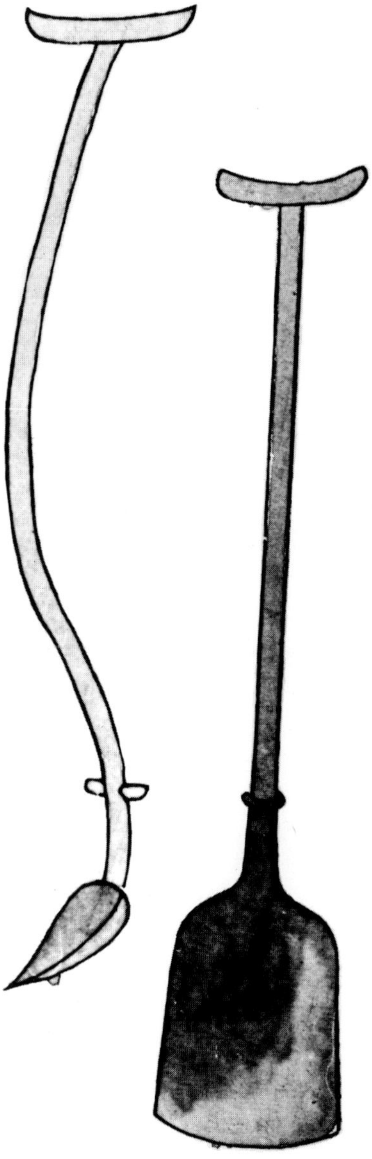

TOP: *Heavy metal-headed hoe-rakes in use in China: from a tomb of the Han dynasty (begun second century* B.C.*).*

ABOVE RIGHT: *A leaf-gathering net.*

RIGHT: *Traditional Chinese wooden tools – a digging stick and a flat-bladed shovel-spade.*

Chapter Five

Essential Operations

IN THE PREVIOUS CHAPTER, I DISCUSSED THE DEVELOPMENT of the most generalized tools used in gardens – tools for breaking up soil and rendering it fit for basic use, for transporting various materials, for permitting access to trees, and for labeling the plantings. This chapter describes some of the essential operations carried out by any normal gardener and the more specialized tools needed for them.

First and most basic are the operations of sowing and planting, which are carried out very much in parallel, depending on the kind of plant involved. The earliest cultivators soon found that, before scattering seed, it was desirable to turn the soil over, to destroy any hard caked surface and to render it more friable and accessible to air and moisture, which encourage seeds to germinate. Thus, in agricultural fields ploughs were used from very ancient times, and in gardens hand implements capable of being used in more confined space. Soil in fields would be reduced to a rough tilth with the aid of harrows, while in the garden hoeing and raking produced a fine tilth. Seeds could either be sown on the surface and lightly worked in or, better in principle, sown in furrows or "drills" (this odd term probably comes from an old general-purpose word for tools).

SOWING AND PLANTING

These furrows could always be made with a hoe, using the corner of a rectangular blade or the point of a special triangular one; there used also to be sickle-shaped hoes for this purpose. Where many seed drills had to be made close together, a tool with several teeth or prongs, like an exaggerated rake, was sometimes used (it is recorded from the sixteenth to nineteenth centuries). Deep furrows such as those needed by beans were made with a spade, or a strong hoe pulled through previously broken soil.

Most seeds would be scattered, or doled out into the drill, by hand, but as time went by various devices were used to make handling easier and distribution more regular. These culminated in wheeled machines which both made the seed drill and deposited seed into it, and might either sow a single line or several at once. These, once again, have their larger counterparts in agriculture.

The need for presowing treatment in some cases was recognized by Theophrastus, who mentioned soaking cucumber seeds in milk or water for quicker germination. The Roman Columella (first century B.C.)

ABOVE: *Flowering pot plants are set around a square pool in a Canton garden, together with some bonsai or dwarfed tree specimens in special shallow glazed pans.*

LEFT: *Flowering plants indoors were potted in ornamental containers on wooden or ceramic stands.*

OVERLEAF: *An open gallery enabled people to walk the length of the boundary wall in this Chinese garden, while pavilions set into the wall at intervals allowed them to sit and contemplate the most beautiful views into the garden or the landscape beyond it.*

ABOVE: *A full-scale meal is brought to a Persian officer on a tree platform by his soldiers. The tree is somewhat fanciful.*

OPPOSITE: *Music accompanies a formal meeting between the Emperor Akbar and an important visitor in a "garden throne" built into a clearly recognizable* chenar *or oriental plane.*

LEFT: *The assiduous maiden braving the weather in this French calendar scene from 1896 is using a long-handled spade with a long narrow blade and no grip.*

BELOW: *In more clement weather another young lady uses a simple wooden dibber to make seed planting holes in a border.*

OPPOSITE: *Brawn and determination were required by late medieval gardeners digging with thick wooden, metal-shod spades. Here a long handle is combined with a D-shaped grip.*

The Romans did not hesitate to use human excreta or "night soil" for horticultural purposes — if perhaps not in small gardens. This mosaic shows men carrying night soil from house to garden.

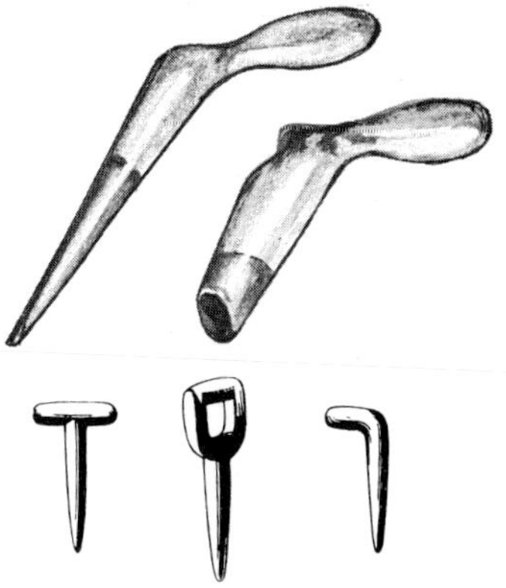

ABOVE: *Dibbers for making a planting hole have been in use for centuries. The simplest is a pointed piece of stick; more efficient ones have handles. The three nineteenth-century examples (above) are of wood; the twentieth-century ones (top) of metal. The hollow dibber lifts out soil; it is recommended for bulb planting.*

LEFT: *Planting holes in the naked rock beside the Temple of Hephaistos at Athens (449–444* B.C.*). The inner row, a meter wide and deep, contained flower pots like those in the foreground, or their remains. The holes held bushes such as myrtle or pomegranate.*

develops this accurate suggestion into the inaccurate one that presoaking in milk or mead makes the resulting cucumbers sweeter. Squaws of the North American Huron Indians made baskets of bark which they filled with rotten wood from old tree stumps. In these they placed pumpkin seeds. The boxes were then hung over a gentle fire until the seeds germinated – a nice early example of what we now call "bottom heat."

In modern times a number of seed merchants have devised means of sowing seeds which have been prepositioned on a strip of paper or some other soluble or easily penetrated material, few of which have really "caught on," although a current method of growing grass in wide strips is being extensively used where instant turf is needed. An extraordinary foreshadowing of this method is again to be found in the writings of Columella, in describing how to form thorny quickset hedges made from

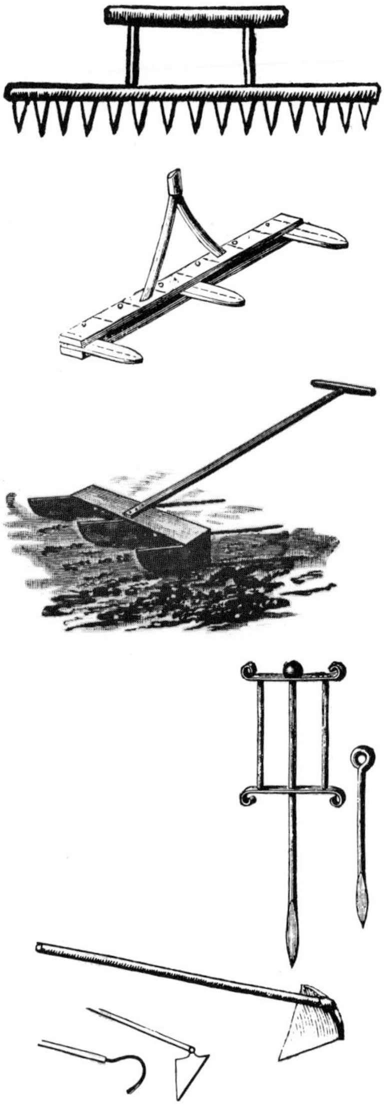

FROM TOP TO BOTTOM: *Before sowing seeds, furrows or "drills" of appropriate depth and spacing are made. In the seventeenth century, a toothed, hand-held drillmaker might be used. By the nineteenth century, a drill-rake had replaced this. The implement below is an American homemade row marker of similar principle. The garden reel and line are indispensable for marking rows if hand hoes are to be used, like the example from the seventeenth century – much resembling the modern American "warren hoe" – or the early Victorian sickle-hoe or triangular drill-hoe at bottom.*

brambles, wild roses and Christ-thorn (*Paliurus spina-christi*). He recommends mixing the ripe seed with a powder made by grinding vetch seeds; after mixing with a little water, this "seed meal" is smeared onto pieces of old rope and, after drying, stored. Deep furrows are then prepared where the hedge is to grow, and these lie fallow over winter. In early spring the seed-smeared ropes are placed along the bottoms of the furrows and covered with a little soil. Once the seedlings appear, sticks are set along the furrows so that the hedge can be trained and supported as required.

In gardens today much seed is sown in boxes or pots and grown on for a time before being planted out. Sometimes peat blocks or peat pots, or compressed soil blocks made in special machines, are used to ease the actual transplanting process. Before these were invented, eggshells were sometimes used in a similar way, and an American manual of 1890 describes how "a safe plan is to sow about five seeds on reversed pieces of sod about 4 inches square. On planting in the ground, insert the sod with the growing plants, and firm the soil in the usual way."

The easiest way to ensure straight seed rows is to use a garden line. In its earliest form, this was doubtless just two sticks with a cord wound around them, but quite early on – as shown in Evelyn's garden tools of 1659 (pages 116–117) – we find a simple reel on a prong, its asset being that it was far tidier, because it allowed the cord to be wound out to the required length, held in place by a pin while the drill was made, and finally wound back neatly onto the reel.

The first reference to even sowing of seed comes from the gardening writer Leonard Meager in his *The English Gardener . . .* of 1670: "if you put your seeds in a white Paper, you may (if the seeds are small) very easily and equally sow them by shaking the lower end of your paper with the forefinger of that hand you sow with; the paper must not be much open toward the end." Today's latest device consists of a small pointed, triangular-sectioned blade in which seeds are placed; rotation of a knurled wheel with the thumb creates tiny vibrations in the blade which feed the seeds to its point and into the seed rows. The principle is identical to that described by Meager.

Little is written about postsowing treatment, but Leonard Mascall in 1572 reminds the gardener to "take good heede that your hennes do not scrape your beddes."

Planting starts with moving seedlings from seed rows into better spaced positions. Columella gives detailed instructions about the best moment for that, as when cabbages or lettuces have six leaves. It was only in the nineteenth century, when delicate bedding plants came into cultivation – needing germination in boxes, moving to other boxes and thence into pots – that special tools for handling them were devised. The early Victorians used delicate tweezers made of ivory to lift the seedlings and a miniature dibber to make its new planting hole. They very soon

learned that seedlings should be moved, after an initial loosening from underneath, by the leaves, and not handled by the stem or roots.

Larger dibbers were in use from antique times; even the early digging sticks could be used in this way. All a dibber is, essentially, is a stick that can be pushed into the ground. The Romans used two-pronged dibbers. Little refinement is needed to give the dibber a pointed or rounded end, and to supply it with a handle of some kind. One modern version is hollow, with an open end, allowing soil to be lifted out to leave a soft-walled planting hole big enough for a bulb.

The trowel, so widely used for small-scale planting today, is in effect a miniature, pointed, concave spade, but its earliest versions did not imitate a spade in shape. They were made from a long narrow piece of metal of semicircular section with a handle. Little change in this tool is seen from its invention in the seventeenth century into the nineteenth; then the old version vanishes and the "miniature spade" (which had been developing alongside it) takes over.

Larger scale planting was always, of course, basically a matter of digging a hole big enough for the plant's roots with a spade or shovel. If the ground was of rock or sand, the planting hole cut in it was then filled with soil or – as in the case of the trees (mostly tamarisks and sycomore figs) planted in front of Queen Hatshepsut's great temple at Deir-el-Bahri (fifteenth century B.C.) – with Nile mud, after being lined with clay. These holes were like great subsurface flower pots. The Egyptians also conserved the water which was carefully and painfully brought to trees by building up a shallow-rimmed basin of mud around each.

Queen Hatshepsut is famous for having instigated the earliest plant-collecting expeditions recorded (about 1495 B.C.). The trophy was thirty-two incense trees obtained from "the land of Punt" (Somalia), which were dug up with soil balls intact and packed in wicker baskets. Straps slung on carrying poles enabled the trees to be carried aboard ship on laborers' shoulders. After the sea journey, they were transported to Luxor and planted in huge pits dug in the rock that formed the upper terrace of Deir-el-Bahri, and also in very large pots. All but one survived the journey.

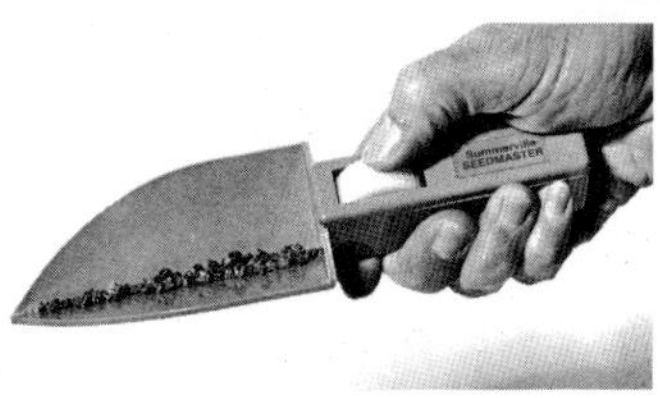

Seed can be distributed by hand or mechanically. Nineteenth-century devices include (top left) a six-row machine for market gardens, which could be used either for seed or potatoes; the hand-held seed-hopper (top), and a small wheeled seed drill. The modern "Seedmaster" shakes seeds out one by one when the knob is turned.

BELOW, FROM LEFT TO RIGHT: *The semicircular trowel was used from Tudor times to the end of the nineteenth century, but then died out. The scoop-shaped trowel of 1706 developed in parallel, into various shapes; a modern pointed version is shown below. At bottom, the handling of tiny seedlings was accompanied by a tiny ivory dibber about two millimeters thick.*

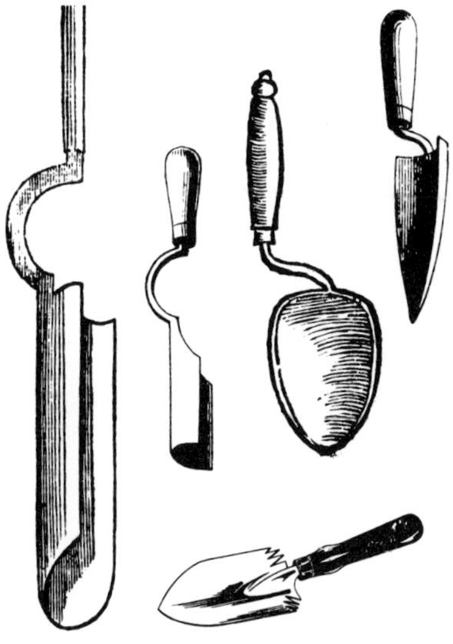

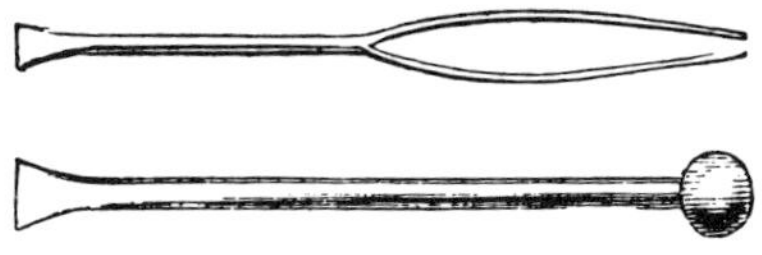

The earliest record of the moving of trees (1495 B.C.). Incense trees from the Land of Punt, destined for Deir-el-Bahri at Thebes, are carried in wicker baskets slung on carrying poles.

The need for a large planting hole in rocky situations was also known to the ancient Greeks. In the excavations of the Hephaistos Temple were found, on three sides, a double row of pits over three feet square and deep, dating from the third century B.C., in many of which were the remains of earthenware pots (see page 212 for explanation). Visitors today can see thriving plants of myrtle and pomegranate in these original planting holes, now refilled with soil.

Xenophon (*c.* 434–355 B.C.) discussed the planting of fruit trees, suggesting that they should go into trenches eighteen to thirty inches wide and deep, and that the soil should be well firmed around the plants.

Theophrastus (370–286 B.C.) also recorded his advice to his fellow Greek tree planters. He stated that any tree to be moved must be vigorous and healthy; the hole into which it is to be transferred should be made before the tree arrives, and must be larger than the ball of soil around the roots, which must be retained as far as possible; he also stressed avoiding damage to the roots. He recommended transferring trees into soil similar to that in which they had been growing, or at least improving the soil in the reception area, which ideally should contain stones that would help in keeping the roots cool.

The assiduous and painstaking Romans have left us much written information, in their extensive horticultural manuals, on how they planted trees. Columella suggested that the planting holes should be made a year in

Planting in medieval times was rather unceremonious: trees and other plants were moved with very little root, and sometimes even in leaf.

advance, or at the very least two months; in the latter case, straw should be burned in the holes to make the soil friable. Planting holes should be "oven-shaped," wider at the base than the top so that the roots could be well spread out and less winter cold and summer heat would penetrate. He also suggested that, before transplanting, trees should be marked with red ocher on one side, so that they could be replanted in the same relation to the sun and prevailing wind. Virgil also made this point.

Olives had to have holes four feet deep, at the bottom of which were placed a layer of small stones and then four inches of soil. The tree was then put in place and its roots covered with well-firmed soil mixed with manure. Columella is very emphatic about preserving the root ball and suggests placing it in a basket to transfer it to its new site. Later we find Pliny advocating turf bound around the root ball to keep the roots in good condition, and reminding us that, if there is any delay in transplanting, roots should never be left exposed to dryness, wind or cold.

The Romans believed in general that trees should have their top growth heavily cut back before being transplanted, unless they were quite young. Seneca, for instance, gave drastic advice which one can hardly believe succeeded, recommending that, with large olives, the trunk should

Vegetable planting in neat rows in a formally laid-out kitchen garden with raised beds (1706).

be cut back to three or four feet, all the side branches should be removed, as should side roots up to one foot from the trunk. Cato recommended that, after cutting back, the wounds should be daubed with manure to prevent decay.

By contrast, tree planting in medieval and later times seems to have been distinctly casual, judging from the number of pictures showing trees with bare roots left exposed to the air, waiting to be planted. Sometimes the gardeners were more careful; there is a medieval picture showing vines being planted apparently complete with the baskets in which they had been raised from cuttings – an early example of the "instant gardening" of this century which uses a container that will rot away in the soil.

Another form of instant gardening in the eighteenth century was the annual planting out of orange trees, or other tender shrubs, which had been kept over winter in tubs in an orangery. Usually they stayed in containers, but on occasion they were "bedded out"; the trees were hauled up on a pulley and the tub knocked off the root ball with an implement.

TREE MOVING

It was in the eighteenth century also that – following the new vogue for landscape gardening, in which instant glades and avenues were desired – the moving of really large trees was carried out by machines of

Unusual informal planting in a mound of rich soil of the same date as that opposite; the plants appear to be strawberries.

various kinds. A machine used, and reputedly devised, by the famous landscape gardener Capability Brown consisted of a long pole firmly jointed onto an axle carrying a pair of cart wheels. Soil would be dug out all around the tree, the pole would be securely fastened to it in the vertical position, and by hauling on the pole the tree would be forced out of the soil into a horizontal position. A small trailer wheel supported the load so that it could be towed away to its new site.

Naturally, such a clumsy method broke a lot of roots and shook off much of the soil. As the English gardening author William Pontey wrote early in the nineteenth century, "such Trees, for several years, grow so slowly, as to remind one of 'stricken deer.'" Despite this, an amazing amount of tree moving was carried out, notably by le Notre for his master Louis XIV at Versailles, but also in many other huge French gardens.

One ingenious method of tree transplanting had been devised by John Evelyn much earlier, but one wonders if it was ever actually carried out. A trench was made all around the tree, and the root ball was undercut as far as possible, blocks being put in at intervals to keep the soil in place. This was done early in winter and, as soon as the weather became really cold, water was poured into the trench. It and the root ball eventually froze

Planting techniques did not improve in Tudor times (right), and even in the eighteenth century (below) trees were moved with very little root. In this picture they are obviously being planted when in full leaf, but the gardeners are apparently removing the foliage to reduce water loss. The whole operation seems somewhat lethal to the trees.

LEFT: *Tender shrubs which have spent the winter in tubs in an orangery being knocked out of their containers before being "bedded out" for summer display (1700).*

BELOW: *Tree moving in progress, 1823. Although some care might be taken in saving the roots from damage, they lost most of their soil and were fully exposed to the air in transit.*

The latter part of the nineteenth century saw all sorts of devices for moving shrubs and trees of varying sizes with minimum root disturbance and exposure. Big trees might have containers actually built around the roots before being lifted out of the ground (below left), if necessary being dragged up by a ramp (below right).

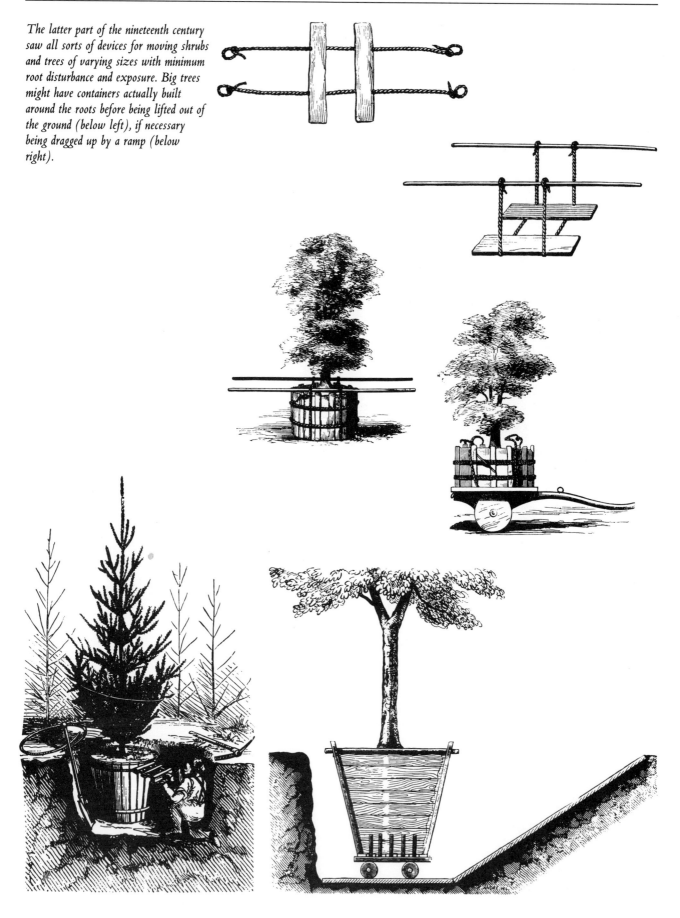

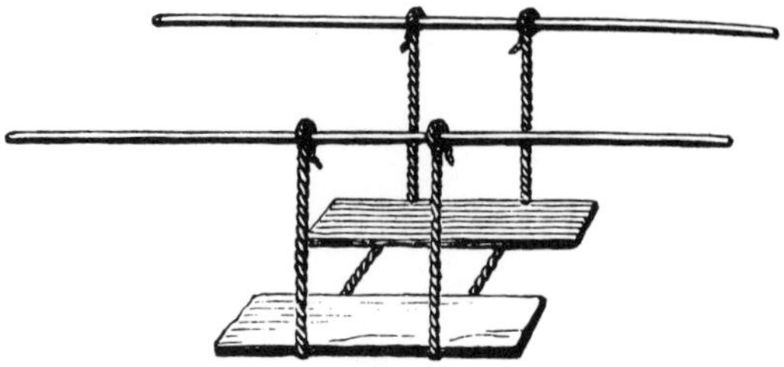

A large tree being moved early this century with the aid of a four-wheeled frame. Pulleys lifted the tree out of the soil after careful excavation, and the roots were protected as far as possible. Guy ropes ensured stability while the tree was in transit.

solid, so that it could be lifted up by a crane without any danger of losing the soil. One can only say that freezing the roots must have been almost as bad as exposing them to the air.

Somewhat similar advice was given by an Indiana lady gardener in 1879, who suggested that plants can "be taken up in the winter when the ground is frozen hard, by digging up a clump of earth with an ax, and the plant put where it is wanted to grow. It will awaken in the spring and not know the change." This would probably work better with herbaceous plants than with trees.

Early in the nineteenth century, the Scotsman Sir Henry Steuart drew attention to the problems of root damage and exposure and, although he continued to use a mechanical transplanter very like Brown's, he took special care not to damage the roots, picking soil away around them – once a trench had been made – with a special light, one-pronged pick, and trying to undercut as much as possible before the transplanter lashed to the tree was brought to the horizontal. Smaller trees would have their root ball covered in sacking or similar material, and in this way many of the rare trees of the Edinburgh Botanic Gardens were transferred to their new site around 1825.

Steuart, like many of his predecessors, believed in digging the trench around the tree a year before it was to be moved, and filling it with fine soil to encourage the production of fibrous roots in this area, outside the root ball that was left. The always adept Dutch, however, realized the amount of damage that even this practice occasioned, and most of their trees for public planting were grown in nurseries in which the trees were regularly transplanted, or had their roots cut back by digging around them every year, so that a small ball of very fibrous roots was produced, exactly as in good modern nursery practice. This had in fact been recommended by Leonard Mascall as early as 1569.

The Dutch made sure that the planting holes were really large, thinking nothing of digging them ten feet square and at least two feet deep, and refilling with rich loam. They also beheaded trees to be transplanted and removed most of the branches, so as to reduce the amount of water lost by the foliage. Scottish gardeners like M'Nab at Edinburgh carried out the same practice. M'Nab also devised a number of carrying devices varying according to the size of the tree. The Dutch also practiced out-of-season planting by the expedient of digging up the trees at the correct time in autumn and transplanting them into soil-filled baskets. (Loudon calls them hampers.) These were then replaced in trenches and the trees lopped as was normal practice. Even in summer they could then be dug up, moved, and replanted where required without any check.

Early in the twentieth century, really large trees were moved with the aid of a four-wheeled "cart," forming an open framework and fitted with pulleys so that the previously excavated tree could be lifted into an upright carrying position, suitable support being provided under the root ball as soon as it parted company with the underlying soil. (One of these machines still exists in England's Royal Botanic Gardens at Kew.) Today, of course, large trees are shifted with the aid of earthmoving equipment and trucks.

TRANSPLANTERS

Smaller transplanters had been in use since the sixteenth century. Richard Bradley, the first professor of botany at Cambridge and a prolific writer of the early eighteenth century, called them "grooves," and they were often referred to as "displanters." These consisted of a tube of metal with a division down one side, hasps to hold it together, and a pull-out securing pin. This would be pushed down around the plant to be moved, if necessary after cutting around it with a semicircular trowel like that shown on page 139, and a pair of handles enabled the whole to be lifted out of the ground. It was then placed in a previously made hole in its new site, or possibly turned out into a barrow or other container, the opening of the hasps loosening the soil ball. In this way, the plants received virtually no

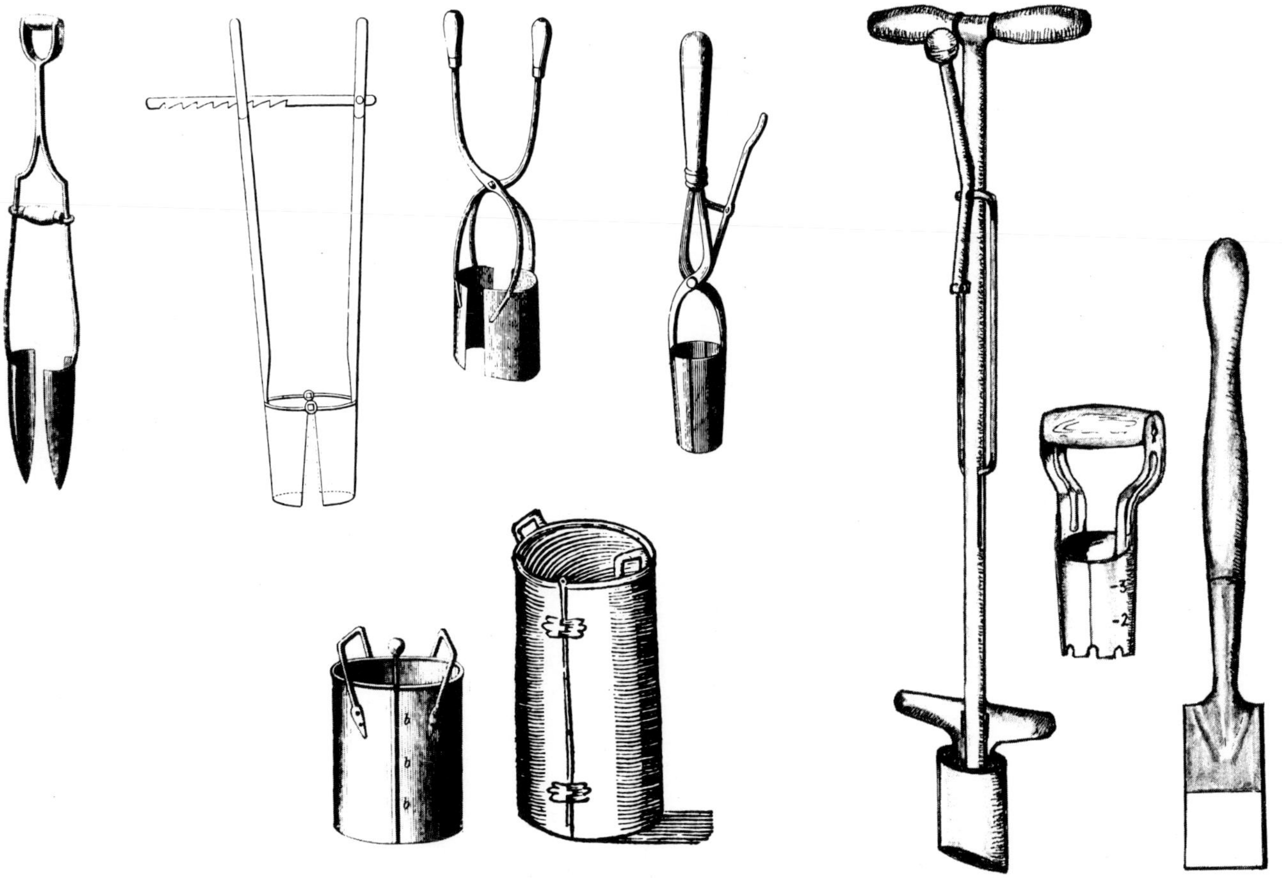

Transplanters for smaller plants have changed little over the centuries since the sixteenth-century examples (lower left). They were usually designed to be pushed down around the plant, which then came up with the root ball intact, to be released by opening up the transplanters. The Victorians improved the mechanics of the operation with levers, ratchets, etc. (above left). The two modern versions (above) are specifically designed for lifting out a chunk of soil before planting bulbs; the long one has a mechanism for ejecting soil. The trowellike tool (above right) is for removing seedlings from seedboxes.

check to growth. More elaborate versions of this simple instrument were made, one having a removable base so that the plant could be kept in the transplanter as long as required.

A number of mechanically operated transplanters of the same basic type were also devised in the early nineteenth century. They were usually formed of two separate semicircular pieces of metal, sometimes trowel-shaped, and were usually operated by a pair of handles; spring-loaded models with a single lever were also made. Such planters were especially used with bulbous plants like tulips, and this is almost the only use modern planters of this type have today. They are often used for placing bulbs in grass, the method allowing a cylindrical clod of earth complete with grass on top to be removed, the bulb dropped into the hole, and the clod replaced firmly above it.

One final planting refinement of the present day is the "bedding box planter," largely used by nurserymen, to enable seedlings to be neatly extracted from seed boxes.

SUPPORT

Plants which have been successfully reared often need subsequent support. The easiest way to help climbing plants is a wigwamlike structure such as the "pyramidal arbor" recorded by Columbus on his first visit to the West Indies – three or more straight branches lashed together at the top. Such structures must have supported the squashes and pumpkins of the pre-Columbian civilizations. It is amusing to note a more elegant version

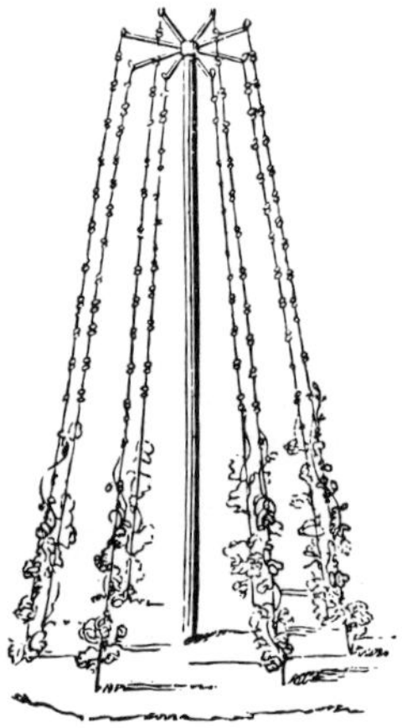

The "wigwam" support for plants was probably based on this "arbor" recorded from the West Indies by Columbus (top). A late nineteenth-century version is shown below.

of it, made of a metal post supporting light chains pegged in a circle, in Victorian times, and we continue to grow beans and the like on similar proprietary devices, or on wigwams formed of bamboo canes.

Where suitable walls were not available, fruit and ornamental trees would be trained on more or less elaborate fences, trellises and wirework, as described in the next chapter – elements which led on to ornamental arbors and topiary work, and which had their origins in Roman times. The Chinese built beautiful lattice fences to support and enhance suitable plants.

The support of small ornamental herbaceous plants and shrubs seems to have begun in the Middle Ages, where illustrations frequently show supporting devices. At their simplest, these seem to have been simple "cages" of sticks and osier which prevented the plant within from falling about. These ranged from "single story" cages to those with three or four squares or, more often, rings of horizontal support fixed to three or four vertical ones. These might be placed around plants in the ground (opposite) or in pots. Lilies and carnations were presumably supported in this way.

"Standard" plants with growths radiating from a single upright stem were treated much as they are today, either with a wheellike structure supported on a pole alongside the plant stem, or an inverted umbrella-shaped structure. In some cases, this seems to have been fixed among the plant's branches rather than on a supporting pole, and sometimes to have consisted of an ornamented, tiaralike circle rather than plain wire or osier. The umbrella, right way up, which we still see occasionally today for rambler roses in particular, is not to be found in medieval pictures, presumably because there were no suitable plants to be trained in this way in those days. But it is clear that a good deal of thought and care went into keeping small ornamental plants erect or tidy with artificial support.

It is not until the seventeenth century that further developments occur. These are concerned almost entirely with "florists' flowers" – the flowers of the European fanciers who bred and developed a handful of flowers to artificial standards for exhibition (more fully described in Chapter 9). Earliest of these was the tulip.

As early as 1614, we can note simple supports of metal wire, twisted into a circle at the top, to preserve the brittle stems of the fancy tulip. These were copied in Victorian times for a variety of flowers. By then the metal loop had been arranged so that its lower end was coiled around the vertical support, enabling it to be slid up or down the plant stem. The late Victorians also devised larger rings for herbaceous plants, which are extremely similar to certain designs on the market today.

Many other methods of support were devised and sold in the nineteenth century. As J. C. Loudon wrote in his *Encyclopaedia of Gardening*, "In pleasure-grounds or picturesque scenes, trees and shrubs

ABOVE: *Quite elaborate plant supports of wood or metal were used in medieval times.*

LEFT: *The Chinese often had double trellisswork fences between which plants were confined.*

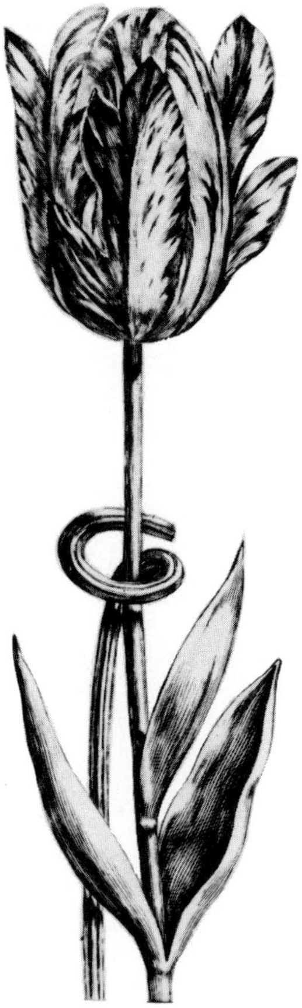

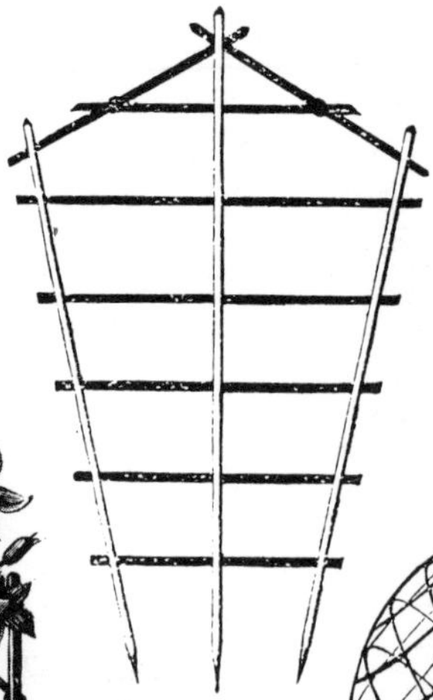

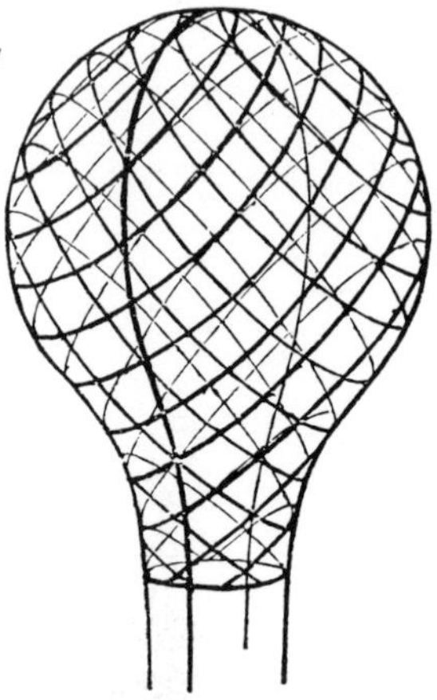

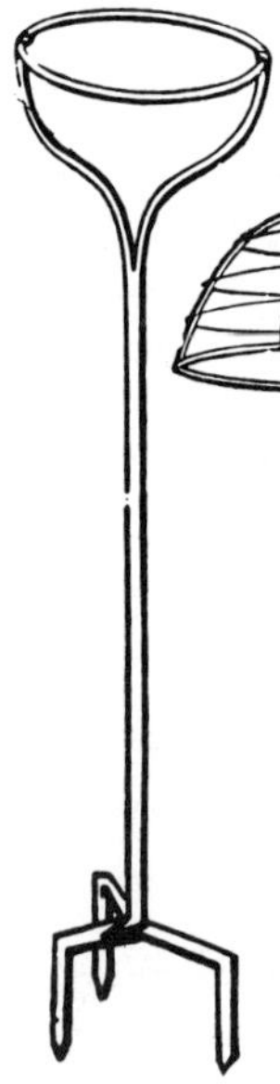

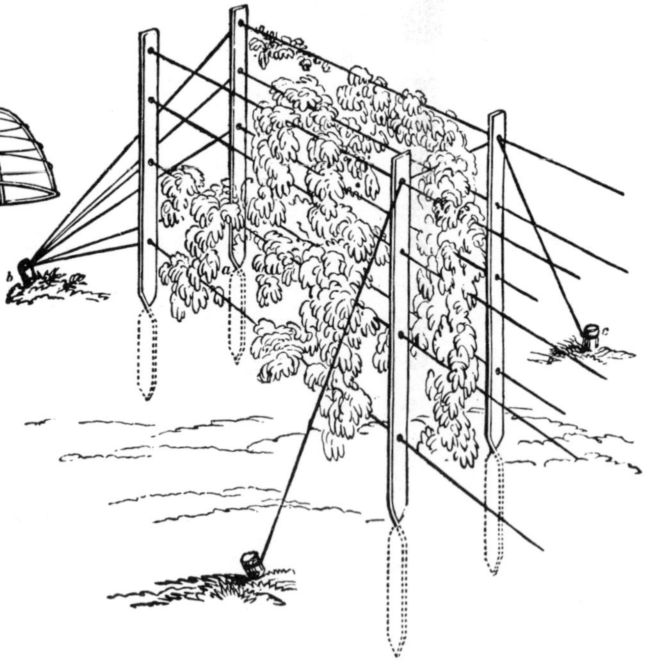

ABOVE: *The tulip fanciers of the seventeenth century supported the stems of their prize flowers with a piece of soft wire bent as shown.* ABOVE CENTER: *This device was improved in Victorian times, both for single-stemmed flowers and for clumps.* ABOVE RIGHT: *A "composite trainer" and, below it, a "balloon trainer."* BELOW: *Trainers for standard and weeping standard roses.* RIGHT AND BELOW RIGHT: *For peas or similar climbing plants.*

should, in general, prop themselves, or each other; but in flower or botanic gardens, flower-borders, green-houses, etc. the greatest degree of art and high-keeping, and a sort of *drilled polish*, ought always to prevail." Loudon concluded, rather acidly: "In all that respects this part of gardening, the French and Germans greatly excel the English, who are herein too apt to look at the end, without regarding the means."

Loudon describes rods from six inches to six feet tall, and also iron stakes, using a good deal of space in listing their lengths, weights and prices. He also depicts a five-sided guard of flat stakes with horizontal tiers of wire, exactly like the medieval ones in principle, and a more elaborate one using similar stakes and wire to form an elongated support for peas or similar plants. Other elaborate arrangements for supporting peas were devised, as well as further metal supports suitable for various kinds and habits of plant.

"Sprays" or branches are also recommended for peas and the like, especially those of beech, hazel and "Scotch elm," although he adds, "for early crops the spray of the resinous tribe, and especially of the spruce and silver firs, is valuable, as producing warmth and shelter, by its numerous chaffy leaves, which are nonconductors."

About ties, he goes on, in his rather ponderous way, "the most general are the ligular threads of bast mats," but for espaliers some use "withs," tarred cords or threads, and he also records the use of rushes and wheat straw in Europe.

WATERING

Above almost all else, plants need water, and this is of course most true in hot countries. Once again we must turn back to the agricultural beginnings of garden watering, with a brief look at irrigation in Mesopotamia and Egypt. Scientific irrigation seems to have been a Sumerian invention; certainly the civilizations of the great valley of the Tigris and Euphrates had to control the raging floods of spring and the parching droughts of summer, and to this end they created lakes and reservoirs and a network of canals, whose regular repair is recorded in the annals.

In Egypt the problem was the annual rising and falling of the Nile, followed again by dryness as the rich, newly deposited mud dried out in the scorching sun. Both civilizations adopted the *shaduf* (or swipe) invented by the Assyrians not later than 2200 B.C. The *shaduf* is a simple but efficient device still to be seen in many countries, working either in rivers or wells, and capable of lifting six hundred gallons per man-day. It is based on a long pole pivoted on a high support. At one end is a bucket; at the other a counterweight. The operator dips the bucket into the water, and the counterweight – often a stone or a lump of clay – enables him to swing it up and around with relatively little effort, to tip the water into a channel.

By the seventh century B.C., the Assyrians were using double-lift *shaduf* systems, the lower lifting water from the river into a pool or channel,

An Egyptian dipping water out by hand, the earliest method. Note the horse pulling the plough – an unusual use of that animal in ancient Egypt.

the second into a higher channel. Both the *shadufs* were pivoted on baked mud uprights, and their operators stood on brick platforms built out into the water.

In a garden, water reaching a tank from a minor channel might be transferred to plants by the simple procedure of dipping jars into it by hand; an alternative method of manhandling water, used in many parts of the world, was to carry two buckets on a shoulder pole or yoke.

There is a charming Egyptian record (probably around 500 B.C.) of the lady Talames instructing her new gardener Petfumont in his duties: "If you intend to be gardener for me in my garden then you are to give water to it. You are to give drawings of water to it in the proper measure of twenty-eight hins of water to the pot. . . . You are to connect the dyke to my garden . . . and you are not to cause me to compel you to do it!"

More mechanization followed the *shaduf*. Sennacherib (705–681 B.C.), very much an engineer, recorded how "that daily there might be an abundant flow of water, I had made copper cables [apparently] and pails, and in place of mud-brick pillars I set up great posts and crossbeams over the well." So was his palace garden watered.

In many parts of the Middle East, elaborate irrigation channels and subchannels were constructed, notably the Persian *qanats*, subterranean

The shaduf *or swipe is a simple counter-weighted device which is one of the most efficient methods of raising water with a single operator.*

conduits leading down from water-bearing strata in the hills. The makers of these (which were often quite deep) had to throw out the debris periodically, and this gave rise to large apertures in the ground which today can be seen from above, or from the air, to form straight lines like scars on the land, often for considerable distances. The *qanat* was invented at least two thousand years ago, and it still supplies many Iranian towns. It has one special advantage over surface irrigation channels: it is much less liable to evaporation and also to blockage by windblown sand.

The Persians also developed Sennacherib's water-raising method in which scoops are fastened to an endless belt stretched between a higher wheel and a lower one. This was usually operated by animals harnessed to a radial yoke and walking around and around, or occasionally to a treadmill. A rather simpler method still used in India, dating from 200 B.C., is the single wheel fitted with scoops, operated through coarse gearwheels, usually by animals walking in a circle.

The well itself, with which we are more familiar, is very ancient in origin. Though usually operated by hand – a tedious operation with a deep well, even when a windlass wheel is used rather than hands pulling on the rope – it is sometimes mechanized by animal power. In India today, this can occasionally be seen: one or two oxen are harnessed to the rope, and walk down an inclined plane to draw up the bucket – typically formed of a complete ox hide, the four corners secured with ropes – which a man then tips into the water channel. Once the water is released, the oxen back up the ramp to lower the bucket again. As Sylvia Crowe remarks, "the prospect is a dismal one for the ox."

Pliny, in Roman Italy, mentions three methods of raising water: one the well with a roller wheel for the rope, another the *shaduf* or swipe (*tolleno*), and a third the pump, *organon pneumaticon*. This, a double-action lever pump operated by suction, was apparently invented by Ctesibius in the third century B.C. There is some argument as to its use in horticulture – although it was certainly used for firefighting – but Pliny's reference seems fairly conclusive. The Romans also used the Archimedean screw, *cochlea*, in which water is raised by turning an enclosed screw in a tube. It can be operated by a handle at the upper end or, as a Pompeiian mural shows, by a slave on a treadmill, but it cannot raise water very high.

During the first century B.C., the Egyptians, as recorded by Strabo, used enormous water wheels and screws operated by 150 prisoners at a time in treadmills. These water wheels seem to have been of the paddle-wheel type, being called *torchoi*, as opposed to the enclosed or compartmented water wheel, or *tympanum*, recorded early in Roman history.

Countries with extensive irrigation systems must maintain these regularly, and must arrive at satisfactory ways of sharing the supply. The disputes to which claims on water give rise can be deduced by the fact that the word *rival* derives from the Roman *rivus*, an irrigation channel.

William Prescott describes astonishing irrigation schemes seen in Peru during the Spanish conquest, including "canals and subterranean aqueducts, executed on a noble scale. . . . Some of these aqueducts were of great length. One . . . measured between four and five hundred miles." As he adds, all this engineering was done without iron tools, using stone blocks fitted together without mortar.

Windmills to raise water seem to have arisen after about A.D. 1200, before grain-grinding mills were invented by the Arabs prior to the tenth century. They started with literal sails of canvas, fixed to a wooden framework, but angled blades of hinged wooden slats, their angle controllable according to the power required, soon replaced these (though in Greece one can still see picturesque cloth-sailed windmills with six small triangular sails). Vertically mounted sails were in use in Persia in the tenth century and were reproduced later in European books, although European representations of such were probably never actually built.

By Tudor times, the Roman double-acting pump was again in regular use in Europe. It might simply dispense water into a channel from a conduit system; another version, fixed in a tub, had a handle one pulled to and fro. Thomas Hyll, in *The Gardener's Labyrinth* of 1577, describes how

OPPOSITE TOP: *The Archimedean screw, known since ancient times, can raise water a few feet.*

OPPOSITE CENTER: *A lever-operated suction pump (left) brings up water from a well in contrast to the more orthodox pulley well (right).*

OPPOSITE BELOW: *Late seventeenth-century designs of windmills for raising water. Although horizontal sails (left) were certainly used very early in Persia, it is doubtful whether they were actually constructed in Europe, where of course vertical, slatted sails (right) were until quite recently a familiar sight.*

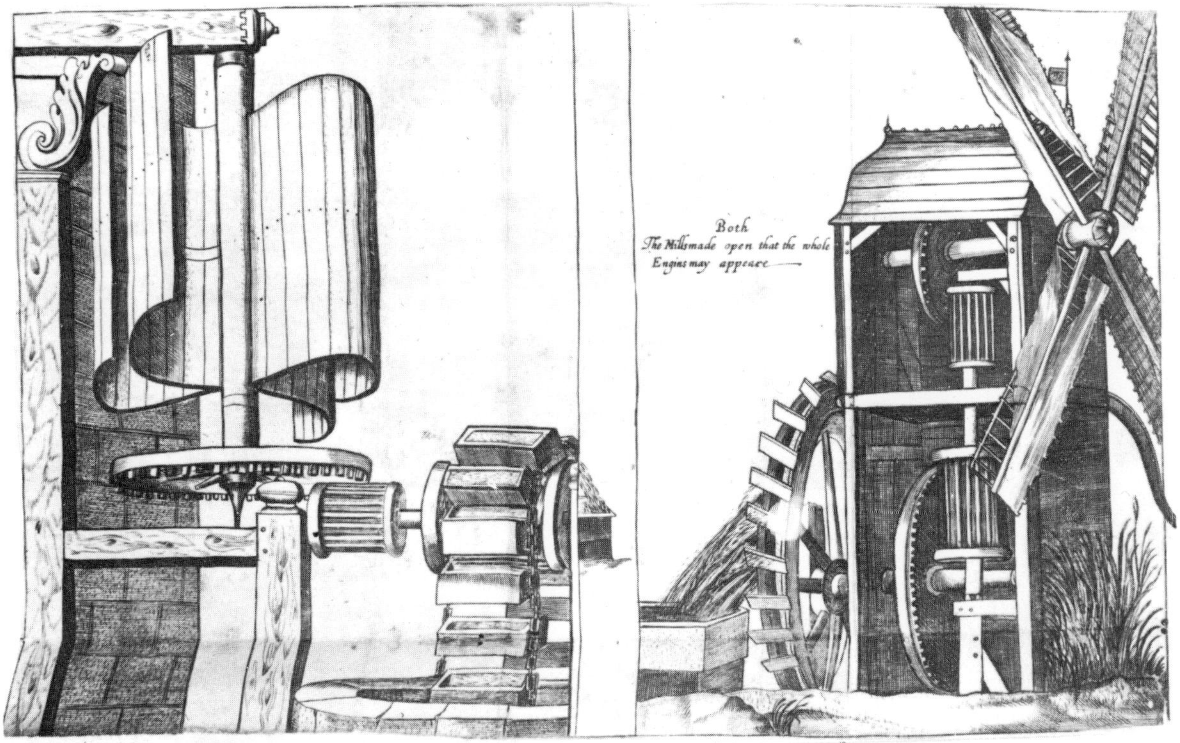
Both
The Millsmade open that the whole
Engins may appeare

An Indian woman clearing debris from a water channel (1600).

this "great Squirt of Tin," looking "like a small cannon," took "mighty strength to handle." Its advantage was that it sent water into the air like a modern sprinkler, to fall over a wide radius like rain. By 1629 John Parkinson was writing that gardens should have "a fountaine in the midst to convey water to euery part of the Garden, eyther in pipes vnder the ground, or brought by hand, and emptied into large Cisternes or great Turkey Iarres, placed in conuenient places, to serve as an ease to water the nearest parts thereunto."

Water was manhandled in the seventeenth century by a method allied to the antique yoke-and-buckets; the yoke was placed on two large wheels which enabled men to trundle two large waterbutts along.

Another method of large-scale watering, in use in the late eighteenth century, was an enormous barrel on wheels, pulled by a horse. This could either be fitted with a single spout, to be directed at will, or with a boom carrying many small sprinkler heads, which could either be positioned lengthwise along the barrel or swung out to cover several feet on either side. These watering carts were used for watering lawns (their rollerlike wheels ensured minimum damage to the grass while the horses were fitted with soft "slippers" for the same reason), for laying dust on paths and in the vegetable garden.

Very early watering pots were made from clay: this perforated example dates from 1470.

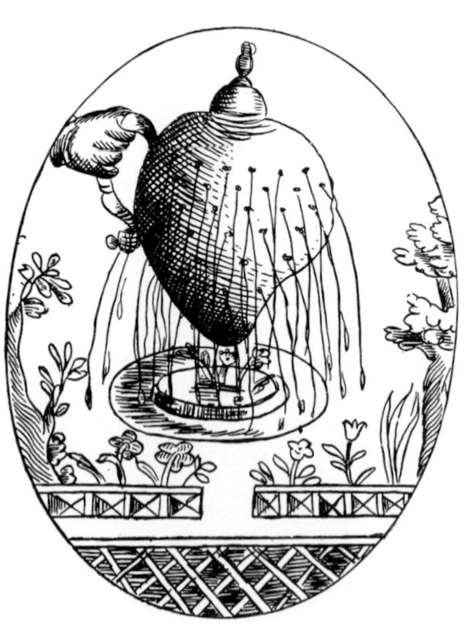

On a smaller scale, hand-carried pots or cans with a sprinkling effect were in use in the fifteenth century. The earliest seems to have been a large jar with a handle, with a covered filling aperture on top and a number of small holes perforated all over it, so that, once full, it would deliver many fine streams of water. By the sixteenth century, this had become more sophisticated, making use of the principle of suction. To quote Thomas Hyll, "the common water potte for the garden beds with us, hath a narrow

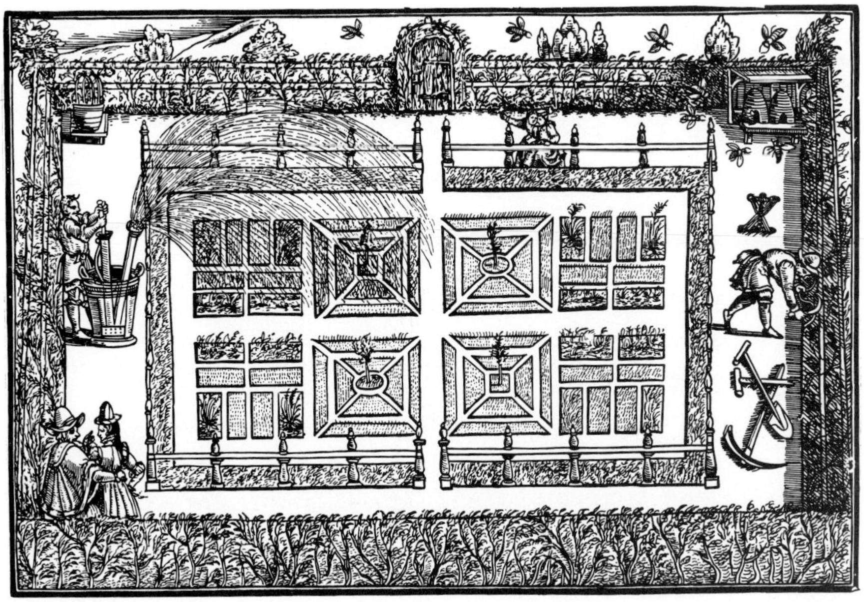

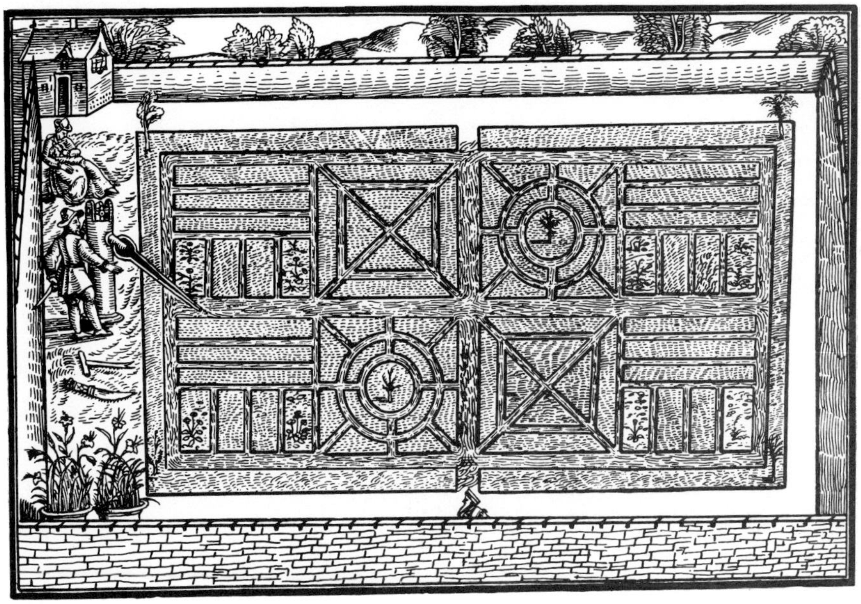

Mechanical watering devices depicted in 1577. Above, the "great squirt of tin," a lever-action pump which could deliver a fine spray a long way. BELOW: *A more orthodox suction pump feeding water conduits – rather unexpected in a Tudor garden.*

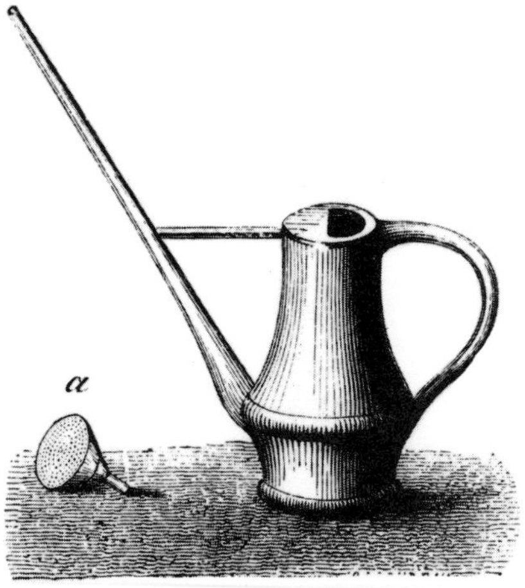

A seventeenth century clay watering pot (right) begins to resemble the modern type. The elegant long-spouted greenhouse watering can (left) is a nineteenth-century U.S. example.

necke, big belly, somewhat large bottom, and full of little holes, with a proper hole formed on the head, to take in the water, which filled full and the thumbe layde on the hole to keep in the aire may in such wise be carried in handsome manner."

The metal watering pots which appeared in the eighteenth century, and resemble modern ones in principle, are foreshadowed in various earthenware jugs with a handle, filling aperture, and perforated spout. Evelyn shows one with two spouts, for some curious purpose, as well as a vessel with a pointed spout at its base, which must have delivered an accurate single stream of water.

By the early nineteenth century, metal watering cans with fine "roses" were made in all kinds of shape, often with "kneed" spouts – in which a sharp angle near the opening allowed the flow of water to be cut off between one pot and the next by lifting the can slightly. More elaborate versions had a sucker valve, which held the water in by suction, next to the handle. There was even a small, flat can with a perforated pipe sticking out of it in the same plane as the body, to water plants on staging close to glass roofs.

The need for care in watering seems first to be expressed by Thomas Hyll around 1570. To avoid drenching seedlings, he says, "The best watering which is certain . . . is to make a hole with a dibble a little from the herb or plant, a slope to the root, and so water the root under ground, for water rotteth and killeth above ground." Worlidge in 1677 emphasized that, if the plants are watered overhead, it should be with a spray of "the smallest or rainlike drops as you can, and not too much, for hasty watring and hasty showers discover them." Hyll also recommended making a circular furrow around plants for filling with water, and a capillary method – using a small container alongside each plant, with a woolen wick to deliver the water slowly. Another method, first recorded in 1672, and useful especially with plants in containers, is to sink a flower pot into the soil and fill this with water, which gradually percolates through the drainage hole. Modern watering gadgets for indoor pot plants are based on similar principles, usually comprising a water container above a vertical tube with a very fine bore.

The rubber hose revolutionized garden watering, especially if used in conjunction with an iron hose reel.

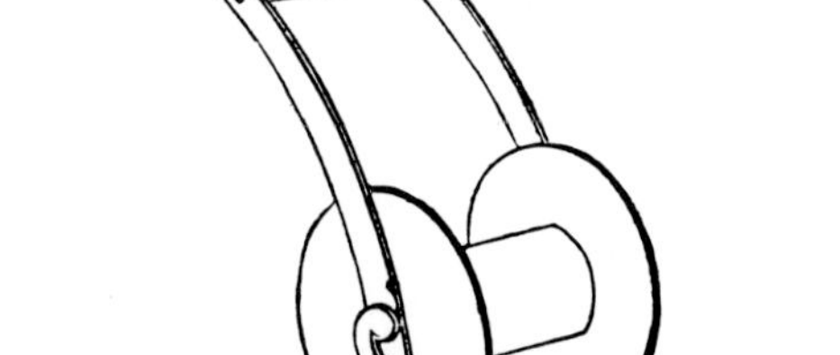

In China development of waterworks parallels that of other tools and techniques. Water is lifted from wells by a *shaduf* – but this is made of neatly fashioned bamboo as are the containers. A windlass well of less sophisticated construction pulls up a wide wicker bucket, its handle looking rather uncomfortable and difficult to use. A kind of bailer, probably made from finely interwoven bamboo or twigs, is handled by two men to lift water from river to paddy field (for most Chinese horticulture, outside the garden proper, is concerned with rice). Simple mechanization comes in with a fan-bladed water wheel turned by hand, or a paddle wheel system forcing water up a square conduit, operated by a man on a treadmill.

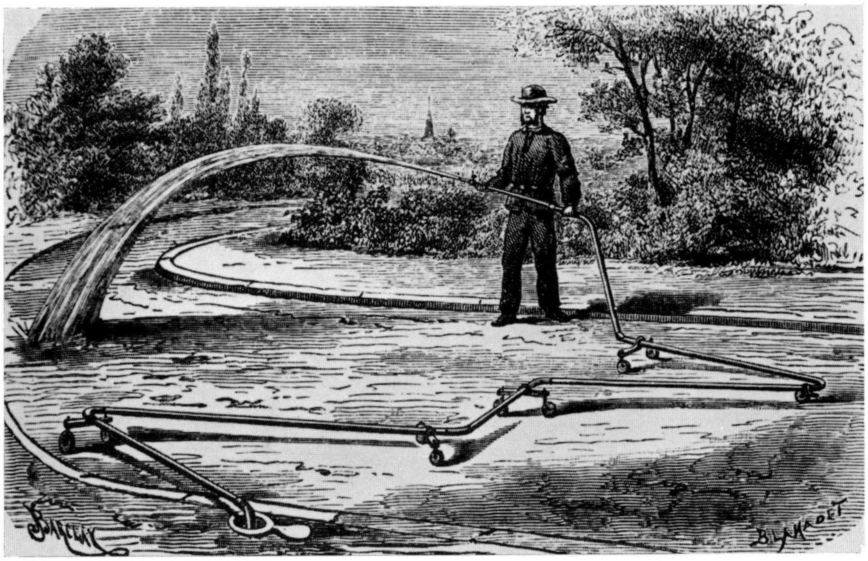

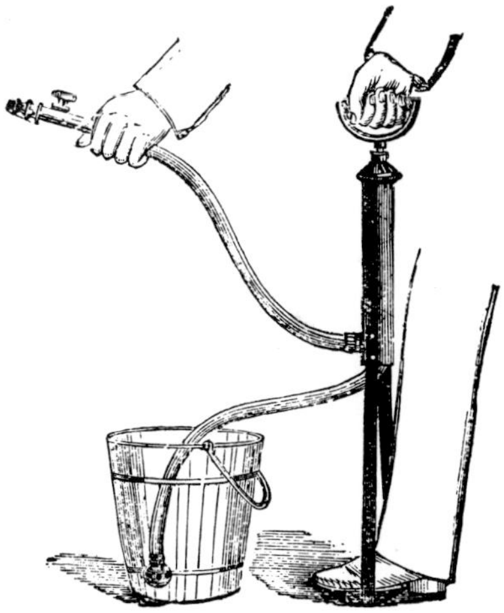

ABOVE LEFT: *A jointed metal "hose" on wheels, or* tuyaux à chariot *(France, late nineteenth century).*

LEFT: *The barrow engine held many gallons of water and was fitted with a powerful pump.*

ABOVE: *For more local use, the stirrup pump delivered water effectively from a bucket.*

Manpower, always cheap in China, is indeed usually employed, but occasionally a waterwheel operates a device, as in larger mechanisms working an endless bucket-and-cord system.

For hand watering of garden plants, a small pan-shaped container on a wooden handle is used, and this can be seen in Japanese illustrations as well. The Chinese also used flask-shaped containers with a very long

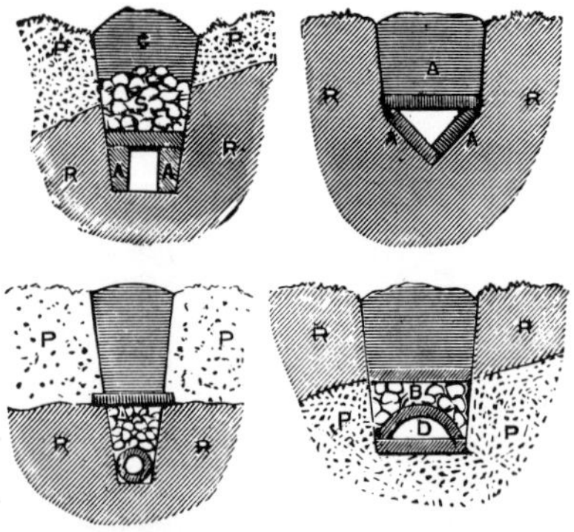

The value of draining many soils was well known to the Romans, and many modes besides their round tile drains have been developed since, as the nineteenth-century examples show (top). For really deep drains, a special instrument with a right-angled prong was used to lay the pipes (above).

straight spout – not, one would think, very efficient, since the air coming back into the container would impede the flow of water. Both methods seem finicky and inadequate.

More sophistication entered the watering world, as we expect, with the use of metal. But the rubber or plastic hose which we so widely use today did not appear until the turn of the century, although canvas hoses were available. Before that, the large-scale waterer might employ a series of jointed metal tubes on swiveling wheels if he wanted any flexibility.

Once rubber hose was available, it allowed the simple syringe to develop into various kinds of stirrup pump, trimmer versions of Hyll's "great Squirt." There were also barrow engines like miniature fire engines, with a pump handle and flexible delivery hose. An earlier version described by Loudon could apparently throw water up to fifty feet as a jet, or less far as a fine shower. Such engines were mounted on a wheelbarrowlike structure or, later, on a pair of large wheels, and could hold twenty or thirty gallons of water – a fair weight to trundle about.

The soil plants go into is, of course, almost as important as water. The Romans were the first to discuss soil quality. They went a good deal by its color, but Columella mentions a "soil test." Dampened soil is kneaded in the hand, and if it "sticks to the fingers of the person holding it, in the manner of pitch, it is fertile." Another test was to dig a hole and then try to replace the soil. If, after treading it in, there was an excess, this was a sure sign of fertility; poor soil would not refill the hole. Another method was to taste a mixture of soil and water after straining it; a sweet taste meant good soil, sour meant poor. "Sweet" ground could also be recognized because it grew plants such as rushes, reeds, grass, trefoil, dwarf elder or brambles. The Romans also understood that autumn cultivation helped the soil to "crumble with the cold and frosts of winter" (Columella).

SOIL AND MANURES

After the Middle Ages, good gardeners were very well aware of the need for soil quality and of the differing needs of plants, as Tusser shows in his lines:

> Ground gravelly, sandy and mixed with clay,
> Is naughty for hops, any manner of way.

It was soon found that soil could be improved, in both its fertility and texture, by adding manure and other materials. The use of manure is recorded from Egypt in the third millennium B.C. However, further east, where winters are hard and long, animal dung was dried for use as fuel, as indeed it continues to be in Turkey, India and many other places. The Persians got around this by making gigantic pigeon houses – not, like medieval dovecotes, to provide birds to eat, but for the droppings, which were periodically dug out and carefully distributed on the fields.

Human excrement, or "night soil" as the books politely call it, was also used in Persia and China, possibly from very ancient times.

Animal manure has been used since early Egyptian times to add both food and "body" to the soil: above, applying it to a garden in 1706. Today we rely too often on artificial fertilizers alone, which can be delivered through distributors like the American one at left.

Certainly the Romans advocated it, to quote Columella's gardening poem in *De Re Rustica*:

> . . . the gardener
> Should with rich mould or asses' solid dung
> Or other ordure glut the starving earth
> Bearing full baskets straining with the weight,
> Nor should he hesitate to bring as food
> For new-ploughed fallow-ground whatever stuff
> The privy vomits from its filthy sewers.

Elsewhere, in more factual vein, he recommends various exact amounts of goat's dung for olives, or of animal manure, pigeon's dung, or human urine for vines, and gives very specific advice about storing manure to retain its goodness. Most of this is in an agricultural context.

The South American civilizations were knowledgeable about different manures, "a circumstance," to quote Prescott, "rare in the rich lands of the tropics. . . . They made great use of guano . . . the stimulating and nutritious properties of which the Indians perfectly appreciated."

North American Indians were on the whole ignorant of manures, mostly moving on to new ground – like so many primitive peoples – when the soil was exhausted. To clear the ground, they used stone hatchets, with which – to quote the traveler Peter Kalm, writing about the Pennsylvania Indians in 1771 – "they cut off all the bark all around the trees with their hatchets, especially at the time when they lose their sap. By that means the trees become dry . . . and the leaves could no longer obstruct the rays of the sun from passing. The smaller trees were then pulled up by main force, and the ground was a little turned up with crooked or sharp branches." Indians on the coast, especially near Long Island Sound, made use of small fish which swarmed in the sea: they made holes in the ground into which a fish was dropped, and on top of this some corn kernels. The Indian chief Squanto taught the Pilgrims this procedure in their first planting season.

Other Indians were able to do without fish fertilizer because they practiced rotation of fields. John Winthrop in 1636 wrote, about the Pequod Indians on Rhode Island, that "The ground seemeth to be far worse than the ground of the Massachusetts, being light, sandy and rocky, yet they have good corn without fish: but I understand they take this course; they have, every one, two fields, which, after the first two years, they let one field rest each year, and that keeps their ground continually in hart."

To the ancients at any rate, the old saying "Corruption is the mother of vegetation" was very much acted upon. It is all the more surprising to find eighteenth-century botanists and gardeners believing that plants fed upon the fine particles of the soil, or on the "juices of the earth," and that plants imbibed these in much the same way as animals, their roots being "but guts inverted."

There is little to say about the application of manure. It was carried in baskets or on carts and spread on the fields, around plants, and in gardens by manual labor. In the eighteenth and nineteenth centuries, barrel carts such as those already described for watering were used to dispense liquid manure, made by steeping dung in water – as first mentioned by Theophrastus for watering potherbs. Theophrastus also knew about the warming effect of dung on the soil, claiming it gave a start of up to twenty days compared with unmanured ground. And he knew which crops benefited from manure and which did not.

The Roman's knowledge of manuring was extensive and sound. They even carried out green manuring, in which lupin seed was harrowed in and the resulting plants turned into the soil at its first digging, to rot and thus enrich the soil.

The Romans did not, apparently, carry out organic mulching – the spreading of suitable material (e.g., rotted garden compost) on the surface of the soil to hold in moisture. They did, however, practice stone mulching with small rocks. Virgil mentions that "I have even found some who loaded heavy fieldstones on top or considerable weights of broken pots; this is protection against cloudbursts and against the hot summer heat which cracks the thirsty fields." Columella recommends stone mulching for grapes and apricots. In modern times, this method has been used successfully, notably in China, where reports as recent as 1977 indicate the successful use of a four-inch mulch of pebbles in areas of low rainfall.

FERTILIZERS

Gradually, other materials besides manure and compost were recognized as valuable. Sir Hugh Plat, English gardener and writer, in 1594 was one of the first to understand that soluble "vegetable salts" were important in plant nutrition. He realized also that salts leach out of manure and recommended that the enriched soil below a manure heap should be spread on the garden after the manure had been taken to the fields. Among the other materials he mentions as valuable are lime, chalk, ashes, bone meal, and dried blood – all very modern.

By 1620 the English gardening writer Gervase Markham is adding to this list with "sope ashes," "hoofes," horn shavings, hair from hides, shredded woolen cloth, and also "all your powdred beef broth, and all other salt broths or brines, which shall grow or breed in your house, and also all manner of soap sudds, or other sudds, and washings which shall proceed from the Laundery."

Europeans seem to have appreciated the value of such materials more than the first American settlers who, curiously enough, often left animal manures to accumulate in noisome quantity without spreading them on the fields. However, the development of the New York vegetable market influenced intensive cultivation in the area, leading to demand for manurial materials. In his *Travels* . . . , the Reverend Timothy Dwight records their zeal:

> Within this period [1789–1804] the inhabitants, with a laudable spirit of enterprise, have set themselves to collect manure, wherever it could be obtained. Not content with what they could make, and find, on their own farms, and shores, they have sent their vessels up the Hudson, and loaded them with the residuum of potash manufactories; gleaned the streets of New York [of street sweepings]; and have imported various kinds of manure from New-Haven, New-London, and even from Hartford. In addition to all this, they have swept the Sound; and covered their fields with the immense shoals of whitefish with which in the beginning of summer its waters are replenished. No manure is so cheap as this, where the fish abound: none is so rich: and few are so lasting.

These whitefish were taken in seine nets in enormous quantities in June and July, and about ten thousand fish per acre were used. Another account of around 1800 describes how "A single net has taken 200,000 in a day. . . . These fish are sometimes laid in furrows, and covered with the plough. Sometimes they are laid singly on the hills of maize, and covered with the hoe. At other times they are collected in heaps, formed with other materials into a compost; carted upon the ground; and spread in the same manner, as manure from the stable. . . . They are sold for a dollar a thousand; and are said to affect the soil advantageously for a considerable length of time." The odor of this type of manuring must have been powerful. (Long Island farmers also made use of seaweed.)

By 1834 J. C. Loudon could list the following manurial materials which had been found of value: animal manure of all kinds, specified separately; animal urine; dead animals if available for any reason; animal blood; fish, blubber, bones, horn, hair, woolen rags, feathers, skin and leather manufacturers' refuse, and human night soil; soot, rape cake, malt dust, linseed cake, seaweed; and "all green succulent plants," preferably dug into the soil as green manure, whether growing or as hedge clippings or ditch cleanings.

Loudon also mentions various "mineral manures," mainly the different kinds of lime, but also sulfate of iron, phosphate of lime, bone and wood ashes, and soda. His text does not suggest a very deep understanding of the use of many of these. Superphosphate – derived from treating bones, or calcium phosphate, with sulfuric acid – was first produced by the Irishman James Murray in 1817, but it was J. B. Lawes, Squire of Rothamsted in England and begetter of Rothamsted Experimental Station, who built up its production, patenting his process in 1842. Superphosphate was the only manufactured fertilizer in England for nearly eighty years. It was used in conjunction with naturally occurring nitrate of soda, and with sulfate of ammonia, a by-product of gas production. After World War I, the chemical industry, stimulated by its new-found knowledge in the explosives field, started turning out mixed fertilizers based on superphosphate and other phosphates, nitrate of soda or of ammonium or similar salts, and potassic salts.

In the United States the beginning of chemical fertilizing seems to have been in the use of limestone, marl, and eventually gypsum on the largely acid soils of much of the country which bedeviled many of the early settlers. Peter Kalm in 1748 noted of limestone: "The people however pretend that this stone is a very good manure, if it is scattered upon the cornfields in its rubbish state, for it is said to stifle the weeds: it is therefore made use of both on the fields and in gardens." In 1818 Edmund Ruffin, a U.S. farmer, advocated the use of shell marl to counter acidity, and others began to use burnt lime.

Franklin and Washington were both early experimenters with chemical fertilizers. Peruvian guano was the first commercially produced fertilizer to be widely used in the United States. These dried seabirds' droppings, imported from the arid Chincha Islands off the Peruvian coast, were first brought to public notice in 1824, but not widely distributed until 1843. The first mixed fertilizer was patented in 1849 by a firm in Baltimore, which rapidly became an important center for the manufacture of superphosphates. In 1852 this material was being sold mixed with guano and with sulfate of ammonia by J. J. Mapes of Long Island, who had previously prepared a useful line of "acidulated bones" for feeding his own land.

The chemical fertilizer industry in the United States went from strength to strength, largely independently of European research; important landmarks were the opening of the South Carolina phosphate rock deposits in 1867, and the importation of German-made potash in 1870. Fertilizers sold in the early years of the nineteenth century contained a fairly high proportion of salts derived from manure. In 1921 the direct synthesis of ammonia from atmospheric nitrogen took place at Syracuse, New York, a very important step forward, followed by the opening up of the huge potash deposits at Carslbad, New Mexico, in 1931. After that, the U.S. fertilizer industry was totally independent of other sources.

Until these chemical fertilizers appeared in stable form (before the war they were so unstable and liable to damage crops that farmers were actually warned against their use), garden plants everywhere were fed with materials such as those earlier listed by Loudon in various traditional ways. Weird soil mixtures were recommended for a few specific plants, mainly those of the florists (like the auricula). One example must suffice: two barrows full of goose dung, steeped in blood; two of sugar-bakers' scum; two of night soil; and two of fine yellow loam. Such mixtures took two years to prepare, being turned over and mixed every month in the open.

Complex soil mixtures are still sometimes recommended, but most gardeners rely on manufactured concentrated foods, either granulated

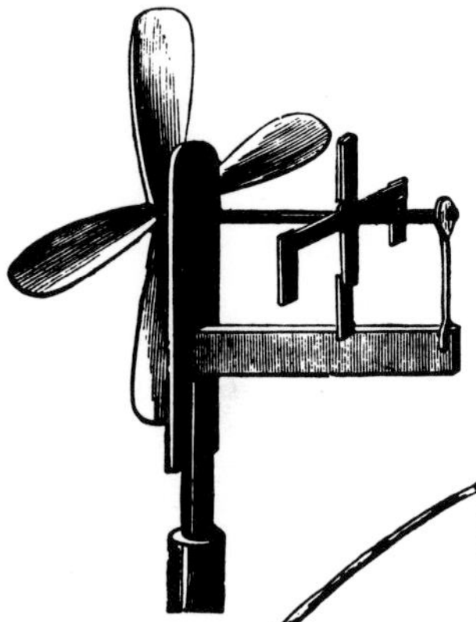

TOP: *"A cherry clack" operated by propeller to make a noise.* ABOVE: *A visual bird scarer for seed rows.*

or liquid. A growing number of people, sometimes unkindly called the "muck and mystery school," refuse to use anything of chemical origin and rely entirely on animal manures and compost made from decaying vegetable matter of all kinds, in the making of which a certain amount of ritual sometimes takes place. Composting, one may add, was well known to both Greeks and Romans, who used animal manures, vegetable wastes, leaves, sewage sludge, house sweepings and domestic food waste. As the writer K. D. White points out in *Roman Farming* (1970), referring to Columella's advice, "modern practice would add nothing to these recommendations, except the use of chemical activators which speed up the process."

One specialized way of feeding plants has led to growing them in a quite distinct and "unnatural" way. Early experiments to discover whether plants obtain their food from soil or water led to others during the nineteenth century, notably those of the French agricultural chemist Jean-Baptiste Boussaingault (1802–1887), who raised crops in pots containing sand and charcoal, to which nutrient chemical solutions were added. By 1920 this *hydroponic* method was universally accepted for the study of plant nutrition. Ten years later the American W. F. Gericke transformed this laboratory technique into one capable of growing plants on a commercial scale, either outside or in greenhouses, in situations where soil and organic

HYDROPONICS

manure were unobtainable. Hydroponic culture has been very widely used, especially to grow food crops in desert areas or for concentrations of landless city dwellers. Today it is becoming popular as a means of growing indoor plants.

Perhaps the greatest advances are being made at the University of Arizona, which has pioneered large-scale gardens enclosed in plastic bubbles in Central America and Saudi Arabia, and at the University of California, whose work has been more for domestic purposes. In the commercial field, the General Electric company's Electronic Systems Division in Syracuse, New York, has developed in Scandinavia and other locations, structures with completely artificial growing conditions as pilot or full-scale models for commercial food production.

Early hydroponic installations had the plants appropriately supported, with their roots dangling in the nutrient solution, but most now use an inert material – sand, washed ash or baked clay granules – to support the roots.

PESTS AND DISEASES

Pests and diseases of plants have been recorded from earliest times; one has only to turn to the locusts of Exodus, which "covered the face of the whole earth, so that the land was darkened, and they did eat every herb of the land, and all the fruit of the trees . . . ."; or to Joel: "That which the palmer worm hath left hath the locust eaten; and that which the locust hath left hath the cankerworm eaten; and that which the cankerworm has left hath the caterpillar eaten."

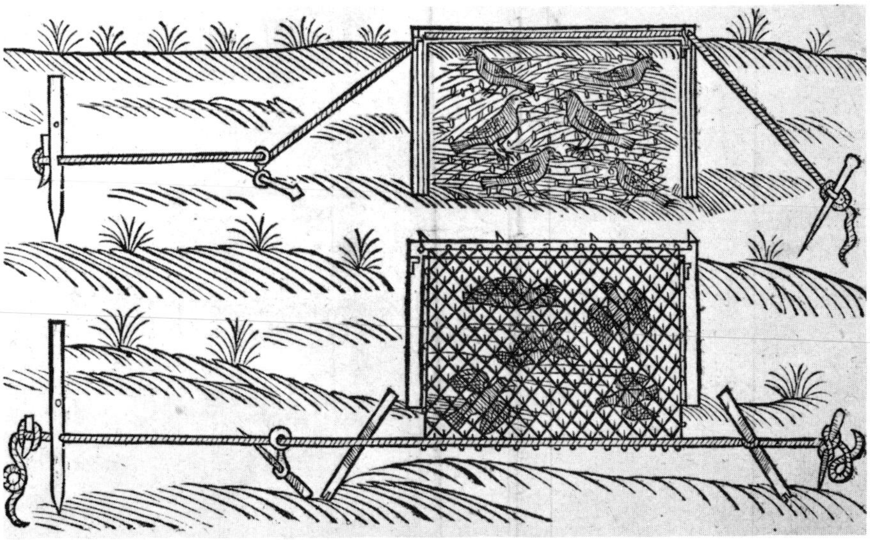

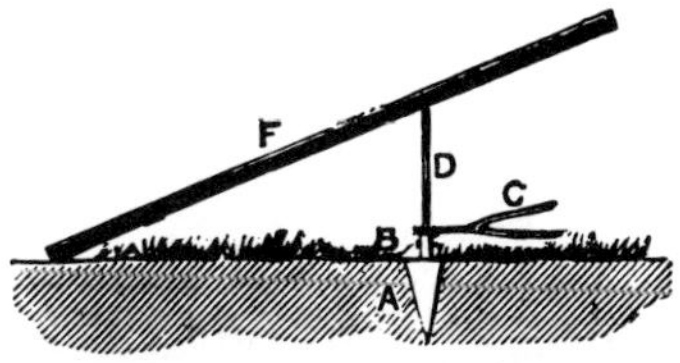

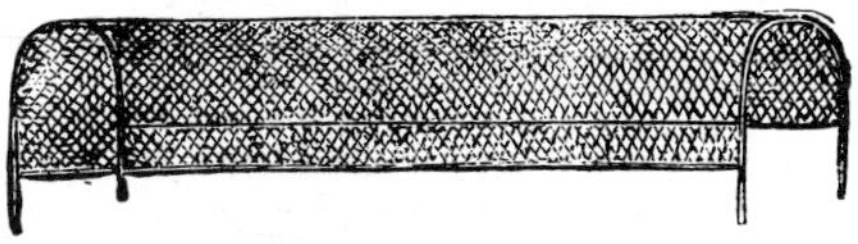

Traps and deterrents for bird invaders. TOP LEFT: *A crow net of 1590, shown set at top, sprung below.* ABOVE: *Early nineteenth-century devices (from top to bottom): a slate poised to fall on a bait-taking bird; a mesh pea guard; seed protectors to be aligned over seed rows with thread strung along the projections; and the inefficient basket trap.* LEFT: *The scarecrow has been in use since the sixteenth century.*

Theophrastus describes many "worms" and grubs of fruit and seeds, and caterpillars eating vines and potherbs; he also mentions "diseases," but in rather vague terms, not quite sure whether they are caused by what we now know to be fungi or by some aspect of weather, climate and cultivation. Later, Pliny believed that diseases emanated from the gods or the stars. Theophrastus mentions rot, mildew and "cobweb," and rust on cereals. As early as 700 B.C., the Romans had a special festival, at which a red puppy was sacrificed, to pray for a rust-free wheat crop. But Theophrastus has few remedies: for caterpillars, grubs and "leek cutters" on vegetables he suggests collecting green fodder or dung around the plants, "the pest being fond of dung emerges, and, having entered the heap . . . is then easy to catch, which otherwise it is not." To deal with "spiders"

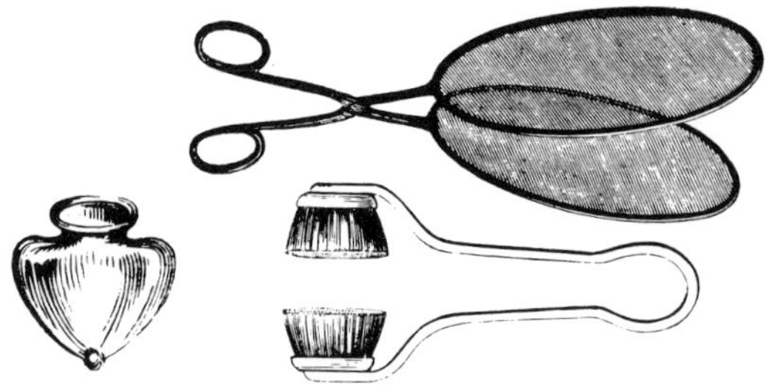
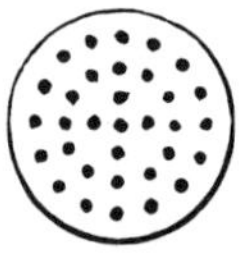
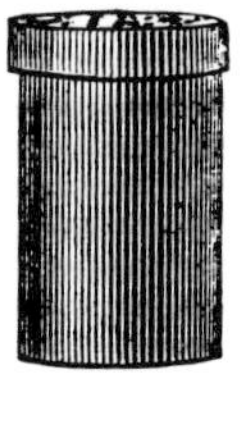
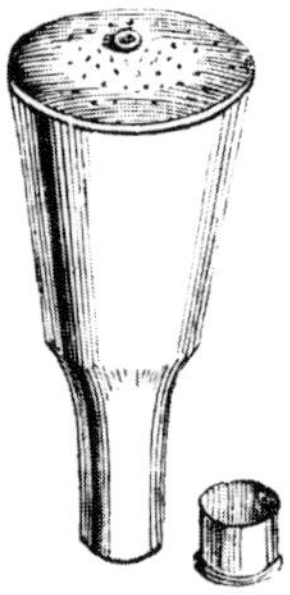

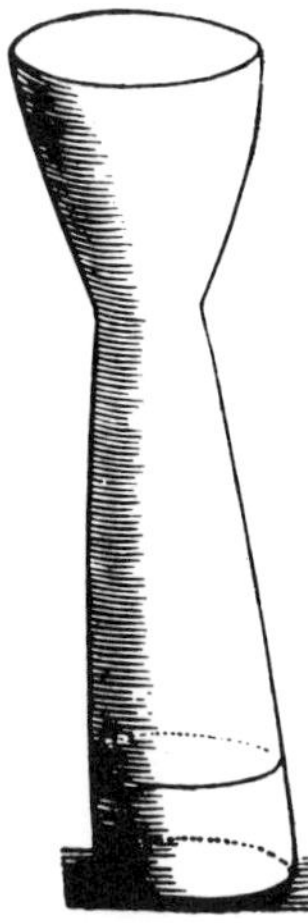
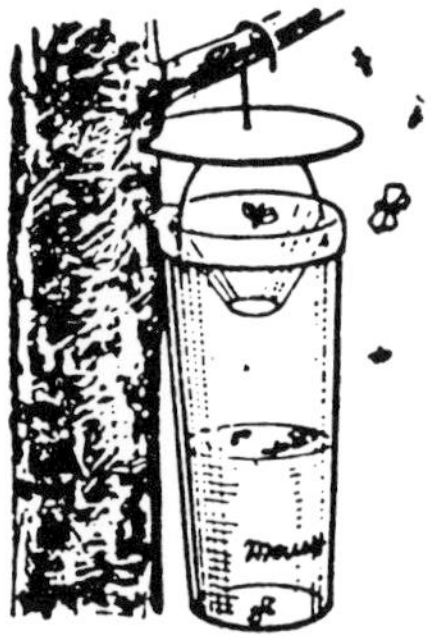

CLOCKWISE AROUND PAGE: *Before effective insecticides were available, wasp jars of different shapes and sizes were used. The one on a branch is a modern French version with phosphorescent rim to attract night insects. An aphis brush and (top) a scissor-action wasp catcher. Two lime and soot dredgers, the right hand one designed to be fixed on a pole. An earwig trap working in the same way as a flower pot placed on a pole, and a section of a simple earwig and beetle trap.*

OPPOSITE TOP: *A series of distributors for insecticides and fungicides, including bellows and puffers for tobacco smoke or dust, and sulfur dust. An early greenhouse fumigator. Early spraying syringes for liquid materials and (bottom, opposite) modern sprayers, which can be hand pressurized or (smaller model) power operated.*

found attacking radishes, "it is of use to sow vetch among the crops; to prevent the spiders from being engendered they say there is no specific." He does not mention the ancient Greek knowledge that wheat rust, obviously a great bane in early days, could be controlled by dusting with powdered sulfur.

Columella likewise describes numerous pests – "tiny ground flea," "greedy ant," the snail, the hairy caterpillar, and "creeping through the garden, canker worms bite and dry up the seedlings, as they go." He mentions placatory sacrifice, "with blood and entrails of a sucking whelp," or the setting up of "the skinless head of an Arcadian ass" at the field's edge, the hedging of fields with bryony, or the pinning of "night-flying birds on crosses." (We still sometimes nail up rows of shot birds and other vermin, but to deter more of the same rather than to placate a deity.)

Another mysterious cure, quoted from Democritus, is for a girl in the throes of her first menstruation ("who for the first time obeys her youth's fixed laws, barefooted and ashamed") to be led three times around the beds, when any caterpillars will instantly fall and die. (How this is to be reconciled with the baleful general effect attributed to women is not described: he says "usually the growth of greenstuff is checked by contact with a woman; indeed, if she is also in the period of menstruation, she will kill the young produce merely by looking at it.")

It is fascinating to find that very similar "pest control" was carried out by the North American Indians. At full noon the squaw stripped naked and walked around the plot she tended, dragging the clothes she had worn that day. This was a magic circle which no cutworm would cross. U. P. Hedrick surmises that this may have been due to missionaries remembering the Roman custom, but it seems unlikely that they would have propagated so pagan a rite.

But much of Columella's advice is good common sense. He recommends picking caterpillars off by hand and shaking vegetables in the early morning, "for, if the caterpillars thus fall to the ground when they are still torpid from the night's cold, they no longer creep into the upper parts of the plants." To prevent leaf-rolling caterpillars, Cato's remedy was to smear around the plants a mixture made by boiling down the dregs of olive

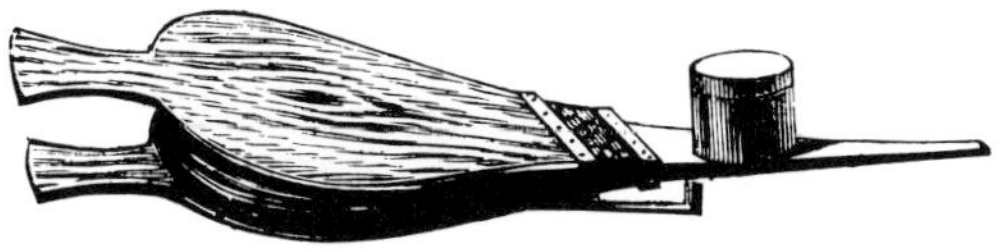

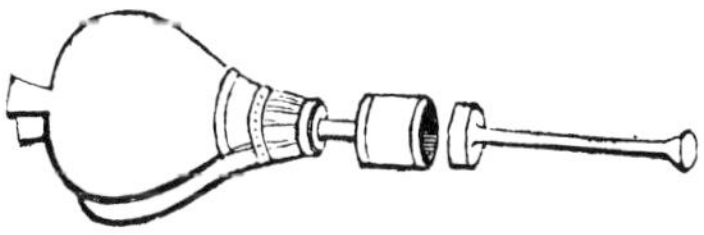

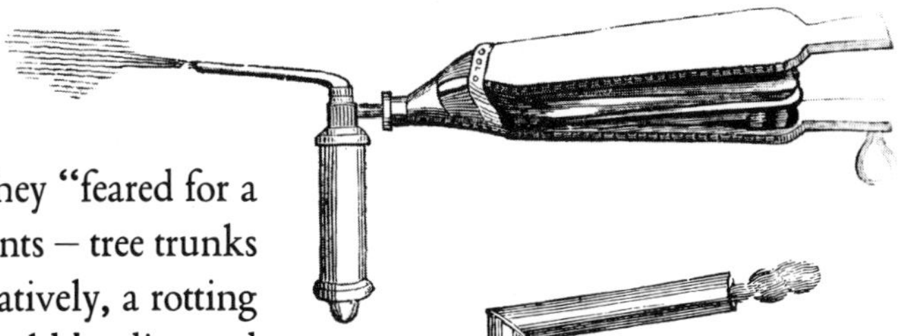

oil, bitumen and sulfur. Against ants – which, because they "feared for a destitute old age," carried off seeds and tender parts of plants – tree trunks were smeared with a mixture of red earth and tar. Alternatively, a rotting fish hung up in the tree would attract them so that they could be disposed of. Sabinus Tiro tells us that heliotrope or bitter vetch sown among crops will deter or kill ants. For deterring moles, filling their runs with dregs of oil lees seems the equivalent of our use of creosote-soaked rags today.

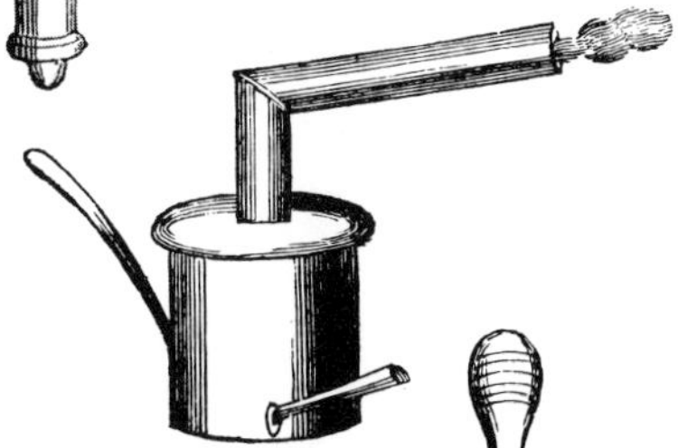

To prevent early pest attack, Columella advises steeping seeds and drenching plants in the juice of the houseleek or horehound; in this he follows the Greek Democritus, who also advocated wormwood. Other Roman seed treatments included rolling them in nitrum (probably carbonate of soda), the deposit from oil presses, "unsalted lees of oil," or in "the powder which is found above an arched roof."

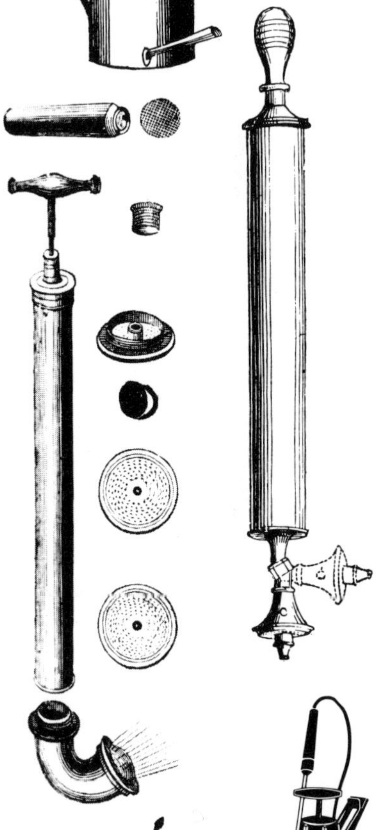

Rather similar treatments recur in Tudor Britain. Mascall, in 1572, refers to "little bestes called Sowes, which have many legs: and some of them be graye, some blacke [these must be aphids], and some hath a long sharpe snowte [these sound like weevils], which be very noysome, & great hurters of young graffes, and other yong trees also, for they cut of in eating the tender toppes of the young cions . . . ." But the only remedy he could suggest was picking then off by hand. However, against "snayles and ants" he recommends laying a mixture of ashes and unslaked lime around the tree, which is then shaken so that the pests fall upon the mixture. He also recommends a springtime fumigation against orchard pests, especially caterpillars, which is done by lighting, on the windward side, fires made of straw, hay, dry chaff, dry ox dung, sawdust, tanners' waste, hair, thatch or old shoes. In 1618, however, we find Lawson recommending hand-picking of caterpillars: "I like nothing of smoake among my trees."

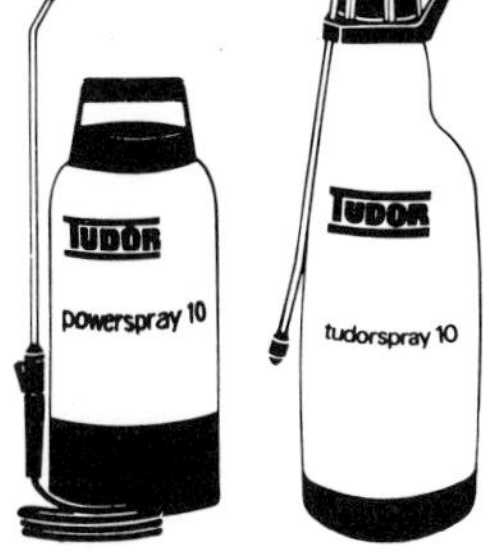

In 1602 the anonymous author of *The Orchard and Garden*, discussing "worms" which develop under the bark of trees, writes, "If you will kill the wormes which grow in the tree, take pepper, lawzell and incense, and mingle all well together with good wine, and pierce a hole into the tree downeward . . . and poure this mixture into it, and stop it with a hawthorne, and the wormes will die." Another remedy was a mixture of ashes or dust with salad oil, rubbed on the bark. If powdered incense was rubbed in when grafting, many believed worms would never eat the fruit. Canker should be removed with a knife, cutting to clean wood and anointing the wound with ox dung, keeping it from the weather by tying bark around it. Pismires or ants were prevented from climbing fruit trees by painting the lower trunk with wine dregs, a mixture of bitter herbs and vinegar, or thin pitch.

This author certainly did not lack observation, for in discussing the caterpillars "which eat the greene, and blossoms of the tree . . . so that thereafter may come no fruit," he explains that their eggs, "hidden as it were in a cobweb, must diligently be serched, and burned from the boughes, before they bring forth other caterpillars. . . . Some were wont to breake them off, and tread them with their feet, but therwith they be not wholly killed. The fire consumeth all things, and therefore it is best to burne them." Nowadays we "burn" overwintering eggs with tar oil wash, and it is still possible to buy quassia extract, a very bitter substance which deters sap-sucking insects on tree trunks, as did the wine dregs or Democritus's wormwood juice. Indeed, there is now great development of insect repellents extracted from local bitter trees (like the neem tree in India). These repellents can be made simply and on the spot by peasant farmers.

Home gardeners today may obtain grease bands to trap certain wingless moths that climb tree trunks, or tie corrugated cardboard around the trunk. An early version of this method can be found in the *Massachusetts Magazine* of 1791: "To prevent Grubs from ascending fruit trees to deposit their eggs. Take a strip of sheepskin about one inch wide with the wool on it at full length; scrape the rough bark off the tree, and nail the skin around it, keeping the wooly side out."

The most entertaining method of controlling small pests I have encountered was the keeping of pet seagulls "for devouring little beasts injurious to kitchen gardens"; so, in 1742, wrote Peter Kalm of the east London garden of Richard Warner.

Ancient pest control in the East is largely veiled in mystery; but the earliest Turkish horticultural treatise, the *Revnaki Rostan* (*Beauty of the Gardener*) of A.D. 1070, includes the use of ashes of oakwood to kill cockchafer grubs, and the sowing of mustard among ornamental plants to repel insects in general. We also have an Arab remedy for slugs dating from around 1300: "Form your beds, strew on them an inch of ashes from the public baths, then lay on your manure and sow the seed: thus the animal mentioned, on leaving the earth in search of the plants, will meet with the ashes and retire confounded." Ashes are still used today, along with other mechanical repellents such as zinc collars.

Tree health was always a source of concern and, apart from "wormes," there was moss. Mascall gives frequent advice "to abate the mosse of the trees, with a great knife of wood or such like, so that ye hurt not the bark thereof." Special curved moss knives were made then and into the nineteenth century. One ingenious twentieth-century device is gloves with wire wool outside, which are rubbed up and down the mossy branches by the operator.

In 1789 William Forsyth, one-time superintendent of the Royal Gardens of Kensington Palace in London, aroused controversy by the claims he made for what was known as "Forsyth's plaister," which he said was capable "of curing defects in growing trees" and could even restore to soundness oaks "where nothing remained but the bark." The "plaister," which after Forsyth's death was proved utterly useless, was made of lime, dung, urine, sand, soapsuds, wood ashes and other materials, and resembled other popular concoctions simply designed to heal wounds in bark. Other concoctions were, and still are, used to try to prevent deer, hares and other creatures from eating the bark of trees, which can of course kill the latter. In 1824 Loudon was, for example, recommending "an ointment composed of powdered sloes and hogs' lard," while "stale urine of any kind, mixed up with any glutinous matter that will retain it on the bark, has also been recommended." He also suggests tarred string, which remains efficacious for smaller plants.

Larger animals were trapped in more or less complicated ways over the centuries. From Tudor times onward, there were many ingenious "traps and engines." In 1618 there was a quite elaborate "portcullis" type of rat and mouse trap. By Loudon's day, the rat trap remained "a box, or enticing engine, of some sort," concealed in leaves or litter and made enticing with oil of anise. Mice were more easily disposed of by a lightly supported stone slab or brick, or a flower pot, buried in the soil upside down under litter. Later an ingenious Victorian devised the "slippery pole" in which food is placed on a central wheel over a bucket of water. Once the mouse reaches the wheel and puts its weight on it, he falls into the water and drowns. Loudon also advises that "a few cats domiciled in the back sheds of hothouses will generally keep a walled garden free of mice." However, as *The Compleat Florist* of 1706 pointed out, "Dogs and Cats ought not to be suffer'd in a Flower Garden. Your Dogs do, by their continual leaping, leave ugly Marks or Impressions upon the Surface of the Ground – and the Cats scattering their Ordure all about, and then scraping the Earth to cover it, grub up many Plants." As both small suburban gardens and pet cats became more numerous, special "cat teasers" of upright nails or tin, and wire "obstacles," became available for fixing on walls to impede the felines' progress.

Moles were ever troublesome. The Roman method of pouring oil lees in their runs was replaced by weird deterrents such as those recorded by Robert Sharrock in 1694: "Take red herrings and, cutting them to pieces, burn the pieces on the molehills, or you may put garlicke or leeks in the mouths of their Hill." Drowning them by filling the runs with water was

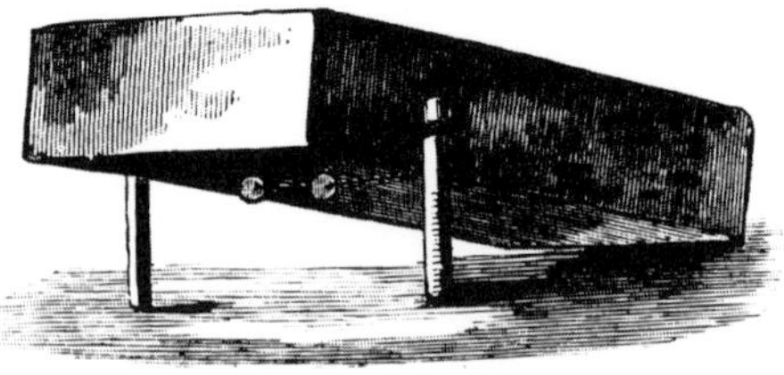

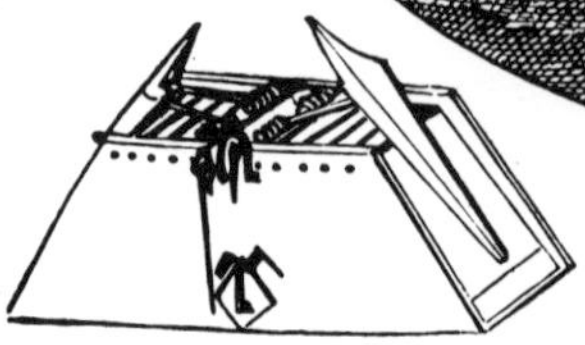

Rats, mice and moles have always been gardeners' enemies, and much ingenuity has gone into destroying them. TOP CENTER: *The portcullis rat trap dates from 1618.* TOP RIGHT: *"A latch trappe for the water Ratte" of 1590 was to be pinned against the rat's hole in the stream or pool bank.* TOP LEFT: *A vicious mole trap of the same date.* LOWER RIGHT: *Nineteenth-century mole trap, and a rat trap.* ABOVE: *Three mouse traps of the same period: the upper two are self-explanatory; the lowest is of some ingenuity – food placed on the wheel entices the animals which are sent spinning into water in the bucket.*

recommended, and by 1710 some quite elaborate traps are described, apart from simpler ones based on the bow principle of driving a sharpened stick into the mole.

Under the heading "Machines for destroying Vermin and for Defense against the Enemies of Gardens," Loudon starts, I regret to say, with "engine traps for man" which "are of two species, the common and the humane." "The common man-trap is a rat-trap on a large scale. . . . This is a barbarous contrivance, though rendered absolutely necessary in the exposed gardens around great towns. . . . The humane man-trap, instead of breaking the leg by crushing, and consequently by the worst of all descriptions of compound fractures, simply breaks the leg, and therefore is comparatively entitled to the appelation of humane. It is not infrequently set in market gardens near the metropolis."

Loudon ends by stating that "the essential vermin engines are the mole and mouse traps, fumigating bellows, and musket." The bellows are discussed later in this chapter; the musket was used both as a destroyer and a scarer of birds.

The early American settlers only knew two "diseases" of fruit trees: one was "meazles," following sun scorch; the other, called "lowsiness," was the result of woodpeckers making holes in the bark. The remedy, to quote the traveler Josselyn in 1674, "is to bore a hole in the main root with an Augur, and pour in a quantity of Brandie or Rhum, and then stop it up with a pin made of the same Tree." (Did this make the birds drunk?)

Birds have always been serious pests, especially for smallholders. To prevent crows pulling up the young corn plants, North American Indians were recorded in 1636 as putting up "little watch houses in the middle of their fields, in which they or their biggest children lodge, and early in the morning prevent the birds . . . ." The human bird scarer was replaced in the sixteenth century – at least in Europe – by the scarecrow, derived from a shot bird left dangling from a pole. In smaller areas, this might be replaced by various kinds of moving or dangling object, by pieces of cord or hose on the ground, which, it is believed, birds think are snakes, or by "clacks" which make a noise in the wind. Ingenious traps were in use by the sixteenth century, and many scarers, traps and killers were devised in the nineteenth century, as well as passive guards of wire mesh or wires strung along the seed rows. The bird-killing, slate-slab trap, very like that for mice, cannot have been very effective; nor apparently were basket traps, which derived from the lobster pot principle. Nineteenth-century spring traps are still used in France today.

Much ingenuity was expended at this time in countering small pests. The aphis brush is rather more subtle, if more time-consuming, than the modern spray gun; the wasp catcher was presumably used in greenhouses devoted to quality fruit like peaches. Earwigs and beetles were often caught in a simple hollow cylinder or a bamboo cane; we have not progressed far from Mascall's advice of 1569 recommending "for Earwigges, shoes stopt with hay, hanged in the tree all night, they all come in." More elaborate was the multiple-tube trap, formed of small iron tubes soldered together "sometimes used by those gardeners to whom expense is not an object." Simpler earwig and beetle catchers were small wooden, metal or earthenware boxes with an upper aperture into which they fell without possibility of escape.

In the open garden, wasps would be enticed into wasp glasses of various shapes, which were half-filled with sweetened water; here again the pests took a one-way trip.

Lime and powdered tobacco leaves, or wood ashes, were often used to deter insects in the early part of the last century, and would be dispensed from a dusting can with small holes at one end. The lid was used when low plants and trees were to be dealt with but, to get the powder into tall trees, a pole was fitted into the filling end. Lime and soot were combined to deter insects getting at seed, and would be "dredged" from a similar can with larger holes.

Another way of dusting over small areas was to use a bellows, the box filled with powder being fitted underneath one of the valves instead of its board. It was also found that dried tobacco leaves, if lit and made to smolder, would discharge a valuable insecticidal smoke. To handle this, a box containing the leaves was fitted between the bellows and its nozzle.

To clean the structures of greenhouses, fumigating pots were used, in which two or three pounds of tobacco would be burned. These were operated from outside the greenhouse with bellows. To enable the spout to penetrate the greenhouse interior, special tin squares with a hole of the right size were fitted into every third or fourth sash, instead of a pane of glass. They were fitted with plugs to close them when not in use.

When sulfur later began to be used for fumigation, the bellows principle was again practiced, and there were also mechanical sulfurators in which the turning of a handle operated a fan to drive the powder out.

Liquid sprays gradually came into use, starting with tobacco water, and continuing at the turn of the century with pesticides made from oils, soaps, sulfur, more efficiently prepared nicotine emulsion, pyrethrum, quassia, hellebore and derris – the last five all deriving from plants.

Fungus diseases were naturally more difficult to understand, and one imagines that a good deal of trial and error took place. In America, there was at first no scientific research of any kind. Prior to 1800 both plant diseases and severe infestations of insect pests were considered by the Puritan New Englanders to be punishments from heaven, and prayers to relieve them would be offered. Other explanations of diseases included "morbid infections of the air," "a surcharge of Franklin's electric fluid"; pear blight was specifically described as "a vegetable apoplexy" due to this last cause. Remedies were thus designed which would draw off this electric fluid or "floating electric current" from the trees. These remedies included hanging pieces of metal, iron hoops or horseshoes in the trees. When, in 1837, the Pennsylvania Horticultural Society offered a prize for an effective cure for pear blight, other suggestions included wrapping the branches with rags soaked in brimstone, soaking the soil with soapsuds, and giving the trees a tonic either by inserting calomel beneath the bark or by driving in iron nails. No prize was awarded!

In England a mixture of lime water and urine was used against mildew in 1802; for severe attacks a concoction of tobacco, sulfur, lime and elder buds was recommended – which is in fact an early version of lime-sulfur wash, still sometimes used today. By 1885 the copper-based Bordeaux Mixture was in use as a fungicide against mildew on grapevines.

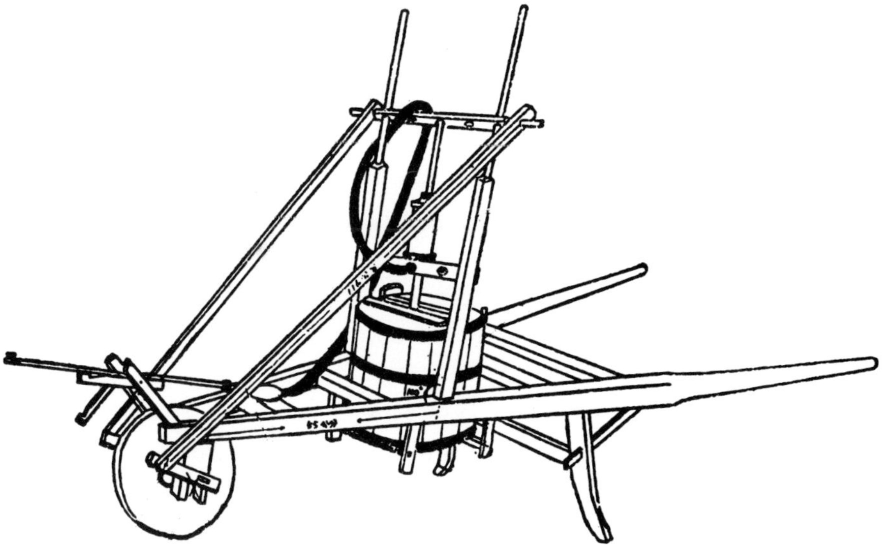

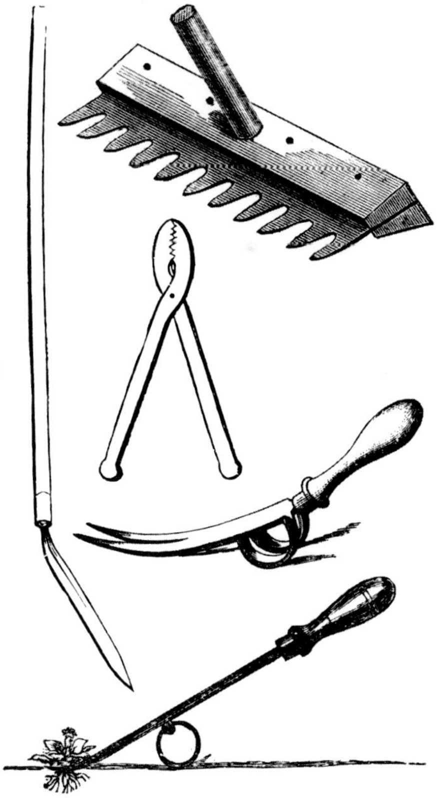

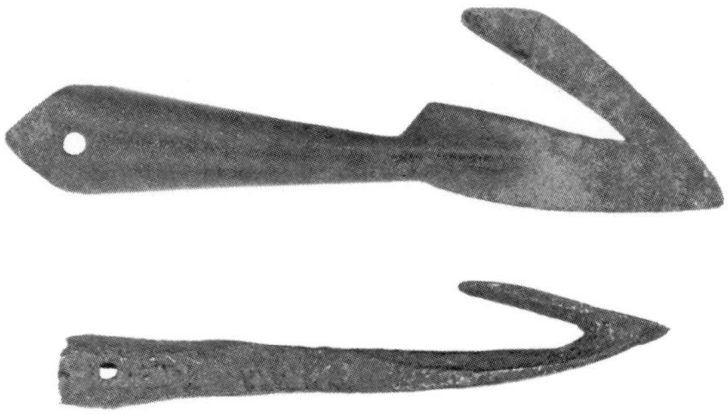

TOP LEFT: *A "grass roots" Chinese wheelbarrow-mounted crop sprayer made almost entirely of wood. The pump, operating in the central tub, is actuated by simple cranks and connected rods fixed on the wheel.*

CENTER: *The business ends of two "weed hooks" at least a century old, designed to remove weeds from cereal crops but also used in large gardens.*

ABOVE, FROM TOP TO BOTTOM: *A daisy rake; weeding pincers; a root extractor; a daisy fork; and (vertical tool) a two-edged daisy knife, used with a to-and-fro motion. (All nineteenth century.)*

LEFT: *A lawn weed extractor that removed plugs of soil, which were then to be replaced upside down.*

To deliver liquid insecticides and fungicides in the garden (as opposed to vineyards, where pump engines were used), syringes of many kinds came into use, ranging from the simple double-acting type in which spray is sucked up by pulling the plunger and expelled by pushing it, to stirrup-pump models in which solution in a bucket was sucked up and expelled continuously as the plunger went in and out.

It was not until 1940 that the first organic insecticide came into use (DDT, now legally banned in most parts of the world), and only in the last few years that efficient pressure sprayers have been available to the amateur. The hand-operated type is pressurized by pushing a handle up and down a number of times before use, and there are now electric rechargeable battery models with "power at the touch of a button." In the greenhouse, pesticides and fungicides are dispensed over a period in electrically heated vaporizers, or can be released from fireworklike "smoke."

WEEDS

Like pests and diseases, weeds are always with the gardener. Use of the hoe or other tool is anciently recommended, as by Columella.

> Then let the careful gardener . . . comb
> The ground with two-pronged fork, and choking weeds
> Cast from the furrows.

While the Chinese poet T'ao Ch'ien (A.D. 365–427) wrote:

> Rising early to weed out the wild and untidy;
> returning with hoe on shoulder and moon on high.

Hoes are the basic handtools for weeding, in all of their varied types. The weed hook was developed to remove weeds from standing wheat, but has been used in herbaceous borders and similar situations. Weeding tongs or pincers, and pivoting root extractors, are fairly recent inventions, although the spud – a tool with a narrow, chisellike blade for cutting weeds off – was invented by 1667, when Samuel Pepys records using one. (The word was later also applied to a digging fork with three broad prongs.) Recent too are devices like the daisy knife and the lawn weed extractor, both to be used from a comfortable standing position.

Today we destroy weeds with many kinds of chemicals, which have become amazingly selective. The first selective weedkillers were intended to destroy broad-leaved weeds in grass lawns, but farmers at any rate now posses an armory of materials that will kill one plant but leave another unscathed. There are also many "total" weedkillers to wipe out all vegetation in an area of intractable weeds, and others, like paraquat, which has been called the chemical hoe, to scorch off top growth.

The use of chemicals for control of weeds, as well as of animal pests and fungus diseases, has recently aroused violent controversy, sparked off by Rachel Carson's *Silent Spring* of 1962. Many are poisonous to man and dangerous if carelessly used, and many seriously upset the balance of nature. It is not my task to arbitrate between chemicals and "natural" methods, and here I am merely recording their arrival in historical terms; further consideration of the problem is made in the last chapter.

Pest control by chemicals is often called warfare, and I must not forget one very warlike garden weapon – the flame gun. Working on the same principle as the blowtorch, its fuel being pressurized before ignition, it delivers a searing flame which is most useful for scorching and killing germinating weeds and for destroying weed seeds in the upper layer of a seed bed.

It is clear enough that there is no easy way to garden, even in this age of mechanization and labor-saving devices. There is a great deal of work involved, from the preparation of the ground, the sowing and planting, to the end products of flower, fruit and vegetables; and throughout the gardener is beset with enemies, whether destructive pests and diseases, or the vagaries of climate and weather. These have always been, and seem likely always to continue to be, the basic ingredients of gardening, making it at once a drudgery, a challenge and a delight. This paradox was neatly expressed in 1931 by the Czech writers Karel and Josef Čapek in *The Gardener's Year*, describing a gardener after a long day's work: "After the sun has set, he sighs with deep content: 'I have sweated today.'"

Chapter Six
Advanced Cultivation

SOWING AND PLANTING, WATERING AND DRAINING, FEEDING plants and dealing with their enemies – all these mark a level of cultivation at which plants are made to give of their best. But they are still, basically, plants growing in natural ways, and giving them support, for instance, is only ensuring that the vagaries of weather do not bring the gardener's efforts to nought.

Advanced cultivation may be said to begin when plants are manipulated, and likewise propagated, in unnatural ways. What the fact says for human nature I am not quite sure, but probably the first plant to be much manipulated was the grapevine.

Wine was probably first made over ten thousand years ago, from wild grapes, and these wild plants were most likely first domesticated by Neolithic farmers somewhere in Transcaucasia, perhaps ancient Armenia, between 6000 and 4000 B.C. New forms of grape were derived from seedlings and from bud-sports (mutations) increased by cuttings, and so the wild grape was gradually superseded by improved forms. From Transcaucasia, viticulture gradually spread into Mesopotamia (where it first appears in records), to Phoenicia and Egypt (where many illustrations exist), then to Crete and Thrace, and next to Greece. From there it was only a step to its introduction in southern Italy and France – probably by the seventh century B.C. at latest. The Romans certainly brought it to northern Europe and Britain by 100 B.C.

The grapevine is an easily molded plant. In its natural state it forms a scrawny bush which throws out arching shoots in all directions. These can be cut back annually to control their spread, or they can be restricted in number and trained in various ways and to great lengths. (The Great Vine at England's Hampton Court has branches up to 110 feet long.) They are superb plants for training over simple arbors, where their dense foliage gives shade in summer, and the bunches of fruit hang down enticingly as the season progresses. The Egyptians usually trained their vines in arching, arbor fashion; by Roman times the possibilities of the plants were being exploited in numerous ways, including the pergola, circular tiers, upright and prostrate bushes. These techniques were handed down in post-Roman times, and we find many medieval depictions of

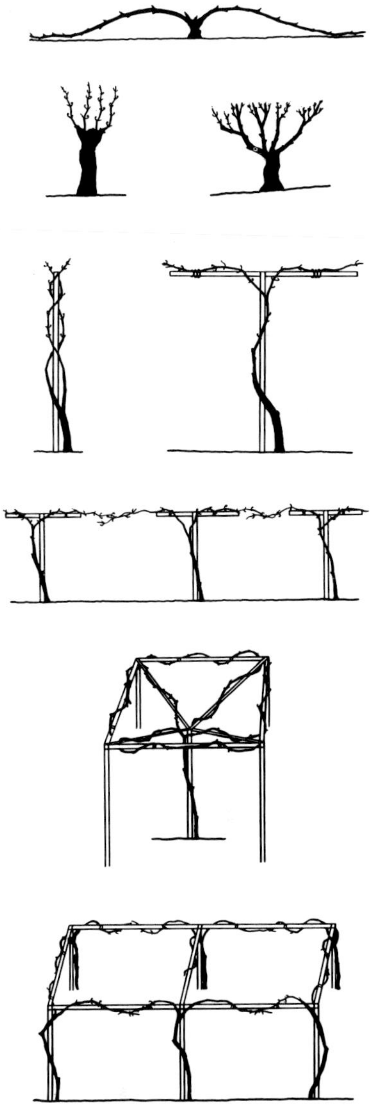

vines trained on arbors or pergolas, and also up mulberry trees, between which horizontal supports were fixed – the latter forming the pattern for a method recommended in a manual published in North America as late as 1826.

The Romans grew other fruits besides the grape – olives, figs, apples, pears and nuts among them. But these seem always to have been grown naturally, as orthodox trees or bushes.

Pruning was, however, carefully carried out. As Theophrastus says, "All trees require pruning; for they are improved by removal of the dead wood." He goes on to quote Androtion, who recommended hard pruning of myrtles, pomegranates and olives, and especially of vines "for promoting both growth and fruitfulness." When it comes to roses, Theophrastus recommends pruning by burning, "for, if left to itself, it grows luxuriantly and makes too much wood."

The main instrument of pruning devised by the Romans was the *falx vinitoria* – as its name suggests, initially for vine culture – derived from the billhook. The plain billhook, *falx arboraria* – a long curved blade with only one cutting edge – was used for lopping branches. But the vine dresser's hook or knife, which Columella describes, was designed to deal with several different tasks. Besides the billhook's long sharp edge and recurved "beak," it had a fine edge for paring and smoothing (*scalprum*), a pointed projection for hollowing or gouging (*mucro*), and a miniature ax blade at the back of the main blade for making straight, defined cuts as in grafting (*securis*). This design, which reappears time and again in sixteenth

TOP LEFT: *In this Roman-occupied farmstead in North Africa, grapes are grown on tiered frames, interspersed with olive trees.*

ABOVE: *The Romans had many ways of training the vine; these were drawn by K. D. White following descriptions of Roman authorities, supplemented by monumental evidence and that of methods still in use.*

The elements of vine pruning depicted in a medieval manuscript (above) and of a trellis-trained vine in a book of the same era (right).

The pergola method of vine training shown in this Renaissance fresco always remained popular.

and seventeenth century manuals of pruning and grafting, in fact remained in use until about a century ago, when the *falx* was replaced by the secateur.

Early pruning operators had a wide range of tools to choose from, including knives, saws and various chisels which were primarily used in grafting (as described later). These gradually became more refined and fewer in number, with more emphasis on knives, and eventually on various kinds of secateur.

Rather curiously, considering the expertise they left behind them at home, the early American settlers hardly ever pruned their fruit trees; in fact, they gave their orchards little care in general, often running pigs or cattle under them to clear the weeds, just lopping the branches so that the fruit was kept out of reach of such livestock. It was not until the early nineteenth century that the widespread belief that pruning was actually harmful began to be reversed.

It seems not to have been until the seventeenth century that any effort was made to take advantage of the plasticity of most fruit trees – if not as straightforward as the grape, certainly as full of possibilities.

FRUIT TRAINING

The earliest methods of training seem simply to have been to grow fruit trees in a single vertical plane – partly, perhaps, for a tidy effect, but also because, if the vertical surface is a south-facing brick wall, it provides shelter and absorbs warmth, some of which is given out at night, so that tender fruit has a much better chance of ripening than if grown on trees in the open. In 1618 William Lawson, a Yorkshire gardener, could write

This primitive pergola in modern Athens will be covered by the vine by the time summer comes, to give welcome shade and later fruit. Note the numerous plants, many of them grown in metal cans.

that the cold climate "provoketh most of our arborists to plant apricocks, cherries and peaches, by a wall, and with tacks and other means to spread them upon, and fasten them to a wall, to have the benefit of the immoderate reflex of the sun, which is commendable for the having of fair, good and soon ripe fruit."

This use of walls must have led to some regularity in training, but it was probably the eighteenth-century desire for maximum formality which led to the regimentation of fruit trees into strict patterns – the fan, the horizontal-tiered espalier, the fuseau and other pyramidal forms, the vase or goblet, the palmette with straight branches upright, horizontal, or crisscross, and so many more. All of these call for a training structure which could be a wall or a series of wires or wooden horizontals between posts. (The word "espalier," which Aldous Huxley once referred to as "crucified fruits," originally referred to this method rather than to the trained tree.) A few called for horizontal structures like open tables, and the spiral – a direct descendant of a Roman vine method – required vertical poles. With careful pruning on the spur system (by which all growth is channeled into bunches of short growths, never allowed to grow more than a few inches during a season and then cut back), virtually any area of wall can be filled, given time and patience.

By the nineteenth century, training fruit trees became a positive obsession. Terracing was used to give wall-trained trees maximum

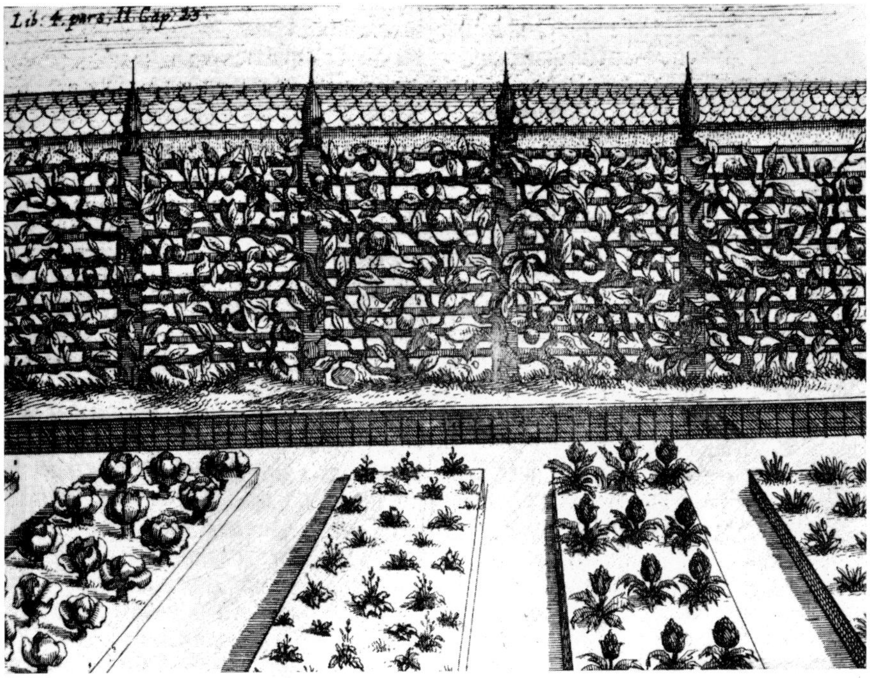

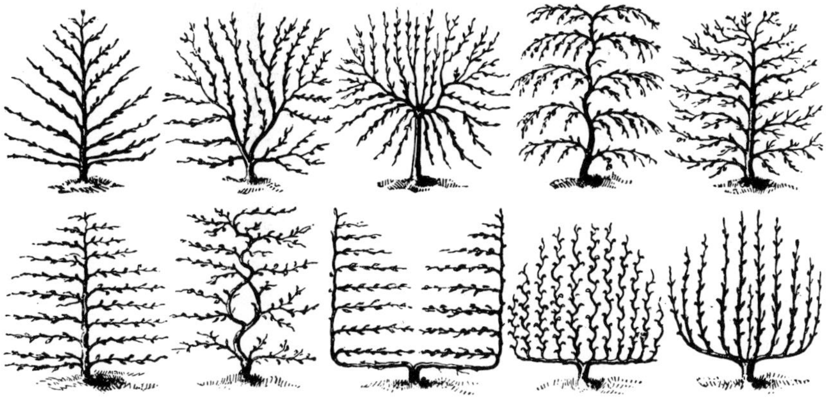

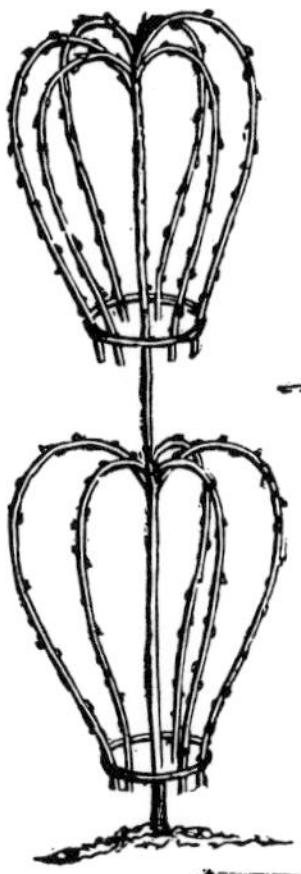

TOP LEFT: *Fruit trees grown on a neat wooden framework against a warm wall in 1706; they have been trained more or less obliquely like the modern single-stemmed cordon.* CENTER AND BOTTOM LEFT: *The amazing plasticity of fruit trees carefully pruned and trained is shown in these Victorian sketches.* ABOVE LEFT: *"Double quenouille" training for fruit trees, one of many decorative methods.* ABOVE RIGHT: *Metal "tables" for horizontal tree training.*

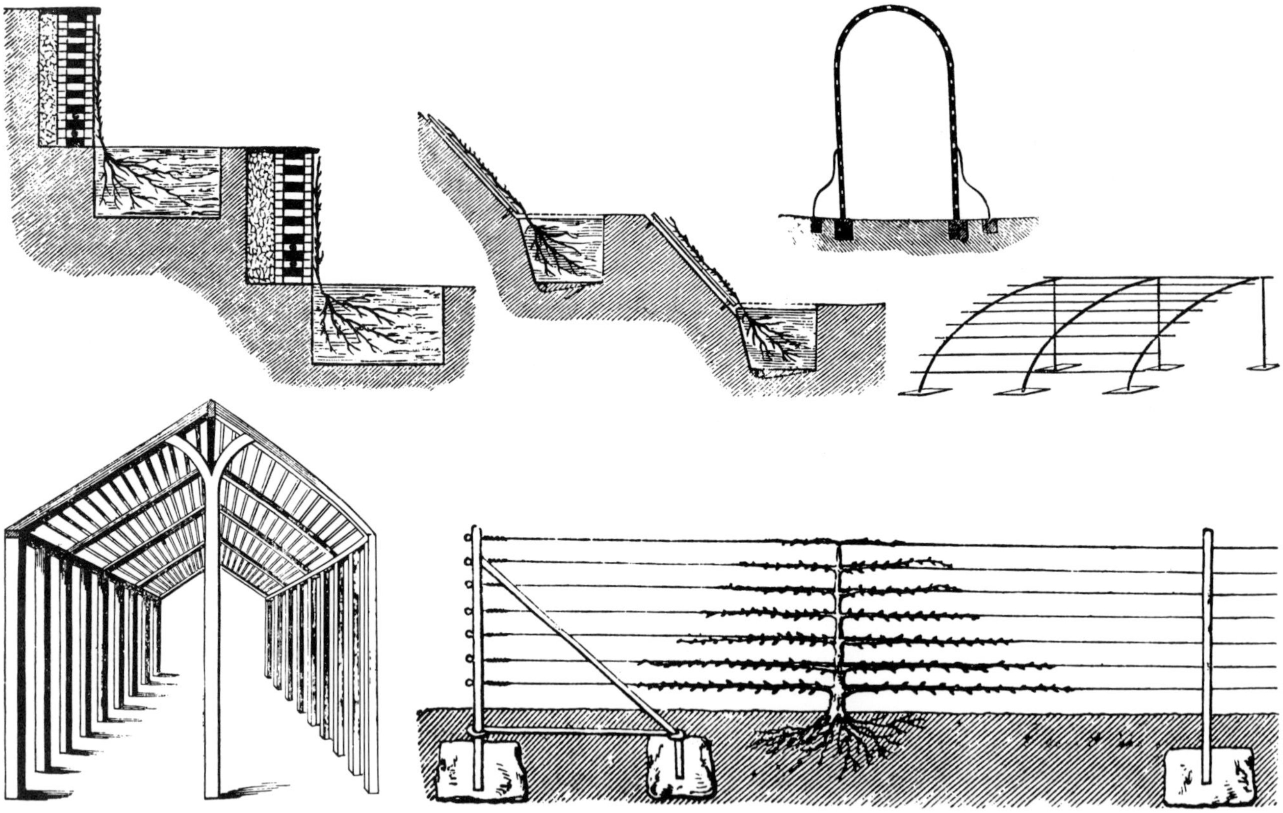

ABOVE: *Further nineteenth-century ideas for fruit tree training: those on terraces receive maximum sun and warmth; the metal and wooden frames ensure both good light and free circulation of air. Metal post and wire structures made neat training much easier as in the espalier shown (lower right).*

sunlight and root room – not only vertical-walled terraces but sloping-walled ones, where the fruit trees were spread-eagled at an angle where they received the sun's rays most directly. Elaborate wire structures and wooden ones like open barns were also erected. Serpentine or "crinkle-crankle" walls were often built, forming a series of warm embrasures even more sheltered from wind than a flat wall. Such embrasures were not new; they were certainly in occasional use in the seventeenth century, and Sir Hugh Plat, in 1594, had made the suggestion – possibly never put into practice – of lining such walls with lead or tin which would reflect additional light.

Training fruit trees implies pruning implements. From the seventeenth until the nineteenth century, most detailed pruning was done by knife. The orthodox pruning knife which gradually evolved still has a characteristic more or less curved blade. But in the nineteenth century scissor-action tools came into being. Some were merely for lopping, and many of these were fixed on long handles and operated by various remote-control mechanisms. Detailed pruning was carried out with secateurs held in the hand, although some experts today still favor the pruning knife, which needs much precision in its handling, not least because it is, or ought to be, razor-sharp.

As with most tools, the variety of different pruning instruments has diminished since the nineteenth century, but the principles remain the same. In the United States, a particularly ingenious and handy tool combines a long-handled remote-control pruner with a small curved saw.

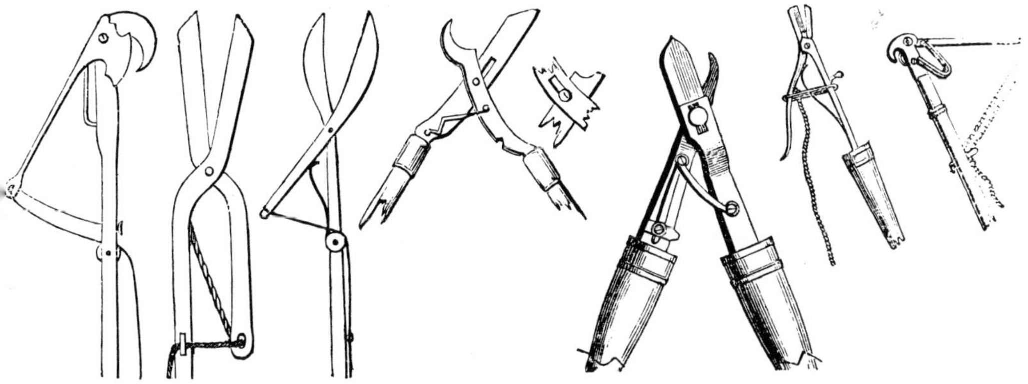

ABOVE: *Nineteenth-century pruning implements include several remotely controlled tree pruners or "averruncators" and (center) two heavy-duty loppers.*

BELOW: *Pruning knives are little changed since early days, but the modern French version is ingenious – it fits over a finger, leaving the hands free for other jobs as well. Nineteenth-century secateurs operated on exactly the same principle as those of today, even if many have now become sleek and streamlined. One modern development, however, has been the development of the "anvil" secateur (bottom right) in which a cutting blade bears down on a flat surface.*

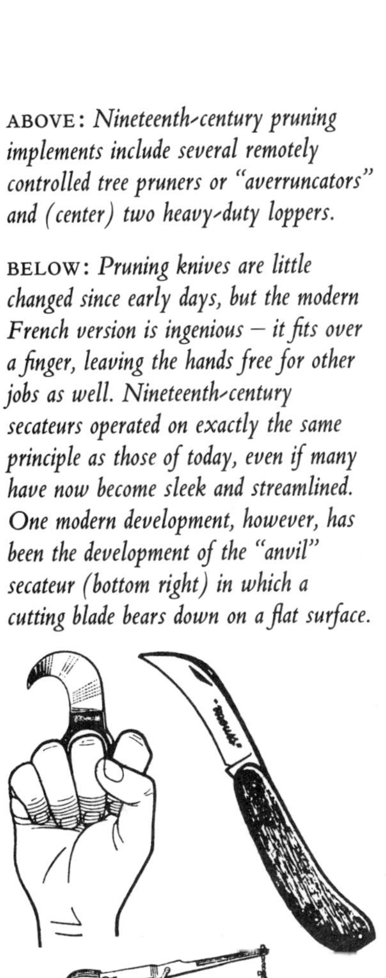

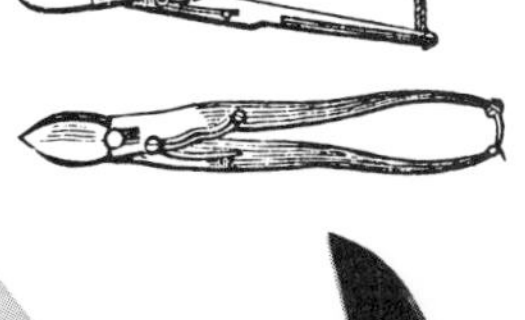

In discussing the historical training of ornamental plants, one should remember that medieval gardeners seem to have enjoyed unexpected corners and secret places in gardens, perhaps because the whole was so shut in by defensive walls. They often had gallery walks around a central courtyard or rectangular garden, they made arched tunnels or rectangular pergolas, and they created arbors. These, like garden houses, were often at a distance from the house "for the more remote it is from your House, the more private will you be from the frequent disturbances of your Family or Acquaintance." All of these had a wooden structure, sometimes of trellis (carpenter's work, as Bacon called it), on which plants would be allowed to grow. At this point pleasure and utility gardening meet, because many of the galleries and arbors were covered with grapevines. However, any suitable plant was used, and sometimes, judging by a list made in 1752, rather unsuitable ones as well: "Jesamin, Rosemarie, Boxe, Juniper, Cyper Trees [cypresses], Savin [prostrate juniper], Cedars, Rose-trees . . . ."

The confusion one may experience in older literature between arbors and bowers is clarified in Richard Bradley's *Family Dictionary* of 1727: "Care must be had that you do not confound the Word Bower with Arbour; because the first is always built long and arch'd, whereas the second is either round or square at Bottom, and has a sort of Dome or Ceiling at the Top." At any rate arbors or bowers, in the sense of a self-contained structure, predominated in the thirteenth century; in *The Floure and the Leafe* we read, "And shaping was this herber, rofe and all, as is a pretty parlour." However, as time went on, it was the gallery and tunnel that developed. Not only were these built around gardens, but sometimes either across them or in the form of a decorative pattern. In some extraordinary instances, a whole series of galleries would be made side by side, reminding one of the arrangements of a wasp's nest. At the Château de Liancourt in France, there were three separate sets of seven, thirteen and another seven galleries all pointing in the same direction. It must have been a curious, not to say an eerie, place.

Galleries around a garden would often be entirely open on the inner side, thus resembling monastery cloisters. More fanciful tunnels

Climbing plants – probably vines – are being trained up this "wall-herber" of 1577 by twining them around the supports.

might have windows in them at intervals.

Obviously the precision of an ornamental gallery meant that it had to be trimmed if it was to remain in keeping with its formal layout, and this is the point at which training and topiary merge. To form a dense gallery, which might in fact not need a support at all, one resorted to pleaching or "plashing," a word derived from the French for braiding or interweaving. The plants needed for pleaching were trees of various sorts, among them notably lime, hornbeam and wych elm, but including willows, cornel (*Cornus mas*, seldom seen today), privet, whitethorn and sycomore, which reacted to a kind of spur pruning very like that carried out on fruit trees rather later. Branches were trained on wire or wooden structures, or bound together, and every year heavy pruning was carried out, so that only the skeleton of the tree, as it were, was left, aligned in the direction the gallery was to take. When eventually the skeleton was massive enough, the annual young growth could simply be trimmed, both outside and inside, to form an ever-denser network of twigs.

Such pleached galleries later became known as alleys or covert walks, and sometimes ended up as a heavily clipped upper story only, with the trunks of the trees supporting the twiggy growth like so many pillars. (An example can be seen today at Hidcote Manor in Gloucestershire, England.) But most of the earlier ones seem to have been made as arched tunnels. The Victorians were fond of alleys and especially of bowers. Many were made of yew or similar evergreen trees, and others of ivy trained over a framework.

TOPIARY

As I have earlier mentioned, the Roman word *topiarius* was applied to the general gardener; but one of his main tasks, as Cicero explains, was to train ivy over walls, trees and terraces. It was not until the first century A.D. that topiary in its modern sense was created. Pliny the Elder (23–79) writes of the use of the so-called Mediterranean cypress (*Cupressus sempervirens*) for trimmed hedges and topiary work, stating that Caius Martius invented *romora tonsilis*, or clipped arbors. Box followed cypress as a prime topiary material in Italy, as Pliny's nephew, Pliny the

Highly mannered galleries of hornbeam form one tunnel around the garden and another in serpentine form, with look-out windows within. Note the seats in the center, each with its separate shelter of hornbeam. This is a French design of the late sixteenth century. A very similar layout, apparently modeled on this design, existed at Elvaston Castle, near Derby, England, as late as 1881.

Younger (62–110), makes clear in a letter describing the garden of his Tuscan villa. From an upper terrace "you descend by an easy slope, adorned with the representation of divers animals in box . . . into a lawn . . . this is surrounded by a walk enclosed with tonsile evergreens shaped into a variety of forms. Beyond it is the gestatio, laid out in the form of a circus, ornamented in the middle with box cut in numberless different figures, together with a plantation of shrubs, prevented by shears from shooting up too high."

After the Dark Ages, Europe returned to topiary through hedges and galleries rather than anything very fanciful. One special form of clipping trees recurs in illustrations – that of making tiers. The device of a metal or wooden pole supporting flat, circular wire baskets almost like trays was popular; the trays would support pots containing flowers in season. These *estrades*, as they were known, may have derived from the symbolism of the May tree; sometimes colorful balls were suspended from them in imitation of fruit. Trees were very often clipped in this way, the

In the estrade, one of the few formal methods of training trees in the Middle Ages, growth is restricted to circular, well-spaced tiers. The fifteenth-century Dutch example, above right, is on a roof garden. Note the accompanying creeper-clad pergolas.

circular, well-spaced tiers sometimes being provided with a metal training hoop presumably attached in some way to the trunk.

By the end of the fifteenth century, advanced topiary was being created in Italy. Box trees in Florence – presumably in Medici gardens – are recorded as being shaped as "spheres, ships, porticos, temples, vases and urns"; the writer goes on to say that "on all sides one sees giants, men, women, animals, apes, donkeys, oxen, a bear and a boat, dauphin, combatants, a harpy, philosophers, Pope, Cardinals and other fancies." During the reign of Henry VIII of England, similar "anticke" work was carried out at Hampton Court, and the author of a book of 1659 writes of such topiary: "About fifty years ago Ingenuities first began to flourish in England." Cypress was first used for such, arising from Italian example, but it proved not fully hardy in the British climate. John Evelyn, writing in 1662, claims to have been the first to bring yew into fashion "as a succedaneum for cypress, whether in hedges, or pyramids, conic-spires, bowls, or what other shapes, adorning the parks or other avenues with their lofty tops thirty foot high, and braving all the efforts of the most rigid weather, which cypress cannot weather."

Hedge and avenue maintenance in the eighteenth century. TOP: *A movable platform for tall hedges.* ABOVE: *Long shears in use.* LEFT: *An immensely tall ladder platform for large trees; note that the pruners are using long-handled sicklelike tools.*

Pleaching could form a solid screen, tunnel, or give a more mannered effect as do the clipped hornbeams forming a "stilt hedge" at Hidcote Manor, Gloucestershire, England – a modern garden but here following the Tudor tradition.

Such "ingenuities" seem often to have been rather restless in character: we read of them made "to the shape of men armed in the field ready to give battle: or swift running greyhounds: or of well scented and true running hounds, to chase the deere, or hunt the hare. This kinde of hunting shall not waste your corne nor much your coyne."

Little is written about the constant trimming which such creations must have needed to keep them shapely, let alone to create. Clipping seems to have been done originally with very sharp but small knives, and must have been very hard work. However, by 1606 *The Countrey Farme* could state – of clipping hedges and knots – "To cut the Border, whether it be of Lavender, Rosemarie, or Boxe, you must use the ordinarie sheeres, which have handles of wood. To cut other smaller and lesse hearbes, you must have sheeres like those which Taylors use." This seems to be the first reference to wood-handled shears with two separate blades. Those "which Taylors use" must have been versions of cloth-napping or sheep-shearing clippers, both of which the Romans invented. The latter, still in use today, have narrowly triangular blades in one piece with a rounded spring.

A small round-bladed sickle was in use on hedges in the eighteenth century, perhaps mainly for finishing off. In modern times, the electric hedgetrimmer has made it possible to maintain hedges and topiary in the face of grave shortages of labor.

For the immensely tall hedges of the most extravagant gardens of

These limes, shown after winter pruning, form a solid screen when in full summer leaf – one might call this modern example "free-style" pleaching.

the eighteenth century, wheeled platforms with ladder ends were used; although usually ten or fifteen feet high, these were sometimes as tall as a two-story house.

By the early eighteenth century, there were several nurseries in Britain which specialized in producing already formed topiary specimens in containers, and some of their original creations are almost certainly still to be seen at Levens Hall, Cumbria, which is one of the oldest surviving topiary gardens in England.

Although it departs from my theme of techniques, the rise and fall of topiary is an entertaining story. Francis Bacon was one of the first to express his dislike of it: "I doe not like Images Cut out in Juniper or other Garden stuffes: They be for Children. Little low Hedges, Round, like Welts, with some Pretty Pyramides, I like well."

In 1712 Joseph Addison was complaining that British gardeners "instead of humouring Nature, love to deviate from it as much as possible. Our Trees rise in Cones, Globes and Pyramids. We see the marks of the Scissars upon every Plant and Bush." Alexander Pope's "laughable catalogue of greens to be disposed of by an eminent town gardener," written for *The Guardian* in 1713, is certainly worth quoting:

> Adam and Eve in Yew; Adam a little shatter'd by the fall of the tree of Knowledge in the Great Storm. Eve and the Serpent very

Two kinds of arbor are shown in this early eighteenth-century engraving – a vine pergola to shelter the water trough and a more intimate structure, apparently built around a central tree, among the knot beds.

A late Victorian arbor made from ivy trained over a metal framework.

> flourishing. The Tower of Babel not yet finished. St George in Box: his Arm scarce long enough, but will be in a condition to stick the Dragon by next April. A Green Dragon of the same, with a Tail of Ground Ivy for the present. N.B. These two not to be sold separately. Edward the Black Prince in Cypress. A Laurustine Bear in Blossom, with a Juniper Hunter in Berries. A pair of Giants, stunted, to be sold cheap. A Queen Elizabeth in Phylyraea [*Phyllyrea*] a little inclining to the green-sickness, but full of growth. Another Queen Elizabeth in Myrtle, which was very forward, but miscarried by being too near a Savine. [A drug obtained from the Savin juniper was supposed to produce abortions.] An old Maid of Honour in Wormwood. A topping Ben Jonson in Laurel. Divers eminent Modern Poets in Bay, somewhat blighted, to be disposed of, a pennyworth. A quickset Hog, shot up into a Porcupine, by being forgot a week in rainy Weather. A Lavender Pigg with Sage growing in his Belly. Noah's ark in Holly; standing on the Mount; the ribs a little damaged for want of Water. A pair of Maidenheads in Firr, in great forwardness.

The landscape garden fashion destroyed almost all the topiary in Britain, although much persisted in France and Italy. Today several notable examples remain, although shortage of labor makes their upkeep difficult. Some of the world's most striking examples are exotic, like the extraordinary sculptured trees at the cemetery of Tulcan in northern Ecuador; based partly on pre-Columbian forms, they are especially remarkable for their amount of relief work.

In the United States, there has been rather less opportunity for topiary because the best materials, yew and box, are not hardy in many northern areas. There are, however, some fine examples, of which the most remarkable technically may well be those at Disneyland. The finest large-scale display is perhaps at the Ladew Topiary Gardens in Maryland, where formal and naturalistic figures are grouped in a number of separate enclosures. The most amusing, if not the grandest, are fox and hounds running across a lawn in a whimsical "pursuit." But what they lack in topiary the Americans have made up for in training trees. Apart from trained fruit trees in espalier and many other forms, examples can be found of forsythia, pyracantha, and even of magnolias trained either as espaliers or in more complex regular patterns. One particular American forte is the use of ivy trained on wires or trellises and trimmed to form narrow "ropes" in crisscross or more complex patterns.

PROPAGATION: CUTTINGS

Seeds are one method of increasing plants – quick and valuable, especially for annuals. But they give variable results in many cases, or they may take a long time to produce worthwhile plants, especially with shrubs and trees. To reproduce these the gardener uses various vegetative methods.

ABOVE: *Perfectly clipped geometric topiary specimens at Augsburg, Germany, in the late seventeenth century, are being enhanced for the summer by orange trees in tubs newly taken out of their winter shelter.*

RIGHT: *The only way we can keep up with extensive hedges in present labor-short times is to use powered hedge-trimmers.*

The most ancient method of vegetative increase is by cuttings – a part of the plant, typically a fairly young shoot, which is pulled or cut off and, being pushed into the ground, takes root. Knowledge of this capacity is probably almost as old as civilization itself and, as with elaboration of training methods, was possibly first practiced extensively with the vine. This we can deduce from the enormous number of varieties which are far more likely to have arisen as bud-sports (mutations), to which the vine is prone, than as hybrid seedlings – if only because there was originally nothing to hybridize with. It may well have seemed natural to primitive farmers that a twig from a living plant would take root and grow; tropical peoples must certainly have found this to happen with many species, and others may have discovered the principle when they took, say, willow

TOP LEFT: *Highly elaborate topiary at Hesse, Germany, in 1631. The varied, complicated knot beds – some of them depicting coats of arms by the use of a variety of contrasting plants – are each bounded by hedges with an outer paling.*

LEFT: *Much of the topiary at Levens Halls, Westmorland, England, quite possibly dates back to Jacobean times. The specimens are in both box and yew, including golden varieties which add contrast to this almost surrealist fantasy.*

ABOVE: *The twentieth-century examples of Longwood Gardens, Pennsylvania, are by contrast almost conventional.*

RIGHT: *These forbidding monsters used to guard the entrance to the gardens of Knightshaves Court, Devon, England. Sadly, economic problems have swept them away.*

ABOVE: *Two diagrammatic examples of hedge clipping machinery adjustable for variously shaped hedges (American, late nineteenth century).*

RIGHT: *Ivy trained and trimmed into narrow "ropes" to form a trellis pattern in a California garden.*

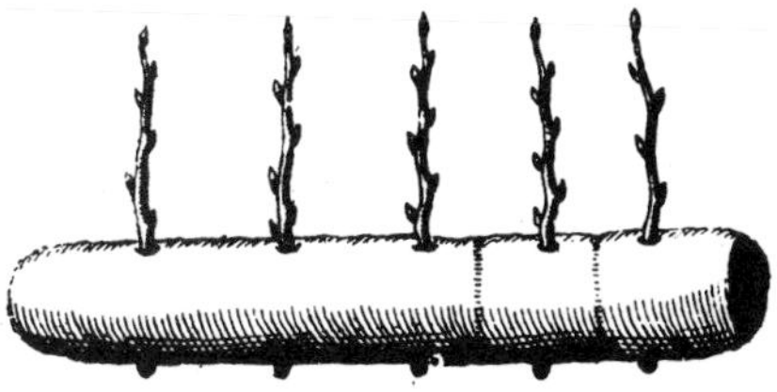

branches and stuck them in the soil to make a fence – which by the next season would have started growing. At any rate, the vine grows very easily from cuttings.

Hippocratic work of around 380 B.C. compares the growth of plants from cuttings and from seeds, and Aristotle mentions different methods of growth. Theophrastus provides the earliest detailed written record of taking cuttings. He mentions growing cabbage from "a piece torn off . . . which has root attached to it," and advocates wherever possible the use of such "Irishman's cuttings," although he realizes that this is not always feasible. If not, shoots for cuttings should be taken low down on the tree rather than high up. He mentions olive, pear, apple and fig as being habitually increased from "slips," as the translator calls them. The easiest to root was the fig, where it was possible "to sharpen a stout shoot and drive it with a hammer, till only a small piece of it is left above ground, then piling sand above so as to earth it up." He also remarks that "the fig progresses more quickly and is less eaten by grubs, if the cutting is set in a squill bulb" (this refers to the huge juicy bulbs of the sea squill, *Urginea maritima*). This method has a late seventeenth-century echo in the practice of making holes, exactly to the diameter of each cutting, in a large willow branch, and pushing the cuttings into them. After the cuttings produced roots, the willow branch was cut into segments. This was supposed to stop decay in the cuttings.

The simplest method of increasing plants (apart from by seeds) is by cuttings. TOP LEFT: *Many trees will root from shoots prepared as simply as this medieval example.* TOP: *An old method of rooting cuttings involved boring holes into a branch of willow or something similar and burying this in the soil.* ABOVE: *More sophisticated methods of Victorian times were rooting cuttings in soil placed between two pots which can be covered with a bell glass to prevent loss of water due to transpiration; watering is carried out through the center pot.*

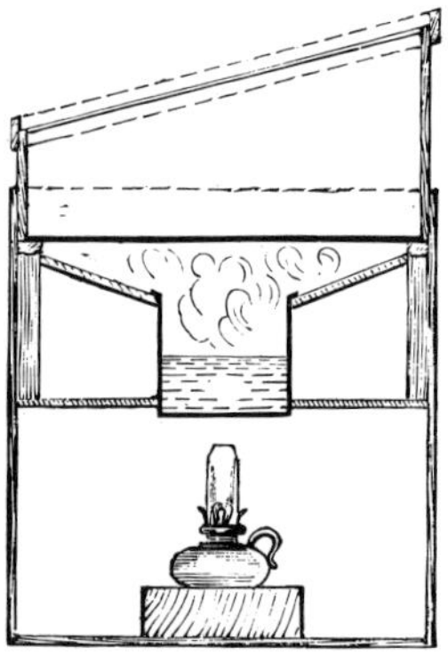

TOP RIGHT: *"The Manner of Cultivating exotic Trees and Shrubs, by cutting their Roots to pieces," from Agricola, 1721. This was mainly applied to citrus trees, which are seen taken out of their boxes at right. In the foreground, the roots are hacked off, and on the table the cuttings are being prepared, a process which includes dipping them into "the noble Mummy," a kind of grafting wax. Behind, roots have been planted in beds and, when shoots appear, in pots.*

Propagating cases were widely used from late Victorian times. TOP: *A small oil lamp heats a reservoir of water to produce steam below the bed for rooting cuttings.* ABOVE: *The "Gardener's Friend" (sectioned center) simply produces warm air directly below the bed which is supported on a strong platform.*

Cuttings without roots, Theophrastus recommends, should be split at the lower end and planted with a stone on top and, where weak shoots are involved, a hole should first be made in the soil with a wooden peg. He also notes that date palms can be propagated by cutting off the top and setting it in moist soil, although the usual method was by seeds – four bound together whose shoots "combine to make a single stem."

Roman instructions for taking cuttings are, as usual, very exact – length and number of "eyes" are specified, and ox dung is recommended for dipping the cut end into, rather as today we use hormone rooting powder. Did this, one wonders, really have any effect?

The Romans mention growing thistlelike plants (possibly acanthus) from roots, but it is not until the end of the seventeenth century that taking root cuttings is shown to be a habitual part of horticultural practice; it was used especially on the citrus trees so popular at that time. The roots were reduced to finger-length, the ends being carefully pared and dipped in "noble Mummy." This was one equivalent of grafting wax, and many complex recipes for making it are given by Agricola and his English translator Bradley (1721). They write: "Formerly I made use of Gum-Copal, but as that is very dear at present, one may employ in its stead the best Virgin-Pitch and a little white Wax; if one mixes a little Aloes amongst it, it will be so much the better, and will be a Preservative against Vermine." After dipping, the root cuttings were put into water so that they would harden and cool.

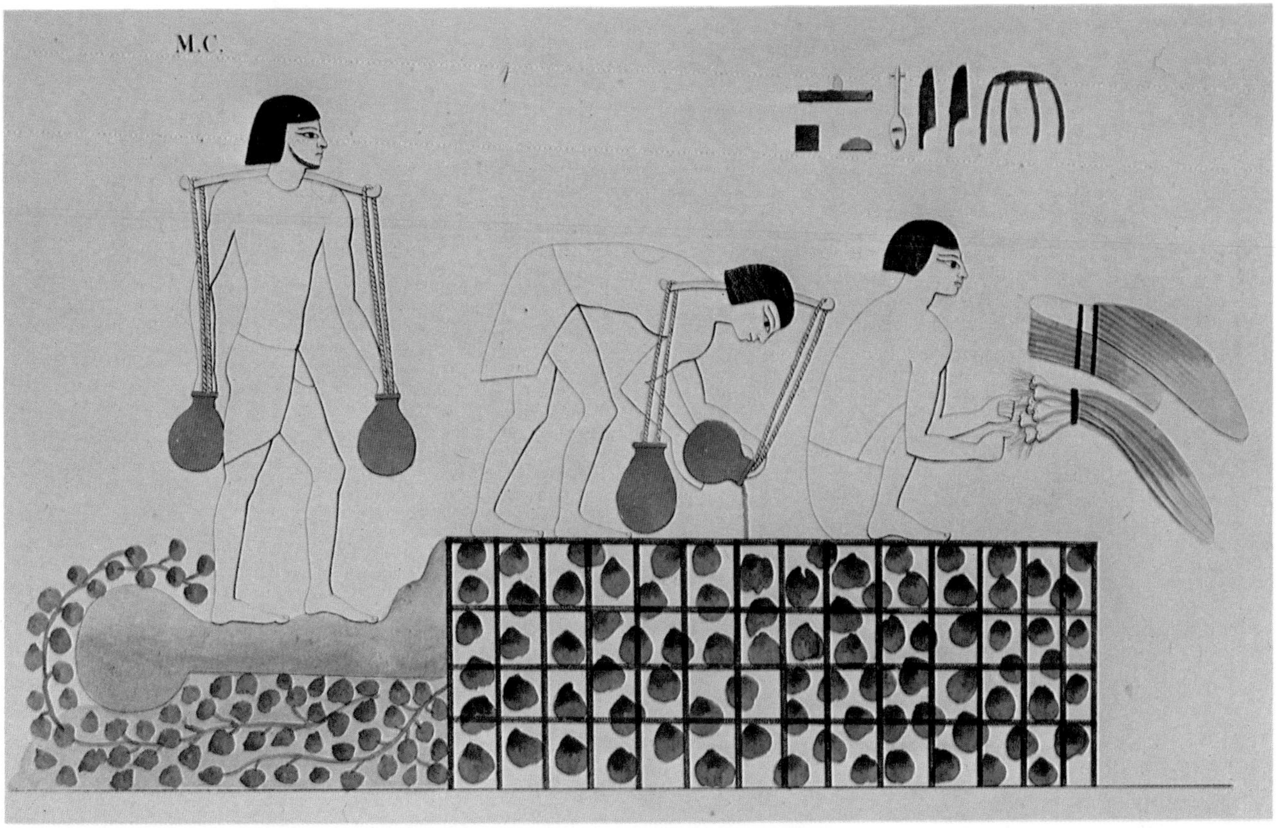

ABOVE: *An Egyptian vegetable plot of about 1900 B.C. Gardeners carry yoked water pots to pour into runnels which crisscross the plot. The man at right is tying vegetables – probably onions – into bundles.*

LEFT: *An almost schematic painting, also from 1900 B.C., of a* shaduf *or swipe, in which the bucket of water is balanced by the counterweight.*

Examples of Eastern irrigation systems, from India (left) and Persia, both showing the typical bucket-wheel for raising water from a well into channels. The Indian example is operated by bullocks going around in a circle, turning a huge wooden cog and ratchet; the human operator sits on the radial arm. The Persian model is altogether more primitive, and may even have been turned by a man.

戽斗

高轉筒車

轆轤
卷七

The need to water paddy fields gave rise to many irrigation devices in China, of which the simplest was the two-handled bailer, probably of finely woven cane (far left). A waterwheel operates the endless bucket-and-cord system (center left), but the device (near left) in which water is forced up an incline by an endless series of wooden paddles in a trough is treadwheel-operated.

BELOW LEFT: *A Chinese well-windlass with a rather clumsy counter-weighted mechanism delivers water into a network of regular channels.*
BELOW: *The Chinese equivalent of the* shaduf, *operating from a well.*
(All these illustrations are from a Chinese horticultural encyclopaedia reprinted in 1639.)

OPPOSITE: *The limited capacity of their watering pots must have kept these Chinese ladies busy. The peony plants are overshadowed by one of those huge naturally sculptured rocks to which Chinese gardeners were so devoted, and are enclosed by a low decorated edging. This is a detail from an eighteenth-century painting called* Spring Morning in the Han Palace.

BELOW: *The Egyptians early discovered how easily the grapevine was trained and often grew it as an arbor or pergola. At left, the grapes are being trodden in time-honored fashion. (About 1900 B.C.)*

BOTTOM: *Another Egyptian painting (before 2000 B.C.) shows fruits being picked from plants trained in a rounded arbor. Though often referred to as grapes, they look more like some kind of gourd or cucumber.*

Some of the most elaborately executed topiary to be found today is located, improbably enough, in the cemetery of Tulcan, the northern frontier town of Ecuador. Part of the layout (top left) is geometrical, but much is sculptural or in deep relief. The topiary trees are Arizona cypress.

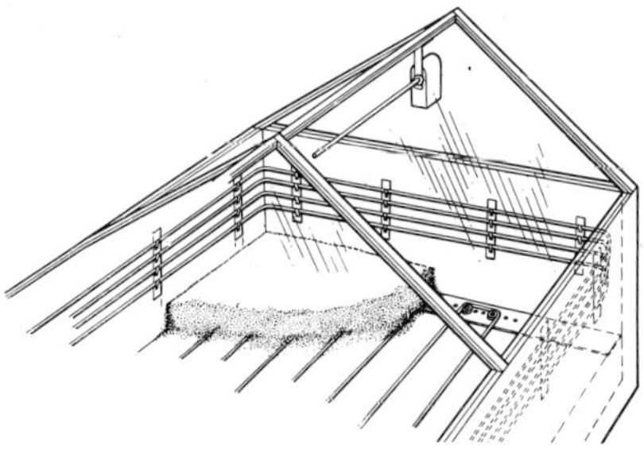

Modern propagators are sophisticated structures with undersoil and air heating and a thermostat to control the temperature. The principle of using heating wires is clearly shown in the diagram.

When clay flower pots came into general use, cuttings would be inserted in these as well as in the open ground. Gradually more refinement entered this method of propagation; the Victorians invented a method of using a smaller pot inside a bigger one, the space between being filled with rooting compost, and the inner pot being used for watering. It was the Victorians too who seem first to have employed bell glasses to produce a moist atmosphere over the cuttings and so reduce their water loss due to transpiration. They also discovered that "bottom heat" was often advantageous for speedy rooting – especially of the many tropical plants which were imported in large numbers in that period – and they devised propagating cases with clear glass lids, heated from a small kerosene or paraffin lamp, either producing direct warm air or heating a reservoir of water which would produce steam.

Today propagating cases are familiar and often sophisticated, although the old bell-glass principle is still widely used, even if the materials are frequently plastics. The more elaborate propagators, whether made at home or bought fully equipped, may have both bottom and air heating, provided by heating cables; these are ideally of low voltage so that the risk of shock to the gardener is obviated. The bottom-heat cables are usually buried under a layer of fine sand, into which cuttings may be pushed directly for rooting, or onto which pots may be placed. The latest models have the heating elements embedded in a plastic base, and it is also possible to obtain flat trays heated in this way.

The closed, very humid propagator is already well on the way to making it possible to root a wide range of plant material, but a modern invention allows propagation to be carried out in an open greenhouse bench and seems to be even more successful. This is the "mist" method: nozzles, designed to produce a very fine spray, are placed at intervals about one foot above the sand level, and are triggered to give a short burst of mist at intervals. Although mechanical methods are used to time the operation,

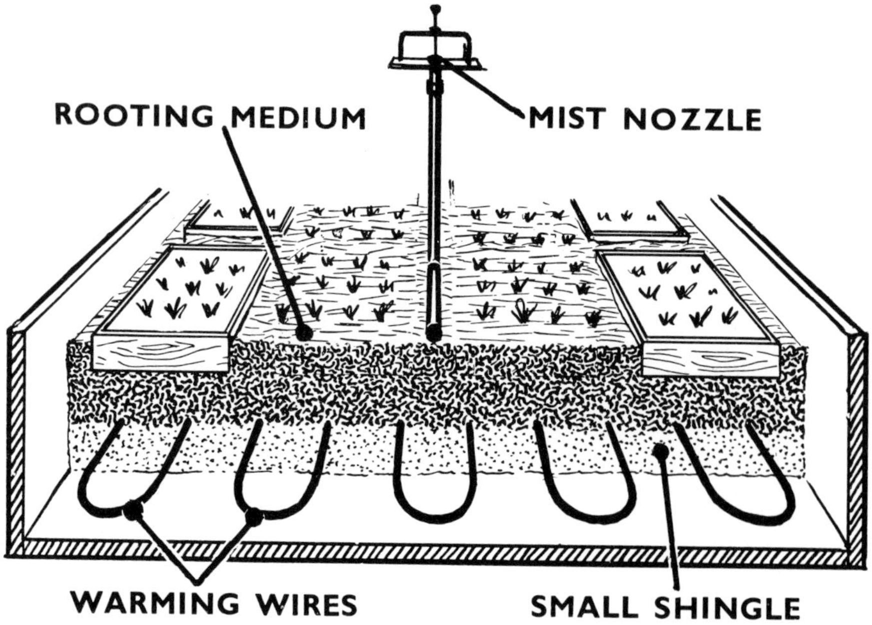

ABOVE: *A mist nozzle in a propagating house with the controlling electronic leaf below it.*

RIGHT: *A diagram of a mist-propagating unit with a nozzle fed from a central water pipe, and soil-warming wires below.*

the most ingenious way, which also reflects most exactly the requirements of the cuttings, is to use an electronic leaf. This carries two electrodes a centimeter or so apart; as long as the gap between them is bridged by water, a solenoid-operated valve keeps the water supply shut off. When evaporation breaks the contact, the valve allows the mist to operate. An equivalent device is an absorbent pad on a balance arm which fills up with water when the spray is on. The increased weight of the pad tips the arm, breaks an electric contact, and turns off the spray. As water evaporates, the pad becomes lighter, and finally the contacts are reconnected to allow the spray to operate again.

LAYERING

Another very basic method of propagation is by layering, in which a shoot from the parent plant is bent down and fixed into the soil in some way, or – especially with low-growing, many-branched plants – soil is heaped over the lower part of the growth. Many plants will put forth roots in the buried area without further ado; some will do so more readily if they are twisted, sharply kinked, or cut open in the part to be buried. Once well rooted, the layer can be cut away and planted elsewhere. Many plants which will not root easily from cuttings do so from layers, the great advantage of which is that rooting occurs while the shoot concerned is still attached to, and being nourished by, the parent plant.

Once again it is the vine about which most is written in Roman times, because it lends itself well to layering. Columella describes three methods of layering – "one in which a rod sprung from the mother vine is planted in a furrow, a second in which the mother vine itself is laid down flat and distributed branch by branch over a number of props, and a third in which the vine is cleft into two or three parts according to the number of different rows over which it has to be trained." (The last method was slow and only recommended in problem cases.) For all three methods, he gives

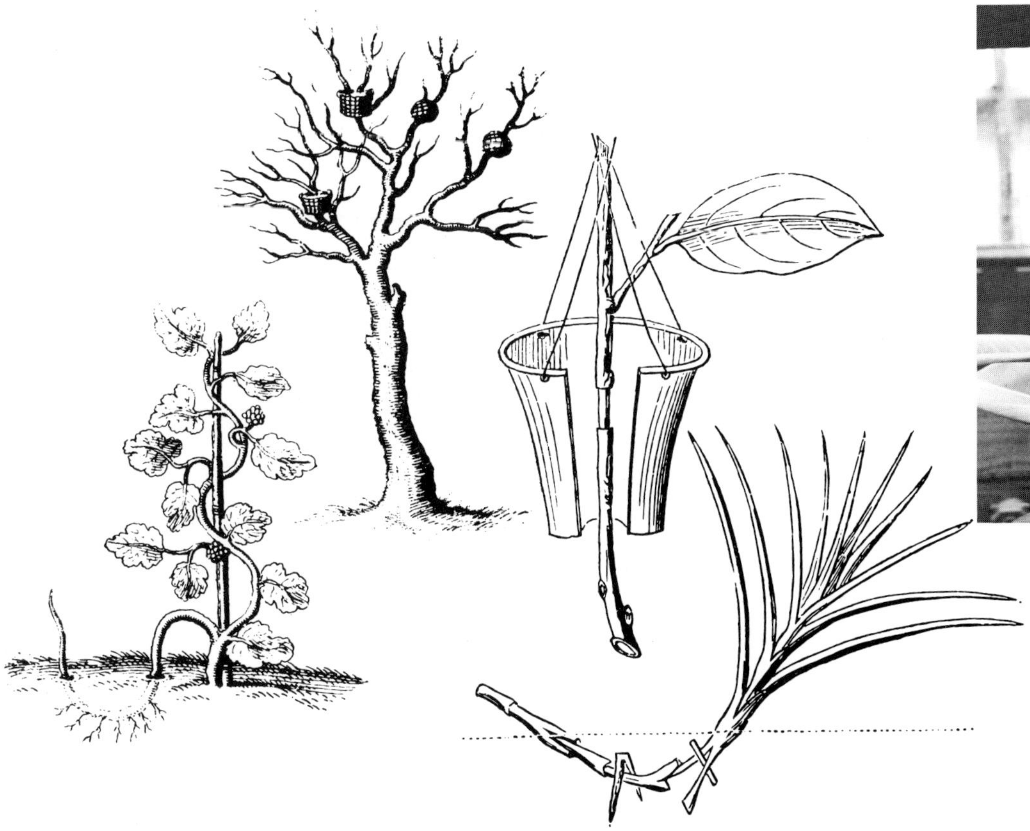

very detailed advice for best results. The furrow or horizontal method, used with quick-growing climbers like clematis and wisteria, will produce a number of new plants on each shoot. Today it is the usual practice to wound the shoot being layered as described above, typically by girdling it or making a "tongue" or "heel" in it, but the Romans believed that to do this would normally weaken the shoot.

Clearly, layering is only applicable to plants with shoots which grow near soil level or can easily be bent down to it. But there is another form of layering, reputedly invented by the Chinese and hence called Chinese or air layering, or circumposition (a word used in 1660). A pot or small basket with a hole in it is carefully drawn over the shoot to be rooted, fixed in an upright position and filled with soil, which must be kept moist. After a period of up to two years, the shoot fills the container with roots, and can then be severed below the container, which is then very carefully removed and the new tree planted. Cato described this method, and reconstruction of pot fragments from the Hephaisteion garden in Athens suggests that this was the method used with the trees grown there in the rock-cut pits, which contain remains of pots at the bottom.

More sophistication with this method comes from cutting the pot into two halves and wiring them together around the branch, or in later times from using a flexible metal pot cut down one side. Now the method has been revolutionized by the use of plastic film: sphagnum moss is placed around the branch at the desired rooting point and bound into place with

LOWER DRAWINGS: *Layering is one of the earliest methods of propagation, probably first used on the vine (left) which needed no preparation. In other cases the shoot to be layered produced roots more readily if wounded or slit in some way, like the carnation (right). Note the method of holding open the "tongue" and the peg to hold the layer in place.*

UPPER DRAWINGS: *When a tree does not produce low branches which can be layered, and is difficult to root from cuttings, air layering is employed. Soil is positioned around previously wounded branches in baskets (left), split pots or, in Victorian times, special metal devices. Today polyethylene film is used, an easy and efficient method (right).*

RIGHT: *The Greeks apparently practiced layering, using entire earthenware pots pushed over the selected twig. One of these is seen pieced together (left) and its base* in situ *after planting (right), as found in the Temple of Hephaistos, Athens. According to Cato, the pot was not broken before planting.*

RIGHT: *In grafting by approach, the tip of a branch from one tree (scion) is grafted on to the beheaded base of another (stock), to be severed when united.*
BELOW: *It is possible to use "loose" scions in water, or in a pot.*

Het af-Zuijgen der Boomen.

One of the simplest methods of grafting is cleft grafting, in which a piece of scion wood is pushed into a slit made in the bark of the stock. Here a Tudor propagator is at work – note the thick coating of wax or grafting clay around the grafts.

thread or fine wire; plastic film is laid over and around the moss, overlapped, and tied firmly at top and bottom. When sufficient roots have formed, they can be seen growing through the moss, and the air layer can then be severed, unwrapped, and potted or planted. With this method, as almost always with older-style air layering, the bark of the shoot is best wounded in some way, by making a cut all around or even removing a ring of bark. Hormone rooting powders, very much a twentieth-century invention, greatly speed up the rooting process. Air layers of this sort were successfully used on many of the trees in the Palm House at Kew Gardens, England, when, a few years ago, it was necessary to remove large parts of the glass to repair the structure, and the trees were too big to be moved elsewhere.

GRAFTING

Cuttings and layers produce new plants on their own roots, identical in all respects to their parent. The Romans would increase a bud-sport on a vine, which had been marked out for particularly good flavor or extra heavy cropping, by rooting that shoot as a cutting. But once it had proved itself on its own roots, the one new plant would not provide enough shoots for rapid increase in the same way. It was then that grafting, in which a piece of the selected variety (scion) is inserted into a well-rooted stem of an ordinary kind (stock), was used.

How the idea of grafting came about is an open question, but the great British authority on the subject, R. J. Garner, suggests that "it seems reasonable to suppose artificial grafting followed upon observation of natural grafting," such as quite often occurs when neighboring wild trees rub together. Natural grafting between trees of the same species was encouraged in the eighteenth century, when trees were twisted and tied

Seventeenth-century propagators carrying out cleft grafting use a thick knife and a mallet to make the incision.

together in their young stages to imitate pillars and balustrades.

The obvious outcome of such observation would be "grafting by approach," in which a shoot of one tree is fastened onto the branch or tip of another with appropriate mutual paring of bark – a method which was much later adopted with the scion as a pot-grown plant – or even cut off and inserted in a bottle of water. Garner goes on to say, "Grafting with detached scions must surely have been a later invention, probably encouraged by the observation of damaged approach grafts."

The Greeks and Romans were clearly fascinated by grafting and had a number of different methods at their command; the Romans grafted roses because they grew too slowly from seed (Pliny). This knowledge was greatly increased by inquiring gardeners in Europe in the sixteenth and seventeenth centuries, some of whom seem to have been quite obsessed with the possibilities, experimenting with far more methods than are currently in use today and employing an impressive array of tools, including a special grafting bench to ensure rapid and accurate matching of stock and scion. As Abraham Cowley wrote in his seventeenth-century poem "The Garden":

We no where Art do so triumphant see
As when it Grafts or Buds the Tree.

It is worth mentioning the various reasons for grafting. One is rapid increase of stock; another the fact that quite often cuttings on their own roots do not do particularly well (the modern rose is an example). So a strong, healthy stock, often a wild species, provides a good root system for the more delicate special fruit or flower one desires to grow. In his *Epistle to the Romans*, St. Paul has a parable about the "graffing" of olives so that the grafts could partake "of the root and fatness of the [wild] olive tree" (see illustration, page 279).

The third main reason for grafting, which the Romans began to recognize, is that stock and scion can interact, especially in the way that a stock can control the vigor and size of the final tree – a discovery to which almost every apple and pear tree in the West today bears witness.

The Chinese were well aware, although much later than the Romans, of the desirability of using a strong wild stock in cultivating one of their favorite plants – the tree peony or moutan. By the eighth or ninth century, new varieties were created in hundreds by hybridizing, and these precious creations were budded onto robust stocks of wild moutan or of the herbaceous peony. In a treatise on the moutan, Ouyang Hsiu wrote, in the eleventh century, "Bud-grafting should be performed in the autumn. . . . The [budded] stock is cut above five to seven inches above ground, when it is surrounded with loose soil and covered with a basket made of bamboo leaves to protect it from the sun and wind: a small portion facing the south is left open for ventilation."

There are enough ways of grafting to fill an entire volume, and the illustrations reproduced here must serve to provide much of the detail. The Romans used several methods: among them were the cleft graft, in which a small scion shoot is fitted into a wedge made between bark and wood in the stock, which has been cut down to a manageable height. As in most kinds of grafting, the edges of scion and stock are carefully pared to make a close fit when placed together. Another Roman method occasionally used today was root grafting by a similar technique, and a third favorite technique was budding, emplastration or inoculation – "graffing in the shield or scutchion" – in which a bud, sometimes with a minimum of surrounding tissue, or sometimes with a square or diamond of bark around it, is placed into an appropriate aperture in the stock. Quite recently a mechanical "budding gun" has been invented.

The ancients knew all the basic essentials for ensuring success when grafting, including the use of a protective "plaster" to help seal the graft and keep it moist and infection-free. They used a mixture of clay and chalk, with a smaller amount of sand, cattle dung and straw kneaded together. All kinds of weird mixtures were made later in Europe, like the

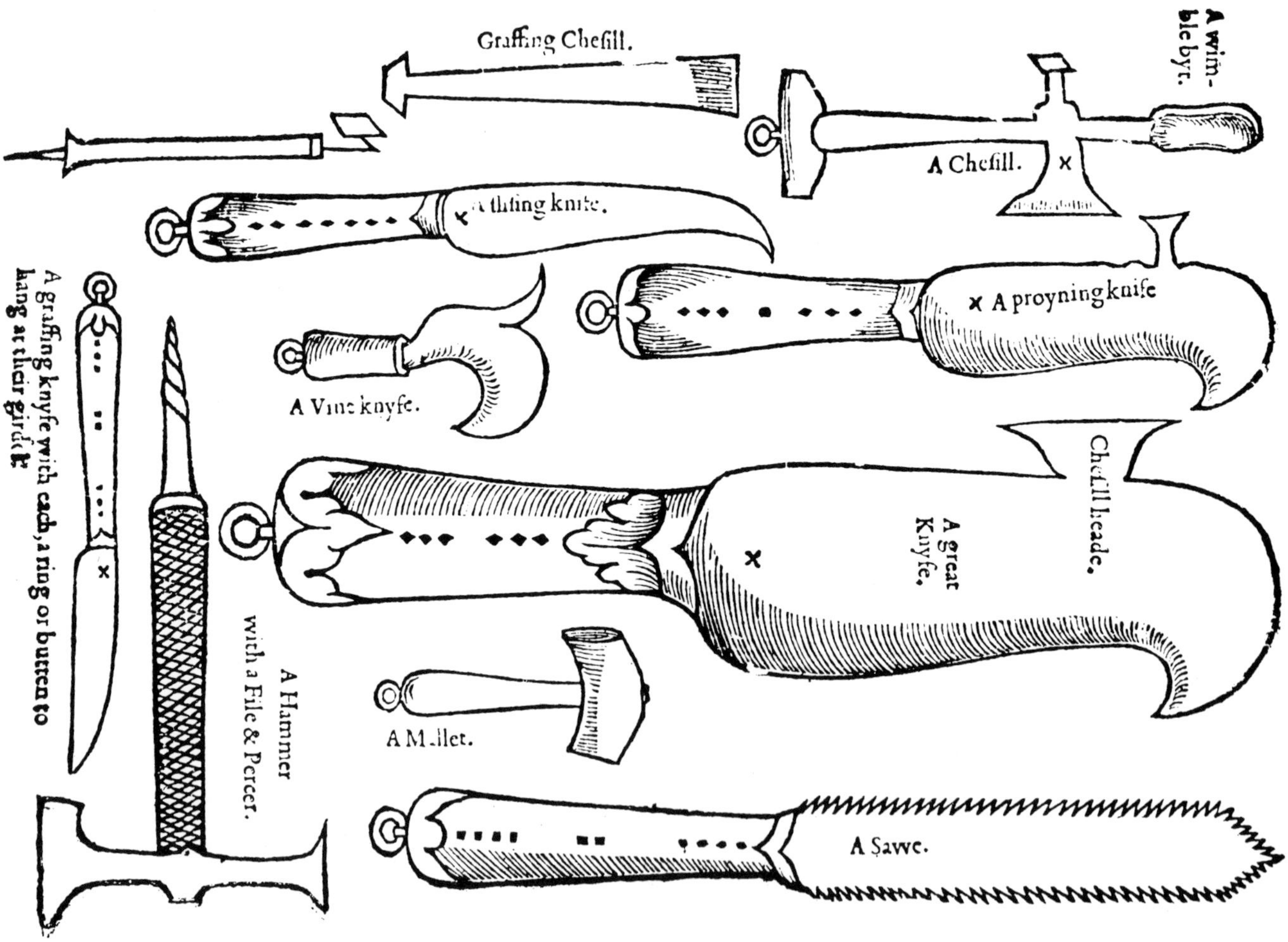

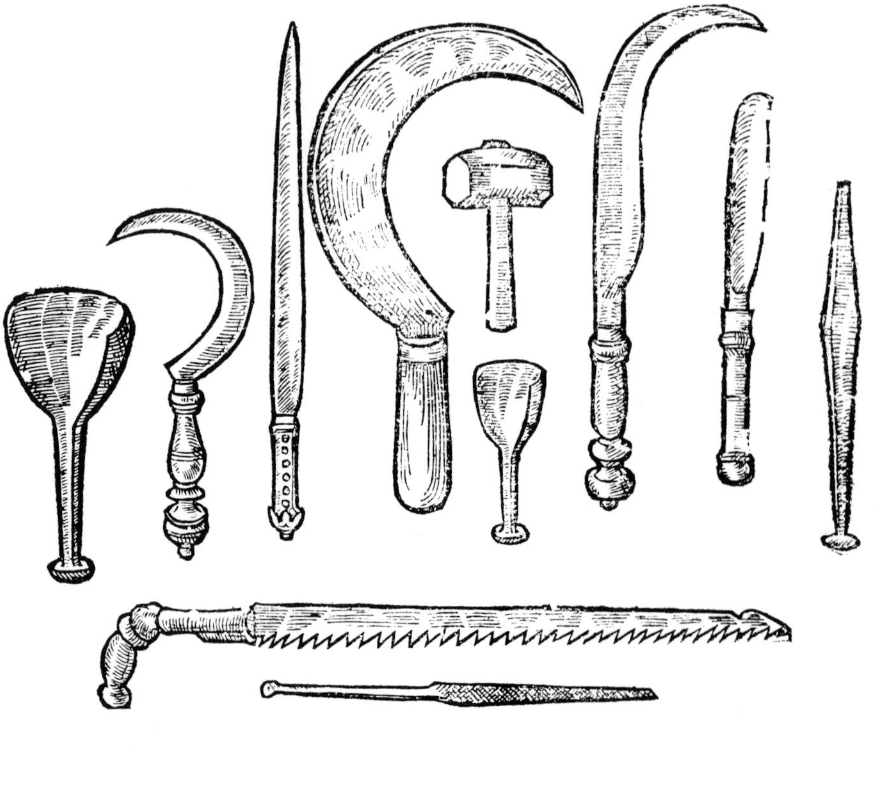

ABOVE: *Tools for pruning and grafting fruit trees of 1572.* RIGHT: *By 1640 the tools have become much more refined, and the "chesill heades" have all disappeared; indeed there is no dual-purpose knife-cum-chisel. The cup-shaped implements are for gouging out buds.*

Instructional sketches of grafting and budding of 1621: at right are splice-grafts, the rest, shield-budding in various stages. Lower right is a ladder on which a grafter could stand when working on tall fruit trees.

"noble Mummy" already quoted. In some parts of Europe, grafting clay – two parts clay, one part cow dung with finely cut hay, kneaded to the consistency of putty – is still used. Today people usually use various kinds of wax: one much-used hot wax contains resin, Burgundy pitch, tallow, paraffin wax and Venetian red; and a cold wax recipe calls for resin, beeswax, talc and methylated spirit. Bitumen emulsions and petroleum jelly are also used. Maybe we have not moved far from Agricola after all.

Mascall, in 1572, after recommending covering the graft with moss and binding it down with cloth, osier or briar, suggests finally that we should "stick certain long prickes on the graffes head among your cyons, to defend them from the crowes, jayes or such like."

As already mentioned, one of the standard grafting tools was the falx descended from the Roman *falx vinitoria*, but the early European grafters had quite an armory of chisels and knives at their disposal. It is interesting to see the apparent change in tools recommended between Mascall's *A Booke of the Arte and maner howe to plant and graffe all sortes of trees* of 1572, which showed eleven grafting and pruning tools, and Parkinson's *Paradisi . . .* of 1621, which only depicted five grafting tools, some of them small and delicate for budding.

Nor surprisingly, many myths about the possibilities of grafting developed, and for a long time there was hesitancy in accepting that only

The few grafting tools recommended by Parkinson in 1621. From top to bottom, a chisel for cleft grafting; a "penne-knife" used in budding; a cut quill for taking a bud; and an ivory tool for the same purpose. Below right, "a shielde of brasse" to keep the budding slit open till the bud is inserted.

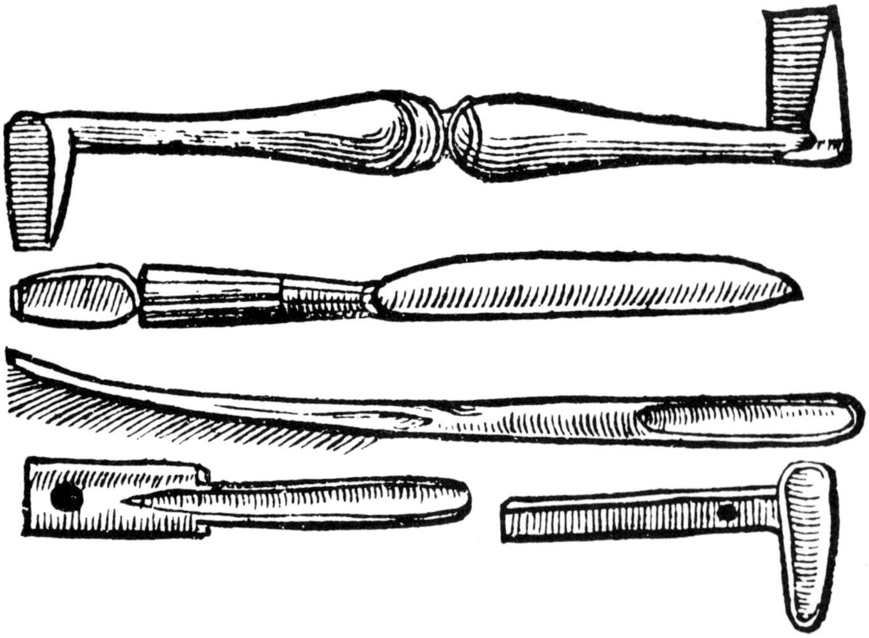

RIGHT: *"The Manner of grafting Roots" of trees, from Agricola, 1721. Some of the grafts have entertaining names, like (B) the "Imperial Incision," the "Count's Incision" and (D) the "Gentleman's Incision," invented by a "Gentleman of Great Curiosity in Gardening. It is plain, but nevertheless very good." In the insert below, the tools and bench used for these grafts, needing a perfect fit of stock and scion, remind one of a cabinetmaker's workroom.*

BELOW: *In root grafting tree peonies, a bud-bearing scion, trimmed at the base, is inserted into a correspondingly shaped incision in the root. The suckering iron at left became necessary to remove suckers from overvigorous stocks, which could otherwise swamp the scion growths.*

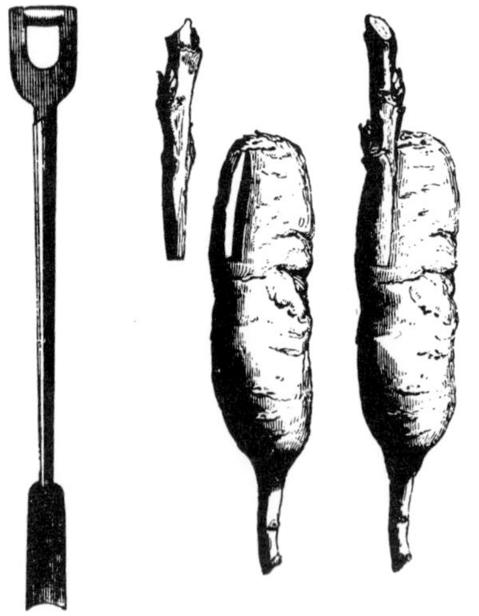

closely related plants would make true unions. Columella gives a detailed description of how to approach-graft an olive upon a fig, and other authorities suggest nuts upon arbutus, apples upon plane, cherries upon elm, and so on. Mascall mentions fig upon peach and, of tree grafting in general, says: "They say one may graffe on coleworts [cabbages], or on cloves, the which I think are but testes." Possibly such beliefs arose from the way in which tree seeds of one species can germinate in a branch crotch of another and live there quite happily. The Romans also believed that grafting onto thorn stock would cause the trees to be struck by thunderbolts (a belief disproved today when pear, cotoneaster and amelanchier are occasionally grafted onto related hawthorn).

In an early seventeenth-century treatise, we have complicated and largely misguided advice on how to graft a cherry so that the fruit will have

The most popular method of budding is called shield budding, in which a growth bud on a "shield" of rind is inserted into a T-shaped cut in the stock and bound into position. LEFT: *A seventeenth-century working diagram.* BELOW LEFT: *A very clear Edwardian one.*

TOP: *Many other forms of bud can be used in methods called patch budding: a Tudor diagram.*

BELOW: *Further methods as elaborated in the nineteenth century. Above, budding with a square shield. Center, with a double shield. Right, a punch used for cutting out shield buds and making the appropriate incision on the stock. Other drawings, various ways of flute budding, in which the scion is a tube of bark carrying buds.*

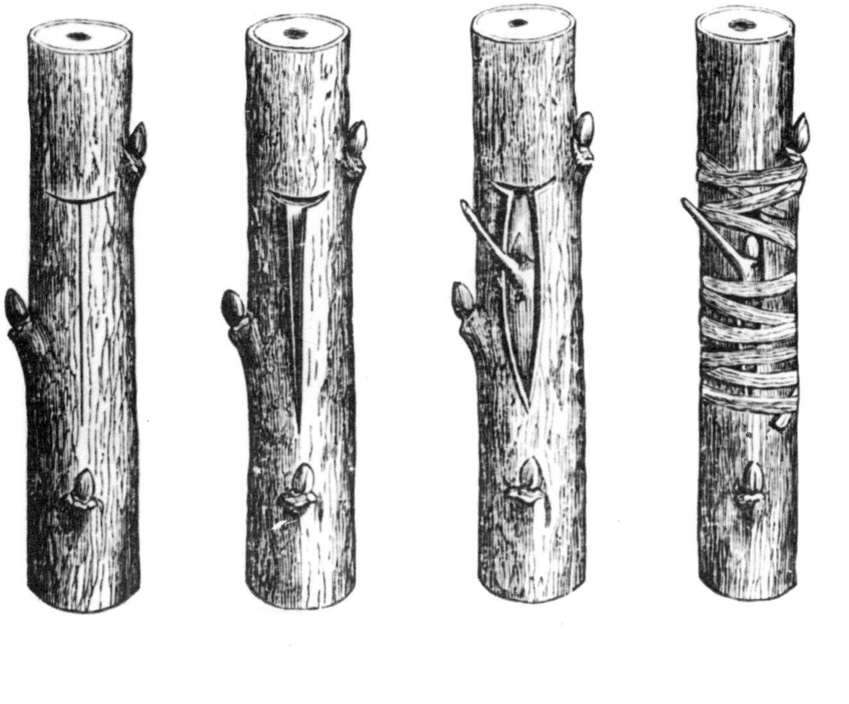

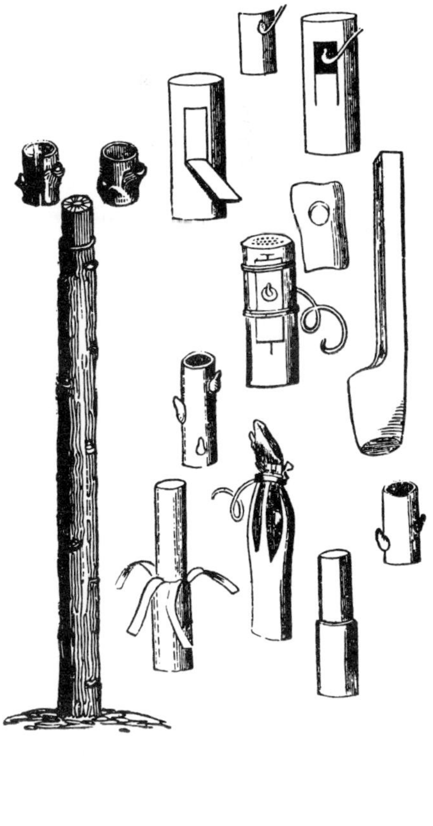

Various methods of taking cuttings and layers. Prominent are "a curious multiplication made by a giant Tree being put in the earth," rooting cuttings by putting them in a pierced willow bough, and, in the tree at right, several air layers. (This and the following three illustrations all come from Agricola's treatise of 1721.)

no pips; how to ensure red apples – either by grafting onto a cherry, or by dipping the scions in pike's blood before inserting an apple stock; how to make medlars sweet – by grafting onto pear; and how to make grapes taste like claret – by boring a hole in the stock and filling it with powdered cloves and cinnamon. Another author suggests that grafting an orange onto a pomegranate will guarantee blood oranges. For a fruit to taste half of pear, half of apple, two appropriate scions are carefully joined together. A vine, it was believed, could be grafted onto cherry, and grafting a rose onto a holly was thought to make it evergreen.

There is some Roman evidence of grafting a single stock with several different kinds of apple or other fruits. Agricola's eighteenth-century treatise devotes quite a lot of space to this principle, but he did not suggest doing it by inserting several grafts upon one stock. His multiple trees were created by fastening together up to five young rooted cuttings by what he called "caressing and embracing," in which each branch has its bark pared in an appropriate place to lie alongside another pared surface when all the cuttings are bundled together. The point of multiple union is then fastened firmly and covered with "mummy," until the shoots grow together and can be planted together in a single container. Such "family trees," as we have called them in this century, were then usually made of citrus and related fruits. One of Agricola's examples shows orange, citron, lemon and "Adam's apple" (*Poncirus trifoliata*) joined together near the short tips. Each separate tree could then supposedly produce any of the various fruits. Mascall suggests "family trees" of various kinds of apple;

Grafting methods shown include two by approach: at left "union or caressing," at right, "embracing or twist grafting." At center, inarching with the scion in a pot – "The Inventor of it certainly had fine Thoughts." At i, "a fine Operation, which is call'd Inoculation with the Scutcheon."

apples and pears; pears, apricots and plums; and black, white and green cherries. Modern family trees are usually of three or four kinds of apple or pear grafted onto a single stock, providing a variety of fruit in a small space and avoiding any problems of necessary cross-pollination.

Just as they did not prune fruit trees, early commercial American orchard growers did not graft them. Their fruit trees were mostly seedlings but, as the fruit was usually used for making alcoholic drinks, this did not matter much. Long before most fruit growers, George Washington enjoyed grafting fruit trees, obtaining scion material from friends, as his diary from 1760 onward shows. It is clear that those friends must also have carried out the "wedding" of stock and scion, as it was often called, on their own estates.

From about 1800 on, all orchards in the north of America, where the hardy fruits grow, were annually visited by itinerant grafters, who gradually introduced named varieties to the orchardists. Nurseries were slow to supply grafted trees for sale, mainly because of this practice, as the pomologist Patrick Barry noted in 1843. But the Prince Nursery on Long Island, which I have mentioned earlier as the first important American nursery, began selling "inoculated" fruit trees in 1791.

GROWTH CONTROL

Grafting does not always provide perfectly controlled growth in the resulting bush or tree. Additional local control can be achieved by creating sap barriers; their effects reflect the movement of "plant hormones" or auxins in the sap. Such control is normally only applied to trained fruit trees in which precision in development is sought. It is

"The manner of joining three or four different Trees together, by what is called Caressing and Embracing, which produces at the same time several sorts of Fruit. After having cuts made where they are to be in contact, the growths are tied and dress'd with Mummy, and fastened to Pickets; and at length the Roots shoot out at the Joint."

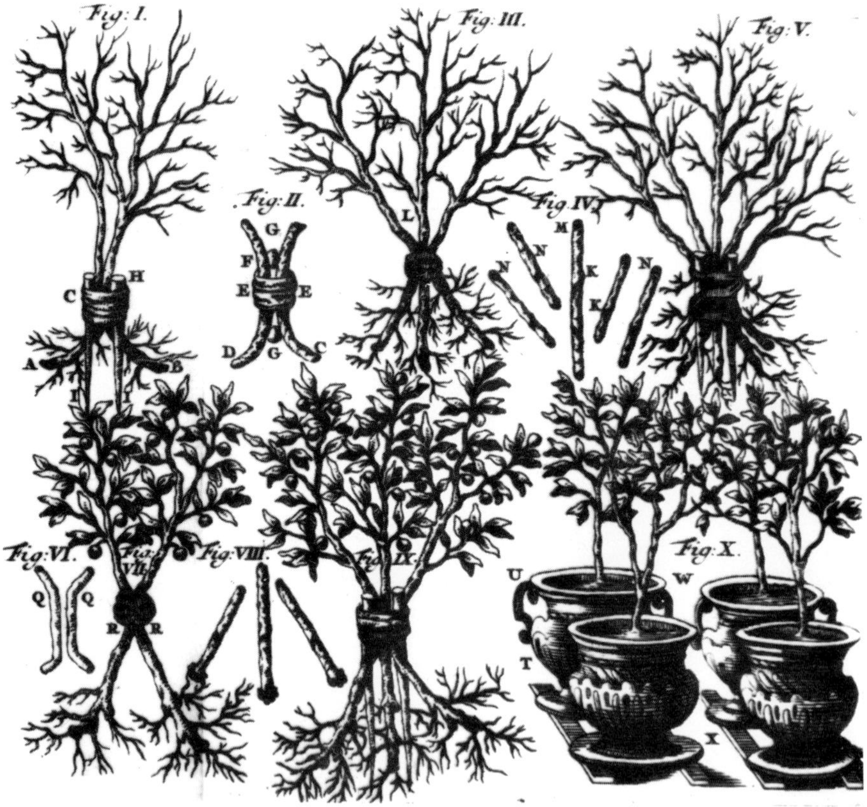

"Universal Multiplication, which is performed with the Graffing-Chizel." Incisions were made in various places on the tree (as at left), and they were then coated with grafting wax, after which roots would form at these places, which might grow into "oyl-cloth bags or tin-boxes" (center), to be subsequently cut from the tree and planted.

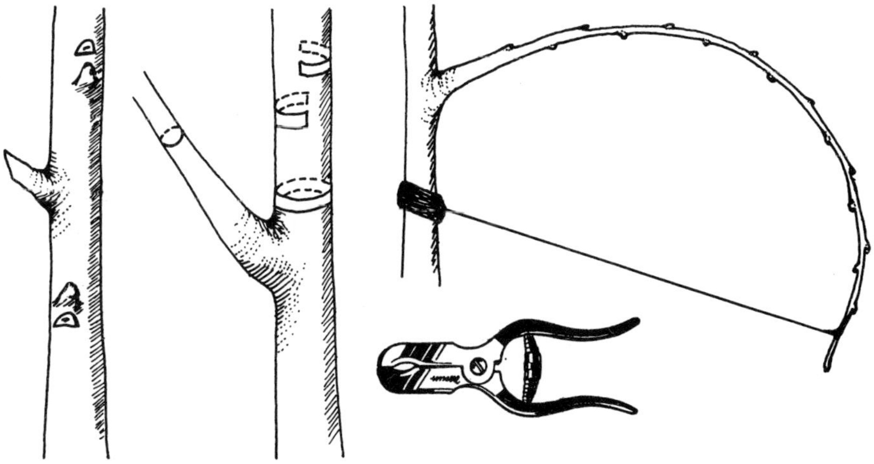

Methods of controlling growth in restricted areas. LEFT: *Making a nick or notch above a dormant bud stimulates it into growth: below the bud, it inhibits growth.* CENTER: *Taking out a complete or partial strip of bark curtails growth and encourages bud formation. A ring cut has a less severe effect. The tool, below, was in use until quite recently to make ring cuts.* RIGHT: *Arching over a branch will encourage flower buds at the expense of growth.*

comprised basically of making a notch or cut, only as deep as the bark itself, above or below a bud. To make this above a bud will encourage it to develop into a wood bud; below, into a blossom bud.

Taking out a complete or partial ring of bark around a young shoot or branch will make it rapidly develop flower and fruit buds; the method called garroting, in which a tourniquet of metal wire is tightened into the bark, is in fact rather less severe on the tree, and is sometimes used to encourage slow-maturing trees to fruit. Cutting into the bark all around the branch with a knife or special tool has similar effects.

Buds on individual branches can be encouraged to produce flowers and fruit rather than growth if the branches are arched or horizontally trained. Columella was aware of this when he described the twisting and tying down of unruly vine shoots. Some Roman methods of improving bearing seem less scientific. One suggestion was to make a cleft in the root and insert a stone. A less violent method was to pour vegetable water or stock around the tree. In the case of cherries, ripening was accelerated by placing a little lime around the roots.

Growth control of quite a different sort was carried out in India, where antique gardening manuals give advice on *dohada*, in which trees and plants are sung or played to, danced around, or sometimes handled or kicked in specific ways to encourage growth. In this century many experiments have been carried out, apparently with conclusively positive results, to show that various sounds and vibrations can indeed stimulate plant growth. Plants are supposed to react more favorably to Bach and classical Indian sitar music than to "acid rock" – at which "they cringe, lean sharply away . . . and die in a few weeks." This sounds like an old Solomon Islands practice of creeping up on enemies' trees before dawn and suddenly uttering piercing yells – guaranteed to destroy them within a month. However, "harsh noises" broadcast experimentally over crops in the United States have actually increased yields.

OVERLEAF: *The ancient Indian practice of* dohada *– singing, dancing and stamping around trees, and occasionally striking them – was supposed to encourage growth. There seems to be a scientific basis for the idea.*

BEEKEEPING

That bees pollinate flowers is relatively recent knowledge, and I do not think they have ever been kept in gardens specifically for this reason.

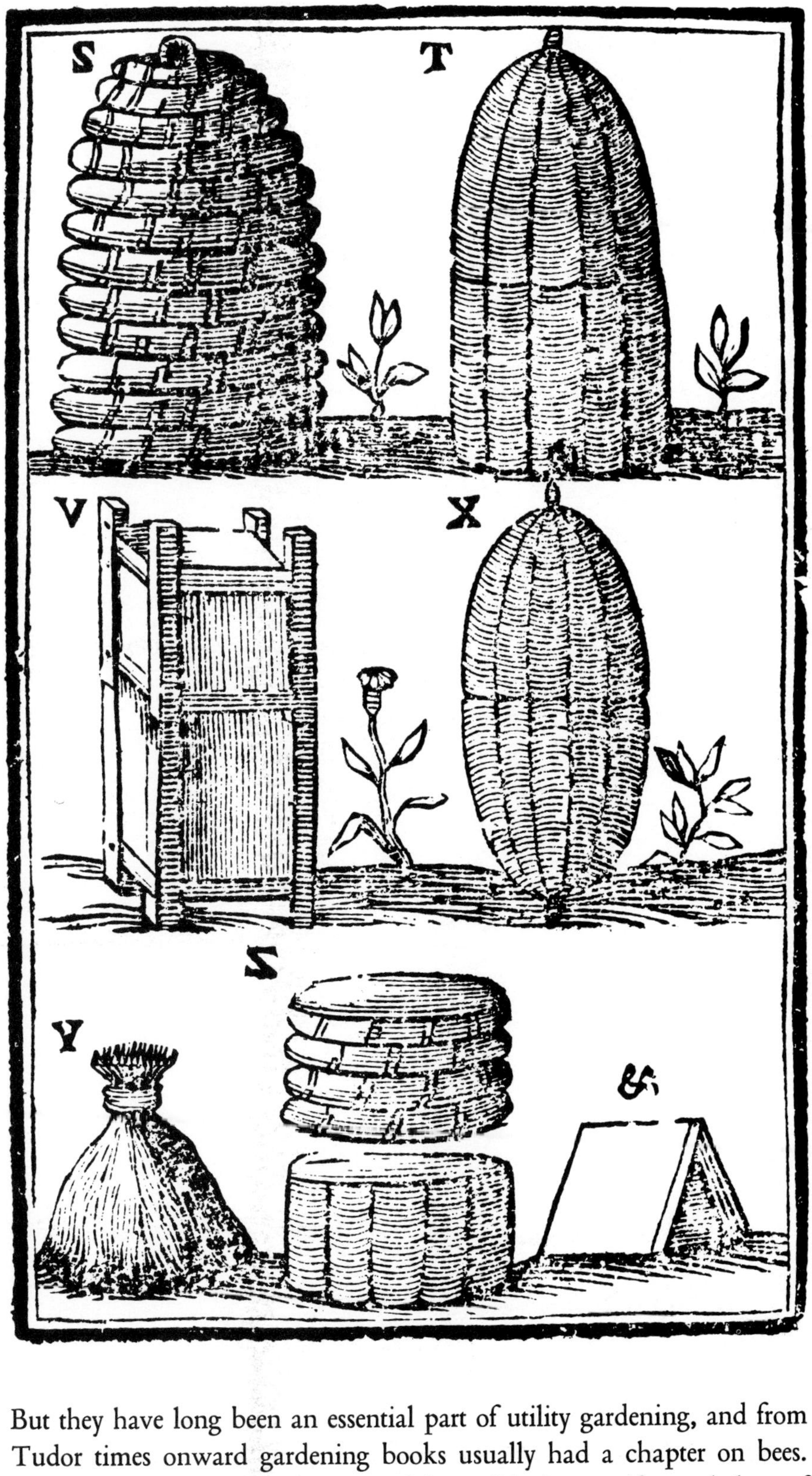

By the eighteenth century, there was a good understanding of bees and how to look after them: several different kinds were recognized. Hives were made of straw, wicker, wood, etc., and several tools, including a fumigator, were in use.

OVERLEAF: *Beekeeping has been associated with gardening since Roman times at least. All kinds of activity are seen in the eighteenth-century engraving: wild bee swarms are being collected (background); at 6, the beekeeper is making sure there are enough bees in the hive, while at 14 "a charivari of several people" is trying to make an errant swarm stop on a branch.*

But they have long been an essential part of utility gardening, and from Tudor times onward gardening books usually had a chapter on bees. Looking after them was the expected duty of the housewife – only later of the gardener. William Lawson, in 1618, wrote, "I will not account her among the very good House-wives, that wanteth either Bees or skilfulness about them."

Bees have certainly been "cultivated" since Egyptian times. The Greeks had hives; Aristotle wrote about them; and the Romans had much to say about how to beekeep. Virgil gives much detail, mentioning hives made of hollow bark and woven from osiers, and listing all the best flowers for bees. Columella devotes an extensive chapter to them, which could hardly be bettered today, except that he calls the queen the "king bee." Roman beehives were made of small bricks, cork bark, or giant fennel stalks. In other countries and climates, all kinds of containers were used; the Russians hollowed out tree trunks, closing the aperture with a board perforated with little holes. "The height of the tree," to quote one authority, "is to prevent bears getting at the honey." Hives of wood and skeps of straw eventually became the most popular.

It was only in the late Middle Ages that beekeepers adopted protective clothing. While today every effort is made to preserve one's colonies, it was customary until the last century to kill the bees with sulfur fumes, or simply to drive them off, in order to harvest the honey. Medium-sized colonies were retained, and fresh swarms were sought in the wild.

Honey bees were brought into North America from Europe very early, in 1638 to be precise, and by 1670 Daniel Denton could write (in *A Brief Description of New York*): "You shall scarce see a house but the South side is begirt with Hives of Bees, which increase after an incredible manner." Another writer in 1698 relates how "the Sweeds often get great store of them in the woods where they are free for any Body." However, the bees were not kept for pollinating fruit trees, but for the honey they produced, which was the chief sweetener available to the housewife, and which was also used in making mead and metheglin drinks.

It is only recently that the bee has been actively "cultivated" to play its vital part, so far not replaced by any modern invention, of ensuring that fruit trees and other groups, such as beans, will bear fruit. Beekeeping is an exception to the general rule that most aspects of cultivation, basic or more advanced, are as old as civilization itself and only gradually become modified and improved over the centuries.

Chapter Seven
Plants under Cover

FROM THE EARLIEST TIMES, GARDENERS WERE AWARE OF THE changes in plants wrought by the seasons, and by degrees they discovered that different areas of a country, and different aspects and degrees of sunshine and shelter in a garden, would influence the dates of starting into growth, flowering, fruiting or cropping. They also discovered that plants brought in from foreign lands often did not behave in the same way as their native species, and that those introduced from warmer climates might often succumb in the local winter. Twin preoccupations thus arose, of obtaining fruit and vegetables out of season, and of successfully cultivating exotic plants in alien climates.

ROMAN METHODS

There is no doubt that the Romans successfully forced various food plants, and also roses, usually on a small scale in "pits" or frames. Such forcing is usually represented as having been done with the aid of thin sheets of mica, although Columella mentions "sheets of transparent stone," which sound more like talc (*lapis specularis*) split into thin plates. Glass was not used until the first century A.D., when it began to be used in the homes of the wealthy. A building in Pompeii has been identified as a *specularia* or stove house: it has masonry shelves on which plants stood, hot-air flues in the walls, and a frontal framework almost certainly glazed with glass or one of its current substitutes.

Martial (first century A.D.) complains in his *Epigrams* that his friend takes more pains to protect his trees than his poor clients. His friend's Cilician fruit trees are protected by glass and get the southern sun in winter and clear light, while Martial himself has to make do with a tiny room without a window to shut. He thinks he would fare better to be a guest of the tree rather than of his old friend, for then at least he would get the protection of a whole window. Elsewhere Martial wrote about the vines in Entellus's greenhouse, which was glazed with plates of talc so as to keep out the cold and form a winter garden. Thus he had a "countryside" bearing fruit in winter – which Martial says anyone would prefer even to the gardens of Alcinous. He also writes of roses and lilies being forced under glass (*vitrum*).

However, such devices were generally considered to be excesses of luxury. Seneca, in one of his habitual biting comments, wrote "Do not

An orangery of 1676 has windows with small leaded panes and an opaque roof. During the summer its occupants are set out neatly in front of the building.

those live contrary to nature who require a rose in winter and who, by the excitement of hot water and an appropriate modification of heat, force from winter the later blooms of spring?" And, as Kenneth Lemmon points out in *The Covered Garden* (1962), "The trouble of running a forcing house, however rudimentary, in the warmer sunny climate of southern Europe could not really have been worth while after the initial novelty had worn thin."

EUROPEAN METHODS

Many centuries passed before any further attempts of this kind are recorded. There is a rather ambiguous record of a garden with unseasonable flowers and fruit, apparently produced by artificial heat, in Padua in 1259; and there is a letter of 1385 which mentions in passing that "in the Bois de Duc in France they grow flowers in glass pavilions turned to the south."

Padua long remained in the forefront of innovation in protecting plants. It has what is almost certainly the oldest botanical garden extant, founded in 1545, and in 1550 one of the officials there, Daniele Babbaro, had built a *viridarium* for sheltering tender plants in the winter. It is generally assumed that this was basically a storeroom, of stone, brick or wood, heated with a portable brazier or perhaps an open fire; but since it was called a "greenhouse" it may have had some glazed windows.

It was, in fact, the enormous value placed on citrus fruits – 169 varieties came to be cultivated – which stimulated the development of plant houses. In most parts of northern Europe, citrus fruits are not winter-hardy. But they are tough plants which will put up with other conditions that would kill many other types of plant. They were therefore, if fortuitously, excellent experimental subjects.

ORANGERIES

As early as 1490, there is mention of citrus plants being

As winter approaches, the trees are brought into the orangery. Note the lugs on the clay urns which allow a carrying pole to be inserted, and the small iron stoves. Watering was arduous in a large orangery, even with the hooped yoke support for the buckets.

overwintered in wooden sheds with the aid of coal fires. In the sixteenth century, they were sometimes overwintered in cellars. The *ambulacrum* built in the Netherlands at Leyden Botanical Gardens in 1599 was another heated shed. The first "orangeries" were only rooms which could be heated in winter; Lord Burghley, Queen Elizabeth's chief secretary of state, made one in 1561 and, as late as 1649, Queen Henrietta, wife of King Charles I, had built an "oringe garden" which was entirely enclosed. The walls of such enclosures might be insulated with mattresses or reeds. Evelyn suggested to his patron that cork would be better, but it does not seem that this was ever used. John Miller, in the early eighteenth century, was recommending roofs with a one-foot thickness of reeds, furze or heather. A plant house at Leyden, built in 1744, had walls and ceilings filled with buckwheat chaff; this was sufficient, as recorded in the severe winter of 1828–1829, to maintain an inside temperature of 30°F when outside it was 4°. John Evelyn, describing in 1658 Sir Francis Carew's orange garden begun in 1580, says that in winter the trees "were protected only by a tabernacle of boards and stoves."

Such "houses of defense" gave the wretched plants no light in winter, and despite their toughness many must have expired. But the practice began to be questioned: the botanist Robert Sharrock commented, in 1654, "It is to be wondered how the gardeners get delicate plants to live by sheltering them in dark places during the winter." A little later we find Evelyn noting that "light is half their [plants'] nourishment philosophically considered."

The first use of glass in orangeries, though limited, was in 1619, when Salomon de Caus (or Caux) made a shelter in Heidelberg,

Germany, to protect the four hundred trees of the Elector Palatine. This was a barnlike structure, 280 feet long, 32 feet wide and high enough to take the thirty largest trees, which were 25 feet tall. Its main structure was wooden, it had a freestone roof, and it was erected every year in late September and dismantled in April. In the walls were a number of small windows; within, four furnaces were kept going all winter.

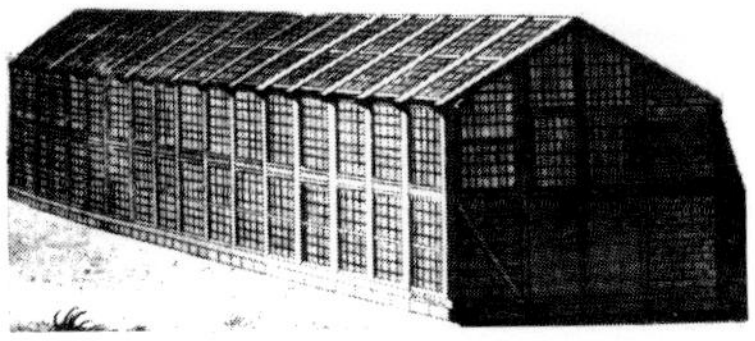

TOP: *As time went on, orangeries acquired more glass, although it was long before the glass-framed roof became usual.*

ABOVE: *An early mobile stove used in Oxford around 1620–1650.*

This was a temporary structure, leaving the orange trees permanently in place in the ground, as was the case with the Carew collection. But it was not long before orangeries became permanent buildings, and their occupants, which stood in front of the edifice in summer, were carried inside when cold weather began. The plant containers would be large, square wooden tubs with metal handles, or huge earthenware urnlike pots with side lugs through which a pole could be inserted, enabling two men to carry them. Later, special wheeled trolleys were designed into which square tubs of standard size could be winched up, and pushed with rather less effort on their twice-annual journeys.

By the last quarter of the seventeenth century, orangeries, or *citronières* as they were called in France, had relatively large windows in at least one wall of the building – the south-facing one – although the roofs remained opaque. This applied to the largest of them all – that built for Louis XIV at Versailles in 1685. It was 508 feet long, 42 feet wide and 45 feet high, with flanking galleries 375 feet long. In it were housed twelve hundred orange trees and some three hundred other tender exotics. But gradually it was recognized that, even in winter, yet more light was needed; walls of glass frames were made rather than windows in masonry, and by degrees glass replaced the solid roofs. The first glass-roofed orangery in Britain seems to have been built in 1696, although it was a very long time before the desirability of glass roofs was generally accepted.

Heating of the orangeries began with braziers, open hearths, charcoal pans, and even large candles. At the Oxford Physic Garden a barrow of open metalwork held a fire and could be wheeled up and down. The first free-standing enclosed stove, made of iron, appeared in Holland in 1670. One has to remember that the mercury thermometer was not invented until 1714, so that the estimation of temperature and fire heat required was risky at best, and the moment to light the fires might be when a saucer of water in the structure froze over.

Obviously open fires and braziers not only dried out the air, but also gave out fumes harmful to the plants. As Evelyn wrote to a friend in 1668, "stoves absolutely destroy our Conservatories." The stove at least had a flue pipe to take the smoke out of the building. Some authorities, like the Dutch van Oosten in 1703, suggested doing without heat altogether, and relying on a building with thick walls and roof, and provided, within the glass, with an inner frame of oiled paper which could be erected as extra insulation. "If the water in the greenhouse is frozen," he

An elaborate two-tiered orangery with glass in both front and roof (Germany, 1706).

wrote, "then you must gently warm the trees or rather the leaves with burning lamps so hung that the flames thereof may not touch the trees."

Gardeners gradually worked out the need of plants for what we call a "buoyant atmosphere" – neither too dry nor too moist – and for "hardening off" before being stood outside when winter was over. As gardening writer John Rea wrote in 1676, "You must on fairer days acquaint them again with the sun and air by degrees."

GREENHOUSES AND CONSERVATORIES

Gardeners of this period gradually came to call their structures either greenhouses or conservatories. They used these words – which John Evelyn was the first to employ in writing – more or less synonymously, for a greenhouse was to shelter the tender "greens," as they called the plants they habitually grew – citrus, pomegranates, myrtles, bay and cypress – and a conservatory was to conserve tender plants. The first building to have been called a greenhouse in Britain seems to have been at Chatsworth in 1697, where the first Duke of Devonshire had built a building with an arcaded front and solid roof – still very much an orangery in principle. At one point Evelyn describes two types of structure – one with a raised floor and a stove below it (as existed at the Chelsea Gardens); the other a less expensive affair in which a wooden frame seven feet high at the back and five feet in front, insulated with dry reeds or rushes, was covered with "common glass frames," such as were already in use over hotbeds, and very like those we have today.

Other refinements which gradually entered into greenhouse

LEFT: *The long sloping windows of the orangery at Oxford Physic Gardens in 1773 made better use of the sun's rays than vertical ones.*

BELOW LEFT: *An alternative use of sloping glass: Thomas Fairchild's near-horizontal greenhouse of 1722.*

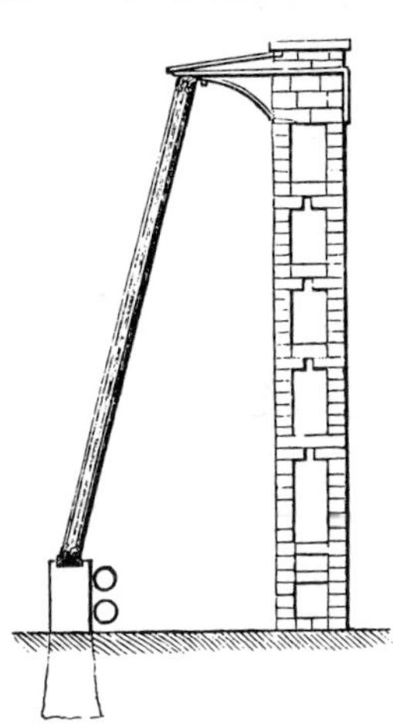

TOP: *A Dutch forcing house, probably for fruit trees, of 1737; it has sloping glass lights and wooden ventilators above them, and is heated by flues in the back wall on the principle of the section shown above.*

construction included ventilation. The frames or sashes holding the small glass panes might either slide or be hinged so that they could be opened widely. Some of the forcing houses had a row of ventilators at the top between the sloping glass front and the vertical back wall. Shading against excess sun was done with cloth or burlap blinds, rolled up with a cord. These were also used for winter insulation, as were thick wooden shutters on older structures. For more light on dull days, it was recommended to paint the back walls white, or glaze them with white tiles.

All these considerations gradually changed the shape of the structures that were made, and one can say that experimentation of various kinds became more and more rapid from the early eighteenth century. One of the earliest structural changes was from barn-shaped structures to sloping, glassed fronts. Such houses were still one-sided, but the angle of the glass made for better use of the sun's rays; the slope varied from nearly vertical to nearly horizontal. In such structures fruit trees grown against the back wall had the double benefit of the sunlight and of heat radiating out from the brickwork, which went on into the night after a bright day. The wheel eventually turned full circle with the back wall again being provided with extra heating through flues within, just as in the Pompeiian *specularia.* This type of greenhouse is still in use today; we call it a lean-to, and it is usually erected when there is no room for a complete structure.

At this point science begins to affect the making of greenhouses. The builder of the hothouse made at Leyden in 1718, Dr. H. Boerhaave, worked out that its front wall should slope at an angle of 52°, so that the midday sun would strike the glass exactly at right angles, and in 1724 Stephen Switzer built a forcing house with the glass at a 45° angle, the vines within being trained up a plane inclined at the same angle behind the glass.

AMERICAN DEVELOPMENTS

The art of protecting plants did not take long to cross the Atlantic. The first American greenhouse was erected by Andrew Faneuil in Boston shortly before 1737 – but only its erection is recorded, nothing of its design. Greenhouses of the orangery type seem to have been constructed at about the same time: in 1737 the Englishman Peter Collinson, writing to the plant collector John Bartram in North America, says "I am told Colonel Byrd has the best garden in Virginia, and a pretty greenhouse, well furnished with orange trees. . . ." In 1760 Bartram wrote to his friend "I am going to build a greenhouse . . . to put some pretty flowering shrubs, and plants for winter's diversion; not to be crowded with orange trees, or those natural to the torrid zone, but such as will do, being protected from frost."

In 1758 Theophilus Hardenbrook advertised in the New York *Mercury* that, among many other kinds of building, he would design "Green Houses for the preservation of Herbs [by which he meant plants in general] with winding Funnels through the Wall, so as to keep them

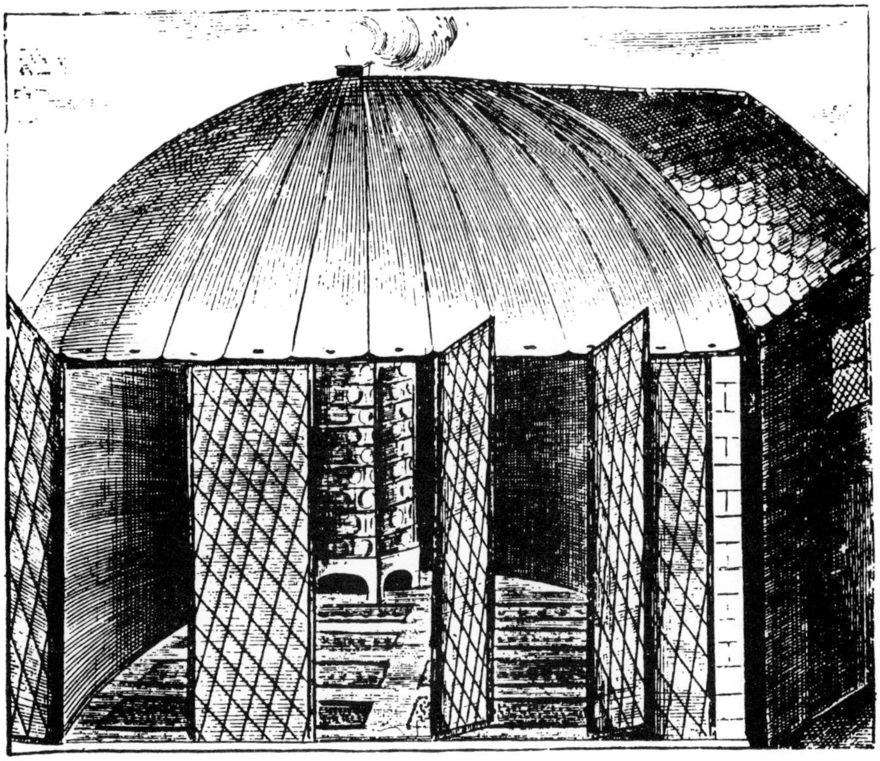

ABOVE: *An early example (1714) of a curved, though solid, greenhouse roof, made of boards and tiles. Large lattice windows give plenty of light to plants grown in soil-level beds and heated by a large hot-air stove.*

BELOW: *The solid-roof orangery principle was still apparent when the earliest greenhouses were erected in America (New York, 1764).*

warm. . . ." The first greenhouse in New York was actually built in 1764 (it is not recorded if Mr. Hardenbrook was responsible). It was a very simple structure with glass only on the sides and ends, the roof being shingled. The glass of such houses was typically fitted in sashes of small panes with thick timber piers in between, and the roofs, also of sashes, were usually removable. The sides were usually high, and in some cases a living room or apartment instead of a roof would be built over the greenhouse – to increase the winter temperature and provide a convenient place for the gardener to live. Commercial greenhouses at this time were made entirely of portable sashes rather like the "Dutch light" structures used today (see page 261), and most of them were of lean-to shape with a high back wall. One of the oldest greenhouses extant in the United States, erected about 1800 at Waltham, Massachusetts, is a very low structure with a barely sloping roof, like a gigantic cold frame. This type of structure was still in vogue in 1827, as one of the earliest engravings of a greenhouse in America demonstrates. By contrast, the first greenhouse erected in Chicago, in 1835 or 1836, was a low three-quarter span building with sashes forming the roof, but with no glass at all in the sides. More orthodox greenhouses followed slowly.

PLANTS CULTIVATED

In the early days much, of course, depended upon what was being cultivated in the greenhouses. At first the scene was dominated by the citrus and other "tender greens" of limited kinds. Gradually, more and more exotics arrived, many of which needed more light and a guaranteed, steady winter temperature "lift" above freezing. Among these were many succulents, and a surprising number of tropical economic plants we seldom see today except in botanical collections, such as guava, pawpaw, coffee, breadfruit, arrowroot and ginger. But the greatest eighteenth-century influence on greenhouses was the cultivation of the pineapple, or "pine" as it was called.

As William Cowper wrote in "The Task," published in 1785,

> Who loves a garden loves a greenhouse too.
> Unconscious of a less propitious clime,
> There blooms exotic beauty, warm and snug.

By the early nineteenth century, a wide range of tender plants was available, but these would still often be grown in separate houses. There might be an orangery, a vinery, a pinery, a peach house and a general house, and if you were a specialist and grew, say, cape heaths, carnations, ferns, palms, pelargoniums or aquatics, there would be a different recommended design for each, with variations in dimensions, heating and ventilation.

CONSERVATORIES

Gradually the words greenhouse and conservatory took on different meanings: the greenhouse was essentially a growing house; the conservatory a structure for enjoyment, where plants, often moved in and out from the other houses according to season, would be on display for those who could wander or sit among them.

The use of the greenhouse structure for entertainment was not new. As early as 1696, the horticulturalist T. Langford wrote, "Greenhouses are of late built as ornaments to gardens (as summer and banqueting houses were formerly) as well as for a conservatory for tender plants, and when the curiosities in the summer time are dispersed in their proper places in the garden the house . . . may serve for an entertaining room." Queen Anne used the orangery at her London Kensington Palace as a "summer supper house."

But these uses presupposed a structure empty of plants. It was about 1760 that Mr. William Belchier conceived, for his small collection of citrus trees, a covering entirely of glass, which could be entered through a pair of glass folding doors from the drawing room, and it was not until 1782 that the word conservatory, in its modern meaning, is recorded in a dictionary. In the first publication of *Red Gauntlet* in 1824, Sir Walter Scott describes a similar structure, adding "I have never seen this before."

In the grandest houses of Europe, the conservatory became vastly enlarged into "winter gardens." As early as 1802, there was one at St. Petersburg in Russia, a three-hundred foot semicircular building, with huge vertical windows and a solid roof, built onto the end of a living room. Chevalier Storch described it:

> As from the size of the roof it could not be supported without pillars, they are disguised under the form of palm trees. The heat is maintained by concealed flues placed in the walls and pillars, and even under the earth leaden pipes are arranged, incessently filled wih boiling water. The walks of this garden meander amidst flowering hedges and fruit-bearing shrubs, winding over little hills and producing, at every step, fresh occasions for surprise. The genial warmth, the fragrance and brilliant colors of the nobler plants and the voluptuous stillness that prevails in this enchanted spot lull the fancy into sweet romantic dreams; we imagine ourselves in the blooming groves of Italy; while nature, sunk into a deathlike torpor, announces the severity of the northern winter through the windows of the pavilion.

Even larger was the Jardin d'Hiver built in the Champs-Elysées in Paris in 1847: 300 feet long, 180 feet wide, and tall as a three-story house. Similar edifices were erected all over Europe.

Such examples led to everyone who was anyone having a conservatory, as well as all the ancillary greenhouses needed to keep it going and the household furnished with exotic fruits. The anonymous compiler of *Famous Parks and Gardens*, a book published in 1880, wrote, "From the beginning of the present century a mania for conservatories has spread contagiously among all the richer classes of the cold or temperate countries of Europe. . . . In the towns and villages of Great Britain, they are attached to all the more pretentious houses – their bowers of foliage and blossom frequently communicating with the drawing or sitting room." In Britain this "contagious mania" was vastly accelerated by the repeal of the glass tax in 1845,* when the price of basic sheet glass (introduced into England from France in 1773) fell to one-seventh of its former price. Loudon

* A glass tax levied upon glass wares of all kinds was first imposed in Britain between 1695 and 1699. It was reenacted in 1746, when it particularly affected the increased manufacture of window and plate glass. The rate was increased at intervals; in 1810 duties on window glass specifically were increased, and in 1812 the rates on all kinds of glass were raised so far that the manufacturing industry was severely affected and began to decline. Reductions then followed until the final repeal of the tax in 1845.

ABOVE: *An "orchard-house aviary" designed by Paxton. The birds are kept from the fruit by an arched wire trellis.*

BELOW: *Ornamental wood staging in a Victorian greenhouse supports plants above hot-water pipes. The low bed in front has its own heating supply.*

comments, "A taste for this appendage to a dwelling is natural to man . . . it adds to his enjoyments and bestows a certain claim to distinction on its possessor." Rather later the prolific writer and editor Shirley Hibberd (1825–1890) was claiming that "a conservatory should be a garden under glass and a place for frequent resort and agreeable assemblage at all seasons."

STRUCTURES

At this time the pressures of interest and fashion, and the vast range of exotics newly available, were the factors that determined the almost incredible developments in all types of glasshouses that occurred in this era. Advice of every kind proliferated; the prospective glasshouse owner was confounded by the initial choice between metal and wooden structures, and by the rival claims put up for houses of every conceivable shape.

Scientific writers poured out information on the best forms of structure and angles of glass to make the most of the sun; and in 1815 Sir George Mc'Kenzie discovered that the optimum structure was a hemispherical one. Expensive as they were, many "domical" or half-dome houses were built. One of the most popular forms of structure, apart from the rectangular, was that described as curvilinear, with glazing bars following a radial curve and converging at the highest point. Many greenhouses and conservatories were built on this principle, the oldest still existing probably being the Palm House at Bicton, Devon, constructed

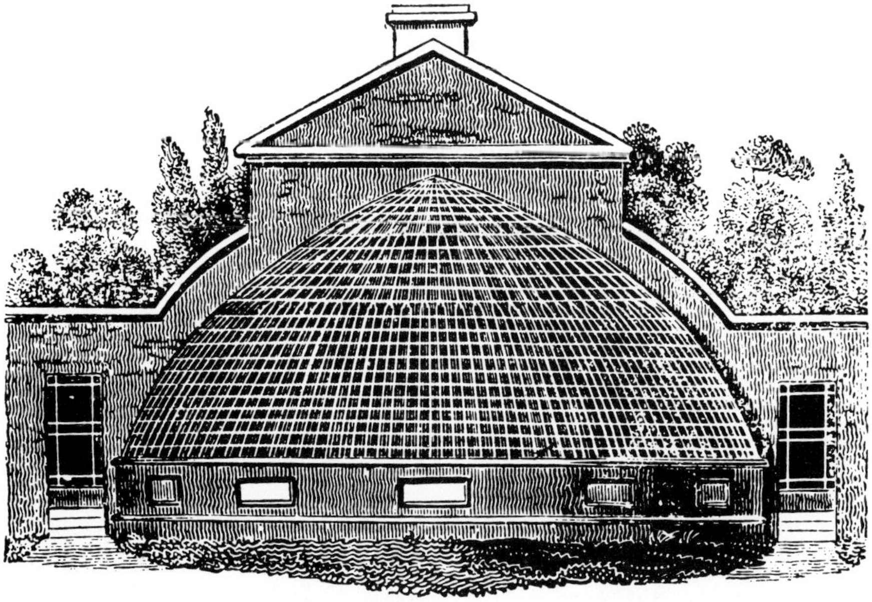

TOP: *This elegant half-dome structure of 1824, erected against a wall, made use of Loudon's flexible glazing bars.*

BELOW LEFT: *An early nineteenth-century greenhouse array with curvilinear roofs, in Hoboken, New Jersey, U.S.A., now sadly destroyed.*

BELOW: *The curvilinear Palm House at Bicton, Devon, England, is possibly the oldest of this type still standing; it was probably built at the end of the eighteenth century, and certainly not after 1838.*

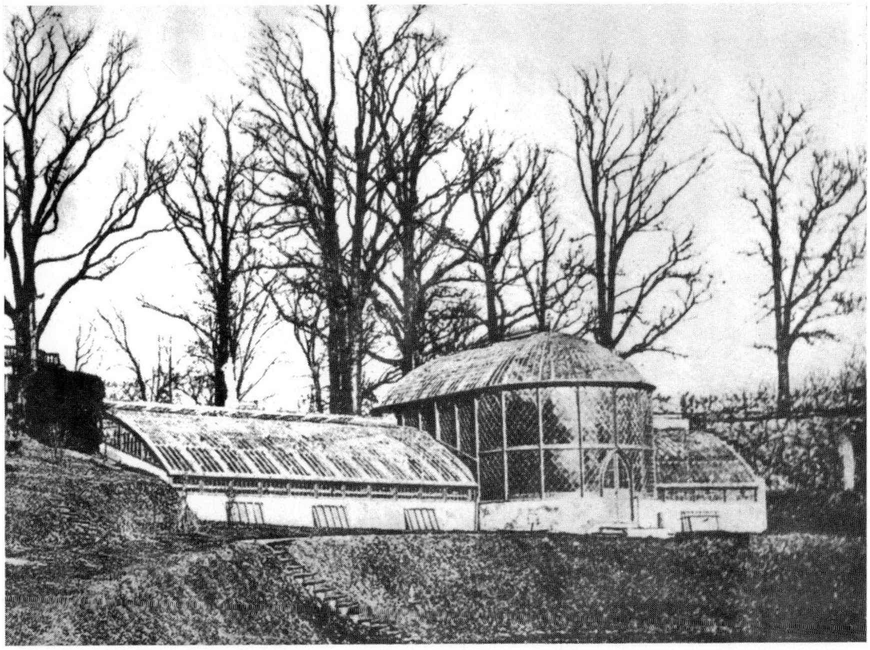

before 1838. In about the middle of the nineteenth century, Henry Winthrop Sargent built a large curvilinear fruit house, seventy by twenty feet and twelve feet high, at Wodenethe, a garden near Fishkill, New York. Until the late 1930s, there was a large structure of similar date at Castle Point, Hoboken, New Jersey, now the property of the Stevens Institute, with curvilinear front and top and curvilinear glazing to the shallowly sloping front bays; it was, sadly, pulled down because of decay.

One could also try the simple pitched roof; the ridge and furrow, in which large areas could be covered with the aid of pillars; the three-quarter span; the cylindrical; hexagonal; octagonal; and the "polyprosopic," the optimum suggested by Loudon, with the roof surface "thrown into a number of faces, these all being hinged at the upper angle and all

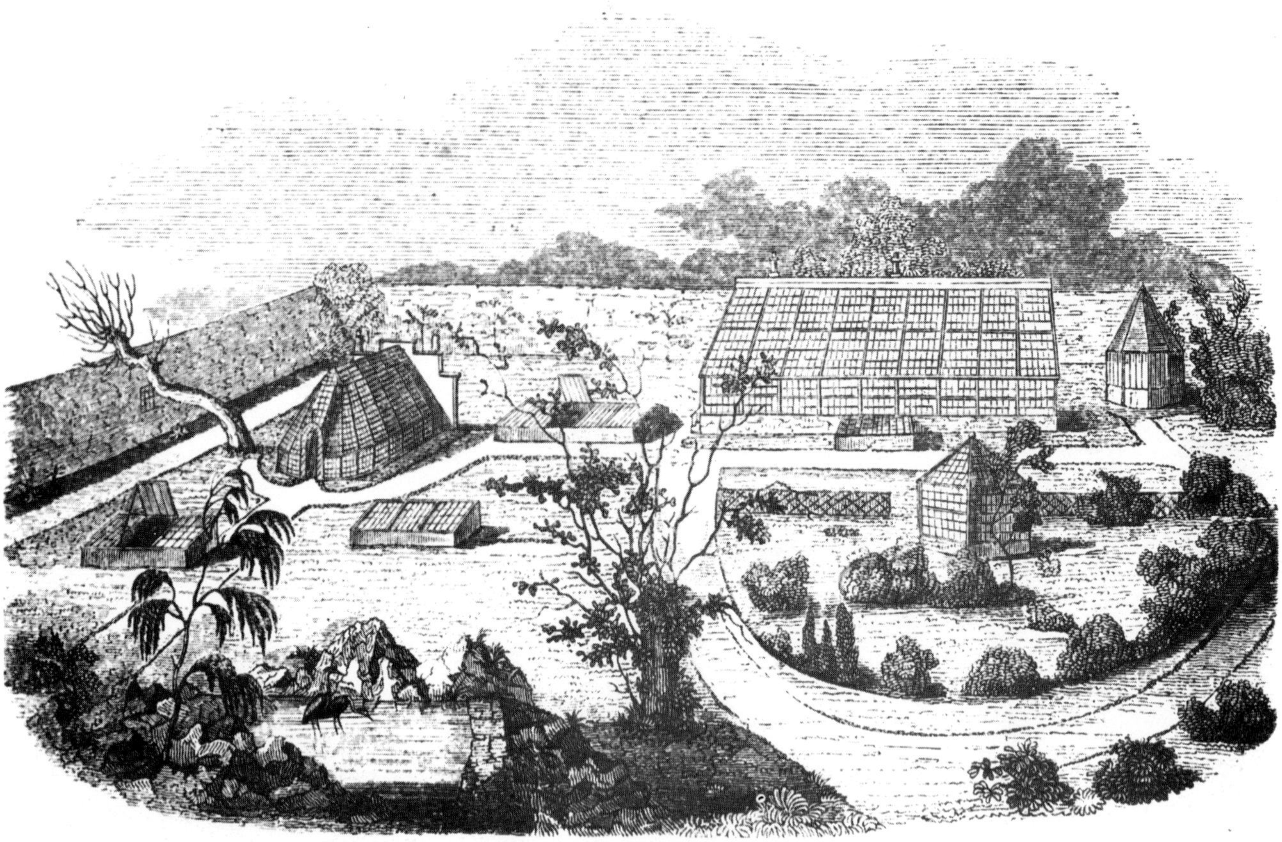

ABOVE: *The gardens of an Edinburgh gentleman of 1836 contained two large glasshouses, several frames and pits, an owl house, eagle house and an apiary.*

RIGHT: *A cross-section of the cucumber house in the Royal Gardens at Frogmore, near Windsor, England, in 1855, is partly built underground, making excellent use of space and available light. The plant beds are heated by hot-water pipes.*

The fernery at Southport Botanic Garden in England is housed in a large greenhouse which incorporates elaborate rockwork, arches and mossy grottoes. It was opened in 1875.

BELOW: *An orangery with classic-style pediment and solid roof, painted by Thomas Robins the Elder around 1750.*

OPPOSITE, BELOW: *In startling contrast, the geodesic domes of the Mitchell Park Conservatory, Milwaukee, enable plants to be grown in a number of controlled environments.*

OPPOSITE, ABOVE: *Two of the plantings under the Milwaukee domes – right, in the desert house; below, in the arid house.*

ABOVE: *A huge Wardian case of "Crystal Palace" type, restored to its original glory on an appropriate stand.*
ABOVE RIGHT: *The author's Warrington case. The container at the top is a reservoir, with a tap and pipe allowing water to reach a metal tray in the base. These cases are rare survivors from the Victorian age.*

RIGHT: *The bottle garden is a modern version of the Wardian case, always creating interest because of the "ship-in-a-bottle" effect produced by the narrow neck. These two gardens, in a whisky demijohn and an antique chemist's jar, were made by the author.*

OPPOSITE, ABOVE: *A comfortable conservatory on Long Island, New York, at second-floor level surrounded by treetops – perhaps designed more for human relaxation than plant cultivation.*
OPPOSITE, BELOW: *A simple modern conservatory in an English garden, designed in traditional style with vertical front, but with a glass roof.*

ABOVE: *An idealized version of a Persian "Paradise," where a stream runs sinuously among the flowering trees and through flower-spangled turf.*

OPPOSITE: *Keeping an eighteenth-century lawn in trim. A garden scene painted by Thomas Robins the Elder about 1750, showing all the contemporary operations of lawn care – scything, rolling, raking, and sweeping up cuttings.*

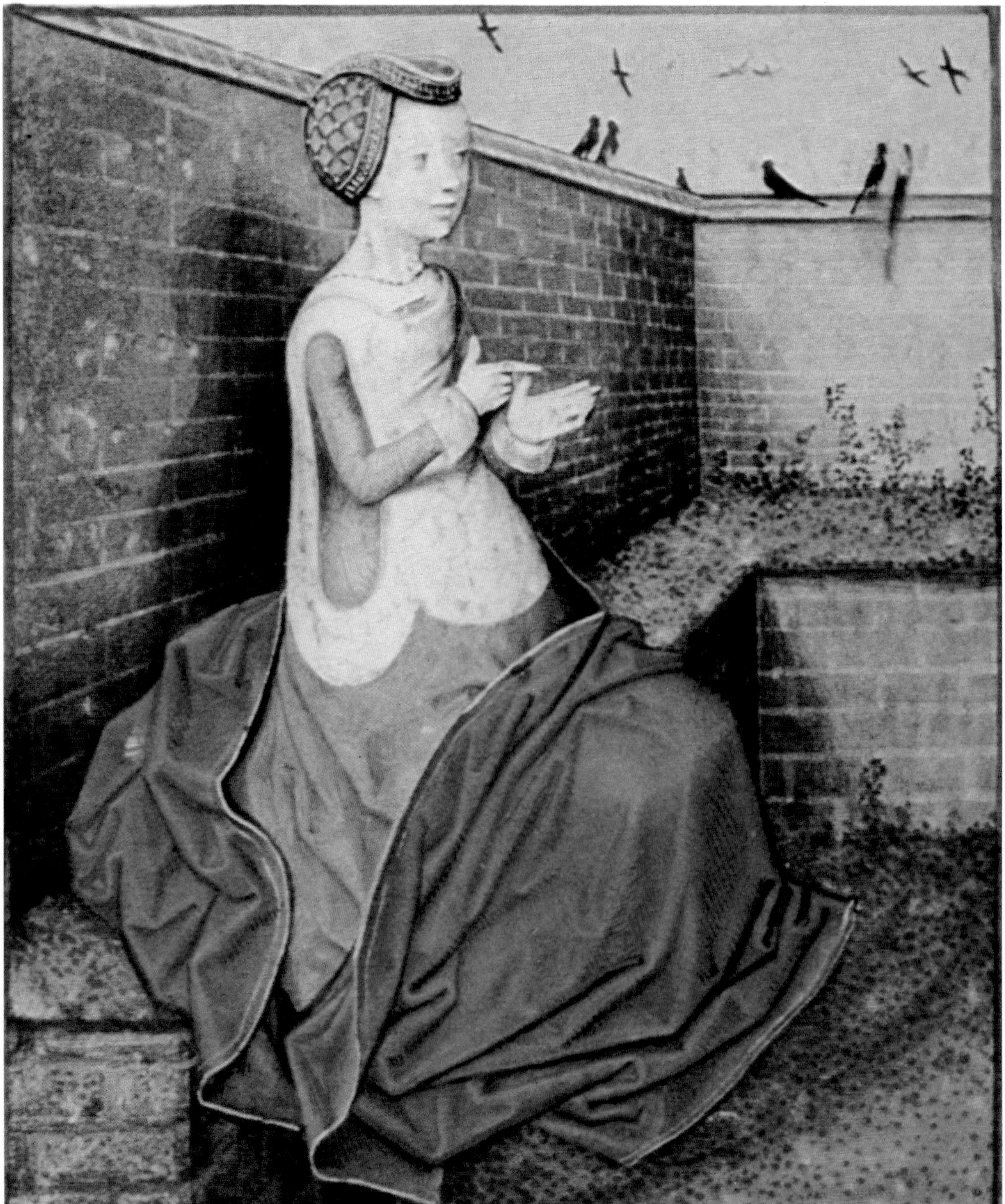

Medieval gardens habitually had turf seats, often supported by a low brick wall; they were sometimes made of chamomile. Perhaps the ladies' voluminous clothes prevented damp getting through.

Sections of late Victorian greenhouses in which cast iron plays an important part. Hot-water pipes heat both air and a deep soil bed in the three-quarter span house (left), and pass under the staging in a more orthodox way (below) in the equal-span house with fine tiered central heating.

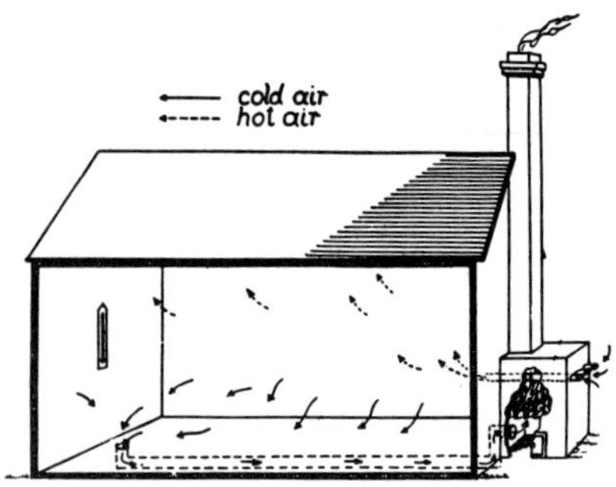

John Evelyn, in the mid-seventeenth century, devised a method of drawing uncontaminated air into a greenhouse: it was sucked through a hole in the floor by the pull of the fire, which heated fresh air being drawn in.

liftable to let in either the sun or the rain." In the mid-nineteenth century, growing grapes became immensely popular in the United States, and in Buffalo alone – as U. P. Hedrick says, "a boom city at this time, and not particularly interested in horticulture" – there were around forty vineries. A contemporary account is somewhat baffling, describing the typical structure as a "span-roof-octagon-curvilinear-lean-to with varied finish and architectural designs." The biggest of these Buffalo vineries was a commercial structure, a lean-to seven hundred feet long and twelve feet wide, housing over two hundred vines.

Sir Joseph Paxton – designer of the Great Conservatory and Giant Waterlily House at Chatsworth (now, alas, destroyed), and later the largest glass construction of them all, London's Crystal Palace – produced many designs at this time. (Whether they were ever built is debatable.) In many of them, sashes sloped right to the ground in an inverted V, and access to the interior was aided by sinking the floor. Structures with sunken floors are known as pit greenhouses, a form derived from the hotbed pit. The floor is sunk so far into the ground that the greenhouse roof is at or just above floor level. In such houses warmth is particularly well conserved because of the insulation provided by the soil, and the glass is less exposed to the wind. Popular in Victorian days, the pit is seldom constructed now, although it has many merits – probably because of the difficult excavation work involved.

GLAZING

Both glass and glazing methods improved out of recognition in the nineteenth century. Glass became clearer and more even, letting through more light without focusing it disastrously in one spot as flaws in older glass often did. Glass made in the United States, however, was very unsatisfactory for many years: it was wavy, spotted and blistered, so that plants grown under it were always liable to scorch. In the nineteenth century, most greenhouse glass was imported to America from France and Belgium. Glasshouse panes came in many shapes – in 1825 Loudon was recommending seven possibilities, each with some supposed advantage in sealing against water and air, and in forcing rain water into a desired spot. Most were flat, but some were curved, like the "corroboranted" pane which had a molded flange; others were made to be fixed like roof tiles on rafters without sash bars. Methods of fixing the glass were also examined; "laps" or clips of lead or copper might be used in conjunction with putty. Sir Joseph Paxton designed a glazing bar which combined a channel for rain water on the outside with others to trap condensation on the inside; it was soon called the Paxton gutter. Originally wooden, these bars were later made of cast iron. He took his inspiration from the enormous ribs on the inside of the giant waterlily's leaves, which may be up to two yards across: "Nature was the engineer," he wrote, "nature has provided the leaf with longitudinal and transverse girders and supports that I, borrowing from it, have adopted."

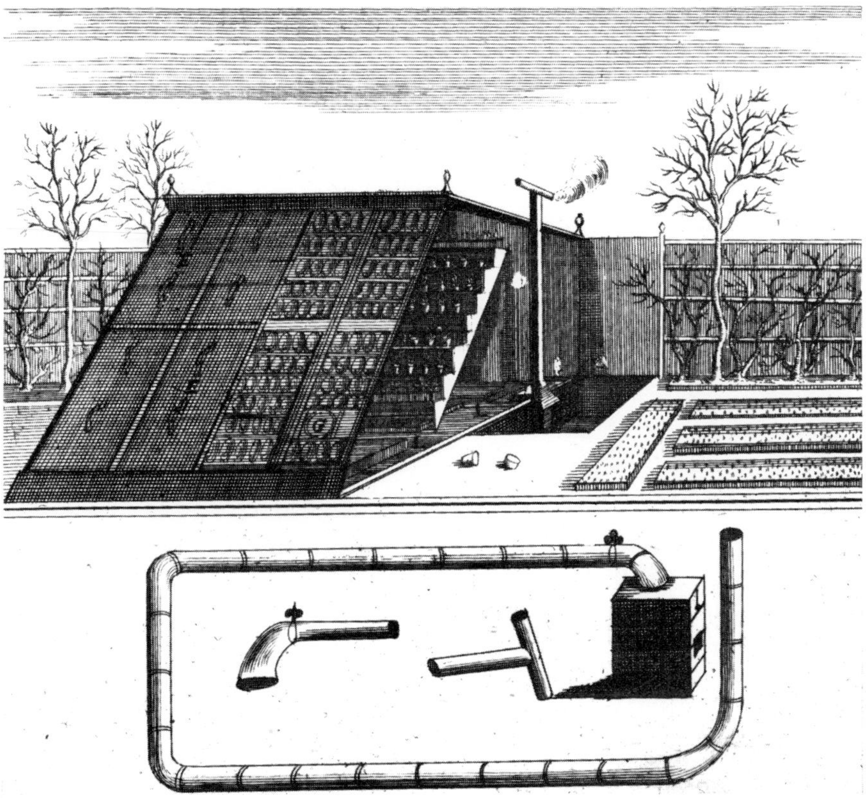

The experimental greenhouse built by G. A. Agricola before 1717 was heated by the hot smoke from an outside stove passing through a looped flue, shown diagramatically below. The windows "for certain reasons were made with round panes," and were built parallel to an oblique staging for pots. Shutters covered the windows when protection was necessary.

Ironically enough, the improvements in glazing led to unforeseen problems – the clearer glass, and the bigger sizes which were used without great numbers of shadow-casting glazing bars, gave rise to sun scorch. Theorizing then began on using glass tinted in various colors; some of the glasshouses at England's Kew Gardens were originally glazed with a pale yellowish green glass. In America, the theory that light filtered through blue was best for plant (and also human) health gave rise to a craze for blue glass. However, it was soon found that clear glass was essential for healthy plant growth, and sun scorch was dealt with by various methods of shading such as we still use today – by incorporating roller blinds of thin wooden strips, or of material like muslin, or by painting whitewash or more sophisticated shading paints on the exterior of the glass as high summer approached. A recent invention is a surface application which goes transparent in rain and opaque in sun.

Plants would be grown in these houses in various ways. In the orangery, of course, they usually lived in large containers, although they might grow in beds in the ground itself. As exotic plants multiplied, the tendency was to grow them massed in pots on shelves, or "stagings," in tiers along the walls, or freestanding at waist level. Vines and fruit trees were usually grown directly in the soil, and sometimes soil beds would be raised to waist level by a retaining wall.

HEATING METHODS

Such arrangements were readily combined with heating arrangements, which by the mid-nineteenth century were almost entirely of

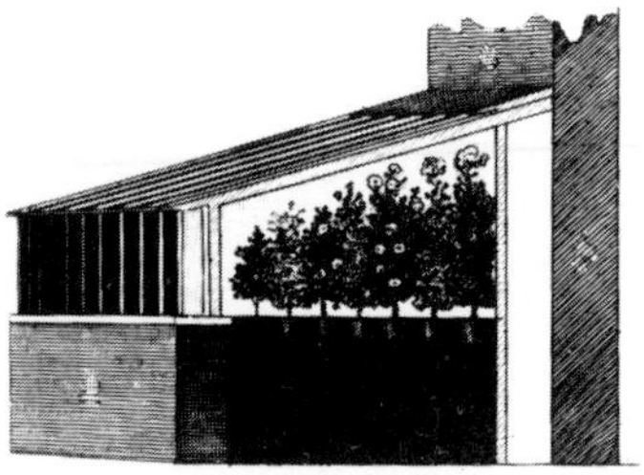

The pots of the "greens" are sunk into a deep pit of tan bark or dung in this eighteenth-century greenhouse.

pipes filled with water heated by a boiler. But before this time less satisfactory methods were employed.

I have already described the elementary means of heating orangeries by open fires, charcoal pans, and finally a standing stove with flue. By degrees the flue system became developed as a means of heating the structure rather than as a way of getting rid of the fumes. John Evelyn, in the mid-seventeenth century, suggested a method by which fresh air was drawn into the greenhouse via pipes of "crucible earth" passing through an oven or furnace outside the structure. A return pipe in the floor at the further end of the greenhouse entered the furnace below fire level and eventually left through a chimney. This had the effect of ensuring a good circulation of air.

Although this appears to be a sensible and satisfactory method, providing warm, fresh air, most of the earlier warm-air systems involved the hot gases arising from the furnace fire passing through the greenhouse in a flue, finally escaping at a higher level outside so that the fire would continue to "draw." Later methods had heated vaults or flues below the floor or, as we have seen, zigzagging in the back walls of greenhouses. In this respect, the early heating systems parallel those of Roman houses and, presumably, the Pompeiian *specularia* mentioned earlier. Of the very low greenhouse of 1800 at Waltham, Massachusetts, mentioned on page 236, Arthur Lyman, great-grandson of the first owner, said that "the smoke and heat of a small fire at the west end is carried in a long flat horizontal flue to the chimney at the east end." A grape house on the same estate was originally heated "by wood fires built in arches of brick at the base of the heavy north brick wall, the heated wall slowly giving out its heat to the house." This house was originally built for tropical fruits and ornamental plants.

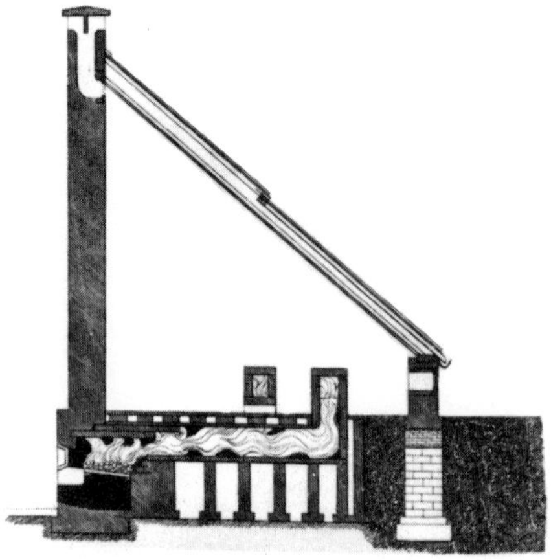

A method much used in the eighteenth and early nineteenth centuries employed flues directly heated by a stove, standing well into the greenhouse structure.

Unfortunately, flues were unreliable and often leaked noxious fumes into the greenhouses almost as badly as the old open methods. Richard Bradley, writing in 1718, describes how he "half-roasted" his plants "with subterranean fires which commonly raised damps, cracked the passages of the flues where it ran and oft filled the house with smoke, which is a great enemy to plants." Of charcoal fires, he writes, "several men have been choked by them, and sparks from them have set fire to the house, but that depends on the care of the gardener." Such fires and flue systems all gave dry heat, which the citrus and other "greens" more or less put up with, and which gardeners thought the newly introduced aloes, prickly pears and the like would enjoy.

A heating revolution occurred early in the eighteenth century, when it was discovered that the bark (usually oak) used by tanners gave off a great deal of heat when it started to ferment after its use in tanning pits, where crushed bark was placed in water.

The first man to use "tan bark" seems to have been Henry

To provide "bottom heat" for rooting cuttings, Agricola devised a double container – the upper part a basket of soil, where the cuttings were rooted, which fitted into a framework containing fermenting dung. The whole was placed at the front of his glasshouse. The dung pit has a lid "which serves to hide the nastiness."

Telende, gardener to Sir Matthew Decker, who raised England's first pineapple "deemed worthy of the Royal table" with its aid in 1720. Telende used a brick-lined pit some 5 feet deep, 11 feet long, and $7\frac{1}{2}$ feet wide, with a glass cover. He put a layer of fermenting dung a foot deep at the bottom and covered this with 300 bushels of tan bark. The bed was prepared in early February; it was ready for use by the end of the month and lasted until October.

The use of tan bark became widespread, and the usual preparation was to add a small quantity of elm sawdust to a load of used bark. It was allowed to heat up for a week and was then placed in the pit, layer by layer, with elm sawdust sprinkled on each layer. Two weeks later pots could be plunged into it. Temperatures of up to 90°F were reached, and not the least advantage was the humidity this method created around the plants.

What seems surprising is the vast amount of tanner's bark that must have been available, for this became the standard method of heating many glasshouses, as well as the pits in which pineapples were often grown. Oak leaves, also used in tanning, could be substituted for bark, and fresh manure was also used for heating up pits and "stoves," as hot greenhouses came to be called. Dung (first used for pits around 1660) was sometimes heaped up outside a raised pine pit, up the outer back wall of a lean-to greenhouse, or even inside a greenhouse. Loudon recommended "finishing off" grapes with a large pile of fermenting manure. However, it did not retain its heat as long as tan bark.

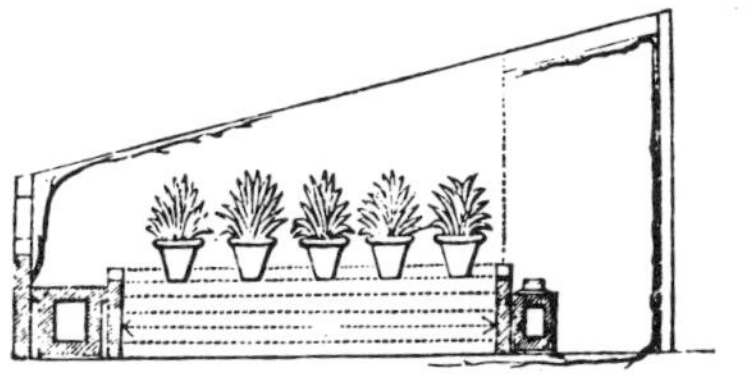

Pineapples were grown in "pine pits" which had to be heated to a considerable degree. The simplest method (top) was to heap dung outside a covered frame. More sophisticated methods used tan bark under the plants, its heat sometimes supplemented with hot-air ducts (above).

The use of dung and especially tan bark was sometimes supplemented by heating flues, and the latter, in improved form, became the most common form of heating in the early nineteenth century. Both the flue pipes and the furnaces that supplied the hot air were greatly improved, the first to avoid fumes escaping, the latter to get more out of the fuel burned. Flues began to emerge from the walls they had been built into, to become raised or even detached air channels within the glasshouse structure, thus delivering their heat where it was needed. They were often topped with flagstones, cast-iron panels, or tiles, and these might have a central channel in which evaporating water would provide humidity.

At this time there was little way in which heat could be controlled except the delayed-action one of stoking up or damping down the furnace fire. Richard Bradley, in the early eighteenth century, advocated a foot depth of sand over an exposed flue. This could be removed to allow heat to escape. It was a century before anyone thought of an air valve – really just an adjustable ventilating aperture – on the furnace inlet.

There is not, unfortunately, the space to expand on the innumerable ideas which were mooted for the design of flues and furnaces; the subject is, perhaps, more akin to engineering than horticulture in any case. The great revolution came with the use of steam and, finally, the more easily controlled hot-water heating. In the eighteenth century, Diderot, in his great *Encyclopédie*, drew his idea of a steam-heated frame; we do not know whether this was ever made. In England the Earl of Derby's gardener heated melon and pine pits with steam in 1792, using perforated pipes within tan beds, so that the steam added to the tan bark's heat. By 1816 several extensive steam-heated glass ranges were in operation, some passing the steam through pipes, others exuding it through small perforations into beds filled with loose stones. The most successful use of steam seems to have been in installations where a one-inch steam pipe ran through the center of an eight-inch water-filled pipe; this method allowed the pipes to work at lower temperatures and to retain their heat at the same level for longer if the fire heat or outside temperature changed materially.

This technique led, naturally enough, to the use of hot-water pipes heated by a boiler, such as are often used today in houses as well as greenhouses. This method could not be put into proper use until it was understood that hot water would circulate in a closed circuit without external pumping, a fact not established until 1818. The first British greenhouse installations were made in the early 1820s, and by the late 1830s a number of boiler systems were available commercially. Enormous numbers of these proliferated as the century progressed, some of them seeming more suitable for railroad locomotives.

Hot-water heating arrived in the United States about 1831, when it was considered freakish. Previously heating had been carried out by horizontal flues in the greenhouse walls, or by hotbeds of fermenting manure, with which pineapples and other tropical plants, and vegetables out of season, were being grown well before the end of the eighteenth century. (The first record of a hotbed is in 1773 in Virginia.) Until about 1850 hot-water heating in the United States was very much a luxury used in the hothouses and vineries of the rich.

Today we see hot-water boilers still in use, fired with coal or, more conveniently, oil, alongside newer methods. Electricity powers tubular heaters – resembling a hot-water system – or fan heaters; gas has made its debut as a cheap, efficient method; and in countless small greenhouses in Europe paraffin (kerosene) heaters keep out the frost. (Some of these are little changed from their late Victorian predecessors; more modern ones often have horizontal heat diffusers.)

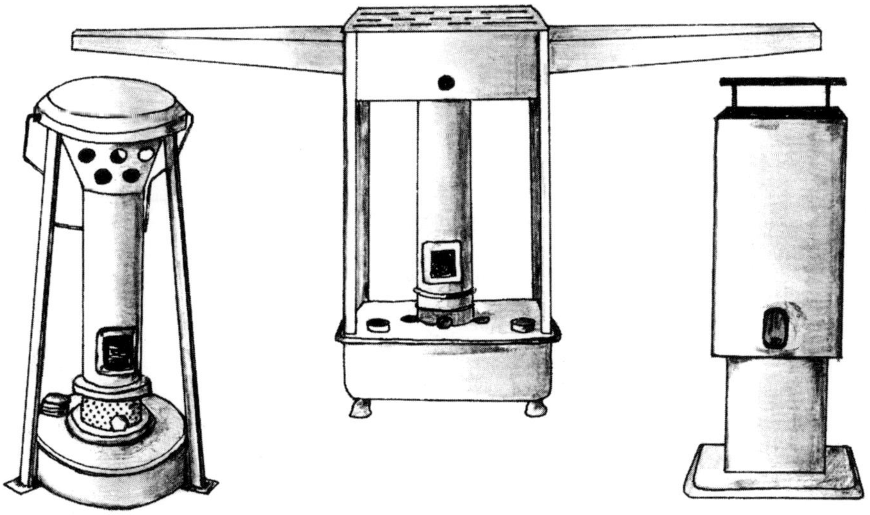

Modern methods of heating smaller greenhouses. LEFT TO RIGHT: *Two paraffin or kerosene heaters, the central one having heat distributors and a gas-burning device.* ABOVE: *An electric fan heater.*

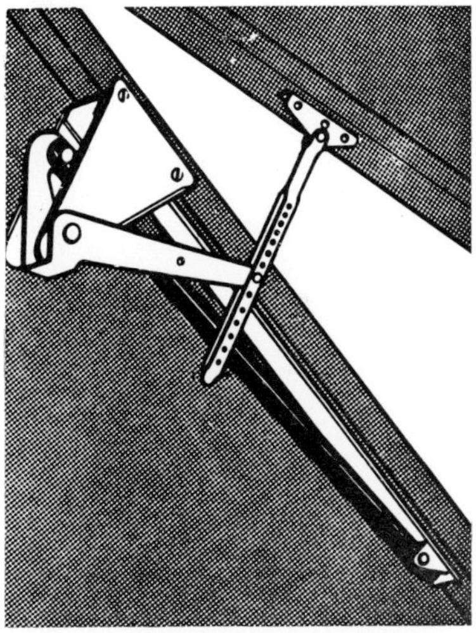

ABOVE: *Today automatic ventilator control is simply carried out by devices in which the piston is directly operated by expansion or contraction of a fluid within, and operates a lever attached to the vent.*

LEFT: One of the earliest attempts at *thermostatic heat control – Kewley's "alarum-thermometer," depicted by Loudon in 1834. It was based on a large thermometer filled partly with mercury and partly with spirits of wine; any change of temperature would move the mercury from one of the ball-shaped vessels to the other, alter the balance of the pre-set apparatus, and ring an alarm bell. Alternatively, wires in the "automation gardener" (below left) could be connected to each end of the balance thermometer, and a water-primed piston (below right) would move accordingly, and could open and shut ventilators.*

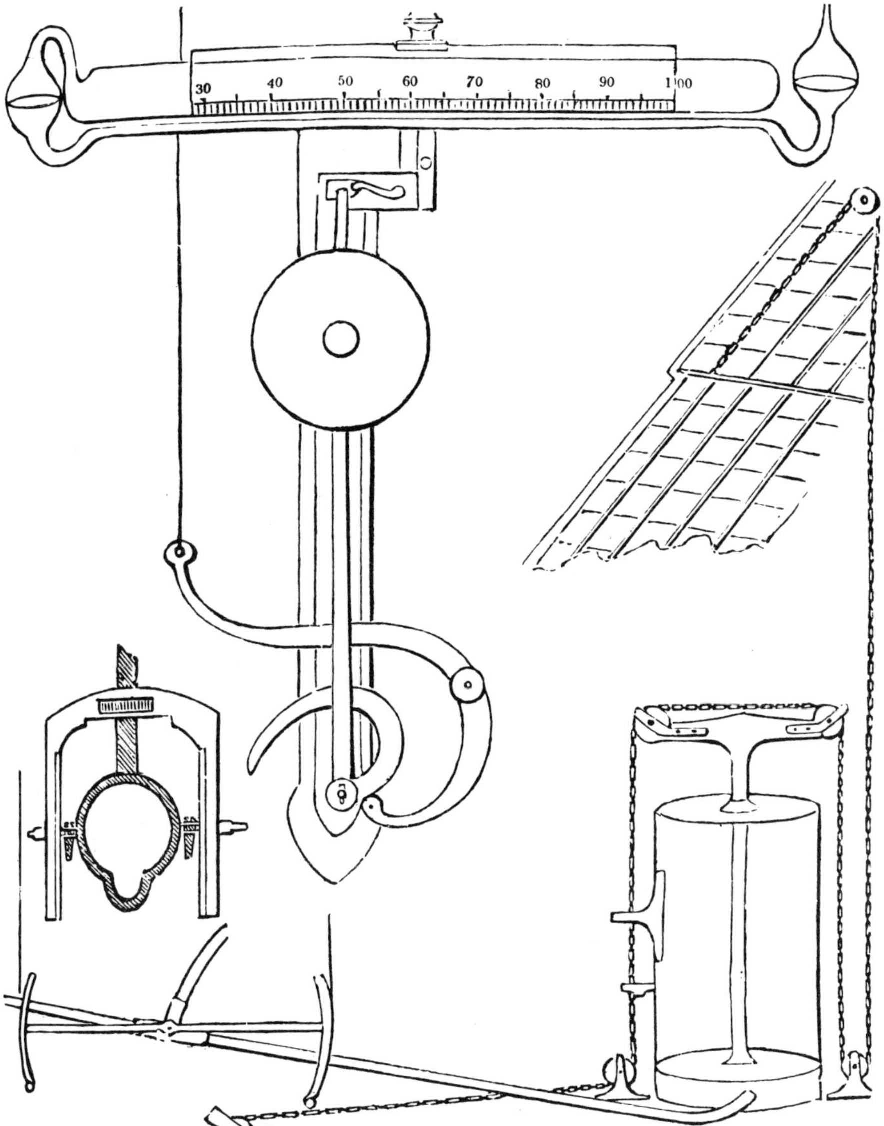

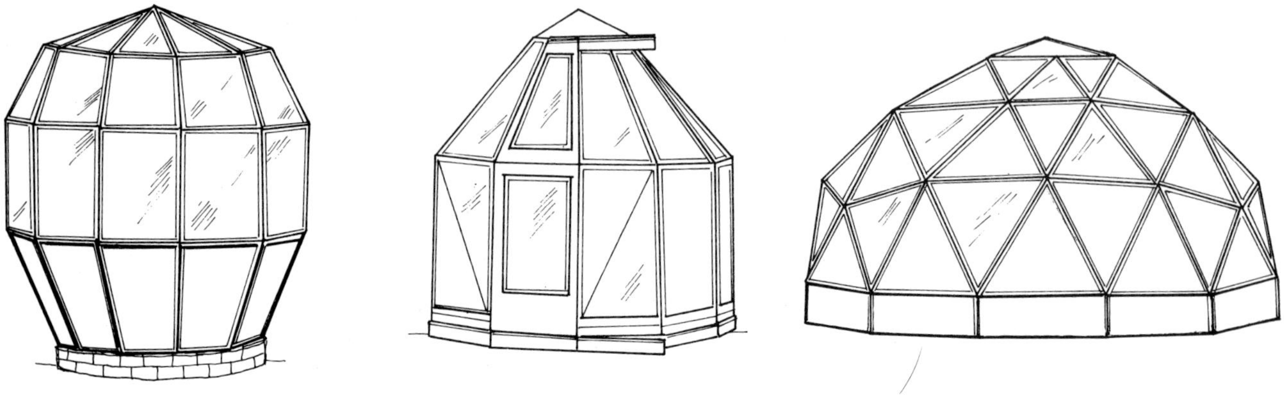

Some recent innovations in small greenhouse design, including a geodesic structure (right).

Electricity has the advantage of being capable of very accurate thermostatic control; oil-fired water heaters can also be controlled in this way, and a different kind of thermostat will control the gas heaters. The desirability of temperature control was of course clear to early nineteenth-century greenhouse designers, but without electricity their inventions were cumbersome, if very ingenious, like the one illustrated on page 255 which could ring an alarm bell or, apparently, actually open and close greenhouse ventilators. Today ventilators can be controlled according to temperature by a much more compact device operating by the expansion and contraction of a gasoline compound in a piston. A further refinement is the use of thermostatically controlled electric fan ventilators with louvers to prevent blowback.

GREENHOUSE SHAPES

Greenhouses themselves have altered little in principle since the late nineteenth century, although construction, especially in metal, has become more sophisticated. The habitual structure remains typically barn-shaped. In recent years, several small, more or less circular greenhouses have been produced but, although attractive to look at, they have severe limitations as efficient places to grow plants. Geodesic greenhouses have become fairly popular on both sides of the Atlantic, and in the United States huge geodesic structures, resembling the Victorian dome, have been built, with astounding control over the internal conditions. But these are for botanical institutions, not for the amateur or commercial grower.

One of the most impressive of these is the Climatron at the Missouri Botanical Gardens – a far cry from the first greenhouses built there a little over a century ago by Henry Shaw, who was inspired to do so after seeing Paxton's Great Conservatory in England. In the Climatron, as in the giant conservatory in Colorado's Denver Botanical Gardens, curtains of air separate the various climes and their permanent natural habitats. In Milwaukee, Wisconsin, there are three separate domes, each completely air conditioned with its own climate. Similar controlled conditions provide a tropical environment at the Boettcher Memorial Center, Denver, Colorado. In Calgary, Canada, another conservatory features tropical birds along with its plants.

ABOVE: *The huge geodesic dome of the Climatron at the Missouri Botanic Garden, in which curtains of air separate naturalistic groupings of plants from different countries.*

LEFT: *An open lattice-covered plant house as used in warmer climates, such as the southern United States, to keep excessive sun and also light frost from the plants.*

In Europe various ideas have been mooted for making more use of limited ground space, including one system in which the greenhouse is tower-shaped and the plants in pots move continually up and down on endless belts. An earlier use of motion, created in order to give plants better access to sunlight, was that of a Massachusetts orchid grower, Albert C. Burrage, who before 1930 built a greenhouse which revolved with the sun.

Plastic houses kept inflated by a small air pump have been used successfully, especially to cover temporary or quick-growing crops. Many cheap greenhouses today use plastic film for a covering, though this suffers from degradation by sunlight and does not last more than five years, often less. It also encourages excessive condensation. However, with such covering the greenhouse structure can be much simpler, lighter and quicker to erect, and interesting curves can be embodied. Stiff plastics such as acrylic sheet and fiberglass are being used increasingly in the United States. One recent U.S. design uses double glazing of rigid acrylic, each glazing panel consisting of two panes with an air space in between, which acts as a thermal insulator and greatly reduces heating costs. Double glazing of greenhouses with glass has been ruled out because of the demands it makes on the structure, and it has in any case been suspect because of reduced light transmission. But this new development is claimed to transmit virtually the same quality of light as a single pane of glass without loss or any discoloration. A material that will genuinely supersede brittle glass is certainly much to be desired.

Another aspect of protection is the open plant house, composed of lattice or spaced laths both on the sides and on top, to keep excessive sun and light frost from plants. This seems to have been developed first in the southern United States in the early part of this century; Netherlands' nurserymen, Japanese bonsai growers and Far Eastern orchidists are among others who use the same idea.

FRAMES AND CLOCHES

The development of the greenhouse was paralleled by that of smaller glass-covered structures, namely frames and bell glasses or cloches. I have already mentioned the Roman use of pits covered with sheets of mica, thin talc or, possibly, glass; the Romans also discovered the value of fermenting dung to heat the pits. Alternatively, well-manured soil was placed in a deep basket which was carried into the sun wherever it was warm enough and was covered with "transparent stone." A refinement was a board on wheels on which the pots or baskets stood, easily moved in and out of shelter. This seems to have been employed by the gardener of Tiberius Caesar who had, according to Pliny, to provide the emperor with the daily cucumber recommended by his doctor. Columella gives a detailed description of the process.

The Egyptian Bolus of Mendes, quoted by Columella, had a more puzzling method of forcing. "He advices us to have . . . fennels and brambles planted in alternate rows, and then, when the equinox is past, to cut them a little below the surface of the ground and, after loosening with a wooden prong the pith of the bramble or fennel, to put dung into them and thus insert the cucumber seeds, so that, as they grow, they may unite with the brambles and fennels, for by this method, they are nourished not from their own roots but from what may be called the mother root; and the stock thus engrafted yields the fruit of the cucumber even in cold weather."

The idea of forcing may even have come from the Greeks, for Plato wrote of their Adonis gardens, that "a grain of seed or the branch of a tree, placed in . . . these gardens acquired in eight days a development which cannot be obtained in as many months in the open air." The implication seems to be the use of a bell glass or similar protective device.

Garden frames, very similar to those of the present day, were widely used in the seventeenth century, as were the glass cloche (left) and other types of framed hand light (above center), shaped for different purposes.

It was the seventeenth century before further use of such devices became at all common, parallel with the development of orangeries. Wheeled "trays" of soil, echoing those of the Romans, are mentioned by Gervase Markham in 1631; these were placed in shelters at night or in cold weather. Glass-covered, dung-filled pits were in use around 1660, and in 1670 wooden-sided garden frames of virtually the same design as those in use today are shown in books. Alongside these were glass cloches, about one foot wide, bell-shaped with a knob for handling on top, certainly in use in 1629, as were hand lights of usually small glass panes set in metal frames. These hand lights were of various shapes and sizes, and one illustration of 1726 shows something very like a modern "continuous cloche" – triangular, with large glass panes a good foot across (page 260).

The earliest examples of cloche and frame were undoubtedly of thick, often green glass, which provided more protection than light transmission. The glass was often replaced with oiled paper, which was also widely used for secondary insulation of orangeries. (Some early reference books depict large machines for preparing oiled paper.) Sometimes pits were covered with solid boards: such covers would be lifted during mild weather to allow light and air to reach the plants.

Cloches were employed in ever-increasing numbers to protect and encourage tender vegetables and fruits such as melons and cucumbers, and also to give crops an early start. They were still in use on some specialized crops such as violets in the 1930s. Hand lights were mostly employed in the garden to cover specialized crops and plants; their variety of size and shape increased in Victorian days, when some were made with detachable tops. The first really elongated hand light is depicted in Loudon's *Encyclopaedia* of 1818. I think this may well have been rather more convenient to handle than the so-called continuous cloches (invented after World War II), consisting of two or more panes of glass held together by an ungainly series of interlocking wires, and very easily broken. Their advantages are that panes can be removed for ventilation, or the cloches staggered slightly so that air can enter, and of course individual cloches can be removed to allow attention to the plants below. Continuous cloches are made in three forms: the tent, of two pieces of glass at right angles; the barn, a tent with two further vertical panes to give added height; and the flat-top barn, of three panes.

RIGHT: *Various advanced kinds of protected cultivation depicted in 1726: glass cloches, a kind of triangular continuous cloche, and at left, wall-trained fruit under large glass lights very like the modern Dutch light in outer dimensions.*

BELOW: *A specialized French fruit and vegetable garden of 1763, in which numerous cloches are used, many on hotbeds of fermenting dung (right), two of which are sloped to receive maximum sunlight. Espaliered fruit trees occupy all the walls.*

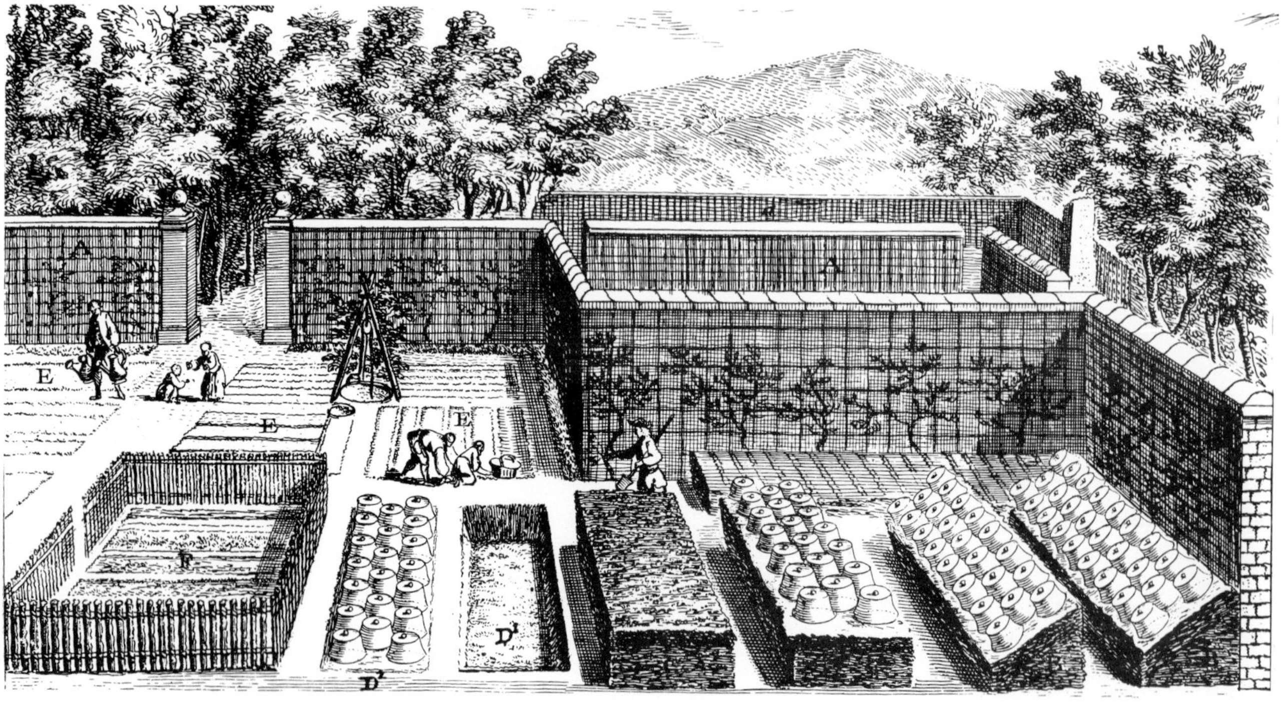

LEFT: *Cloches in use in a sheltered melon garden which has raised beds and trained wall fruit (1703).*

BELOW: *In the nineteenth century, hand lights proliferated in many shapes. Bell glasses might have a ventilation cap; metal-framed lights were used to protect tender shrubs and smaller plants including vegetables. The swiveling lid was designed to give ventilation or access when the base was frozen to the ground.*

BOTTOM: *A very early form of continuous cloche.*

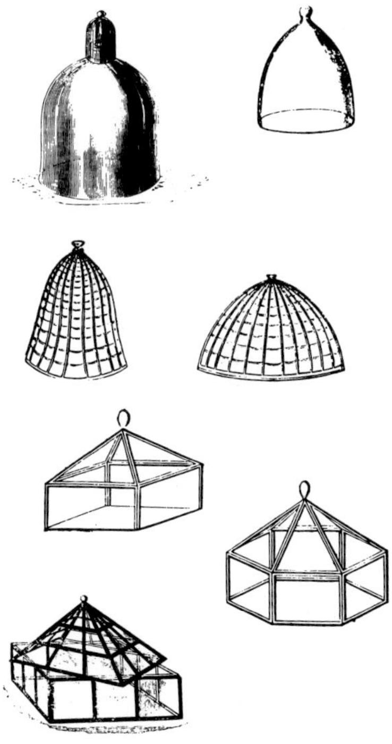

The breakability of glass cloches led to others of more durable, if more opaque, glass substitute, which can in fact be bent into a V form without any framework wires. Other glass-avoiding cloches are made of both rigid and soft plastic sheeting, the soft being used in long lengths to make "tunnels." Both are supported on hoops of wire. Tunnel cloches are widely used by commercial growers, as are greenhouse-sized structures of simple timber or metal framing covered with polyethylene, and both are easily moved from crop to crop. Plastic cloches are much easier to store than glass ones, and although plastic has a limited life, torn plastic is cheaper to replace than glass.

Garden frames are used partly to grow tender and out-of-season crops, partly to protect tender plants during the winter, and partly to give seedlings raised in the greenhouse an interim period of "hardening off" before they are transferred to the open garden. Glass frames were in extensive use in London market gardens in 1748, when the Swedish traveler Peter Kalm described them, protected at night from cold with "Russian matting," itself covered with straw.

Although the basic design of the frame has changed hardly at all from the seventeenth century, being essentially a raised box with a sloped glass lid or "light," there have of course been some variations on it. The most important was a reduction in the number of panes in what was for long the standard size of light, 6 by 4 feet, so that much more light could penetrate. The so-called Dutch light, usually 59 by $30\frac{3}{4}$ inches, is a simple wooden frame with a single piece of glass, inserted without putty. Both in weight and light transmission, it is better than the ordinary frame light, and lends itself also to the construction of quickly erected greenhouses; but the large panes are easily broken and quite expensive to replace.

As late as 1935 these large cloches (above) were in use over violets in Sussex, England. Plastic sheet over wire hoops forms the modern continuous "cloche" (below), though the metal-framed ones of glass sheets are still in use (right).

LEFT: *An elaborate – and perhaps hypothetical – late Victorian strawberry house made up of many framelike units.*

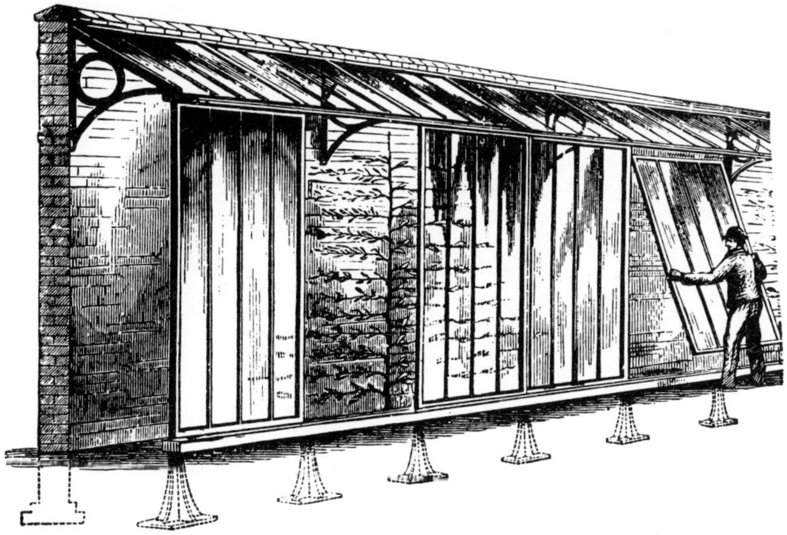

BELOW LEFT: *A sophisticated structure of similar date to protect wall-trained fruit trees: when frost threatens glass panels are placed in position.*

Frame structures are today made of wood, brick, concrete or metal. Besides the traditional one-way slope of a long light, frames with a pitched roof were in use in Victorian times, the lights being hinged at the apex. Pitched-roof frames of simpler construction are popular today; some sophisticated models have sliding, metal-framed roof lights on solid walls.

FROST PROTECTION

Glass protection has been adapted in various ways which cannot be classified as greenhouse, cloche or frame. One of the more sensible was the provision of temporary protection for fruit trees. Whereas such fruits as peaches and nectarines were habitually grown in lean-to greenhouses, these and more hardy fruits were often, as we have seen, trained against outside walls. But spring frosts are always a hazard to flowers or newly set fruit, and the late Victorian suggestions for glass panels or burlap curtains, which could be set in front of the trees when needed, in conjunction with a narrow overhanging roof, are ingenious and valuable. Less practical seems "Ingram's strawberry house" which is really a series of frames piled one on top of the other; the idea of making good use of vertical space and available sun is fine, but how the frames are reached or watered is not explained.

Fruit trees can also be protected against frost in other ways, and on walls a drape or screen of fine mesh netting or muslin gives a little more protection; burlap and thin plastic give a good deal more, especially in windy weather. The possibilities of this method were understood in the early eighteenth century; it acts mainly by trapping the day's residual heat. Opaque covers must, of course, be removed each morning.

On a commercial scale in orchards, it is possible to heat the air on frosty nights by making slow-burning fires on the windward side and among the trees; recently special "smoke pots" have been available to release heat over several hours. Some installations use large fans which dispel frost by bringing down warmer air from above the trees. The most modern method is to use water sprinklers. As long as these are constantly on during the period of frost, the latent heat of freezing (however anomalous that may sound) will actually keep ice-encased buds and flowers just above the temperature at which damage occurs. The frost sprinklers can double as irrigators during the summer. In the United States, all of these methods have been employed, in particular to protect the citrus crops in Florida during periods of severe frost.

In the seventeenth century, straw "hats," shaped like glass cloches, were used to keep frost from strawberries and other small fruits. Today we are less neat and usually protect the strawberry flowers from frost by heaping straw over the plants; this must of course be pulled back every morning. Straw, dried bracken or similar material is habitually used to keep frost from tender deciduous shrubs, which are bound up in the straw in the autumn, sometimes in an outer layer of burlap or polyethylene sheet. Such methods have been in use for several centuries. Similar protection can be given to tender herbaceous plants, although often a heap of sand or ashes will keep frost from their roots. Alpines which dislike winter wet rather than the cold are often covered by a glass pane held above the plant on short supports.

The Victorians used prefabricated wicker covers for tender plants, and also wicker windbreaks, for much damage is caused by searing cold winds. Once again the principle has long been recognized; in 1691 there is a description by J. Gibson, in *Account of Several Gardens near London*, of Sir Henry Capel's garden at Kew, where "stood out his orange trees and other choicer greens in two walks about fourteen feet wide, enclosed with a timber frame about seven feet high and set with silver firs hedge-wise which are as high as the frame, and this to secure them from wind and tempest and

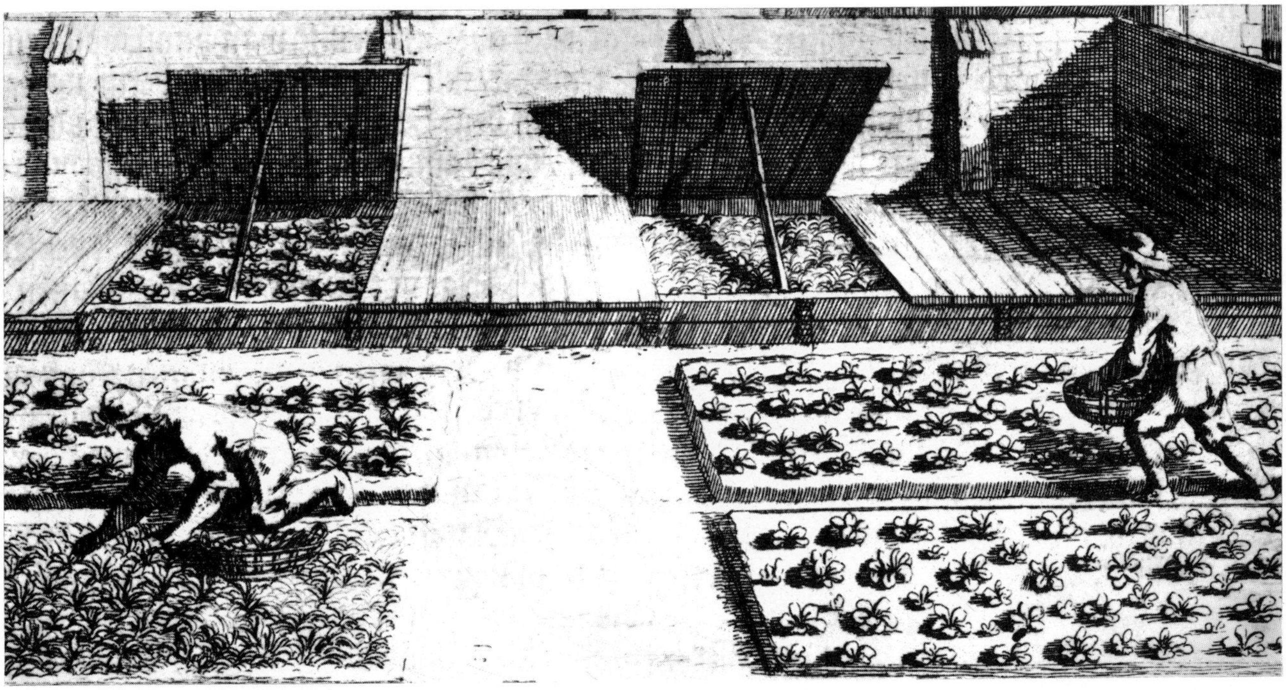

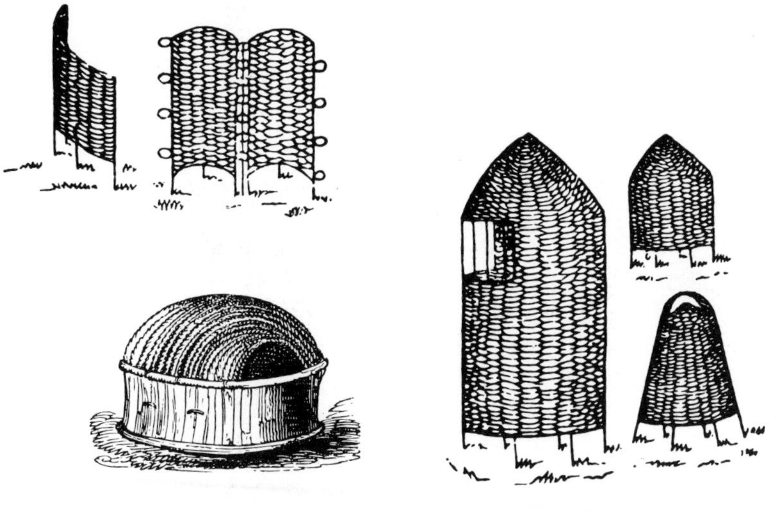

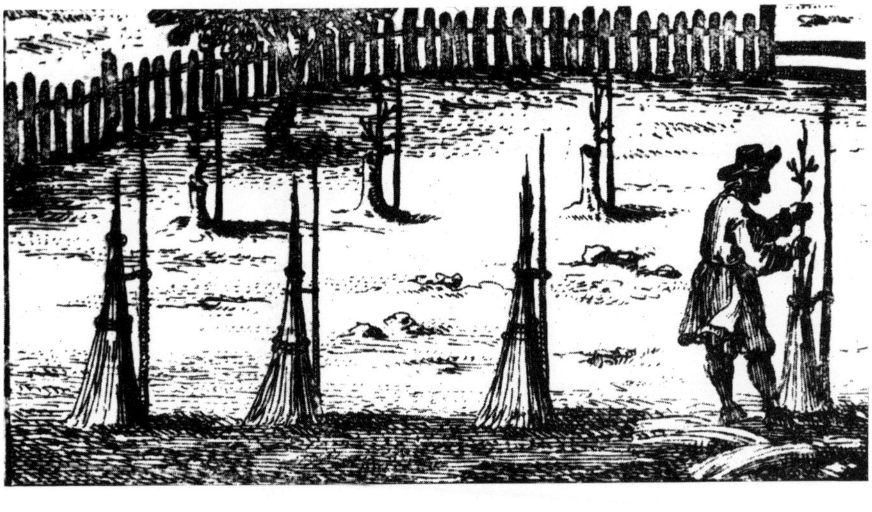

ABOVE: *The most basic form of protection is solid shuttering, let down to cover the frames on cold nights (1706).*

LEFT: *Victorian wicker windbreaks, and wicker covers for tender plants – they might be packed internally with bracken or straw.* BELOW LEFT: *Straw "wigwams" protect young fruit trees against winter cold (1703).*

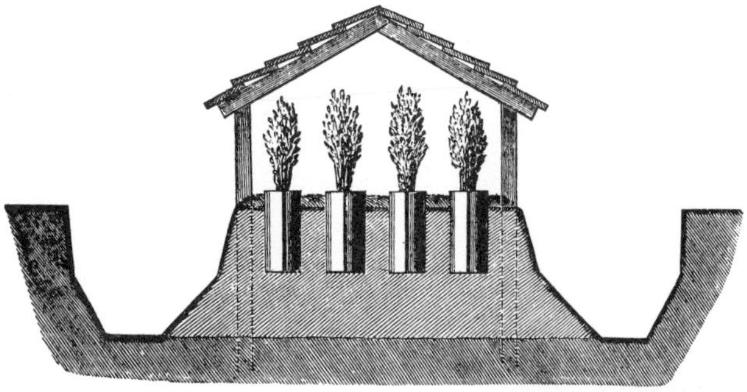

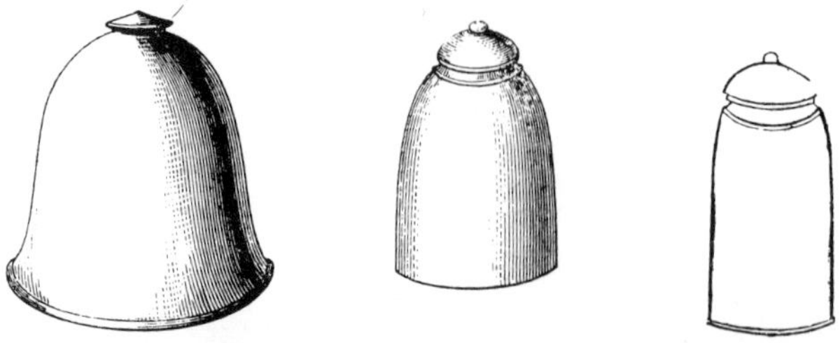

TOP: *Late celery blanched in the usual way, by earthing up around the stems, is protected from frost by a portable roof.*

TOP RIGHT: *Opaque forcing pots often had specific functions: the first two are for endive and seakale respectively; that at extreme right, with a lid, and those in the photograph are for rhubarb.*

ABOVE: *The partly open cover is for "ferns, mosses and fungi."*

sometimes from the scorching sun." Mr. Gibson describes myrtle hedges which, being planted in the ground, could not be taken into shelter, but were covered with "painted board cases."

FORCING AND BLANCHING

Much of the use of greenhouse or other glass protection can be lumped under the term "forcing," which can either mean the production of flowers and fruit out of season or their accelerated production. This is usually carried out simply by applying heat, although other conditions may also need careful control.

A special aspect of forcing is the production of blanched vegetables. With plants such as sea kale and chicory, specially grown roots can be dug, bundled and stored in the right conditions for some time. When placed into soil with a little warmth, they will sprout the desired blanched growth. This may be done in winter where frost can be fully excluded, or in the ground when the vegetables are in a more normal growth cycle. Rhubarb stems are much better if blanched, and it is habitual to blanch celery by "earthing up" – heaping soil around the stems as they grow. Other vegetables blanched by excluding light are endive and – rarely today – dandelion for salads.

Out-of-season blanching is usually done in cellars, dark sheds, or under the greenhouse staging, where a flap of opaque material can be used to exclude light. In the open garden, various "blanchers" were formerly often used. Loudon described these as "any close utensil that, when whelmed over a plant, will exclude the light." A blancher was typically

Forcing out-of-season vegetables in a cellar (1703). The produce at right looks, however improbably, like globe artichokes.

shaped as a bell glass or, for large plants like rhubarb, could have vertical sides. They were usually made of earthenware, often with a removable lid so that the produce could be examined, and they only exist today as antiques.

Variations on the blanching pot included "protective shades," which might have an aperture cut in one side or be perforated all over. These admitted some light and were recommended, a century ago, for transplanting tender plants and for cultivating alpines.

Modern methods of growing plants out of season have become very scientific. Bulbs may be subjected to specific periods of chilling, or in some cases of exposure to warmth, or a combination of the two, before they are started into growth in a high temperature, which is sometimes done with minimal light or under artificial light. Chrysanthemums, poinsettia, kalanchoe and other plants which are known to flower either in long- or short-day seasons have their growth controlled by imposing artificial day-lengths upon the plants. This may mean total shading for twelve hours when natural day-length is longer, or providing artificial light during the night when natural days are shorter. It has been proved that artificial lighting can be very weak, or be on for only a brief period in the night.

ABOVE AND TOP RIGHT: *The "repository" and the "blooming stage" used by auricula fanciers in the late eighteenth century and into the next. Shutters were used against heavy rain in summer, to be replaced in winter by glass frames, also used in the blooming frame.*

RIGHT: *A massive "awning" used to cover carnations, and also hyacinths, once they had come into flower. The saucers around the plank supports are to prevent access by earwigs.*

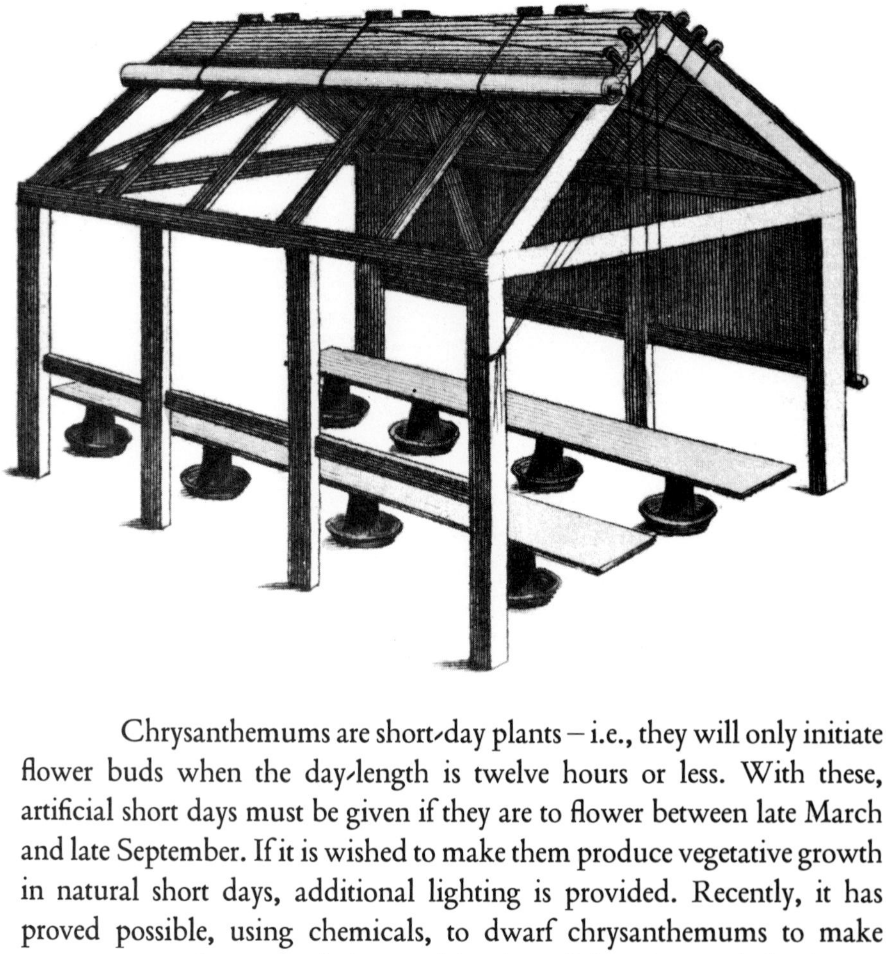

Chrysanthemums are short-day plants – i.e., they will only initiate flower buds when the day-length is twelve hours or less. With these, artificial short days must be given if they are to flower between late March and late September. If it is wished to make them produce vegetative growth in natural short days, additional lighting is provided. Recently, it has proved possible, using chemicals, to dwarf chrysanthemums to make compact pot plants. And the combination of dwarfing and day-length control has resulted in a very exact science, with the number of days' growth required known for each variety grown.

FLORISTS' PLANTS

This kind of cultivation takes one back to the great days of exhibiting "fancy" plants in the seventeenth and eighteenth centuries. (For a further description of this, see Chapter 9.) Flowers were developed by breeding to certain general specifications of size, regularity of form, and pattern of markings. The "rules" were laid down by the "fanciers" or "florists," as they were called. The cultivation of these plants gave rise to complex methods, each grower trying to improve upon the norm. I have already mentioned the extraordinary recipes devised for composts (page 167). To grow each flower to perfection, special covering structures were built, and often specific shading devices were used.

The cultural complexity of the auricula structure opposite was later reduced to keeping the plants in "common hotbed frames" as above.

For the auricula, for example, both a summer and a winter "repository" were mandatory, as well as a "blooming stage." The first criterion of the repository was a deep layer of ashes or a series of square tiles to keep earthworms from entering the pots. Rows of bricks were then placed on this base to raise the pots and allow a good circulation of air around them. On a framework of posts and horizontal bars were then placed shutters, which could be closed over the plants on a central rail if there was heavy rain or scorching sun, while allowing adequate air circulation through the open ends of the structure. The winter repository was similar, but the shutters on the south side were replaced with frames of glass, because it was necessary to keep the plants covered for longer periods, while light must be allowed to reach them.

When the plants were in flower, they went into the "blooming stage," which consisted of four or five shelves, slightly staggered in height, and covered with the glass frames later to be used in the winter repository. The purpose of this arrangement was to regulate the amount of strong sun reaching the plants. The front of the structure was normally left open, but in unfavorable weather it was "defended by frames of wood covered with canvas."

Such instructions date from the end of the eighteenth century. By 1838 we can read that "the London florists at present for the most part keep their auriculas in common hotbed frames." The anti-earthworm precautions continued to be observed in these shallow pits. In summer the frame lights would be lifted well above the plants on bricks, to allow full air circulation, but in winter "the frame is let down to rest on the basement, and exclude the cold."

Hyacinths were planted into specially prepared soil beds and, in early stages of growth, hoops over the bed could be covered with mats or canvas in heavy rain or frost. When most of the flowers were showing color, an "awning" was erected over the plants. This consisted of a strong frame of wood over which roller blinds of "Irish or Scotch sheetings, or Russia duck" would keep out rain and cold wind while admitting plenty of light.

When carnations came into flower, they were covered in exactly the same kind of structure – the same one could be used, since carnations bloom much later. The curious objects shown under the staging planks (opposite) are "supporters" standing in shallow lead or earthenware vessels filled with water; these were meant to stop earwigs reaching the

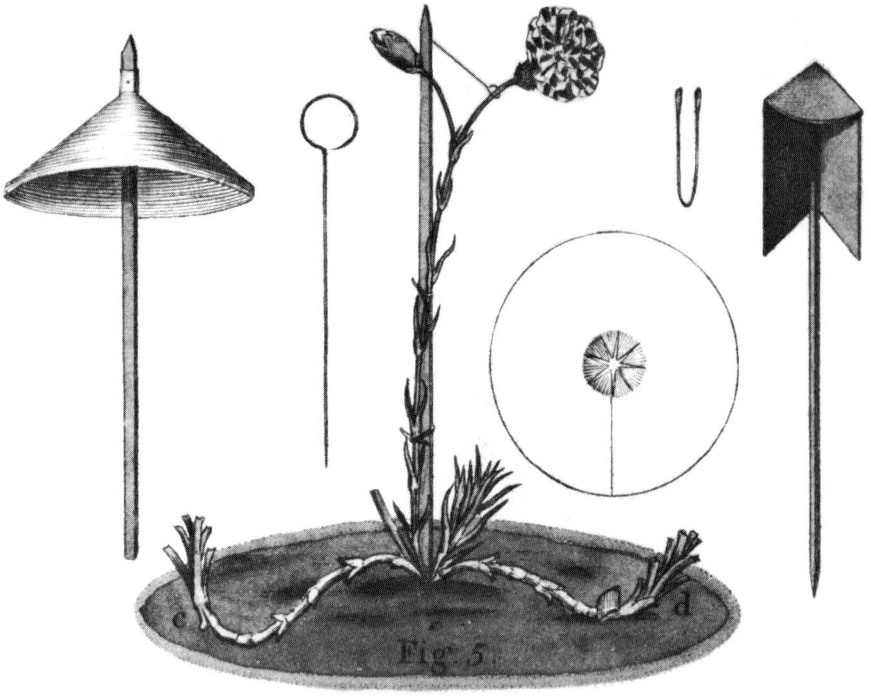

As they came into bloom, carnations – supported by a special wire pin – could be shaded from the sun by a paper cap; to prevent the calyx splitting, a card collar was folded round it. The carnation plant is shown being layered.

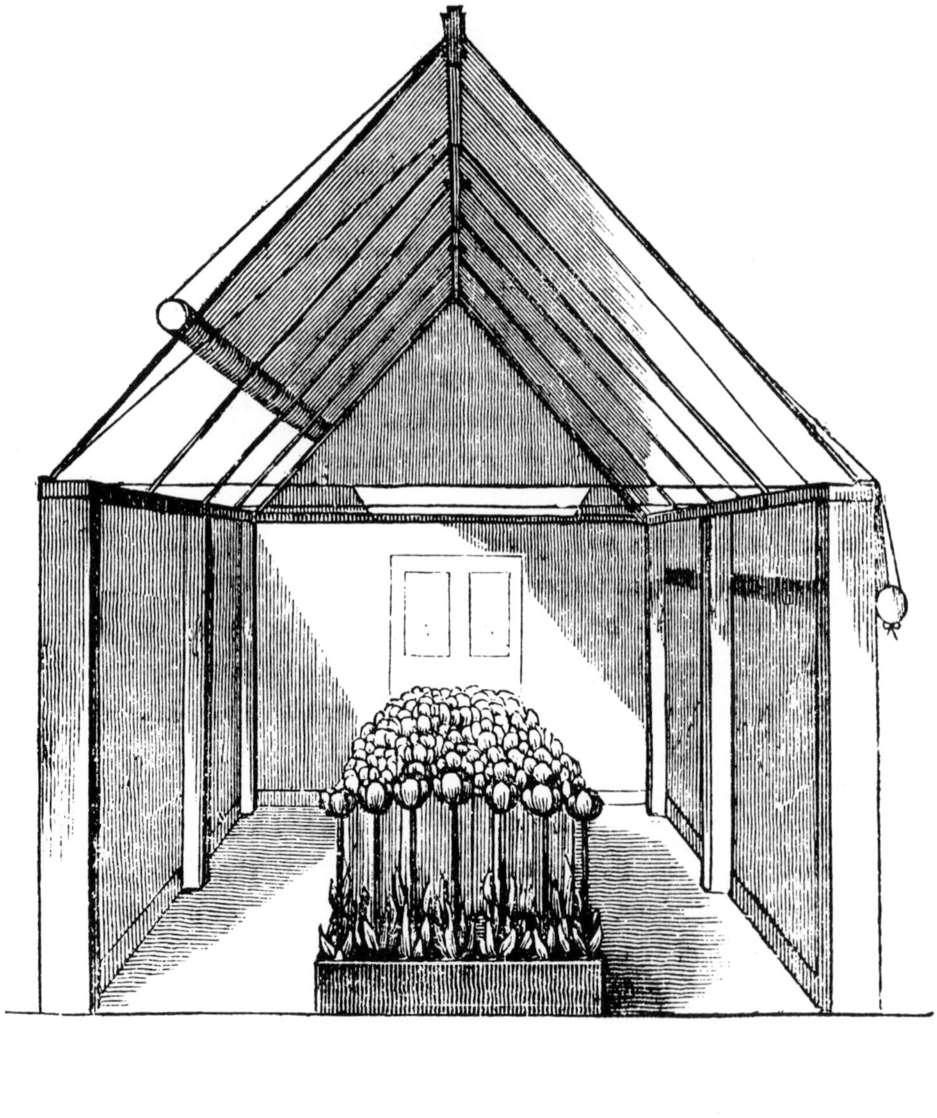

RIGHT: *A grandiose awning for tulips in flower, equipped with roller blinds and a sheet of calico to intercept stray drops of moisture. Those unable to afford such a structure made do with a smaller version (below). (Both around 1800.)*

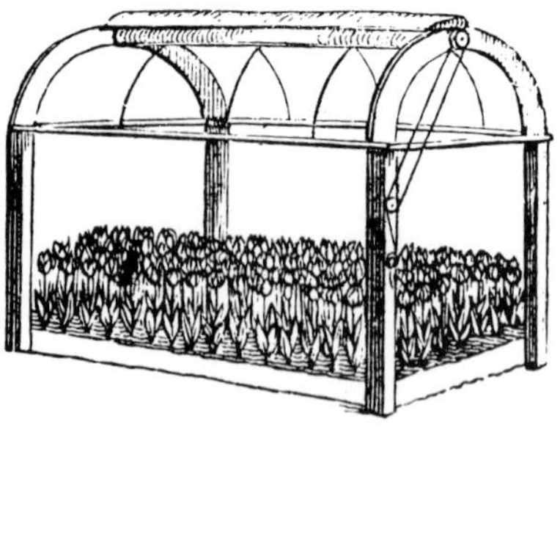

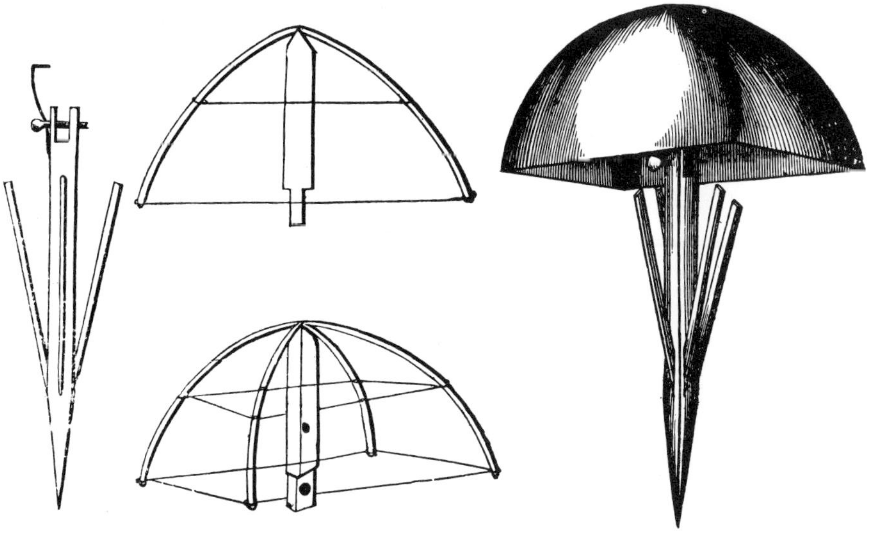

LEFT: *An elaborately framed cap of oiled paper designed to shade dahlias and similar flowers from rain and sun (late nineteenth century).* BELOW: *A modern patent protector of wire and plastic for show chrysanthemums.*

flowers. Before the plants were in full flower, the stems were, first of all, very carefully supported, and the opening buds protected from rain by a circular or triangular hood. When the flower began to expand, a card collar was placed below it, fixed onto the calyx.

The same principles were carried out with tulips. As the buds developed, an umbrella-shaped shade on a stake was placed over each; the cone was made of "cartridge paper done over with equal parts of spirit of turpentine, linseed oil, and boiled oil. This will render the paper quite translucent, while it will be proof against rain." At full bloom, a protective awning with roller blinds was installed. In between the roof of blind material and the tulip bed was suspended a sheet of light calico to intercept drops of moisture that might penetrate; "the white color of the cloth adds much to the softness of tint in the colors, and to the semitransparency of the petals." For those unable to afford a grandiose awning "lofty enough to allow of being walked under," a low structure of wooden or iron hoops, also equipped with a roller blind, would suffice.

When the cruder dahlia or georgina, as it was then called, arrived on the exhibition scene – from 1813 it became the major florists' flower, with around 1,500 named varieties listed by 1830 – it was still necessary to protect it from rain damage, and to this end more or less elaborate paper caps were placed over the flowers. Those who cultivate dahlias and similar flowers today do much the same, although sometimes with less finesse. Chrysanthemums, for instance, are habitually protected in large paper bags, and controversy has been heard over the pros and cons of inflating the bag before putting it over the bud or allowing the expanding flower to push out the bag.

GLASS INDOORS

The final aspect of growing plants under cover is that of protecting them indoors, in living rooms, against the hostile atmosphere there – dry, draughty and often carrying fumes. The principle of the closed glass container was invented independently by the Scot Alan D. Maconochie in

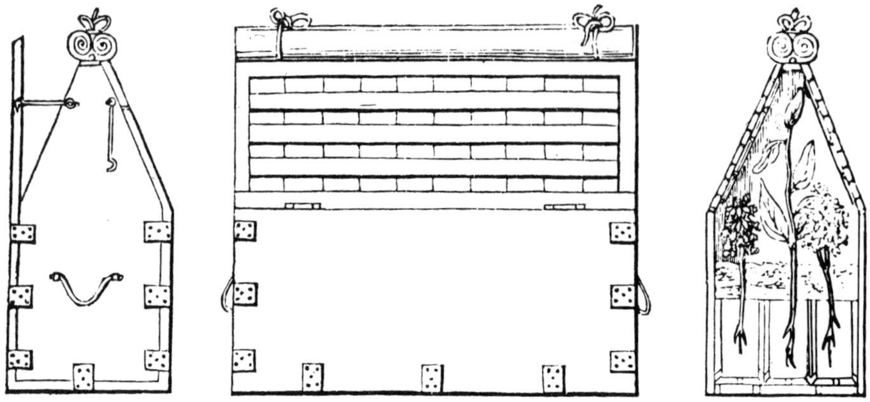

The most valuable use of the closed or Wardian case was to keep plants shipped from distant countries alive. ABOVE: *An early example.* ABOVE RIGHT: *This later nineteenth-century model, similar to those still in use today, has slatted shutters to protect the glass, and roller blinds to keep out scorching sun.* BELOW: *A splendid "Ornamental Stand for Hall" of the late nineteenth century.*

1825 and the London doctor Nathaniel Ward in 1829. Maconochie tried plants in a large goldfish bowl after reading of European experiments, and followed this up with a miniature wooden greenhouse. Ward stumbled upon the principle by accident. The Scot did not publicize his discovery; Ward did. He rapidly improved on his methods and grew a variety of plants successfully in his house.

Plants can survive in closed containers for several years, for the moisture they give out is condensed and returned to the soil, while the balance of oxygen and carbon dioxide in the air is maintained by the photosynthetic process. In fact, the containers create their own climate, and save the plants from dry, fume-filled atmospheres and draughts.

From this discovery of the closed glass container arose two distinct aspects of horticulture. In some ways the most important was the use of the Wardian case by plant collectors. Before its introduction, plants carried on board ships suffered enormous mortality on long journeys from far countries. In closed cases, ninety-nine out of one hundred plants were likely to survive, without need for watering or other attention. Apart from thousands of ornamental species, the Wardian case made possible the introduction of the tea plant to India (from China) and quinine-producing plants to the Old World (from South America).

The second, more widespread use was in the English Victorian drawing room, where the mania for Ward's Cases was everywhere apparent. They became fashionable in the United States at least by the 1860s. Early examples rather resembled miniature greenhouses, or were rectangular structures with glass panes in a simple frame. There was also a vogue for bell jars and glass domes, often on elegant bases of composition stone. Metal framing led to an incredible variety of shapes, upright or elongated, with peaked or dome-shaped towers, flat or semicircular outline. There was the Crystal Palace Case – "a noble adornment to an entrance hall" – of which a splendid and enormous example still exists in Scotland at the People's Palace museum, Glasgow. There was the Tintern Abbey Case, in which the ruined west window of the Abbey – somewhat scaled down – formed the centerpiece. It was some eight feet square.

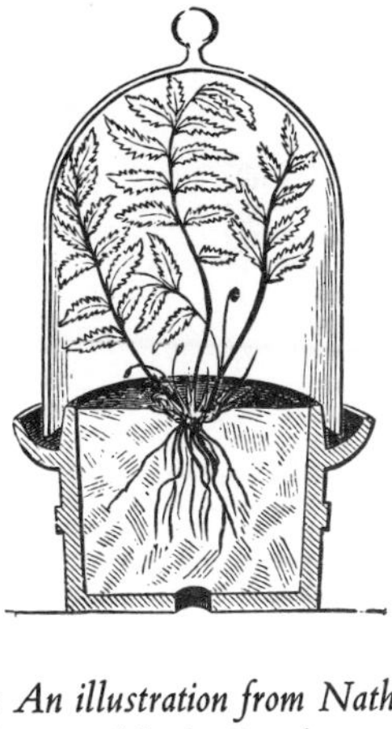

LEFT: *An illustration from Nathaniel Ward's original book,* On the Imitation of the Natural Conditions of Plants in Closely Glazed Cases. TOP LEFT: *Other early glazed cases looked like scaled-down greenhouses.* ABOVE: *Others were simply glass domes or bell glasses on more or less elaborate stands.*

RIGHT: *Plant case and aquarium combined in a window case, with access from the room behind, and a free-standing example.* BELOW: *A Wardian case of unusual design dating from roughly 1860, recently found in Glasgow.*

RIGHT: *A late Victorian indoor conservatory of imposing size, placed against a large window.*

This modern American terrarium with plants in a large plastic bowl is designed to form a handsome table.

The first, and always the most important, plants to be cultivated in these cases were ferns, and for some time they were known as fern cases. In one of his classic books, *The Fern Garden* of 1869, Shirley Hibberd wrote, "In the heart of a great city where gardens are unknown and even graveyards are desecrated by an accumulation of filth, the fern case is a boon of priceless value." (Why he had to bring in graveyards one cannot imagine!) Some of the later cases combined ferns with fish; water filled the lower part, while ferns grew on a pile of rocks projecting in the center. Constructions of this kind came to be known as Warrington cases. Some of these cases were provided with a reservoir on top, a tap controlling the flow of water through a pipe to the waterproof tray on which the glazed part stood. (Such is the principle of an antique case which I was fortunate enough to find in a junk yard.) Cases were also built out from windows, glazed on the inside as well as out; hardy ferns were usually grown in these. At other times this double-glazed window case projected into the room, terminating at the window. Wardian cases were flimsy and bulky and, when their vogue petered out toward the end of the nineteenth century, most of them must have been broken up. At any rate, very few examples still exist.

A modern American metal-framed terrarium of medium size.

Today there is a new vogue for the closed case, which seems to have started in the United States just before World War II. These cases are called terrariums. They include the bottle garden, the making of which seems to the uninitiated to be as mysterious as the ship in a bottle (although it is in fact quite simple). Such cases come in all shapes and sizes; as well as bottle-shaped, they can be rectangular, circular, or greenhouse-shaped. They are usually composed of acrylic and framed in metal. In both the

A modern British terrarium entirely of acrylic plastic. It has a lid for access.

United States and Europe, specialists such as orchid and African violet growers can buy large rectangular metal- or wood-framed cases, often with heating and fluorescent lighting built in, which are in effect miniature greenhouses.

Recently many homes, especially in Denmark and Germany, have been fitted with "plant windows." These were also invented in the nineteenth century, and are composed of two glass vertical walls, one formed by the outside window, the other by a sheet of glass inside the room. And you can now buy ready-made "window garden greenhouses," with shelving for plants, to be fitted outside a window, just like the Victorian examples if rather starker in outline.

Today thousands of people all over the world enjoy the possession of some type of glazed structure – whether indoors or out. The future of such "plants under cover" may be one of full automation for commercial growers, but the average amateur gardener truly enjoys the process of manipulating his plants in the artificial climate he provides for them – whether he merely alternates tomatoes and chrysanthemums or has a collection of exotic orchids or rare succulents.

Chapter Eight
The Lawn

TODAY A GRASS LAWN IS A FEATURE OF ALMOST EVERY GARDEN, though more so in the United States and Britain than in most other countries. Grass has certainly been an important part of gardens in Europe since the Middle Ages. Evidence for its use before that is surprisingly vague. One might imagine that the Romans had lawns, but apart from a brief mention by Pliny, when describing his villa at Tusci, the records yield no reference. Pliny refers to what appears to have been a small lawn on an upper terrace, in which flower beds edged with evergreens were cut. Elsewhere he describes a soft mossy carpet kept moist by a fountain playing over it. The heat of Mediterranean summers must have discouraged the use of ornamental grass.

We have to turn to medieval authors before we have any account of turf extensively used as a feature. Boccacio mentions a meadow spangled with flowers, and this was obviously the medieval standard. Monasteries had grassy plots, often with fruit trees growing in them. Grassy areas were needed for tournaments and other games, just as they are today.

The first detailed account of preparing turf comes from a famous work called *Opus ruralium commodorum*, or *The Advantages of Country Living*, by Petrus de Crescentius, or Crescenzi. (In fact this work was one of the earliest really popular books on husbandry, including gardening. Completed around 1306, many manuscript copies were circulated before its first printing in 1471 – after which there were 52 further editions.) In this work the author recommends digging out all weeds and roots, scalding the soil with boiling water to prevent further weeds germinating, and then laying turf brought in from the wild. Then the sods are beaten with wooden mallets or "beetles" (still used in laying turf today), and trodden with the feet until the grass is almost invisible, after which fresh, even growth should appear. The resulting sward should, he says, be cut twice a year; if it got out of hand it was simply returfed, which usually occurred every three or four years.

The French *Maison Rustique* of 1564, translated into English in 1600, amplifies his description. After the initial preparation, this text suggests that the turves should be laid grass side downward, "and afterward daunced upon with the feete, and the beater or pauing beetle

A medieval stylized version of a "flowery mead."

lightly passing ouer them, in such sort as that within a short time after, the grass may begin to peepe up and put foorth like small haires; and finallie it is made the sporting greenplot for Ladies and Gentlewomen to recreate their spirits in."

Such was the preparation of the "orchard" or "pleasaunce" of this period, briefly mentioned in Chapter 2. The turf was apparently liberally filled with tall-growing wild flowers. It seems on the face of it impossible that such plants could survive all the traffic, but they appear in every illustration of such grassy areas, and one must assume, even allowing for artistic license, that they were there. In the *Maison Rustique* we read, "flowres for nosegaies shall be set in order . . . some of them upon seats." These meadows became known as flowery medes, and are more or less contemporary with – although almost certainly not influenced by – similar flowered meadows favored by the Persians. The latter, to quote the French Chevalier Chardin on his visit in 1668, were grass actually "sown with a mixture of flowers in natural confusion." The Emperor Babul recorded in 1519 that in one of his gardens the "lawns were one sheet of trefoil."

In these recreational areas, turf was apparently the favored material upon which to sit. These visitors sat on the sward, or on low artificial mounds, or on benches of built-up soil (even when these were supported by planking they would be turfed). One might imagine that the turf would more often than not be damp, but it is seldom that the old illustrators show even a cushion to protect against this; maybe their voluminous clothes protected the ladies, but the tight linen hose of the gentlemen cannot have kept much damp out. Some of the old pictures show turf seats supported by projecting boards or even a spiky-topped piece of wattle fencing, with the people sitting on these edges without worrying – more artistic license, perhaps.

The flowers grew on the seats also, but by the early seventeenth century it became more fashionable to plant seats and banks with chamomile; not only is this compact and low growing, but it gives out a delightful aroma when crushed. Also, as Falstaff says, "The more it is trodden on the faster it grows." Aromatic seats are still occasionally made; there is one in the herb garden at Sissinghurst Castle in southern England, and chamomile lawns are sometimes planted, as at Buckingham Palace, although their establishment is laborious. John Evelyn gave directions for their maintenance. Bacon mentioned other fragrant plants for the purpose: "But those which perfume the air most delightfully, not passed by as the rest but being trodden upon and crushed, are three; that is, burnet, wild thyme, and water mints. Therefore you are to set whole alleys of them, to have the pleasure when you walk or tread."

The medieval mount, especially its top terrace, would be covered with turf. Grass walks were also much loved, and there is a record of one, raised 6 feet above ground level, 9 feet wide and 130 feet long, in the

Improbable flower-spangled grass in the well-known "Mary Garden" or "Paradise Garden" painted by an unknown fifteenth-century Rhenish artist. Besides typical features of a medieval garden, it includes many Christian symbols, such as the grafted tree in the foreground (see also page 215).

English county of Sussex during the sixteenth century. There is also a hint of a grass path in the wall painting in the subterranean room in the Villa of Livia in Rome; at any rate the path is shown green.

During the sixteenth century, the English game of bowls, which needs a closely cut grass area, became steadily more widely played. Bowls began to supersede archery as a pastime, and also led to excessive gambling; hence an act of 1541 imposed a fine on anyone playing bowls outside his own orchard or garden, while landowners with land of the yearly value of £100 or more had to obtain a license to play on their own private greens. All this activity led slowly to better turf being developed, although it has been suggested that the alley Drake played on in 1587 was actually of chamomile.

The French took over the words "bowling green" and made them into *"boulingrin"* – which was not for bowls, a game they did not play (their *boules* is played on flattened soil) – a word that came to mean a sunken grass area, in the center of a woody dell or *bosquet* and often centered with a fountain.

RIGHT: *Any cutting of grass before 1830 (when the lawnmower was invented) had to be carried out with the scythe (1757).* BELOW: *Women helped the scythers by sweeping and gathering up the grass cuttings.*

By degrees ornamental grass came to be mown; in his famous essay of 1625 Bacon calls for "closely mown lawns . . . because nothing is more pleasant to the eye than green grass kept finely shorn." It is clear, too, that the scrolls of knot gardens and the plots of English parterres were often of grass around this time, and for this to have looked attractive it must have been closely trimmed. Grass plots were always hemmed in with vertical wooden planks. Turf was obtained from the wild ("the best . . . are had in the most hungry Common, and where the grass is thick and short") and cut with a turfing iron. The grass was kept short by "Mowing and Rowling." Mowing was of course carried out with the scythe, an instrument which has hardly changed in design since Roman times. Edgings and knot scrolls were trimmed with shears. A little later we find John Evelyn recommending that grass walks and bowling greens should be mowed and rolled every fifteen days. Uneven turf was to be dealt with by using a "turf beater or rammer" during moist weather.

By 1706 we find, in an originally French book, suggestions for different kinds of sward – "by Turfs, by Spanish Clover Grass, by Hay Seed, by the Seed of Sainfoin, and by that of Medick Fodder," and, as I have noted, chamomile lawns were much in vogue.

The advent of the landscape garden in the early eighteenth century called for much larger areas of closely cut grass – whether in the areas around a mansion, where the sward would link imperceptibly, across a ha-ha, with the animal-cropped turf beyond; or in more formal layouts where, perhaps, broad grass stretches would lay along alleys of trees or beside canals. The scythe was now wielded with increasing precision, aided by the brush and roller, and shears and edging irons came into general use. Though manpower was cheap, really large areas were rolled by horsepower, but "care must be taken that the horses should be without shoes and have their feet covered with woolen mufflers." So wrote the anonymous author of *The Gardener's New Kalendar* of 1758.

After the landscape era, in the early days of the nineteenth century, lawns rapidly became very much smaller, but their maintenance called for the same tools and principles. The scythe man's drudgery is made obvious, if unintentionally, in this definition of a lawn from *Hints on Ornamental Gardening* by J. B. Papworth, published in 1823.

> By the lawn is meant that portion of the grass plat which lies between the house and the pasture, which is constantly kept mown, forming a verdant carpet on which the building stands. . . . The lawn is usually separated from the pasture by a light iron fence – from parks by a ha! ha! or sunken fence or terrace . . . its embellishments are beds of choice shrubs and flowers formed upon it of various shapes, and by single evergreen trees or shrubs growing from the grass. The lawn is in general very much restricted in point of size, from the labor that is imagined necessary to keep it mown: but this is a great error – perhaps proceeding from the silly habit that the mower has of indicating his industry by the frequent use of the grit stone in sharpening his scythe: and generally at the time of the morning when such noises are most tormenting.

MOWING MACHINES

The scythe mower must have vanished rapidly from the garden scene after 1830, the year in which Edwin Budding invented the cylinder or reel mower. Budding was an engineer in the textile trade, where a small cylinder of spiraled blades was used to trim the nap of cloth. It must have occurred to him in a blinding flash one day how similar the cloth pile was

RIGHT: *Rollers were used in eighteenth-century lawns, both to maintain general smoothness and specifically to flatten worm casts the day before scything.*

BELOW, FROM TOP DOWNWARD: *A roller barrow of 1890 – "a light, elegant, and useful combination"; verge and grass shears; and garden scythes (all nineteenth century).*

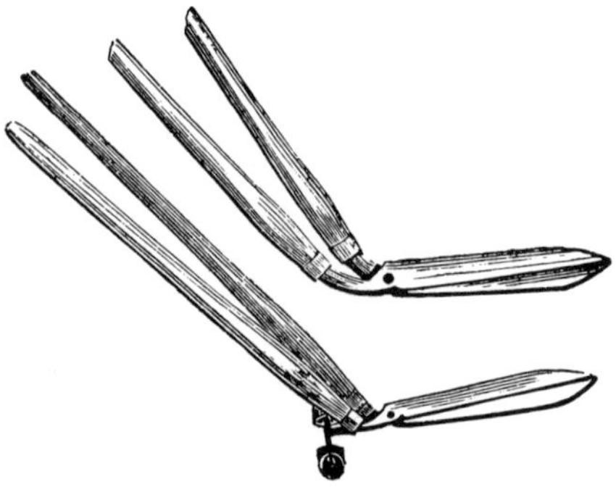

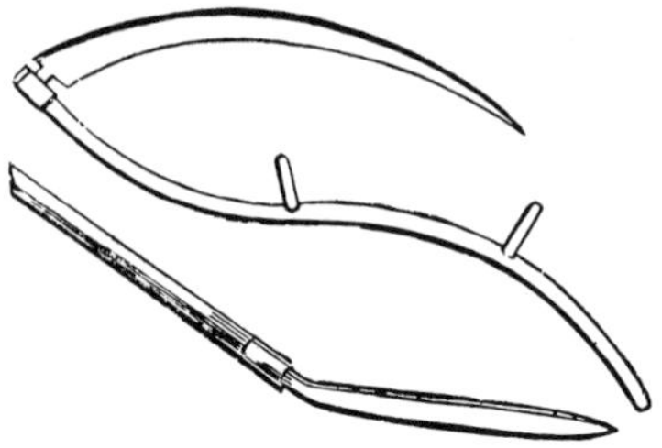

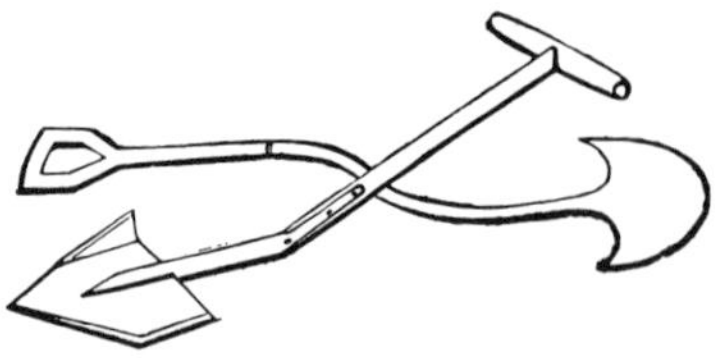

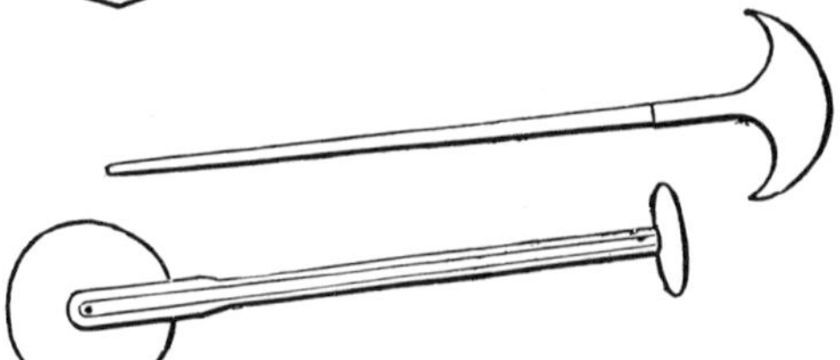

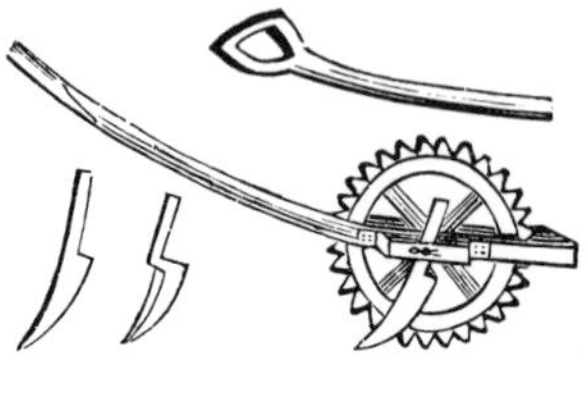

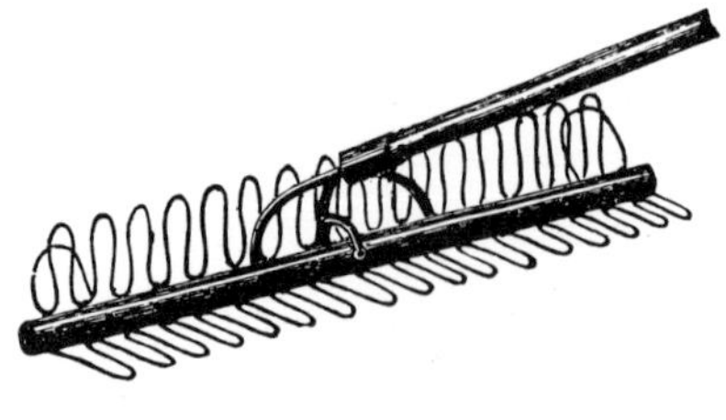

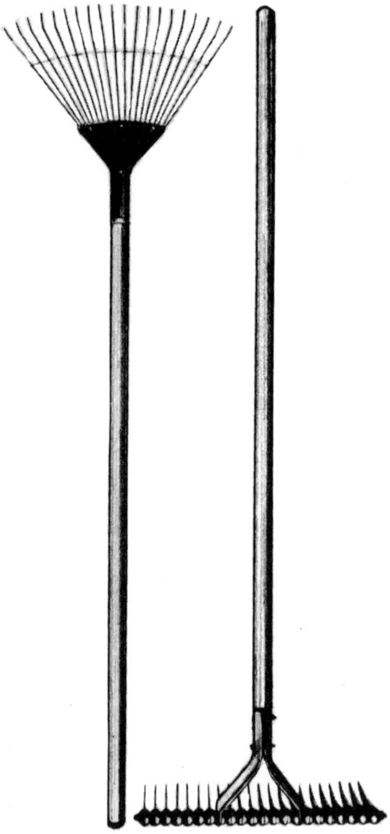

MIDDLE COLUMN, FROM TOP DOWNWARD: *A lawn scraper to remove worm casts; turf spades; verge cutters or "turf-racers"; a patent wheeled verge cutter (all nineteenth century); a lawn rake.*

FAR RIGHT: *A modern lawn wire rake and a "lawn comb" for getting out moss and debris.*

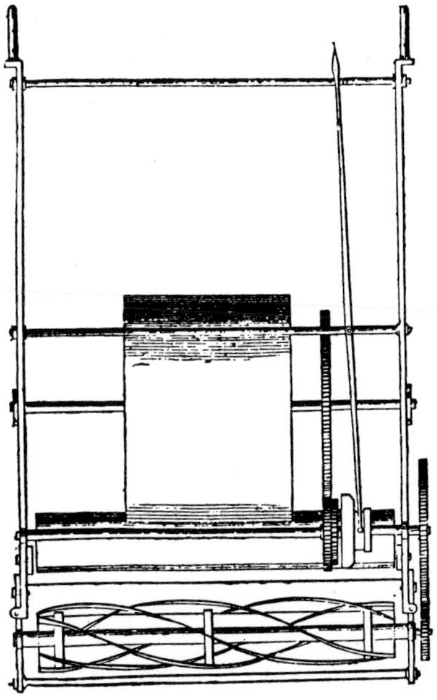

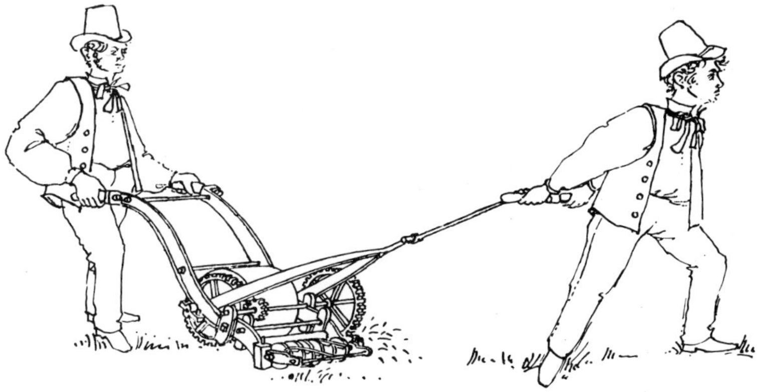

TOP LEFT AND RIGHT: *Revolution in mowing. Thomas Budding's first lawnmower of 1830 was derived from a machine which cut the nap of cloth.* LEFT: *Many early mowers were designed to be pulled as well as pushed. This is another Budding model.*

LEFT: *This 1890 mower was designed to be pulled by a donkey, pony or horse according to the width of the cut. "As the machine makes little noise in working, the most spirited animal can be employed without the fear of it running away, or in any way damaging the machine." This model was controlled by a man walking behind it.* BELOW: *An early version of the "ride-on" mower, also of 1890.*

TOP: *An American mower advertisement of 1878; the machine has the orthodox several-bladed cutter.*

ABOVE CENTER: *This "Archimedean" American mower of 1890 has a single blade; it was advertised as doing double the work for half the effort.*

ABOVE: *The "Multum in Parvo" mower of 1890 was available in sizes from six to ten inches wide and had a grass box.*

to the grass in a lawn – and presto (after some nocturnal experiments, the sound of which puzzled his neighbors), there was the cylinder or reel lawn mower. Its spiral blades caused one make to be called Archimedean (after the Archimedean screw mentioned on page 156). Of his patent invention, Budding wrote that "grass growing in the shade and too weak to stand against the scythe may be cut by this machine as closely as required, and the eye will never be offended by those circular sears, inequalities, and bare places so commonly made by the best mowers with the scythe, and which continue visible for several days." He adds that "Country gentlemen may find, in using the machine themselves, an amusing, useful and healthy exercise." I suppose he would have been proud, were he alive today, to see his invention and its descendants moving across almost every garden in several countries every weekend.

Mowers were made in all sizes, from a six-inch cut upward; many were designed to be pulled as well as pushed, and in due course horse-drawn machines were available. Grass boxes were optional; Budding's original version had one. The roller was placed at the back, and for a long time it was deemed better not to have a front roller, which – as an early advertisement points out – flattens the bents, or long stiff stems. The early mowers all had relatively large rollers at the back; later on, popular models were made with two side wheels and only a small front roller. This does not give such a good finish and the wheels can score the grass if it is wet, but such mowers are lighter and cheaper.

The cylinder mower was adapted to gasoline-driven motor power around 1900. Today there are gasoline-engined and electrically driven versions; electricity may be supplied from the main supply via a cable or, much less frequently, from a battery. Some motors just turn the cylinder while the operator pushes; others propel the whole machine as well. On a large scale, there are gang mowers pulling several cylinders so that a wide swath can be cut at once.

Some early mowers had solid blades, but these must have added to the weight. The number of blades on the cylinder varies according to the coarseness of the grass to be dealt with and the fineness of finish desired; it is a matter of number of cuts per yard. For rough work, the mower may have only four blades and give around 25 cuts per yard; for the smoothest grass, as on bowling greens, a power-driven machine may have ten blades and make 130 cuts per yard. Standard "home" mowers are likely to have five or six blades and give from 40 to 70 cuts per yard – the higher number if power-driven.

The most interesting development in grass cutting of recent years has been the rotary mower, in which a blade spins horizontally under a safety hood. This blade is often relatively blunt, or just sharpened at the ends, relying on its speed to sever the grass blades. Rotary mowers are most useful for rough or coarse grass, and will readily cope with long or wet grass

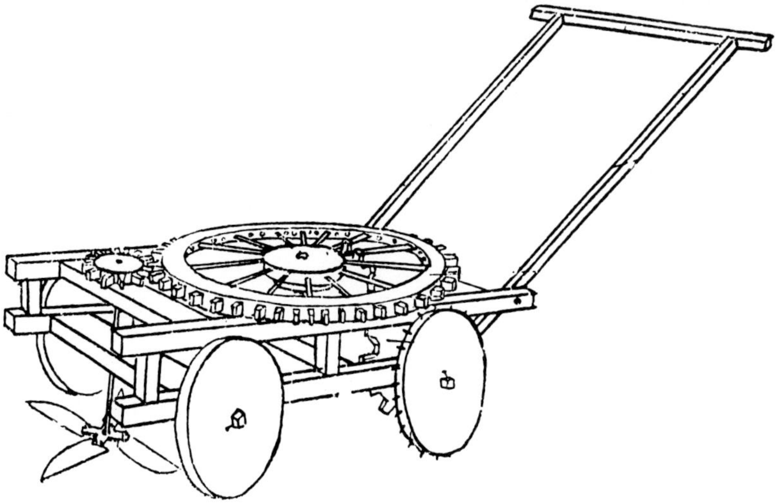

ABOVE LEFT: *A minute side-wheel machine of around 1860 (from a private family album).*

BELOW LEFT: *A modern Chinese do-it-yourself adaptation of the rotary mower, made almost entirely of wood. A gear wheel on the rear axle meshes with the horizontal cog wheels. It is an example "of utilization and adaptation of traditional style of engineering and craftsmanship to meet modern needs" (Needham).*

BELOW: *A very wide American cylinder mower of the late nineteenth century.*

which defeats the cylinder. But they do not produce the "banding" of the cut sward which is an attractive feature with cylinder mowers. Tiny powered versions of the rotary mower are used for cutting on banks or in difficult corners. In the United States and Canada, rotary mowers now far outnumber the other type.

The rotary mower has been further developed by adopting the air-cushioning effect of the Hovercraft. In this type of machine, the cutting blade works in conjunction with a fan which brings air under the hood and forces it out around the sides. These mowers do not normally have the wheels with which ordinary rotaries are fitted; the slimness of the hood allows the mower to be slipped under low branches, and the air-cushioning effect means that it can be moved freely in any direction, be swung along a bank from the top, or even lowered over steep banks on a rope.

ABOVE: *The modern air-cushion or hovercraft mower has a rotary blade (insert left), and a fan motor which creates a cushion of air so that no wheels are needed. It can be swung readily in any direction and on sloping surfaces; for steep banks it is maneuvered on the end of a rope.*

RIGHT: *A modern power-driven, rotary-bladed "ride-on" mower. Surprisingly maneuverable, it will go right up to trees or verges, while enabling large areas to be cut without effort by the operator.*

Other mowers for rough conditions include the flail, or hammer knife, and the sickle bar. In flail machines the cutting blades are small and hinged; the grass is chopped up more than with fixed blades and lies more or less evenly, unlike the method of standard rotaries which throws the grass out at one side, either as a swath on the surface or into a collecting bag. The sickle bar or power scythe is like a giant version of hair clippers, with a reciprocating bar carrying small triangular blades working against a fixed one. It uses the same principle as agricultural reaping machines and hay cutters.

Much smaller versions of the "hair clipper" had been invented in late Victorian times for dealing with edges and areas of grass difficult to reach with a mower. They were also used for clipping ivy, shrubs, and shaping topiary and edgings. Today there are a number of hand-held power-driven trimmers using the same principle, with only four or five teeth on each blade, some operating from rechargeable batteries. One model is designed either to be held in the hand or fitted onto a lightweight two-wheel chassis equipped with a long handle. Another small model employs a whirling nylon cord which can actually touch solid objects without damaging them, and can thus remove grass and weeds surrounding such objects. These nylon-line trimmers have become very popular.

Local grass trimmers old and new. TOP: *A reciprocating-bar version of 1890.* ABOVE: *Modern battery-powered electric shears.*

The most recent development of the lawn mower, whether cylinder or rotary, is the "ride-on," in which the operator sits upon a self-propelled machine. It is, of course, designed for large areas, but many models are at the same time remarkably maneuverable.

LAWN MAINTENANCE

Alongside the development of mowers, a large range of other lawn maintenance devices came into being. The wheeled edge trimmer of previous centuries was fitted with a small roller and, in recent years, has become available in a powered form. The early principle of spiking the grass with a fork for aeration was elaborated in various ways. The hollow-tined fork was one advance, taking out small cores of soil so that grit or fertilizer could be replaced in the holes. Less laborious are the various spiked rollers and rotary slitters; and for small-scale use the French invented a pair of hinged, spiked clogs which could be strapped to the shoe, spiking as one walked. Distributors for fertilizers and top dressings are available, as are horizontal "sprinkle bars" for the controlled release of liquid lawn chemicals of various kinds.

Finally, there are a large number of modern ways of watering the lawn, much developed from the hinged metal *tuyaux* of the nineteenth century or the earlier water barrow. The ordinary hose was first equipped with a simple rotary sprinkler; but the round watering pattern this produces leads to dry patches or overlaps as the sprinkler is moved; the newer oscillating sprinkler covers an oblong area. There are gadgets which will "walk" along a hose laid in a prearranged line, sprinkling as they go.

TOP AND MIDDLE: *British and American edge trimmers around 1890.* ABOVE: *A modern device with vertical and horizontal cutting edges.*

RIGHT: *The electric "Grassmaster," with rotary blade and skids for ease of pushing into difficult corners.*

Other watering devices employ a permeable canvas hose, or a rubber or plastic hose or steel pipe, with many small perforations. A luxury method of watering is to have a series of "pop-up" sprinklers which are sunk just below the turf level and are connected to buried water pipes: when the supply is turned on, the pressure pushes up each sprinkler so that it can operate. Timing devices for turning the water on and off in such installations are also available.

As well as watering in dry weather, grasses need feeding, which is usually done with a granular or water-diluted liquid fertilizer. Major changes have taken place in the feeding of lawns in the past few years, notably in the United States. For years lawns had been fed with balanced fertilizers applied in solution, needing two or three applications during the growing season. The period of effectiveness was extended by making the fertilizer granular to retard its dissolving. However, the great breakthrough came with the introduction of slow-release ureaform (urea-formaldehyde), which continues to supply available nitrogen the whole season so that the gardener can get by with only one feeding per year.

Alongside feeding comes weed control, because many of the

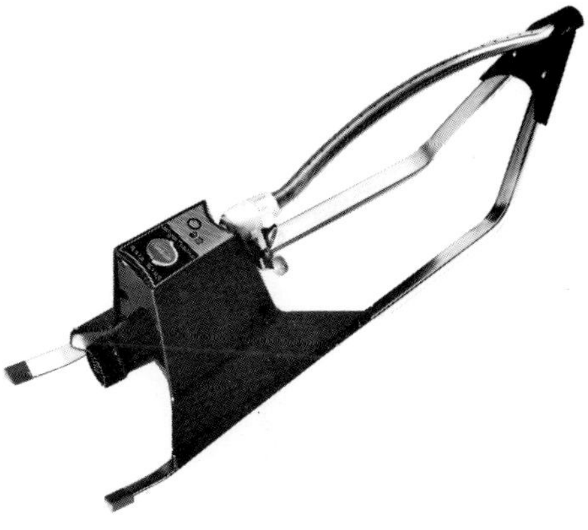

ABOVE LEFT: *This rotary sprinkler is designed to crawl slowly but steadily along the hose laid out in a suitable line for watering a lawn and neighbouring beds.* TOP: *A stationary oscillating sprinkler which waters a rectangular area.* ABOVE: *a rotary model.*

chemicals originally used for killing weeds and moss will benefit the grass in the long run. Today most reliance is placed on a whole array of hormone or selective weedkillers, so-called because they select the broad-leaved weeds and do not harm the grass. They act by disrupting the growth pattern of the weed plants, which literally tear themselves apart. Different selectives must be used where certain pernicious weeds appear – such as mecoprop against trefoils and yarrow, or ioxynil against speedwell. Weedkillers are often combined with fertilizer mixtures, and there are different formulations available for autumn and spring application.

TURF QUALITY

Lawn care is not, of course, entirely connected with mechanical and chemical aids. The quality of the turf is a key factor in a good lawn. One of the first mentions of this is in *The Gardener's New Kalendar* of 1758, which tells us that "there is great difficulty in getting good seed; for that from a common haystack is by no means proper," and also insists that it should come from "the grass of a clean upland pasture." However, the author prefers turfing which "does the business sooner and much more perfectly," and tells us that "the only proper mixture with the grass, in turf, is the white trefoil. . . . These mix well with the grass and form a fine thick bottom." This advice is anathema today, when we can buy special clover killers for lawns, but I can testify that it is in fact good.

It was not until the turn of the eighteenth century that seedsmen could begin to provide reasonable grass seed mixtures. Alexander MacDonald, in 1807, suggests obtaining "those kinds which strike deep root, spread out laterally in their tops and are permanent and capable of

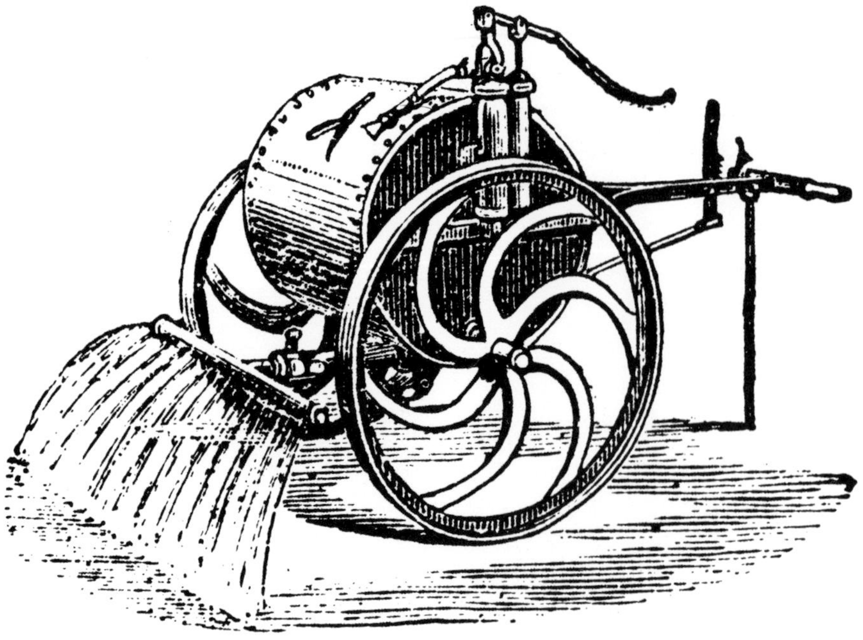

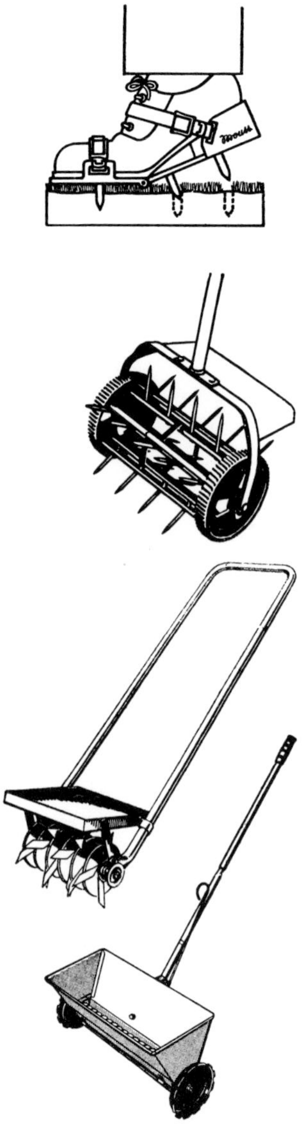

TOP RIGHT: *The "water-cart and garden engine" of 1890, holding thirty-five gallons, was used both to water lawns as shown and, by use of the pump, to operate a hose.*

ABOVE: *Some modern aids to lawn maintenance: various designs of aerator for spiking or slitting the turf and, bottom, a fertilizer distributor.*

resisting the effects of heat." However, at this time seed was much more expensive than turf.

But the realization that a good lawn depended on good grass varieties, and the increasing shortage of natural turf, led to research on wild grasses and their most desirable strains. The botanist W. J. Beal initiated evaluation of turfgrass species and their mixing at the Michigan Agricultural Experiment Station in about 1880. J. B. Olcott – who always referred to turf maintenance as "grass gardening" – set up turf gardens in Connecticut in 1885, and worked in conjunction with the Connecticut Agricultural Experiment Station from 1890 until he died in 1910. Many more research centers were set up in the United States in the following years, largely in conjunction with the Department of Agriculture. Many of their studies were in relation to golf courses, and the British Sports Turf Research Institute, founded only in 1929, arose for the same reason.

Today a wide selection of grass mixtures for varying conditions is available from carefully selected seed. Innumerable newly named strains of Kentucky bluegrass, ryegrasses, bents and fescues have been introduced in the northern half of the United States and in Canada. In the South, Bermuda grasses, zoysias, St. Augustine, centipede, carpet, and Bahia grasses are used, while in the dry Plains states experiments are going on with buffalo and other native grasses. This parallels similar work in Australia.

In warm climates quite different plants may be used, like dichondra which is favored in the western United States. Other plants, apart from chamomile already mentioned, have been tried in temperate countries, including pearlwort, corn spurrey and even moss, but these are basically quite unsatisfactory for anything except pure visual ornament. The Japanese make beautiful moss lawns, but they are not for walking on.

Natural turf is now very difficult to come by, but especially in the United States many firms are now engaged in producing turf (or sod) by modern methods. This is sold in garden centers by the square foot or in long rolls. One new method of producing turf is to sow on thin sheets of foam rubber in shallow trays containing water and fertilizer granules. After six weeks it can be laid and is fit to play games on within three months.

With its need for cutting at least once a week, sometimes more in the growing season, and for all kinds of other attention from time to time, a lawn can be one of the most intensely looked after parts of a garden. It is an area on which many mechanical and chemical industries concentrate their inventiveness. The recent use of synthetic turf for playing fields must worry these industries, but there is at present no sign that amateur gardeners are taking it up.

It used to be said that it took centuries to make a really fine lawn, and that only the English had the art. Certainly few English homes are without lawns today, and most gardeners spend much time upon them. But in the United States and Canada, home lawns are perhaps of even greater importance, since properties are less often enclosed, as many are in Britain, and front lawns between the house and the street usually take the place of dooryard gardens.

Chapter Nine
Specialization

THE URGE TO COLLECT IS A DOMINANT ONE IN THE HUMAN race. We may collect stamps, shells, paintings, books, china – or flowers. Most collections are passive; they are sets of more or less permanent objects which do not change except as the collector may reorder them. Flowers, however, are transient; to keep them alive is a distinct kind of specialization calling for a great deal of care and work.

From the Sumerians and Egyptians onward, people have made collections of herbs, although these were of course for medicinal and possibly magical purposes. The desire to make botanical collections of as many plants as possible is evident quite early in history. Aristotle had one in his Athenian garden which he left to Theophrastus, and where that early botanist made many of his observations.

The first true flower specialists seem to have been the Chinese, whose devotion to the chrysanthemum began in the fourth century A.D. By A.D. 700 the rich so coveted new varieties of the moutan or tree peony that one hundred ounces of gold were paid for a single plant. Herbaceous peonies, apricots (notably forms of *Prunus mume*), hollyhocks and waterlilies followed, and camellias were collectors' pieces by the fifteenth century at the latest. The Japanese likewise collected plants with many variations, including the maple, plum and cherry, camellia, azalea and water iris. Both civilizations also specialized in bonsai or dwarfed trees.

The Persians cultivated wild bulb flowers, notably the tulip, and the Turks were assiduous growers of a few flowers – the rose, carnation, cyclamen, hyacinth, tulip, daffodil and jonquil in particular. In the late sixteenth century, the daffodil was considered king – or queen – of garden flowers, and its first great specialist was the Grand Mufti of Suleyman the Magnificent, who died in 1574.

But the tulip was not far behind in importance, and probably much ahead in popular appeal. Tens of thousands of wild tulip bulbs were dug up annually to be planted in royal gardens. It was this flower which gave Europe its first specialty. By 1562 it reached what the modern writer Wilfrid Blunt has called its "spiritual home" – Holland; and it reached England in 1578. Dutch "tulipomania" raged from about 1634 to 1637, when values of bulbs, especially new seedlings, soared to bizarre heights.

One of the most extreme examples on record is of the exchange of a single tulip bulb for two loads of wheat, four loads of rye, four fat oxen, eight fat pigs, twelve sheep, two barrels of butter, one thousand pounds of cheese, two hogsheads of wine, four barrels of special beer, a silver beaker, a suit of clothes and a complete bed. No wonder that it expired so rapidly. Tulipomania also gave rise to "tulipophobia," a "disease" which attacked Everard Forstius, professor of botany at Leyden who, according to Wilfrid Blunt, "could not see a tulip without attacking it furiously with his stick."

The Turks, incidentally, went on growing tulips assiduously and, in the early eighteenth century, there was something approaching tulipomania in Turkey. Here tulip shows were rather different from the Dutch ones. To quote Wilfrid Blunt again:

> ... important domestic events ... were celebrated if they occurred in springtime by a more intimate kind of tulip show held in one of the courtyards of the Grand Seraglio in Constantinople. For this purpose a great amphitheater of wooden stands was erected, fitted on both sides with shelves to support vases of cut flowers. Among the vases were placed lamps, glass globes filled with different colored waters, and cages of canaries; and here and there the flowers were grouped into pyramids, towers or archways, or drawn into patterns upon the ground like carpets. At sunset the Grand Seigneur caused kalvet (the state of complete privacy) to be announced, and the outer gates of the courtyard were closed. Then, as the fortress cannon fired a salute, the doors of the harem were flung open, and in the sudden magic light of a thousand sweet smelling torches borne by eunuchs, the women would "rush out on all sides, like bees settling on the flowers and stopping continually on the honey they found there." To the shrill cries of the eunuch gardeners and to the roar of the cannon were added to the joyful ululations of the concubines.... For the most part they had but one object to accomplish – to attract the attention of their royal master.

How different must the scene have been at the early shows of the artisan tulip fanciers in the early part of the nineteenth century, which were largely held in public houses. (The Wakefield and North of England Tulip Society – the only one of its kind still in existence – was founded in 1836.) There is even greater contrast with the earlier fanciers' shows, especially those of pinks staged by the Paisley weavers, who made beautifully patterned fabrics and whose florists' club, as recorded by their local clergyman, was notable for its peacefulness and sobriety, always finishing its meetings at 10:00 P.M.

But tulips were only the first of the "florist" flowers which were bred according to strict rules to specific size, form and coloring. The tulip was followed in the late eighteenth century by the auricula, polyanthus, carnation, pink, hyacinth, anemone and ranunculus. These were the eight main groups then defined as florists' flowers, all of which were grown almost exclusively by artisans to be exhibited for prizes on the show bench. The tulip, its focus shifting from the well-to-do to the workman, declined in popularity because bulbs remained very expensive; but this did not, for instance, stop one Luke Pope, a victualer who lived from 1740 to 1825, collecting varieties at £50 (about $250) a time.

The number of new varieties bred was remarkable. A catalog of 1769, for instance, lists around 1,100 named varieties of ranunculus, a difficult flower now only grown occasionally as a summer-flowering "bulb"; 810 varieties of tulip; 575 double hyacinths; 208 anemones; and 132 bunch-flowered narcissi.

During the early nineteenth century, these florist flowers were joined by other "fancies," including violas and pansies, dahlias (then often called georginas), crocuses, bulbous and later tuberous irises, fritillaries, lilies, hippeastrums (amaryllis), ixias, gladioli, peonies, chrysanthemums and, surprisingly, pyrethrums, which are now run-of-the-mill border plants. However, only in a few of these cases were the plants grown chiefly for exhibition.

The switch in flower specialization from the rich tulipomaniacs to the working man is a fascinating piece of sociology. As *Flora Domestica* comments in 1843, "The auricula is to be found in the highest perfection in the gardens of the manufacturing class, who bestow much time and attention on this and a few other flowers, as the tulip and the pink. A fine stage of these plants is scarcely ever to be seen in the gardens of the nobility and gentry, who depend upon the exertions of hired servants, and cannot therefore compete in these nicer operations of gardening with those who tend their flowers themselves, and watch over their progress with paternal solicitude."

The first tulip specialists of Britain grew their plants under the cover of complicated structures as described in Chapter 7, often in pots though also in beds. Their effect on garden design was negative. As Derek Clifford has written, the fascination of the tulip "was felt by the connoisseur and the collector rather than by the gardener working as an artist. In practice tulip culture militated against other flowers for, when the beds were not occupied by the bulbs, there was nothing else sufficiently vivid in hue to take their place. It was to compensate for the absence of the gaudy tulip that gardeners took to filling their flower beds with balls and sheets of covered glass."

Most of the early florists' societies faded out, to be replaced in more recent times by new or different ones. The oldest specialist society still in existence, as far as I can discover, is England's National Chrysanthemum

Society, which started as the Stoke Newington Chrysanthemum Society in 1846. The Northern Auricula Society was founded in 1872, and the National Rose Society in 1876. There are at present over forty specialist societies in Britain, some minute and struggling bravely to maintain the old florist standards, others of much greater popularity, like those for dahlias, chrysanthemums, fuchsias and, of course, the rose. Competitions for the heaviest gooseberry have been going on for over 150 years.

In England some of the "fancies" are still largely the province of manual workers; others attract people of different social habit. Daffodils, rhododendrons and camellias are perhaps considered the most "aristocratic" flowers in Britain. One of my acquaintance claims he can tell which flower is being exhibited at the Royal Horticultural Society by studying the visitors.

The first specialist florist society in North America seems to have been the American Rose Society, founded in 1899. Others followed; but starting from societies devoted to agriculture and general natural history, Americans originally favored large regional societies, of which the first was the New York Horticultural Society, founded in 1818 (and thus almost predating the august Royal Horticultural Society, founded in Britain in 1804). It only continued in existence, however, until 1837. The Pennsylvania and Massachusetts Horticultural Societies were founded in 1827 and 1829 respectively; and the first organized flower show in the United States was held in Philadelphia in 1829. One of the first specialized U.S. shows was one for Indian azaleas held by the Massachusetts Horticultural Society in 1835. Today United States horticultural societies parallel those in Britain in specialization and exceed them in number.

One of the most popular groups of plants today is the rose. This was always a favorite English cottage garden subject, and in the nineteenth century it became a suburban one. In 1826 Loddige's famous Hackney, London, nursery was listing 1,393 species and varieties. There can hardly be a British garden today without some roses in it, although there are relatively few entirely devoted to this flower, as there were in late Victorian and Edwardian times, when rose gardens entirely separated from the rest of the layout would be planted with a formality reminding one of the parterre. The rose is probably the oldest ornamental plant cultivated in North America, having been brought over very early in the history of white settlement. The earliest notable book on its culture in America, Robert Buist's *The Rose Manual*, was published in 1844, a good indication of wide popularity by that date. The American Rose Society was founded in 1899; what is now the Royal National Rose Society was founded in Britain in 1876. As with the rhododendron, no special cultural knowledge is necessary with the rose; it grows on most soils, likes heavy feeding, and needs pruning in specific ways according to the class of rose grown.

The breeding of numerous climbing roses, together with large-

The rose, always a favorite cottage garden plant (right), was usually planted with heavy formality in the spacious gardens of the rich (below).

ABOVE: *In the ultra-modern Los Angeles State and County Arboretum, concrete has been extensively used – for the platform under a wooden roof giving a shady sitting area, to delineate the pool and create the cylindrical forms within it. It is a garden for modern living where plants are used mainly as decorative adjuncts.*

PREVIOUS PAGE: *Early specialists: the Turkish gardeners' guilds decorated floats on which they demonstrated their skills in the procession celebrating the accession of Sultan Murad III in 1582. The parade wound its way through the streets of Constantinople and along the Bosphorus. These gardeners are mainly bulb growers.*

OPPOSITE: *Rock gardening has innumerable adherents in North America, Britain and Europe. In this present-day U.S. example a rocky stream has been created among shrub and tree plantings.*

ABOVE: *This small modern Danish garden has been designed for minimum upkeep. Paving has entirely replaced lawn and almost all the planting is of conifers – evergreens which give a variety of forms and colors throughout the year.*

OPPOSITE: *Because of problems of upkeep paving has replaced lawn in this tiny garden in London, surrounded by houses. But many elements of the traditional larger garden remain – grass reduced to an edging, a pool with a tiny fountain, bedding plants, trees and tumbling roses.*

ABOVE: *A London rooftop garden concentrates on greenery rather than flowers, with lawn, box edging and trees.*

OPPOSITE: *This New York rooftop is an amazing oasis of flowers packed into containers around a tiny lawn. It eclipses other efforts around it, although the house behind has apparently become a jungle.*

OVERLEAF: *Limitations of space have not stopped this California city dweller packing a multitude of features into his high-fenced backyard (designed by Thomas D. Church) – wooden decks and steps, metal pavilion, outdoor lights, a small statue, and plants wherever possible. Such small plots may be inevitable in tomorrow's cities.*

The only aim of the flower exhibitor is to produce perfect blooms: his plot is arranged accordingly. ABOVE LEFT: *This enthusiast grows gladioli, dahlias and sweet peas.* TOP: *Chrysanthemum specialist protects his blooms with paper bags today.* ABOVE: *Before World War II he was using oiled paper caps.* LEFT: *Where space allows, many gardens devote separate areas to one kind of plant, such as the modern bearded irises here; they are planted decoratively but also fulfill the needs of shows and exhibitions.*

flowered clematis, around the turn of the century was largely responsible for the re-creation of pergolas, a construction made in large numbers up until 1939. The less vigorous climbers bred since World War II do not need pergolas. Whether too many roses in a garden are a good thing is seldom questioned. However, as the contemporary English author Richard Gorer has written, it is effectively a hardy, permanent bedding plant, and like tender "bedders" it has no charm for many months of the year. As Shirley Hibberd wrote in 1871, "The question will occur where a rose garden should be formed, within view of the windows or far away. We reply, 'far away'; for a rose garden should be in its season a wonder to be sought, as, when its season is past, it is a wilderness to be avoided."

Other modern "fancies" include the iris, the delphinium, the day lily (*hemerocallis*), the gladiolus, pinks, and others of which breeders have produced a large number of varieties, and to which individual parts of a garden are often allocated.

Both dahlia and chrysanthemum have been very popular in the United States and these were among the earliest to have exhibition classes, at a show in 1830. Ironically, the Mexican dahlias came to the States from Germany. The so-called China Aster, another German import, was at various times particularly popular. Each has its specific cultural needs, of course, and neglect causes deterioration. Cultivation certainly affects the quality of the bloom in delphiniums, and even more so in other examples of garden mania or monoculture, especially if the aim is exhibition, as with the dahlia, sweet pea, gladiolus, and particularly the chrysanthemum. With these, propagation, feeding, disbudding, support and flower protection are among essential activities to produce prize-winning blooms. The exhibition chrysanthemum provides work for its grower almost every day of the year – specialization with a vengeance. The flower exhibitor's garden is seldom attractive to the outsider.

COLLECTIONS

In the rest of this chapter, I want briefly to examine the way in which certain types of specialization have actually affected the form of gardens and, in some cases, the way in which gardening is carried out. Perhaps the earliest type, apart from herbal and botanical gardens, was the formation of *pineta* – collections of conifers. In Britain and Europe, these gathered momentum from the importation of seeds in the early nineteenth century and were greatly stimulated by introductions from the plant collectors David Douglas and, later, William Lobb, from North and South America respectively. Conifers have transformed the British landscape, and many old estates and gardens contain huge trees a century or more old, including the outlandish monkey puzzle, so beloved of the Victorians. And, as in the United States, there are massive commercial plantations. The earliest U.S. pinetum was begun in 1851 by H. H. Hunnewell at Wellesley, Massachusetts; although soon followed by others, it was for many years unsurpassed.

The first great collection of rhododendrons and azaleas in the United States was again that of Hunnewell, whose main aim was to discover which species and varieties would grow successfully in the difficult New England climate.

Gardens in Britain were particularly affected by the flood of rhododendron introductions, begun in 1818 when Nathaniel Wallich introduced *R. arboreum.* This gave rise to a spate of hybridizing, producing new rhododendron hybrids, "azaleodendrons" and the Ghent azaleas – first of the unending deciduous garden varieties. This breeding was reinforced by the introductions of botanist Joseph Hooker from 1848 on, and those of innumerable later collectors, notably from the Himalayas.

I do not think it is exaggerating to say that the multitude of seedlings, germinating like mustard and cress from the seed sent home, rapidly transformed many Britsh gardens into unplanned woodlands – full of spectacular rarities but resembling laurel groves for months of the year. Rhododendron gardening is not particularly difficult: it basically just demands an acid soil. But the collecting mania associated with it has undoubtedly infected several generations of gardeners with what the writer C. E. Lucas-Phillips has called "a curiously twisted sort of snobbery. To have an alkaline soil, in the eyes of these people, is rather like belonging to the wrong club."

Another single-species collector's item in Britain in the mid-nineteenth century was the willow; the numerous species of *Salix* were gathered into *salicetums* or sally gardens, a mania which has not persisted.

Sometimes collecting manias arise for unexpected reasons. The great boom for collecting and growing camellias started with the appearance of Alexander Dumas's *La Dame aux Camélias* in 1848, followed by the play *Camille* and the opera *La Traviata* which were derived from it.

Although American gardens had the advantage to start with of a vast and very beautiful native flora, more and more plants were introduced to the United States during the nineteenth century. Before this, exotic introductions arrived with the Spaniards, English, French, Dutch and the other settlers. Anything from farther east came almost entirely via European centers, notably English nurseries who sent out many collectors. A few very keen American gardeners on the eastern seaboard asked ship captains to bring them new plants, and a number were introduced in this way.

The first real plant-collecting mission from the United States was the sending of James Morrow with Commodore Perry's expedition to Japan in 1853. Hostile natives sometimes boiled seeds before handing them over to Morrow, but he brought back a number of interesting species. In 1861–1862, the American amateur collector George Hall visited Japan, and he later spent many years in China, introducing a good number of ornamental plants directly from the Far East.

An example of late nineteenth-century bedding, using large quantities of annually raised plants.

Later, Harvard's Arnold Arboretum, founded in 1872, was responsible for vast numbers of introductions, first by the original director, Charles Sprague Sargent, and perhaps most notably by E. H. Wilson who introduced around one thousand first-rate ornamental plants, including many new rhododendrons, as a result of his expeditions to the Far East. He started collecting in 1899 for the English firm of Veitch & Sons, and it was not until 1907 that he collected for the Arnold Arboretum.

BEDDING PLANTS

The latter part of the nineteenth century also saw a vast influx of plants to both Europe and North America from South and Central America and South Africa. Among these were hosts of what we now call "bedding plants" – usually tender perennials which can be kept going in a warm greenhouse or be raised annually from cuttings or seeds. Their brilliant flowers and foliage soon led to annually raised specimens being grown outside during the summer while the stock plants remained under glass. With something of a return to the symmetrical beds of the Tudors, and the subsequent knots and parterres, gardens were cut up into small beds which were packed with new, colorful treasures. These beds were usually geometrical and arranged in symmetrical patterns, but sometimes less formal, kidney- or tadpole-shaped for instance, or made to represent – to passing birds at any rate – the shape of baskets or urns. Often the plants were low growing, and the result was called carpet bedding, in imitation of Turkish and Persian carpets.

The beds were often edged with low "basketwork" of cast iron or osier. Actual "baskets" were often placed as a centerpiece – made of concentric tiers of metal or rustic woodwork, rising several feet and up to fifteen feet across. Large urns might also be used. This "bedding out" became the implacable fashion for a long period.

The trigger seems to have been the introduction of *Verbena venosa* and other tender species from South and Central America from 1830 on. This was followed by the breeding of dwarf scarlet pelargoniums (which most people still call "geraniums"), the importation of which in England happily coincided with the repeal of the glass tax in 1845 (see page 237). This made greenhouses far cheaper to build, and in the new greenhouses bedding plants could be raised in the appropriate thousands.

Subtropical bedding, tree ferns, monsters and other exotics planted out for the summer in Battersea Park, 1864.

In the United States, formal bedding experienced a great burst of popularity, especially immediately before and after the Civil War. Carpet or geometric bedding, as it was called, was most practiced, but there was also a considerable vogue for "fancy bedding," in which houses, animals, clocks, calendars and names of townships (as at railroad stations) were created out of plants.

In 1875 one two-acre south London garden is recorded as being bedded with sixty thousand foliage plants of seventeen kinds, the resulting spectacle, according to a contemporary account, being one in which "brilliancy combined with chasteness." The propagation necessary for such plantings, and that required to fill the ubiquitous conservatories, was at first all done on the spot; nurseries for mass producing bedding plants did not come into existence until about 1860. There were, incidentally, then far more varieties of "bedder" available in the United States and Europe than there are today.

Shirley Hibberd started the probably inevitable swing in fashion against bedding in 1871, to be followed by the louder fulminations of the famous gardener-writers William Robinson and Gertrude Jekyll, who preached a return to more naturalistic and even "wild" gardening. By the 1880s, bedding was mainly confined to grand houses and public places; rising costs were responsible for its final eclipse. Now bedding of any kind is only seen in the United States occasionally, and then primarily in places like the Boston Public Garden. In Canada it has held its own a little better, particularly in British Columbia.

It is a little odd that in Robinson's famous book, *The English Flower Garden*, there should be a place for an engraving of subtropical bedding, a very unnatural form of display enjoyed in earlier, less cost-conscious decades. It was first used, apparently, in Britain, in Battersea Park in 1864. Later, perhaps under Robinsonian influence, plants which had to be taken into the greenhouse every autumn were replaced by hardier ones with a tropical appearance – bamboos, yuccas, acanthus, fatsia and so on – which remained permanently in place.

ROCK GARDENING

Wild gardening, to quote Robinson, "is applied essentially to the placing of perfectly hardy exotic plants under conditions where they will thrive without further care." Among the hardy exotic plants then becoming more popular were alpines and other rock-loving plants. These, however, demand rather more care than Robinson's herbaceous perennials and shrubs. They are sensitive to soil acidity, aspect, excessive moisture at the roots, degree of drainage and much more.

The use of rock in gardens seems to have begun in England in 1772, when the "Perfector Horti," or director, of the Apothecaries' Garden at Chelsea (now the Chelsea Physic Garden) placed there some forty tons of old stone from the Tower of London, and lava brought from Iceland by Sir Joseph Banks, with a topping of flints and chalk. There was no attempt to imitate nature; the result – it still exists – is a heap of stones, the lava looking like the fused bricks the Victorians were so fond of, and the present curator says that it must be in the running for the ugliest rockery in Britain. This was the precursor of many such collections of stones, which were known as "stoneries" or "lapideums," and might – to quote contemporary accounts – be "a hillock of flints and fused bricks," or "a goodly assemblage of large stones, and perhaps old roots and trunks of trees, lying loosely together on a mound of earth." They seem to have been built largely for their own sake rather than for growing plants. An anonymous

"What to avoid" in rock gardening – an unclassifiable monstrosity sketched in the Botanic Gardens, Regents Park, London, in 1872.

BELOW: *An early attempt at naturalistic rock gardening, The Mer de Glace and Alps at Chamonix simulated at Hoole House, about 1838.*

article of 1831 stated that "rockworks in general, are made on too small a scale, and more resemble heaps of stones, with the interstices filled with weeds, than the protrusion from the soil of a portion of real rock, decorated with ornamental plants."

One of the earliest natural-looking rock gardens in England, although little is known of it, was built by William Beckford, author of the Gothic fantasy *Vathek*, in a quarry at Fonthill, Wiltshire, very early in the nineteenth century. And by 1839 there was a well-established garden at Redleaf, in Kent, whose owner exposed a natural outcrop of rock and built others forming, among other features, a rocky precipice. Here, however, shrubs were grown rather than rock plants.

The Matterhorn in miniature, complete with model chamois, topped the massive rock garden at Friar Park in 1880.

Others attempted to imitate the mountains more than details from them. Such was the representation at Hoole House, Cheshire, of the Mer de Glace and the Alps at Chamonix, built during the 1830s. At first they kept disintegrating and took some years to stabilize, but by 1838 they were covered with creeping and alpine plants, with some larger shrubs. The impressive spectacle was, however, rendered somewhat absurd for being the backdrop to a series of round beds set in grass, arranged in straight lines. According to Loudon, who described Hoole in 1838, the planting positions were carefully devised to grow "the most rare and beautiful alpines . . . each placed in a nidus of suitable soil, and the surface protected from the weather by broken fragments of stone, clean-washed river gravel, the debris of decaying rock, moss, or other suitable substances, according as the object was to retain moisture; to evaporate moisture . . .; to increase the heat, in which dark fragments of stone are used; or to diminish it, which is effected by the employment of white pebbles, which, by reflecting the light, keeps the ground cool." When Robinson saw Hoole in 1868, it was still in good order, but beehives in the form of Swiss chalets added to its incongruities.

ABOVE AND OPPOSITE: *Many massive rock gardens were built in the first half of this century. Both these photographs were in fact taken at the Chelsea Flower Show grounds, that above before World War II, the other in 1952. Here massive rock gardens were created in a few days and then demolished.*

By 1890 one could see, at Friar Park near Maidenhead in southern England, the fantastic rock garden of millionaire Frank Crisp, with a total of 7,000 tons of rocks, weighing up to 6½ tons each. It had at its summit a miniature Matterhorn surrounded by snowfields simulated in alabaster, complete with model chamois which one could observe through a telescope.

A second rock garden at Friar Park, reached through artificial caves and grottoes, was built entirely of artificial rocks made of concrete, "given stratification marks by scoring them with a piece of broken wood, brushed over with a stable brush to give them a striated and slightly roughened surface, dusted with sand and finished off with a spray of oxide of iron, or some such pigment" (*Alpine Garden Society Bulletin*). They were, in fact, extremely realistic.

By the end of the nineteenth century, there was a real urge to cultivate rock plants for their own sake. The first steps toward their proper understanding were taken by the Swiss Henri Correvon from 1875 onward. However, many early rock gardens of lesser stature than Friar Park often owed much, unfortunately, to recollections of the early "stoneries." It was such that led Reginald Farrer – forceful doyen of rock gardeners and alpine-plant collectors – to classify them in 1907 as "almond puddings," "dog's graves" and "Devil's lapfuls" – of which "the chaotic hideousness of the result is to be remembered with shudders ever after."

In North America rock gardening never reached the exuberance

or grandiosity exemplified by Friar Park, but it did go through its "raisin pudding" stage with heaps of soil and stones in the middle of the lawn, or even of stones arranged for their own sake, as in a once-famous Ohio garden which, around 1836, had a circular pool surrounded by a miniature Devil's Causeway apparently devoid of plants. But that is now past, and true rock gardeners still practice their hobby, seriously begun early in this century. Like the Alpine Garden Society in Britain, the American Rock Garden Society is very much alive.

A good large-scale rock garden attempts to simulate nature by an arrangement of reasonably large blocks as if naturally stratified (such as one can see in the rock garden at Kew, begun in 1882, and countless others). The rock gardens built, planted, admired and pulled apart all in a few days in lavish flower shows for many decades were, and still are, despite economic stringency, remarkable achievements.

But today the pressures both of economics and of space restrictions have led to much more compact ways of growing alpines and other rock plants. It is now possible to buy artificial hollow rocks, which at least reduce delivery costs. The first transition from the massive rock garden was to the flatter rock and scree, ending up almost entirely as a scree or moraine – a bed of very porous soil, deeply drained, and sometimes provided with subirrigation – in which a few rocks appear mainly for appearance.

This has been followed by the making of rock beds or "billiard tables," as they are called by specialists, in which exterior walls of flat rock

Gradually fewer and smaller rocks were used in rock gardens, which ended in scree beds, with much better growing conditions for the plants.

LEFT: *The first raised rock-plant beds, or "billiard tables," were made at the Savill Garden, Windsor Great Park, in 1951.*

BELOW: *A small raised bed in a private garden.*

Further examples of raised beds showing use of unusual materials – right, roof tiles and, opposite, railroad ties.

A garden of terraces formed of peat blocks with a stone edging. Center, after construction; right, a couple of years after planting.

slabs, broken paving stones, tiles, or even railroad ties support a bed of porous soil appropriate to the plants to be grown, above a deep drainage layer. As we find so often in gardening history, it has all been done before; several Victorian writers advocated their use, and there is a description in *The Floral World* of 1868 of one constructed in a north London garden, where a bed of light soil raised a foot above the surrounding ground, with a two-foot drainage layer, permitted the growing of choice alpines in a garden of unsuitable clay soil. Shirley Hibberd suggested making beds as high as four feet, which seems excessive.

The resurgence in the use of raised rock plant beds today stems from those built at England's Savill Garden, Windsor Great Park, in 1951. There are four of them, each with different soil mixture and acidity, and with buried water supplies of different kinds. Such beds, and, on a smaller scale, sink gardens, preferably made in old stone sinks, allow a quantity of rock plants to be grown in small compass and under much closer control than on a large rockery, where one feels that often the plants are decorating the rocks, and where their attention may need minor mountaineering.

PEAT GARDENING

Akin to rock gardening, but more recent, is peat gardening. Walls of peat blocks to hold in a bed of peaty soil are first described in 1927, in an article about Logan Gardens, Stranraer, in southwestern Scotland. The Logan feature was in effect a rock garden built of peat blocks instead of rock. A similar construction followed at the Royal Botanic Garden, Edinburgh, a few years later, and this public model focused attention on the possibilities. A peat garden provides, to quote Alfred Evans, "a much sought after environment seldom met with in a rock garden whether in sun or shade." In fact, the crevices which many rock plants enjoy, and the rock they like to spread over, are not present in a peat garden; the plants that flourish there knit the moist peaty soil mixture together with their roots, and the walls become covered with vegetation. The peat garden is better for plants enjoying cool, shady positions than is the rock garden.

WATER GARDENING

Water gardening is another aspect of specialization whose greatest development, in terms of deliberate cultivation of aquatic plants, has taken place in this century. Sumerians, Egyptians, Jews, Romans, Arabs, Chinese, and medieval monasteries all had ponds for fish, which were an important part of the diet; and water has been used for decorative purposes since ancient times, notably in hot countries.

The ancient Egyptians cultivated waterlilies in their formal pools. The Chinese were growing them, in urns and vases as well as pools and lakes, by the tenth century A.D. (They were practicing pisciculture in the fifth century B.C.) The Japanese followed suit: in his *History of Japan* of 1728, Engelbert Kaempfer wrote that the Japanese garden "is commonly square, with a back door, and wall'd in very neatly, like a cistern, or pond, for which reason it is call'd Tsubo, which in the Japanese language signifies a large water trough or cistern. There are few good houses or inns, but what have their Tsubo . . . with alive fish kept in it, and surrounded with proper plants, that is such as love a wat'ry soil, and would lose their beauty and greeness if planted in a dry ground." The Japanese sometimes grew a few aquatics in their symbolic gardens, in which water – whether a lake or the tiniest bowl – almost always played an essential part. Water-loving irises might decorate the banks; reeds and waterlilies the water itself.

Still water in the garden was decried by Bacon, who wrote, "Pools mar all and make the garden unwholesome and full of flies and frogs." The first comparatively recent mention of water gardening I have found is from Richard Bradley, in *New Improvements of Planting and Gardening* of 1717: "I am persuaded, many curious Persons, would have made Plantations of Water-plants, in their Gardens long since, if they had known how to do it." If, he goes on, there are no ponds, rivers or springs to plant them in, he recommends "either large Garden-Pots glazed within-side, and without Holes in their Bottoms, or else cause some Troughs of Wood to be made, of Oaken Boards, about two Inches thick; such cases should be six Foot long, two Foot wide at the Bottom, and two Foot and a half deep, if they are for large Plants that grow under Water, or shallower for such as do not require deep Waters; the Corners and other Joints of such Cases, should be strengthen'd with Iron, the Insides well pitch'd, and the Outsides painted." He then describes the amount of soil needed for various plants and explains how to plant them.

Soon afterwards Philip Miller, in his famous *Gardener's Dictionary* of 1731, wrote, "In some gardens I have seen plants cultivated in large troughs of water, where they flourish very well and annually produce great quantities of flowers, but as the expense is pretty great (their insides

Although the first mention of growing water plants in relatively modern times is in 1717 – Bradley's wooden trough method is shown below – their widespread cultivation is very much a twentieth-century development, and a well-designed pool (left) is always an attractive garden feature.

requiring to be lined with lead to preserve them) there are but a few people who can be at that charge." In 1786 the introduction of *Nymphaea odorata* from North America stimulated a few more Englishmen to cultivate waterlilies. But it was the flowering of the giant waterlily from South America (*Victoria amazonica*) at Chatsworth in 1849 which triggered off a short-lived craze for growing whatever waterlilies could be obtained, both tropical and hardy. All the early seeds and roots of the giant waterlily were sent to Kew; and some thence to Chatsworth. It was from the Chatsworth stock that the plant was distributed to gardeners in Europe and the United States – where the first flower opened in 1851 in Pennsylvania. As in Europe, this created a short-lived fad for growing waterlilies, several of which, such as that mentioned above, are native to North America. The great range of waterlilies we have today is largely the result of breeding by the Frenchman Marliac-Latour who began breeding in 1860, but did not obtain any notable results until 1875, and by George Pring at the Missouri Botanical Garden in this century.

The great water gardens of the world, from ancient until quite modern times, are made mainly of stone, including marble. Medieval pools seem more often to have been made of puddled or rammed clay, often supported by osierwork. Clay was usually essential in informal ponds, while near the end of the nineteenth century concrete began to be used, usually to form the bottoms of pools. The Victorians sometimes used wrought iron for small ornamental pools. It was not until the beginning of

A revolution in pool making has occurred in little over a decade with the use of flexible plastic linings which stretch to fit the excavation when filled with water (right), and of preformed fiberglass shapes (above).

the twentieth century that pools began to be made entirely of concrete, revolutionizing their possibilities in the smallest gardens.

A comparable revolution is with us today, for during the last decade plastic or preformed materials have been used to line ponds. This started with polyethylene sheet spread out over a carefully smoothed and graded excavation, but even so liable to perforation and deterioration. Heavier-duty polyethylene was more successful, and various other materials were tried, of which the most reliable today, with minimum perforation risk and reasonably long life, are butyl-rubber and nylon-reinforced p.v.c. sheeting, often doubly laminated. These materials are very flexible and will accommodate to fairly abrupt changes of angle such as are demanded by planting shelves at different levels. In fact, the material is placed over the pool excavation, held fairly taut by paving slabs on the edge, and gradually filled with water. This stretches the liner, which molds itself to the shape of the excavation. It is normally retained at the edges under paving slabs, surplus being trimmed off, but it can be tucked under thick turf.

Such plastic material can be used over very large areas. For smaller-scale pools, preformed resin-bonded figerglass "shapes" are available in rectangular or informal designs in wide variety, usually incorporating two levels so that waterlilies and marginal plants can be accommodated.

The number of water plants available for cultivation has vastly

The pleasures of water can be enjoyed even in restricted spaces with the "bubbler" in which a tiny jet, powered by a small electric pump, splashes into water, cobbles or over stone or concrete shapes.

This attractive "drip" pours water from an urn into a small orthodox pool.

increased since the turn of the century, when, for example, an important book like Thomas Mawson's *Art and Craft of Garden Making* (1900) mentions only ten more or less aquatic plants and five waterlilies. It was during the first part of the twentieth century that enthusiasm for water gardening spread through the United States, and it was in 1902 that Amos Perry staged his first exhibit of aquatic plants at England's Royal Horticultural Society show. It was Perry's Nursery which very rapidly brought serious water gardening to general notice, and made available water-loving plants in large variety.

At present many amateur gardeners treat water less for growing aquatics than as a garden feature, adding to the basic pool, however formed, with cascades (also available in preformed shapes, usually in lamentable patterns), pump-driven fountains, submerged lighting and so on. One pleasant innovation of recent years has been the "bubbler," in which water comes up either in a slow flow or a small jet, through a block of cement, stone, or a tray of cobblestones. This is usually just decoration with the sound and sight of moving water, but the bubbler among cobbles allows one to add a few plants.

Concrete and plastic pools are usually made with a ledge about six inches below the surface so that shallow-water plants can be grown. It is, however, only in a natural or clay pool or along a stream that plants liking wet but not submerged root conditions can be grown at the margins. A bog garden can be formed without necessarily having a pool, either in naturally marshy conditions or, artificially, by forming a depression and covering it with plastic sheet with a few holes made in it, then filling with appropriate soil. Attaining the right conditions is not always easy; it is no good filling the soil-filled depression with water, which causes stagnant anaerobic conditions and, if the soil is only partly moistened, it can dry out surprisingly quickly in summer. Some form of subirrigation coupled with a drainage system is often needed in this minor, specialized offshoot of water gardening.

GREENHOUSE PLANTS

Under glass more specialization has always been carried out, starting with the citruses which were the "guinea pigs" for glasshouse development, the succulents which followed them, and all kinds of exotic pot plants which began to become popular once greenhouses became widespread in the early nineteenth century (including plants like Cape heaths and proteas which we consider difficult to cultivate today). The orchids, with their sumptuous or extraordinary appearance, and their incredible variety of form, filled many greenhouses. Especially in America, it can be said that orchid growing has steadily become more popular without suffering the vagaries of fashion which have affected, for instance, the camellia, dahlia and aster.

Ferns were another Victorian speciality to which whole houses were devoted, and one which rapidly became popular with people on every

A modern bog garden on the edges of a tiny stream and (below) a bog garden pictured in Robinson's English Flower Garden *(first published 1883).*

Mrs Hibberd's Fern House at Stoke Newington, England, 1870. Plants like ferns, which demand particular growing conditions, lend themselves well to collection.

Epiphytic plants like orchids, and the bromeliads shown here at Kew Gardens, prefer to be grown on pieces of bark or tree trunks as they do in nature.

In an alpine house like that at the Royal Horticultural Society Garden, Wisley, severe frost is kept out, but otherwise the house is unheated and freely ventilated.

Attractive plants can be displayed all the year round with the help of a plunge bed in a frame where the plants are kept when out of bloom.

economic level: John Smith of Kew wrote in 1866 that even "the hard-working mechanic" could afford a fernery. The fashion for ferns was, once again, rapidly reflected in the United States.

Today succulents, begonias, pelargoniums and fuchsias are prominent among greenhouse specialties. So are alpines, grown in almost cold houses. (Heat is only used to keep out the most severe frost which could freeze the soil and crack the pots.) An essential adjunct to a greenhouse alpine collection is the plunge bed, where the pots are sunk rim-deep in weathered ashes, or coarse grit, when out of flower, to conserve moisture – a principle anticipated by an amateur writing in *The Floricultural Cabinet* for 1849. Some plants may be covered in the height of the summer if they need a resting period, a special necessity for Asian bulbs, which expect a wet spring and a baking hot summer, and which are usually grown in special raised frames which can be completely sealed from rain in the summer.

Greenhouse plants are most often grown in pots, but there have been some notable naturalistic plantings. One of the earliest recorded is that of Mr. Dillwyn Llewellyne, whose Welsh conservatory, early in the nineteenth century, was based on Schomburgk's description of waterfalls on rivers in the South American jungles. A cascade of warm water poured over rockwork into a final pool; a small island and surrounding rocks were thickly planted with tropical ferns, club mosses and orchids. He anticipated modern methods by growing orchids either on cork blocks hanging in the humid atmosphere or in baskets. Around 1880, an English gardener built an entire rock garden under glass in Wimbledon.

One fine naturalistic garden from this period still exists in Britain: this is the fernery at Southport Botanic Garden. Opened in 1875, it was advertised a little later as "unique . . . with its fairylike foliage, mirrors, grottoes, waterfalls and fish pools. Fine panoramic views from the balcony and garden eminences."

Naturalistic plantings under glass have today become one of the important methods of display in large botanical gardens in many parts of the world, ranging from miniature deserts of stone and sand to mock forests where epiphytes grow – often fixed onto artificial trees made of cork bark. Such plantings exist in several U.S. centers, notably those mentioned in Chapter 7 at Denver, Milwaukee and Missouri. And there are smaller ones at the Royal Botanic Gardens of Kew and Edinburgh in Britain.

Such greenhouse plantings are the counterpart to the outside "wild garden," and provide a rather different aspect of specialization from the monocultures of passionate practitioners described earlier in this chapter. It is such specialists who really get down to the quirks of individual plants, providing essential knowledge which gradually passes on to the ordinary run of gardeners.

Chapter Ten
Today and Tomorrow

WE LIVE IN AN AGE OF EVER INCREASING POPULATION AND hence ever greater demands upon land. As the last quarter of the twentieth century begins, gardening is perhaps more at the mercy of social and economic pressures than ever before. It has become harder for many people to garden actively as housing concentrates increasingly on apartments or houses with very tiny backyards or plots. Those with more space have, since World War II, found it increasingly difficult, and expensive, to obtain the extra help needed to maintain large gardens.

These generalizations seem to hold true in most countries, even though gardening habits vary greatly from place to place. Statistics from various sources provide the following figures, which should be regarded as approximations, from about 1974 to 1976:

In Britain, 80% of households have some kind of private garden, compared with 70% in Ireland, 67% in Holland, 63% in Denmark, 49% in West Germany, 45% in France, 30% in Switzerland, 15% in Italy, and 7% in Spain. The latest estimate for the United States is that 51% of households carry out some gardening; this means roughly 80 million gardeners. Gardening is increasing rapidly in the United States, as well as in Canada, and figures show a 10% increase between 1971 and 1975.

In the United States, gardens vary from some 8,000 square feet ($\frac{1}{5}$ acre) to 42,000 square feet (1 acre) or larger in more affluent areas. The average size of a British garden is not large – around 2,000 square feet ($\frac{1}{20}$ acre). Only one garden in twenty in Britain is over half an acre. In overpopulated Holland, gardens average 1,650 square feet, but gardens in France, Belgium, Germany, and Scandinavia are at least twice as large. Moreover, many Continental households have a second home with a garden, which is very much the exception in the United States and Britain.

To a lot of people, gardening has always been virtually a way of life, an almost automatic occupation once one has acquired a house – even if a proportion of gardeners are always reluctant ones. Wars and more recent periods of economic stringency have for many years focused European gardeners onto gardening and food production in particular. In the United States, problems of both economy and security have quite recently tended to make people stay at home much more and, in such an

"... how close-pent man regrets
The country, with what ardour he contrives
A peep at Nature, when he can no more."
(William Cowper, 1784)

"introvert" situation, the idea of self-sufficiency and the pleasure of seeing plants around one have had the added impact of novelty.

In looking at the present and the future, two distinct aspects of gardening thus become apparent. One is the optimum use of small spaces; the second, the continuing use of larger spaces with a minimum of labor. In discussing these pressures, it is impossible to disentangle the methods of gardening from the design aspect; they are today more closely intertwined than ever before, for each depends upon the other.

The extreme case of lack of gardening space, the "hard facts" of living in apartments, has encouraged more people to grow indoor plants, the production of which is today a massive industry. Holland's over thirteen million inhabitants, for instance, buy over three hundred million indoor plants a year; and house plants are fully as, or possibly even more, popular in the United States than are outside gardens. In many countries indoor plants are used very much as an essential part of the furnishings, while in Britain they are seldom more than extras or ornaments. With the rise of the indoor plant, there is more emphasis on specialized methods of culture with indoor greenhouses and illumination. Such specialization also includes hydroponics, a technique of cultivating without soil, mentioned in Chapter 5 and, for the more conventional pot-plant grower using soil, aid comes from gadgets which estimate the need for watering with an electrical probe. A new device even audibly signals lack or excess of water and nutrients, and there are also indoor light meters.

Apartments with balconies have shown people the possibilities of growing many plants in small containers, ranging from roses to tomatoes, and even including water plants in small tubs. Specially devised small lean-to glass- or plastic-covered greenhouses allow more delicate plants to be grown in such places. Many apartment buildings, especially in the United States, are stepped back in tiers which provide large terraces and, of course, where flat roofs exist, gardens upon them allow great scope, even for growing small trees. It is a curious thought that Rockefeller Center in New York stands on the site of the Elgin Botanical Garden, and its roofs clothed in gardens are probably the highest hanging gardens in the world, created nearly five thousand years after the ziggurats of Mesopotamia.

In the outdoor garden, the very small yard or plot has led to two distinct trends. One might be called *multum in parvo*, the packing in of as many features and plants as possible. Some small suburban gardens may boast a terrace, lawn, pool, pergola, beds and borders, and a vegetable plot, and grow a large range of plants. Even in unpromising paved yards, a variety of containers, from old cans to tin baths, may be pressed into service, to be replaced by the more sophisticated with elegant plant containers set off with small pieces of sculpture.

Even though in such confined spaces the rock garden, for instance, is scaled down to a sink, it is remarkable what tiny gardens can grow. The London garden illustrated on page 332, for instance, is seventeen feet square, and the lowest wall surrounding it is eight feet high; the other walls, being the sides of adjoining buildings, are much higher. The picture gives some idea of the range and luxuriance of the plants accommodated, which include a fan palm, a maidenhair tree, a fig tree, a mulberry, a great range of leafy and flowering climbers (making the most of the garden's vertical dimension), and a variety of frost-tender plants in containers. It also has a tiny pool and slow-dripping fountain.

Secondly, small-compass gardening has certainly made people consider the long-term value of the foliage and outline of plants, rather than their short bursts of brilliant flower. A good small garden today is more likely to be composed in terms of the form, texture and architectural effect of its plants, rather than of their color. This applies very much in the Mediterranean or in California, for example, where bold succulents and xerophytes are perfect "structural" plants. However, some small gardens are now very much formalized, with a minimum of planting, the main design being created by patterned paving and contrasting materials, plant containers, internal walls, small regular pools, and so on. This is a trend especially in Europe, while most British gardeners are too much interested in plants to accept such reduction in their numbers. In the United States, both types of garden exist, the more formal being more prominent on the

West Coast, where some stylized gardens show considerable Japanese influence.

Such stylization is naturally less prominent in larger gardens. In these the emphasis today is more on labor-saving planting. The Edwardian herbaceous border of the early twentieth century – frequently scores of yards long and ten or twenty feet wide, full of tall plants that needed individual support – and rose gardens have largely disappeared. Such gardens were followed by a swing toward tree and shrub planting, although shrubs have definite drawbacks as the mainstay of garden display. They have a serious shortage of potential interest from July to October, and are not without their problems while becoming established, when weeds invade the ground between them. A more careful study of herbaceous plants brought to the fore many which could be grown with little attention, some, such as the Mediterranean spurges and acanthus, being as permanent as shrubs, others being more or less self-supporting, with really worthwhile flowering periods. The breeding of new varieties has emphasized the trend toward shorter, self-supporting, long-blooming perennials.

Many people have placed their faith in ground cover as a means of reducing maintenance, especially weeding. Ground cover implies the use of close-growing, wide-spreading plants among taller ones. But the very spreading powers of these "ornamental weeds," as they have been called, results in the need for eventual restriction, and deep-rooted and invasive "true" weeds are not always suppressed. The use of ground cover, which is especially valuable between shrubs, is effectively an aspect of wild gardening, desirable or not according to one's taste. The results can be very attractive, and probably mean less frequent attention than bare-soil gardening, in which every weed is in principle an annoyance. Again, Californian gardeners seem to predominate with this type of planting. A 1976 report suggests that "instant" ground covers, prepared on the same principle as grass sod, but from cuttings, would soon be available in the United States.

In the United States, in both large and small gardens, the average use of bedding plants now tends to be restricted to small beds or ornamental containers, where a limited outlay will create a bold splash of color which will last for a long period – especially in summer when it is most desirable – and create focal points among plants chosen less for their flowers than for other attributes. However, the increasing cost of plants is resulting in more people growing their own, perennials as well as annuals, from seed.

Since 1974 there has been a great upsurge in vegetable growing (which is of course almost entirely from seed), simply because of inflation and rising prices. In Britain and other parts of Europe, those without gardens often make use of allotments – plots assigned by the local government – and today virtually all the allotments in Britain have been taken up. In the United States, similar facilities are provided in

The tiny suburban garden (above) crams together lawn, pool and pergola, and certainly manages to produce the important element of surprise. The lady (left) is determined to pack as many plants as possible into a cement yard.

Another minute garden in which plants are crammed into tiny beds and stone sinks (foreground).

BELOW: *It is almost unbelievable that this elegant, plant-filled garden occupies a sunken backyard only seventeen feet square; it is surrounded by tall buildings and its lowest wall is eight feet high.*

"community plots." These may be cultivated by individuals and their families, including senior citizens, sometimes associated with schools and colleges, and sometimes provided by corporations, as at the RCA Think Tank at Princeton. In some places, such as Chicago, they are actually cultivated communally. It was estimated in 1976 that community gardening – a very recent development in the United States – was occupying about three million people on thirty thousand sites. Many of these are on public land, and they have opened up previously unused areas such as ground underneath power transmission lines. A similar scheme is gaining momentum in Canada.

Before the recent economic crisis, about half of British gardens had a vegetable plot of some sort; the figure is probably over 70% today. In France, three-fourths of the gardens have always grown food, and about half grow food and nothing else. Fruit is almost as prominent as vegetables in French gardens: over 50% of gardens grow some, compared with 34% in Britain. In Germany, only 17% of gardens grow vegetables, but over 40% have strawberries. Over 40% of American gardens include vegetables, but only one in five of these grow fruit, of which strawberries and apples are the most popular. As in Britain, tomatoes outclass everything else in popularity. Although there was a slight decline in 1976–1977, there seems little doubt that the enormous upsurge in home vegetable growing will continue. It saved U.S. gardeners $12 billion in 1976, and is to a large degree tied in with home canning and freezing. This recent upsurge is due in part to rising costs and the current gospel of self-sufficiency and in part to the worries of many, whether well-founded or not, that bought vegetables are polluted by excessive use of insecticides and fertilizers.

Alongside this last feeling, organic gardening today has an increasing appeal. Organic gardening is based on the use of homemade compost from vegetable waste, animal manure, leaf mold and other natural materials, and never makes use of artificial fertilizers. It is combined with pest and disease control achieved with materials of natural and not of synthetic origin, and it makes use of insect predators or interspersing crops with special plants which may deter pests and, perhaps, diseases. The "father" of organic gardening was the Englishman Sir Albert Howard (1873–1947), whose ideas, derived from coping with farmers' problems in India, crystallized in books published in the 1940s. As mentioned earlier, Rachel Carson's *Silent Spring*, published in 1962, focused world attention on the dangers of certain agricultural chemicals, and especially the way they accumulated so that dangerous excesses arose after periods of time. There is a great deal of good sense in organic gardening, especially on the private garden level and, if it has collected the name "muck and mystery," it is, perhaps, because some of its publicists have practiced it as if it were a religion – the "mystery" has become more important than the "muck."

In the small garden today, the work problem is usually an inverted one – the active gardener does not have enough to do. But in gardens over one-fourth acre, where concentrated plant growing means much detailed work, it is both difficult and expensive to obtain even unskilled help, and trained gardeners are few and far between. So owner/gardeners are more and more forced to do all the work themselves. Only 6% of British gardens have expert paid help, although in Holland, with far fewer gardens, 40% of gardeners have it. This new development comes as less of a shock in America; the percentage of "do-it-yourself" gardeners has always been high. In order to cope with this problem, gardeners can rely, on the one hand, increasingly on naturalistic plantings of shrubs, trees and the more trouble-free perennials, and can allow formerly mown grass to revert to occasionally cut meadow. On the other hand, they can use a vast armory of technical aids, many of which I have mentioned briefly in this book.

Powered mowers, for instance, reduce mowing time immensely, and the "ride-on" has almost made it a pleasure. If neat edges to plant beds are desired, power trimmers are available, or edges can be maintained with metal strips. In some ways the lawn today might be thought anomalous. The American William G. Kendrick wrote in 1966 that the lawn was "a living fossil in a modern human zoo," in a passage recently used to preface an essay on "energy conservation on the home grounds" – the use of naturalistic plantings instead of grass. The lawn creates more drudgery than any other part of the garden, yet very few gardeners are willing to dispense with it, for it provides not only a pleasant surface for leisure activities, but also a valuable contrast to flowering plants. In the United States, practically every suburban house has at least a front lawn; 82% of British gardens include lawn, but only 40% of French ones. The lawn's replacement by paving in very small gardens is usually because they have high enclosing walls or fences which make it difficult to grow grass well, and also, being in the nature of "outdoor rooms," it is desirable to have a hard surface which does not become soggy after rain, and can be walked on readily at all times – even in winter.

Especially in the United States and in Europe, there is a trend toward using the garden for "leisure activities," and the barbecue raises its curious form in many layouts.

Engine-powered cultivators, just as power mowers, are available in sizes from one-horsepower mechanical hoes to almost farm-size tractors; but these have much less impact on the average gardener since they are basically of value only to those with large vegetable gardens or smallholdings where plants and crops can be arranged in long straight lines.

Whatever the organic school may say, the chemical industries have provided further invaluable assistance for gardeners. Fertilizers of many kinds make feeding plants easy, though perhaps at the expense of making many gardeners forget about the desirability of making compost. Fertilizers may be granular, powdered, in pill form or liquids to be diluted, and come in various different formulations. Slow-release materials, in

"Must one foresee a multitude of paved yards . . . with plantings reduced to a square yard or two of small plants and patterns of stones?"

which nutrients leach for from three months to five years, are also available, mainly in the United States. Some fertilizers are bulked up with organic materials; others are combined with lawn weedkillers.

Peat is widely available for use on its own or in food-enriched composts with special wetting agents incorporated; shredded tree bark is a recent introduction with similar qualities. In the United States, where mulching is much practiced, tree bark is now being widely sold for mulching purposes along with pecan, rice, peanut, cocoa and buckwheat hulls, bagasse (shredded sugar cane), ground corn cobs, and pine straw, all of which are more regional in availability.

Other materials which help gardeners overcome problems of unsatisfactory soils are conditioners, which make soil more workable, increasing porosity and permeability to water. Some are based on inert materials like lignite; a seaweed derivative is widely used in Britain; and in the United States a number of polyvinyl and cellulose compounds have been used, although their cost has kept most of them out of the garden market.

Weeds, pests and diseases can be combated with many chemicals. There are total, superficial and selective weedkillers, the latter invaluable for use in lawns since they kill broad-leaved weeds but do not harm grass. Insect and fungus killers can likewise be broad-spectrum or fairly selective, and the systemic materials, which actually penetrate the plant's tissues and thus give protection against organisms large or small, which may suck or otherwise penetrate, give longer protection than those which merely coat the plant surfaces. They are also generally harmless to insect predators.

There are over two million greenhouses in Britain, a higher per capita number than anywhere else. Most of them are entirely devoted to growing tomatoes, chrysanthemums, or both. Although the proportion in North America is less, the number of greenhouses in use has risen very rapidly in the last few years. A 1977 survey suggested about 285,000 backyard greenhouses in the United States.

Apart from improvements in greenhouse design, the various aspects of maintenance – temperature control, ventilation, watering and shading – can now all be carried out automatically if desired, although this is expensive. The propagator has a wide range of sophisticated propagating cases and special techniques, such as misting, at his command, and also synthetic hormone compounds to accelerate rooting. Plant cultivation and leisure can be combined in the sunroom, the modern equivalent of the conservatory.

Although glass is still the most widely used light-transmitting material, polyethylene and polyvinylchloride sheeting have been used for inexpensive structures and, especially in the United States, fiberglass and rigid acrylic sheet for more orthodox ones (as described in Chapter 7).

Even in the uncertain climate of Britain and northern Europe, there is today increasing use of the garden for purely leisure activities. A terrace or patio has become an increasingly frequent feature, existing in over 50% of German gardens. In places like California, a terrace is practically standard equipment with every individual home, and in Florida a screened version originally called a "Florida room" is popular. In U.S. patios there is a preference for wooden or concrete "decks," often above ground level. Other results of using the garden for pleasure are attractive mass-produced garden furniture, swimming pools of various sizes, decorative lighting for use at night, including illumination of the pool, and a range of *al fresco* dining equipment, starting with the barbecue which is *de rigeur* in many European and American gardens.

Increasing leisure use of the garden naturally affects its design rather than the methods used for its cultivation, but the wish for more time to be spent at leisure – whether within or beyond the garden – has been partly responsible for the increasing use of short cuts and mechanical aids. The wish to curtail the hardest work has surely also been influenced by the increasing part played by women in the actual work of gardening. It is true that the woman used to have a major share: Thomas Tusser had words for it back in 1577, although then it was probably more of a duty than a pleasure:

> In March and April, from morning to night,
> In sowing and setting, good housewives delight.

But gardening became a man's world, especially when plenty of paid help was available, up to World War II. Since then things have changed: recent surveys show that the wife does most of the work in 31% of British gardens, and as much as her husband in another 26%, although man insists more on his way in the industrial Midlands and beyond the Scottish border. In Italy and Ireland, women are more usually responsible for most gardening; in France, Belgium and Germany, it is still the men. In Canada, the situation is roughly the same as in Britain, while in the United States, if one makes generalizations, the lawnmowing, vegetable and fruit gardening and heavier work are more often done by men, the indoor and the ornamental gardening by women.

Can one foretell the future of gardening and its techniques? Looked at in terms of continued population increase, it looks rather depressing; a recent calculation suggested that by A.D. 2800 every square yard of England and Wales would be urbanized, while northern Europe would reach that state even sooner. And present building trends suggest that new houses will be built with ever smaller surrounds, if not frequently in the larger gardens of older houses.

In Canada and the United States, the squeeze is fortunately not so tight and, for the present at least, the birthrate has dropped. As we have seen, suburban plots or "lots" are relatively large, and gardening is on the

A New York balcony greenhouse – an oasis of sun, warmth, flowers and greenery.

increase in terms both of participants and of space used. But some day there will doubtless be the same crunch as in Europe.

Must one foresee a multitude of paved yards, even if glass dividing walls give them more light, with plantings reduced to a square yard or two of small plants and patterns of stone and paving? It is a depressing thought which any plant lover will fight against, and which counters the increasing need to grow some of one's own food.

One can be fairly certain, however, that technology will continue to assist the gardener, although it is difficult to imagine any new invention which will go much further toward reducing work or enhancing results. Looking back, one sees a gradual evolution in tools and techniques which has only been accelerated today by the advent of portable power sources, by a better understanding of cause and effect, and by the endeavors of chemists. As I mentioned at the start of this book, the ancient origins of many of our garden tools and practices are astonishing.

In a way, this is a pleasant conclusion to the gardener, who is not normally an ardent technologist or scientist. In recalling primitive beginnings of cultivation, one is reminded of man's constant instinctive urge to have plants around him, to select those that are most attractive to him, and to grow them to the best of his ability. Our gardens are echoes of the primeval green world in which our ancestors lived and evolved, a world which we are all too busy destroying today. Without green and flowering plants for pleasure as much as food, the world would be a much poorer place. As Ruskin wrote, "flowers seem intended for the solace of ordinary humanity." On the practical side, a community gardener in Chicago expressed her pleasure thus: "You know, I've never gardened

LEFT: *Smaller gardens mean more interest in plants with interesting forms, textures and leaf colors which remain attractive much of the year, as in this British example.*

BELOW: *There need be no dearth of flowers and climbing foliage even on a narrow balcony, like this New York example which even boasts a weeping willow tree.*

Plants, privacy, a place to sit and a place to eat – these are the attributes of this New York City garden.

before. Before this I never even knew how cucumbers grew. It's just amazing to see these vegetables grow. It's a happy experience – a whole new world."

Not everyone enjoys gardening, of course. One wonders, for instance, what experiences prompted Emerson to write that "A garden is like one of those pernicious machineries which catch a man's coat-skirt or his hand, and draw in his arm, his leg and his whole body to irresistible destruction." But most who write about it abstractly rather than practically are enthusiastic. It is a lifetime occupation, and one in which the gardener is always looking forward. As Karel and Josef Čapek wrote in that much-to-be-recommended book *The Gardener's Year*, "We gardeners live somehow for the future; if roses are in flower, we think that next year they will flower better; and in some few years this little spruce will become a tree – if only those few years were behind me! I should like to see what these birches will be like in fifty years. The right, the best is in front of us. Each successive year will add growth and beauty. Thank God that again we shall be one year further on!"

The happy gardener is most beautifully evoked, perhaps, in Virgil's *Georgics*: "I remember I saw an old Corycian who had a few acres of waste ground, not fertile for ploughing nor suitable for cattle, crops or a vineyard. However, here and there among the thorn bushes he planted his vegetables, and around them lilies, verbena, and the slender poppy, and he equaled by his devotion the wealth of kings. Returning home late at night, he loaded his table with unbought feasts."

OPPOSITE: *Whatever methods and tools a gardener may use, they are employed only to fulfill his constant instinctive urge to have plants around him, for solace quite as much as food. A small paved British yard epitomizes the garden as an oasis.*

Acknowledgments

To several individuals I owe a debt of gratitude for help in preparing this book. The original idea of a book on these lines came from Maurice Michael, who also did a great deal of the essential work on picture research. Miss Barbara Midgley gave me much help with the detail of classical and medieval horticultural practices; she also read the manuscript and made most useful comments upon it. Mr. Edwin P. Steffek in the United States and Mr. Richard Gorer both read the manuscript and made valuable comments. When the manuscript was nearly finished, the late Earl of Morton read it on behalf of the Royal Horticultural Society and his favorable report was most encouraging. Edward Bacon gave me some valued help on historical and archaeological background.

The illustrations and the old, often very rare books used for reference have come from several sources, in particular The Lindley Library of the Royal Horticultural Society, where personal thanks are due to the librarian, Peter Stageman; the London Library; the British Library; and the Trustees of the British Museum. My wife Alyson, and Denys Baker, made a number of drawings based on miscellaneous originals.

Others who have kindly supplied photographs or transparencies or allowed the reproduction of published material, or have provided help on specific details, are listed opposite.

Amateur Gardening
The American School of Classical Studies, Athens
Theresa Atkins
Morley Baer
Biblioteca Apostolica Vaticana, Vatican City
Biblioteca Nacional, Madrid
Bibliothèque de l'Arsenal, Paris
Bibliothèque Nationale, Paris
British Insulated Callenders Cables Ltd.
The Bodleian Library, Oxford
Pat Brindley
Brooklyn Botanic Garden
The Chester Beatty Library, Dublin
Country Life
The Daily Telegraph
Verlag L. Däbritz
Dome Enterprises Inc.
Editoriale La Scala, Florence
Trustees of the Will of the late J. H. C. Evelyn
Fehr'sche Buchhandlung, St. Gallen
Arthur L. Finney, A.I.D., West Medford
The Garden Club of America
John L. Gilbert
Glasgow Museums and Art Galleries
Gottscho-Schleischner Inc.
Miles Hadfield
Sonia Halliday
J. Harris
Judy Harrison
The Harry Smith Horticultural Photographic Collection
Michael Holford
Homes and Gardens
The India Office Library
Institut Royal du Patrimoine Artistique, Brussels
N. D. P. James (The Clinton Devon Estates)
A. D. Johnson
Mrs. L. Laman
Landschaftsverband Rheinland, Cologne
Norman McGrath
The Macmillan Company
Metropolitan Museum of Art, New York
Metropolitan Toronto Central Library
Milwaukee County Park Commission
Missouri Botanic Garden
Ian O. Morrison (Botanic Gardens Museum, Southport)
Mount Vernon Ladies' Association of the Union
Mousset Frères
Musée des Antiquités Nationales, Château de Saint-Germain-en-Laye
Museum of London
Museum of Turkish and Islamic Art, Istanbul
Hans Namuth, Photo Researchers Inc.
Naprstek – Museum of Asian, African and American Cultures, Prague
The National Gallery, London
New York Public Library
Prince of Wales Museum of Western India, Bombay
Royall House Association of Medford, Massachusetts
Rheinisches Landesmuseum, Bonn
Rijksmuseum, Amsterdam
Gerald Rodway
Alison Rutherford
School of Oriental and African Studies, University of London
Societé des Amis de la Bibliothèque d'Art et d'Archeologie de l'Université de Paris
Staatsbibliothek, Preussischer Kulturbesitz, Berlin
Staatliche Museen Preussischer Kulturbesitz, Berlin
Städelsches Kunstinstitut, Frankfurt-am-Main
Allan Stirling
Principal de la Ville de Strasbourg
Topkapi Saray Museum, Istanbul
D. H. Trump
Union Centrale des Arts Decoratifs, Paris
K. D. White
Fred Whitsey

Select Bibliography

Anonymous — *The Flower Garden.* London, 1838.
ANDRÉ, Edouard — *L'Art des Jardins.* Paris, 1879.
AGRICOLA, G. A. — *see* Bradley.
BACON, Francis — *The Essayes or Covnsels . . .* (including Essay on Gardens) 1627.
BAILEY, L. H. — *The Standard Cyclopedia of Horticulture.* New York, 1928, 1963.
BARRY, P. — *Barry's Fruit Garden.* New York, 1883.
BEETON, S. O. — *The New Book of Garden Management.* London, n.d. (about 1900).
BERRALL, Julia S. — *The Garden.* London, 1966.
BIELIĆKI, Marian — *Zapomniany Swiat Somerów.* Warsaw, 1966.
BLITH, Walter — *The English Improver, or a New Survey of Husbandry.* London, 1649.
BLUNT, Wilfrid — *Tulipomania.* London, 1950.
Tulips and Tulipomania. London, 1977.
BRADLEY, Richard — *A Philosophical Treatise of Husbandry and Gardening . . .* translated from G. A. Agricola. London, 1721.
New Improvements of planting and gardening . . . London, 1717 etc., 1739.
The Experimental Husbandman & Gardener . . . translated from G. A. Agricola. London, 1726.
The Gentleman and Gardener's Kalendar. London, 1718.
Survey of The Ancient Husbandry and Gardening. London, 1725.
ČAPEK, Karel and Josef — *The Gardener's Year.* London, 1931.
CATO, M. P. — *De Agri Cultura De Re Rustica* (2nd. century B.C.) Various excerpts, and in Schneider, q.v.
CAUSE, D. H. — *De Koninglycke Hovenier – Nederlantze Hesperides.* Amsterdam, 1676.
CECIL, Evelyn — *A History of Gardening in England.* London, 1910.
CHIPIEZ, C. — *History of Art in Ancient Egypt.* London, 1883.
History of Art in Chaldaea. London, 1884.
COLUMELLA, Lucius J. M. — *De Re Rustica* (1st century A.D.) (translated by E. S. Forster and E. H. Hefner). London, 1955, and in Schneider, q.v.
CONDER, Josiah — *Landscape Gardening in Japan.* New York, 1893, 1912, 1964.
CRESCENTIUS, Petrus de (CRESCENZI, Pietro d') — *Opus ruralium commodorum,* 1304, 1306. Various translations including F. Sansovino, Venice, 1561.
CRISP, Frank — *Mediæval Gardens.* London, 1924.
CROWE, Sylvia, and Sheila HAYWOOD — *The Gardens of Mughal India.* London, 1972.
DEZALLIER D'ARGENVILLE, A. J. — *La Théorie et Pratique de Jardinage.* 1711.
DIDEROT, Denis — *L'Encyclopédie . . . des Sciences, des Arts, et des Métiers.* Paris, 1763.
DWIGHT, T. — *Travels in New York and New England.* New Haven, 1821–1822.
ESTIENNE, C., and M. I. LIEBAULT — *L'Agriculture et maison rustique . . .* (translated by R. Surflet, q.v.). Paris, 1569–1570.
EVELYN, John — *Kalendarium Hortense.* London, 1666.
The Compleat Gard'ner (translated from de la Quintinye). London, 1693.
FARRER, Reginald — *The English Rock Garden.* London, 1919.

GROEN, J. van der — *Der Nederlantsen Hovenier.* Amsterdam, 1696, 1721.
GARNER, R. J. — *The Grafter's Handbook.* London, 1960.
GORER, Richard — *The Flower Garden in England.* London, 1975.
GOTHÉIN, Marie Louise — *A History of Garden Art* (translated by Mrs. Archer-Hind). London, 1928.
GRIMAL, P. — *Les Jardins Romains.* Paris, 1969.
HAYAKAWA, Masao — *The Garden Art of Japan.* New York, 1973.
HADFIELD, Miles — *A History of British Gardening.* London, 1960, 1969.
Topiary and Ornamental Hedges. London, 1971.
HEDRICK, U. P. — *A History of Horticulture in America to 1860.* New York, 1950.
D'HERVEY ST. DENIS, Baron Leon — *Recherches sur l'Agriculture des Chinois.* Paris, 1830.
HESSE, H. — *Neue Garten Lust.* Leipzig, 1714.
HIBBERD, Shirley — *Rustic Adornments for Homes of Taste.* London, 1857, 1870.
The Fern Garden. London, 1869.
HILL (HYLL), Thomas (also under the pseudonym DIDYMUS MOUNTAIN) — *The Gardener's Labyrinth.* London, 1577.
The Profitable Arte of Gardening . . . London, 1568, 1574.
HOHBERG, Baron Wolfgang Helmhard von — *Georgica Curiosa.* Nürnberg, 1707.
HYAMS, Edward — *A History of Gardens and Gardening.* London, 1971.
JAMES, John — *Theory and Practice of Gardening.* London, 1712.
JEFFERSON, Thomas — *Garden Book, 1766–1824* (edited by Edwin Morris). Philadelphia, 1944.
JOHNSON, Edward — *Wonder Working Providence of Sion's Saviour in New England.* London, 1654.
KAEMPFER, Engelbert — *Amoenitatum exoticarum* . . . Lemgovia, 1712.
History of Japan. London, 1727.
KALM, Peter — *Travels into North America* . . . (translated by J. M. Forster). London, 1770–1771.
LAWSON, William — *A New Orchard and Garden,* including The country housewife's garden. London, 1618, 1623, etc.
LEMMON, Kenneth — *The Covered Garden.* London, 1962.
LIGER, Louis — *Le Jardinier Fleuriste.* Amsterdam, 1706; Paris, 1768. (translated as *The Retir'd Gard'ner,* by Gentil, London, 1706, 1717).
Le Nouveau Theâtre D'Agriculture. Paris, 1723.
LOCKWOOD, Alice G. B. (editor for The Garden Club of America) — *Gardens of Colony and State.* New York, 1931.
LOUDON, John Claudius — *An Encyclopaedia of Gardening.* London, 1822, 1834.
The Horticulturist (originally *The Suburban Horticulturist*). London, 1849.
MACDOUGALL, Elisabeth B., and Richard ETTINGHAUSEN (editors) — *The Islamic Garden.* Washington, 1976.
MARKHAM, Gervaise — *A Way to get Wealthe.* London, 1638.
The Countryman's Recreation . . . London, 1640.
The English Husbandman. London, 1613 and 1614.
MASCALL, Leonard — *A booke of the Arte and maner, howe to plante and grafte all sortes of trees.* 1569.
MAWE, Thomas, and John ABERCROMBIE — *Every Man his own Gardener.* London, 1767.
MAWSON, Thomas H. — *The Art and Craft of Garden Making.* London, 1912.
MEAGER, Leonard — *The New Art of Gardening.* London, 1697.
MILLER, Philip — *The Gardener's Dictionary.* London, 1731–1739, etc.
M'INTOSH, Charles — *The Book of the Garden.* Edinburgh, 1855.
The Practical Gardener and Modern Horticulturist. London, 1828.
NEEDHAM, Noel Joseph — *Science and Civilisation in China.* London, 1954–
NUSSEY, Helen G. — *London Gardens of the Past.* London, 1939.
PADILLA, Victoria — *Southern California Gardens: An Illustrated History.* Berkeley, 1961.
PARKINSON, John — *Paradisi in sole, Paradisus terrestris* . . . London, 1629.
PLAT (or PLATT), Hugh — *The Jewell House of Art and Nature* . . . London, 1594.

PLINY (PLINIUS, C. C.), Caius, the Elder (23–79 A.D.)	*The Natural History of Pliny* (translated by J. Bostock and H. T. Riley). London, 1855–1857.
POPE, Alexander	"Essay on Verdant Sculpture" (*The Guardian*, No. 173). London, 1703.
PRESCOTT, William Hickling	*History of the Conquest of Mexico.* New York, 1843.
	History of the Conquest of Peru. London, 1847.
QUINTINYE, J. B. de la	*Le Parfait Jardinier* . . . (translated by John Evelyn, q.v.). Paris, 1595.
REA, John	*Flora; sea, de Florum Cultura.* London, 1665.
ROBINSON, William	*The English Flower Garden*, London, 1883 etc.
ROHDE, Eleanour Sinclair	*The Story of the Garden.* London, 1932.
ROSELLINI, V. F.	*Monumenti dell'Egitto.* Rome, 1832–1838.
SCHNEIDER, Gottlieb (editor)	*Scriptores Rei Rustica* (Cato, Columella and Varro, q.v.). Leipzig, 1744–1747.
SERRES, Olivier de	*Le Theâtre d'Agriculture, et Menage des Champs.* Paris, 1600.
SINGER, Charles, E. J. HOLMYARD, A. R. Hall, and Trevor I WILLIAMS, (editors)	*A History of Technology.* Oxford, 1956.
SIRÉN, Osvald	*Gardens of China.* New York, 1949.
STEUART, Sir Henry of Allanton	*The Planter's Guide* . . . Edinburgh, 1828, 1848.
STRABO, Walahfrid	*Hortulus* (written about 842). Pittsburgh, 1966.
SURFLET, Richard	*Maison Rustique, or The countrey farme* . . . (translated from Estienne and Liebault, q.v.). London, 1600.
SWITZER, Stephen	*The Practical Fruit Gardener* . . . London, 1724.
	The Practical Kitchen Gardener . . . London, 1727, 1731.
TAYLOR, Geoffrey	*Some Nineteenth Century Gardeners.* London, 1951.
	The Victorian Flower Garden. London, 1952.
THOMPSON, Robert	*The Gardener's Assistant* . . . Edinburgh and London, 1859 etc.; and with Moore, T., London, 1878.
TUSSER, Thomas	*Five Hundred Points of Good Husbandry.* London, 1573, 1931.
VARRO, Marcus Terentius	*De Re Rustica* (37 B.C.) (translated by H. B. Ash, E. S. Forster, and E. H. Heffner). London, 1955, and in Schneider, q.v.
VOLCKAMER, J. C.	*Nürnbergsche Hesperides.* Nürnberg, 1708.
WALPOLE, Horace	*Essay on Modern Gardens* (written 1770). London, 1785.
WARD, Nathaniel Bagshawe	*On the growth of plants in closely glazed cases* . . . London, 1842.
WHITE, K. D.	*Roman Farming.* London, 1970.
WOOD, William	*New England's Prospect.* London, 1635; Boston, 1868.
WORLIDGE, John	*Systema Horticulturae.* London, 1677.

Index

INDEX OF COLOR PLATES

A simple modern flat-roofed conservatory in an English garden.
Rare survivors from Victorian times – a Wardian case and a Warrington case.
Two modern bottle gardens.
An idealized version of a Persian "Paradise," with a stream running through flower-spangled turf.
Keeping a lawn in trim around 1750 – scything, rolling, raking and sweeping up cuttings.
A medieval turf seat on a low brick wall.

Following page 296:

Early specialists: Turkish gardeners' guilds in a Constantinople parade of 1582.
A modern rock and stream garden in the U.S.
Concrete is extensively used in an ultra-modern garden in Los Angeles.
A small modern Danish garden designed for minimum upkeep.
A tiny London yard which yet retains many elements of traditional larger gardens.
A New York rooftop garden provides an amazing mass of flowers.
A London rooftop garden which concentrates on grass and trees.
Space limitations have not stopped a multitude of features being packed into this minute high-fenced California backyard.

Page numbers in italics refer to illustrations.